T0146208

NUDGING HEALTH

NUDGING HEALTH

Health Law and Behavioral Economics

EDITED BY

I. GLENN COHEN
PETRIE-FLOM CENTER,
HARVARD LAW SCHOOL

HOLLY FERNANDEZ LYNCH
PETRIE-FLOM CENTER,
HARVARD LAW SCHOOL

CHRISTOPHER T. ROBERTSON
UNIVERSITY OF ARIZONA,
JAMES E. ROGERS COLLEGE OF LAW

FOREWORD BY
CASS R. SUNSTEIN

JOHNS HOPKINS UNIVERSITY PRESS
BALTIMORE

Johns Hopkins University Press
2715 North Charles Street
Baltimore, Maryland 21218-4363
www.press.jhu.edu

Library of Congress Cataloging-in-Publication Data

Names: Cohen, I. Glenn, editor. | Lynch, Holly Fernandez, editor. | Robertson, Christopher T., 1975– , editor.
Title: Nudging health : health law and behavioral economics / edited by I. Glenn Cohen, Holly Fernandez Lynch, Christopher T. Robertson.
Description: Baltimore : Johns Hopkins University Press, 2016. | Includes bibliographical references and index.
Identifiers: LCCN 2016005167 | ISBN 9781421421001 (hardcover : alk. paper) | ISBN 9781421421018 : (pbk. : alk. paper) | ISBN 9781421421025 (electronic) | ISBN 1421421003 (hardcover : alk. paper) | ISBN 1421421011 (pbk. : alk. paper) | ISBN 142142102X (electronic)
Subjects: | MESH: Health Policy—economics | Economics, Behavioral | Health Behavior | Choice Behavior | Legislation as Topic—economics
Classification: LCC RA971.3 | NLM WA 525 | DDC 362.1068—dc23
LC record available at http://lccn.loc.gov/2016005167

A catalog record for this book is available from the British Library.

Special discounts are available for bulk purchases of this book. For more information, please contact Special Sales at 410-516-6936 or specialsales@press.jhu.edu.

Johns Hopkins University Press uses environmentally friendly book materials, including recycled text paper that is composed of at least 30 percent post-consumer waste, whenever possible.

To Peggy Hoffman, Doug Hutchinson, and the late Dan Meltzer.
Cherished teachers whose lessons echo in my mind to this day.
IGC

To Adrian and Theodore Lynch, my favorite people to nudge—
and sometimes shove.
HFL

To Jamie Cox Robertson, whose nudges are always welcome
(and good for my health).
CTR

In Memoriam: Professor Jeremy Blumenthal, JD, PhD,
Syracuse University College of Law

CONTENTS

FOREWORD

Cass R. Sunstein

Choices and Default Rules

Consider the following problems:

A private company is deciding among three options: to enroll people automatically in a health insurance plan; to ask them to opt in if they like; or to say that as a condition for starting work, they must indicate whether they want health insurance, and if so, which plan they want.

A doctor is deciding whether to suggest a default treatment for a cancer patient or instead to outline a series of options for that patient, to present them in a neutral fashion, and to ask the patient to choose for herself.

Having adopted a wellness program, an employer is deciding whether to select an "opt-out" design, presuming employee participation (but allowing them to elect not to do so), or instead an "opt-in" design—or alternatively to require employees, in January of every year, to say whether they want to participate.

In these cases, and countless others, an institution is deciding whether to use some kind of default rule or instead to require some kind of active choice. For those who reject paternalism and who prize freedom of choice, active choosing has evident appeal, perhaps especially in the domain of healthcare. Indeed, active choosing might seem far preferable to any kind of default rule. Hospitals and doctors frequently think so, emphasizing the idea of "patient autonomy"—an idea that can be connected with the central argument in John Stuart Mill's great essay *On Liberty*.

In recent years, there have been vigorous debates about freedom of choice, paternalism, behavioral economics, individual autonomy, and the use of defaults (Conly 2012; Thaler and Sunstein 2008; Bubb and Pildes 2014; Camerer et al. 2003; Wright and Ginsburg 2012; Rebonato 2012). Invoking recent behavioral findings, some people have argued that because human beings err in predictable ways and cause serious problems for themselves, some kind of paternalism is newly justified, especially if it preserves freedom of choice, as captured in the idea of "libertarian paternalism" (Camerer et al. 2003; Sunstein and Thaler 2003). These arguments have evident applications to health-related policies of many kinds. Others contend that, because of those very errors, some form of coercion is required to promote people's welfare, and that the argument for choice-denying or non-libertarian paternalism is much strengthened (Conly 2012; Bubb and Pildes 2014). These claims raise special problems in the area of health and healthcare, whether the question involves food safety, insurance plans, the design of wellness programs, or the relationship between doctors and patients.

A possible concern is that those who oversee or provide healthcare are prone to error as well, and hence an understanding of behavioral biases argues against paternalism, not in favor of it (Glaeser 2006). In particular, the "knowledge problem" (meaning an absence of sufficient information) potentially affects all decisions by government (Hayek 1945), including officials who are involved in healthcare, and behavioral findings seem to compound that problem, because they suggest that identifiable biases will accompany sheer ignorance. Hospitals, insurance providers, and doctors can fall prey to the knowledge problem as well. Because patients have superior knowledge of their own values, tastes, and situations, the knowledge problem might well argue for active choosing.

It might also be objected that on grounds of both welfare and autonomy active choosing is desirable even if people have a tendency to err (Wright and Ginsburg 2012). On this view, people (emphatically including patients) should be asked or allowed to choose, whether or not they would choose rightly—not least when their health and well-being are on the line. For all sides, the opposition between paternalism and active choosing seems stark and plain, and indeed it helps to define all of the existing divisions. Some insurance providers, and some hospitals and doctors, seem to insist on the opposition.

My central goal here is to unsettle that opposition and to suggest that it is often illusory. In many contexts, an insistence on active choosing is a form of paternalism, not an alternative to it. This is emphatically true in the context of healthcare. The central reason is that some people choose not to choose.[1] Sometimes they make that choice explicitly (and indeed are willing to pay a considerable amount to people who will choose for them). They have actively chosen not to choose.

Sometimes people (including some patients) have made no explicit choice; they have not actively chosen anything. But it is nonetheless reasonable to infer that in particular contexts, their preference is not to choose, and they would say so if they were asked. They might fear that they will err. They might be aware of their own lack of information (Coupe and Noury 2004) or perhaps their own behavioral biases (such as unrealistic optimism) (Sharot 2011). They might find the underlying questions confusing, difficult, painful, and troublesome—empirically, morally, or otherwise. They might not enjoy choosing. They might be busy and lack "bandwidth" (Mullainathan and Shafir 2013). They might not want to take responsibility for potentially bad outcomes for themselves (and at least indirectly for others) (Bartling and Fischbacher 2012; Dwengler, Kübler, and Weizäcker 2013). They might anticipate their own regret and seek to avoid it. In the medical context, patients might be under considerable stress, and prefer some kind of default rule, or strong suggestion, for exactly that reason.

But even when people prefer not to choose, many private and public institutions favor and promote active choosing on the ground that it is good for people to choose. To this extent, active choosing counts as paternalistic. *Choice-requiring paternalism* might be an attractive form of paternalism, but it is no oxymoron, and it is paternalistic nonetheless. That form of paternalism is particularly common in the medical context. In a sense, it overrides patient autonomy, though it purports to operate in the name of that ideal.

If people are *required* to choose even when they would prefer not to do so, active choosing counts as a species of non-libertarian paternalism in the sense that people's own choice not to choose is being rejected. We will see that in many cases those who favor active choosing (including doctors and health insurers) are actually mandating it, and may therefore be overriding (on paternalistic grounds) people's choice not to choose (ironically, people sometimes place an excessive value on choice, leading to welfare losses [Botti and Hsee 2010]). When people prefer not to choose, required choosing is a form of coercion—though it may be the right form, at least where active choosing does not increase the likelihood and magnitude of errors, and where it is important to enable people to learn and to develop their own preferences.

If, by contrast, people are *asked whether they want to choose*, and can opt out of active choosing (in favor of, say, a default rule), active choosing counts as a form of libertarian paternalism. In some cases, it is an especially attractive form. A doctor might ask people whether they want to make a choice among treatments, or instead rely on the standard approach. A company might ask people whether they want to choose the privacy settings on their computers, or instead rely on the default, or whether they want to choose their electricity supplier, or instead rely on the default.

With such an approach, people are being asked to make an active choice between the default and their own preference, and in that sense, their liberty is fully preserved. Call this *simplified active choosing*. Simplified active choosing has the advantage of avoiding the kinds of pressure that come from a default rule (Johnson and Goldstein 2013), while also allowing people to rely on such a rule if they like. In the future, we should see, and we should hope to see, adoption of this approach by a large number of institutions, both public and private, and it has strong claims for adoption in the medical domain.

The remainder of this chapter is organized as follows. The following section explores how, and in what settings, active choosing might be required. The third section draws attention to choice-requiring paternalism and shows that it is not a contradiction in terms. It explains that when people choose not to choose, active choosing counts as a form of paternalism, one that runs into both welfare-based and autonomy-based arguments in favor of freedom of choice (including the choice not to choose). This point holds even for simplified active choosing, though the standard objections to paternalism are weakened as applied to that approach. The final section draws some conclusions.

Serving Health? Varieties of Choice

Many of those who embrace active choosing believe that consumers of goods and services, and indeed choosers of all sorts (including patients), should be free from government influence, or perhaps from the influence of private institutions of all kinds (Rebonato 2012). Of course, they recognize that in markets producers will impose influences of multiple kinds, but they contend that when third parties are not affected, and when force and fraud are not involved, government should remain neutral. They reject paternalism (Rebonato 2012; Wright and Ginsburg 2012). Perhaps it is legitimate to provide accurate information, so as to ensure that people's choices are adequately informed. But if public officials, hospitals, or doctors seek to "nudge" (Thaler and Sunstein 2008) people in their preferred directions in other ways—by imposing default rules or embracing paternalism of any kind—they are exceeding their appropriate bounds.

Three Possibilities

But what does active choosing entail?[2] What does it mean to "require" people to indicate their preferences? What does it mean for the healthcare system to do so? Those who insist on the inevitability of default rules will object that there is no good answer to this question. Even if choice architects seek to promote active choosing, they have to specify what happens if *people simply refuse to choose*. Isn't the answer some kind of default rule?

The question is a good one, because some kind of default rule is ultimately necessary. Choice architects have to establish what happens if people decline to choose. But this point should not be taken to collapse the distinction between active choosing and default rules. To see why, consider three possibilities.

1. Criminal or civil punishment for those who refuse to make an active choice.

In most contexts, no one contends that if people fail to make a choice, they should be imprisoned or otherwise punished. The sanction for that failure is that they do not receive a good or service (see [2] and [3] below). But there are exceptions. In some nations, including Australia, Belgium, and (before 1970) the Netherlands, people have been subject to civil sanctions if they fail to vote (Hill 2006), and in that sense they may be punished for refusing to make an active choice. So too, the Affordable Care Act (ACA) requires people to make a choice about health insurance, subject to punishment if they fail to do so (26 U.S.C. §5000A; 29 U.S.C. §218A).

With respect to active choosing, both of these cases do have a wrinkle: people are being forced to choose along one dimension (for whom to vote and which health insurance plan to obtain), but are being prohibited from choosing along another dimension (whether to vote or to obtain health insurance). But insofar as one kind of choice is being required, we may fairly speak of coerced choosing.

We could imagine other contexts in which people would face sanctions if they do not choose, though admittedly such cases look more like science fiction than the real world. Consider cases in which people must decide whether to become organ donors (or face criminal penalties) or must choose privacy settings on their computer (subject to civil sanctions if they do not). The fact that sanctions are rarely imposed on people who choose not to choose (including in the medical context) might be taken to suggest an implicit recognition that in a free society, such choices are generally acceptable and indeed a legitimate part of consumer sovereignty. One reason involves information: people know best what they want, and others should not choose for them, even if the choice is not to choose (Waldfogel 2009). The question is whether this point holds in the particular context.

2. Active choosing with respect to a related or ancillary matter as a condition for obtaining a good or a service (or a job).

Sometimes active choosing is mandatory in a distinctive sense: unless people make an active choice on some matter, they cannot obtain a good or service, even though that good or service, narrowly defined, is not the specific topic of the choice that they are being asked to make. We can imagine a continuum of connections between the matter in question, for which an active choice is being required, and the specific good that has already been chosen. There would be a fairly close connection if, for example, people were told that unless they indicate their preferences with respect to health insurance, they cannot start work. So too, there would be a close connection if people were told that unless they create a password, or indicate their preferences with respect to privacy settings, they cannot use their computers. And indeed, both of these cases are standard. By contrast, there would be a weaker connection if people were told that they could not obtain a drivers' license unless they indicate their preferences with respect to organ donation. The connection would be even weaker if people were told that they could not register to vote unless they have made a choice about their preferred privacy settings on their computers.

In the final two examples, there is not a tight connection between the matter on which people are being asked to make a choice and the good that they are specifically seeking (Dickert-Conlin, Elder, and Moore 2011). In some cases, the choice architect is requiring an active choice on a matter that is genuinely ancillary. Note that in imaginable cases that fall in this category, the requirement of active choosing has a strongly coercive dimension insofar as the good in question is one that people cannot easily reject (such as a driver's license, a job, or a right to vote). The choice architect is, in effect, leveraging that good to ensure an active choice on some other matter.

3. Active choosing among goods, services, or jobs as a condition for obtaining a good, a service, or a job.

For most consumption decisions, people are given a range of options, and they can choose one or more of them, or none at all. Unless they make a choice, they will not obtain the relevant good or service. When people visit a website, a restaurant, or a grocery or appliance store, they are generally asked to make an active choice. The default—understood as what happens if they do nothing—is that no product will be purchased. People do not receive goods or services unless they have actively chosen them. The same point holds for the employment market. People are not typically defaulted into particular jobs, at least not in any formal sense. They have a range of options, and unless they take one, they will be unemployed. In this respect, free markets generally require active choosing.

There is nothing inevitable about this situation. We could imagine a situation in which sellers assume, or presume, that people want certain products, and in which buyers obtain them, and have to pay for them, passively. Suppose, for example, that an employer has sufficient information to know that Johnson would do best with a particular health insurance plan—and defaults Johnson into that system accordingly (subject to personal adjustments). Indeed, that approach is hardly uncommon. One reason is that Johnson may not have a great deal of expertise about which plan is best—and hence a default is very much in his interest.

Choice Architects: Insurers, Hospitals, Doctors, and Beyond

As the examples suggest, both private and public institutions might choose (2) or (3), though of course only the government can choose (1). It should be clear that active choosing is far from inevitable. Instead of imposing active choosing, an institution (including a health insurer or a hospital) might select some kind of default rule, specifying what happens if people do nothing. Of course (2) and (3) also come with a kind of default rule: unless people make an active choice, they will have no good, no service, or no employment. But other approaches are possible.

For example, those who obtain driver's licenses might be defaulted into being organ donors, or those who start work with a particular employer might be defaulted into a healthcare plan. Alternatively, those who make an active choice to purchase a particular product—say, a book or a subscription to a magazine—might be enrolled into a program by which they continue to receive a similar product on a periodic basis, whether or not they have made an active choice to do that. The Book of the Month Club famously employs a strategy of this sort (Bowal 1999).

To take an example far from the medical context: suppose, for example, that a private institution knows that people who purchase product X (say, certain kinds of music) also tend to like product Y (say, certain kinds of books). Suggestions of various kinds, default advertisements, default presentations of political views, and perhaps even default purchases could be welcome and in people's interests, unfamiliar though the link might seem. For example, the website Pandora tracks people's music preferences, from which it can make some inferences about likely tastes and judgments about other matters, including politics (Singer 2014).

We could also imagine cases in which people are explicitly asked to choose whether they want to choose (people usually opt to choose [Bartling and Fischbacher 2012]). Patients might be asked: Do you want to make a series of choices, or do you want to be defaulted into those that seem to work best for most people, or for people like you? Do you want to choose your own health insurance plan, or do you want to be defaulted into the plan that seems best for people in your demographic category? In such cases, many people may well decide in favor of a default rule, and thus decline to choose, because of a second-order desire not to do so. They might not trust their own judgment; they might not want to learn. The topic might make them anxious. They might have better things to do. They might want to appoint some kind of surrogate, or to allow for such an appointment.

Simplified active choosing—active choosing, with the option of using a default—has considerable promise and appeal, not least because it avoids at least many of the influences contained in a default rule (Rebonato 2012), and might therefore seem highly respectful of autonomy while also giving people the ability to select the default. For cell phone settings or health insurance plans, active choosers can choose actively if they like, while others can (actively) choose the default.

Note, however, that this kind of question is not quite a perfect solution, at least for those people who genuinely do not want to choose. After all, they are being asked to do exactly that. At least some of those people (including some patients) likely do not want to have to choose between active choosing and a default rule, and hence they would prefer a default rule to an active choice between active choosing and a default rule. Even that active choice takes time and effort, and imposes costs, and some or many people might not want to bother. In this respect, supposedly libertarian paternalism, in the form of an active choice between active choosing and a default, itself has a strong non-libertarian dimension—a conclusion that brings us directly to the following section.

Choice-Requiring Paternalism
Paternalism, Welfare, Autonomy

Is it paternalistic to require active choosing, when people (for example, employees or patients) would prefer not to choose? Is it paternalistic for health insurers and doctors to require people to choose?

To answer these questions, we have to start by defining paternalism. There is, of course, an immensely large literature on that question (Coons and Weber 2013; Dworkin 1988). Let us bracket the hardest questions and note that while diverse definitions have been given, it seems clear that the unifying theme of paternalistic approaches is that a private or public institution does not believe that people's choices will promote their welfare, and it is taking steps to influence or alter people's choices for their own good (Bernheim and Rangel 2009).

What is wrong with paternalism, thus defined? Those who reject paternalism typically invoke welfare, autonomy, or both (Rebonato 2012). They tend to believe that individuals are the best judges of what is in their interests, and of what would promote their welfare, and that outsiders should decline to intervene because they lack crucial information (Hayek 2014). John Stuart Mill himself emphasized that this is the essential problem with outsiders, including government officials. In Mill's view, people have more knowledge of what will promote their own well-being than anyone else, and outsiders are likely to rely on general presumptions that might be wrong or in any case misapplied to particular situations. Mill's goal was to ensure that people's lives go well, and he contended that the best solution is for public officials to allow people to find their own path (Mill 1859 [2002]; Hayek 2014).

This is an argument about welfare, grounded in a claim about the superior information held by individuals. It applies to patients, who have unique access to their own tastes, values, fears, hopes, and situations. But there is an independent argument from autonomy (Wright and Ginsburg 2012) which emphasizes that even if people do not know what is best for them, and even if they would choose poorly, they are entitled to do as they see fit (at least so long as harm to others, or some kind of collective action problem, is not involved). On this view, freedom of choice has intrinsic and not merely instrumental value. It is an insult to individual dignity, and a form of infantilization, to eliminate people's ability to go their own way (Conly 2012). The interest in patient autonomy stems in part from an insistence on this point.

Choice-Requiring Paternalism

Whether or not these objections to paternalism are convincing (Conly 2012 ; Sunstein 2014), there are legitimate questions about whether and how they apply to people whose choice is not to choose. On reflection, they apply quite well, and so choice-requiring paternalism is no oxymoron. People might decline to choose for multiple reasons. They might believe that they lack information or expertise. They might fear that they will err. They might not enjoy the act of choosing; they might like it better if someone else decides for them. They might not want to incur the emotional costs of choosing, especially for situations that are painful or difficult to contemplate (such as organ donation or end-of-life care). They might find it a relief (Ullmann-Margalit 2000), and in some contexts even fun, to delegate. They might not want to take responsibility (Dwengler, Kübler, and Weizäcker 2013). They might be too busy (Mullainathan and Shafir 2013). They might not want to pay the psychic costs associated with regretting their choice (Brown, Farrell, and Weisbenner 2012). Active choosing saddles the chooser with responsibility for the choice, and reduces the chooser's welfare for that reason. This point emphatically holds in the medical context.

In daily life, people defer to others, including friends and family members, on countless matters, and they are often better off as a result. In ordinary relationships, people benefit from the functional equivalent of default rules, some explicitly articulated, others not. Within a marriage, for example, certain decisions (such as managing finances or planning vacations) might be made by the husband or wife by default, subject to opt-out in particular circumstances. That practice has close analogues in many contexts in which people are dealing with private or public institutions (including hospitals and doctors) and choose not to choose. Indeed, people are often willing to pay others a great deal to make their choices for them. But even when there is no explicit payment or grant of the power of agency, people might well prefer a situation in which they are relieved of the obligation to choose, because such relief will reduce decision costs, error costs, or both.

Suppose, for example, that Jones believes that he is not likely to make a good choice about his healthcare plan, and that he would therefore prefer a default rule, chosen by someone who is a specialist in the subject at hand. In Mill's terms: doesn't Jones know best? Or suppose that Smith is exceedingly busy, and wants to focus on her most important concerns, not on a question about the right health insurance plan for her, or even about the right privacy setting on her computer. Doesn't Mill's argument support respect for Smith's choice? In such cases, the welfarist arguments seem to argue in favor of deference to the chooser's choice, even if that choice is not to choose. If we believe in freedom of choice on the ground that people are uniquely situated to know what is best for them, then that very argument should support respect for people when they freely choose not to choose.

Or suppose that Winston, exercising his autonomy, decides to delegate decision-making authority to someone else, and thus to relinquish the power to choose, in a context that involves health insurance, medical care, privacy, or credit card plans. Is it an insult to Winston's dignity, or instead a way of honoring it, if a private or public institution refuses to respect that choice? It is at least plausible to suppose that respect for autonomy requires respect for people's decisions about whether and when to choose. That view seems especially reasonable in view of the fact that people are in a position to make countless decisions, and they might well decide that they would like to exercise their autonomy by focusing on their foremost concerns, not on what seems trivial, boring, or difficult (Duflo 2012).

But are people genuinely bothered by the existence of default rules, or would they be bothered if they were made aware that such rules had been chosen for them? We do not have a full answer to this question; the setting, and the level of trust, undoubtedly matter. But note in this regard the empirical finding, in the context of end-of-life care, that even when they are explicitly informed that a default rule is in place, and that it has been chosen because it affects people's decisions, there is essentially no effect on what people do. Here is the particular instruction:

> The specific focus of this research is on "defaults"—decisions that go into effect if people don't take actions to do something different. Participants in this research project have been divided into two experimental groups.
>
> If you have been assigned to one group, the Advance Directive you complete will have answers to questions checked that will direct healthcare providers to help relieve pain and suffering even it means not living as long. If you want to choose different options, you will be asked to check off a different option and place your initials beside the different option you select.
>
> If you have been assigned to the other group, the Advance Directive you complete will have answers to questions checked that will direct healthcare providers to prolong your life as much as possible, even if it means you may experience greater pain and suffering.

When given this instruction, people are not less likely to follow the particular default. Here, then, is a finding, at least in the context of end-of-life care, that people are not uncomfortable with defaults, even when they are made aware that choice architects have selected them (Loewenstein et al. 2014).

Alienating Freedom?

To be sure, we could imagine hard cases in which a choice not to choose seems to be an alienation of freedom. In the extreme case, people might choose to be slaves or otherwise to relinquish their liberty in some fundamental way (Sneddon 2001). In a less extreme case, people might choose not to vote, not in the sense of failing to show up at the polls, but in the sense of (formally) delegating their vote to others. Such delegations are impermissible (Rieber 2001), perhaps because they would undo the internal logic of a system of voting (in part by creating a collective action problem that a prohibition on vote-selling solves),[3] but perhaps also because individuals would be relinquishing their own freedom. Or perhaps people might choose not to make choices with respect to their religious convictions, or their future spouses (Batabyal 2001; Conly 2012), and they might delegate those choices to others. In cases that involve central features of people's lives, we might conclude that freedom of choice cannot be alienated and that the relevant decisions must be made by the individuals themselves.

Which cases fall in this category is a complex question (Conly 2012). But even if the category is fairly large, it cannot easily be taken as a general objection to the proposition that on autonomy grounds people should be allowed not to choose in multiple domains. Healthcare can be understood as a context in which we generally do respect choices not to choose, at least in the sense that patients frequently defer to doctors, even or perhaps especially when the stakes are high.

Justified Paternalism?

The choice not to choose may not be in the chooser's interest (as the chooser would define it). For that reason, choice-requiring paternalism might have a justification in terms of the chooser's welfare. Perhaps the chooser chooses not to choose only because he lacks important information (which would reveal that the default rule might be harmful) or suffers from some form of bounded rationality. A behavioral market failure (understood as a nonstandard market failure that comes from human error [Sunstein 2014]) might infect a choice not to choose, just as it might infect a choice about what to choose.

A non-chooser (including a patient) might, for example, be unduly affected by "availability bias" because of an overreaction to a recent situation in which his own choice went wrong (Reber 2012). Or perhaps the chooser is myopic and is excessively influenced by the short-term costs of choosing, which might require some learning (and hence some investment), while underestimating the long-term benefits, which might be very large. A form of "present bias" (Sunstein 2014) might infect the decision not to choose. People might face a kind of intrapersonal collective action problem, in which such a decision by Jones, at time 1, turns out to be welfare-reducing for Jones at times 2, 3, 4, and 5.

But for those who reject paternalism, these kinds of concerns are usually a justification for providing more and better information—not for blocking people's choices, including their choices not to choose. In these respects, the welfarist objections to paternalism seem to apply as well to those who insist on active choosing. Of course, welfarists might be wrong to object to paternalism (Conly 2012). But with respect to their objections, the question is whether the choice not to choose is, in general or in particular contexts, likely to go wrong, and in the abstract, there is no reason to think that that particular choice would be especially error-prone. In light of people's tendency to overconfidence, the choice not to choose might even be peculiarly likely to be right, which would create serious problems for choice-requiring paternalism (Huffridge 2004). In the medical context, we lack evidence that the choice not to choose will go wrong—and in view of the fact that patients often lack information or are under stress, the choice to choose might itself result in mistakes (acknowledging that people's tastes, values, and situations greatly matter, which strongly argues in favor of retaining freedom of choice, whether or not it is exercised).

Consider in this regard evidence that people spend too much time trying to make precisely the right choice, in a way that leads to significant welfare losses. In many situations, people underestimate the temporal costs of choosing, and exaggerate the benefits, producing "systematic mistakes in predicting the effect of having more, vs. less, choice freedom on task performance and task-induced affect" (Botti and Hsee 2010, 161). If people make such systematic mistakes, it stands to reason that they might well choose to choose in circumstances in which they ought not to do so on welfare grounds. We can easily imagine analogies in the medical context.

My aim is not to endorse the welfarist rejection of paternalism; it is only to say that the underlying arguments apply to all forms of paternalism, including those that would interfere with the decision not to choose. To be sure, some welfarists are willing to interfere with people's choices; they may well be libertarian or non-libertarian paternalists (Conly 2012). The central points are that the standard welfarist arguments on behalf of freedom of choice apply to those who (freely) choose not to choose, and that those who want to interfere with such choices might well be paternalists. And from the standpoint of autonomy, interference with the choice not to choose seems objectionable as well, unless it is fairly urged that that choice counts as some kind of alienation of freedom.

Cases

In which cases would it be paternalistic to reject a choice not to choose? Begin with category (1) above. Suppose that people are subjected to criminal punishment if they do not choose (for example, to vote or to purchase healthcare) and that they wish not to choose. To know whether paternalism is involved, we need to identify the reason people are being forced to choose. If people face some kind of collective action problem, and if coercion is meant to solve that problem, paternalism is not involved. But if public officials believe that it is best for people if they choose, and if they are punishing people in order to ensure that they do what is best for them, then we have a case of paternalism. Everything turns on the reason for the punishment.

Whether or not people should be forced to vote or to purchase healthcare, there is a plausible argument that in both contexts, the goal of coercion is to solve a collective action problem. But we could easily imagine cases in which people are being forced to choose on the ground that it is good for them to do so, even if they think otherwise. Some of those who support both compulsory voting and the "individual mandate" for health insurance believe exactly that. In the latter context, the idea might be that people suffer from inertia (Keller et al. 2011) or fail to make a choice that will protect them in the event that things go unexpectedly wrong.

Now turn to (2), which seems to involve many of the most interesting cases. In those cases, some choosers undoubtedly have a second-order preference not to choose, and active choosing interferes with or overrides that preference. Nonetheless, choice architects are imposing a requirement of active choosing in circumstances in which some or many people, faced with the option, would choose not to choose. Is active choosing paternalistic for that reason?

As before, the answer turns on why choice architects are insisting on active choice. In the case of organ donation, paternalism is not involved. The goal is to protect third parties, not choosers. So too with a case in which a choice architect favors a default rule that reduces environmental harms; in such cases, third parties are at risk. But suppose that as a condition for entering into an employment relationship, people are asked or required to make an active choice with respect to their healthcare plan; suppose too that choice architects believe that it is good for them to do so, even though prospective employees disagree (and would prefer to be defaulted). If so, then choice architects are acting paternalistically. In such cases, those who insist on active choosing are hardly avoiding paternalism; they are engaging in it.

It might seem puzzling to suggest that paternalism might be involved in (3). How can it be paternalistic to say that you do not own a pair of shoes, a tablet, an automobile, or a fish sandwich unless you have actively chosen it? The question is a good one, but it should not be taken as rhetorical; everything depends on the reasons that underlie the creation of a particular system of choice architecture.[4] To be sure, there are many justifications for free markets and active choosing, and a number of them have nothing to do with paternalism. Some of those justifications speak of efficiency and others of autonomy. But suppose that we think that active choosing is a way to ensure that people develop certain characteristics and tastes. Suppose that the idea is that choosers gain independence, self-sufficiency, and a sense of initiative, and that a system of active choosing (subject to background entitlements) is desirable for exactly that reason. That would be a paternalistic justification, and it might well apply to some choosers in the context of healthcare.

This view is hardly foreign to those who emphasize the importance of freedom of choice; it plays a significant role in Mill's own defense of liberty (Mill 1859 [2002]). It is also a cousin of an early defense of free markets, memorably sketched by Albert Hirschmann, which emphasizes that free commerce creates a certain kind of culture, in which traditional social antagonisms, based on religion and ethnicity, are softened as people pursue their economic interests (Hirschmann 1997). For at least some of those who prize active choosing, the concern is not softening of social divisions, but the development of engaged, spirited, informed people. Those who favor active choosing often embrace a form of liberal perfectionism, embodied in the idea that the government legitimately promotes certain desirable characteristics, on the ground that it is best for people to have those characteristics (Raz 1986; Rawls 1993).

To the extent that active choosing promotes independence, self-sufficiency, and a sense of initiative, it might be preferred on perfectionist grounds, even if people would choose not to choose. We might think that this view has strong appeal in the medical context, where it may be desirable for people to exercise agency. One question is whether exercising agency has good, or not-so-good, effects on the prospects for recovery. Perhaps those who favor patient autonomy have ideas of this kind in mind; they are concerned with the value and side effects of the exercise of agency.

To be sure, it is not exactly standard to see those who embrace free markets or freedom of choice as favoring any kind of paternalism, and it is often wrong to see them in that way, because other justifications are available and because people often do in fact have a first-order desire to choose, certainly in cases that fall in category (3). But suppose that private or public institutions favor active choosing, and reject mandates or default rules because they want to influence people for their own good.

Recall our working definition, which suggests that paternalism is involved when a private or public institution does not believe that people's choices will promote their welfare, and it is taking steps to influence or alter people's choices for their own good. If people have a second-order desire not to choose, and if active choosing overrides that choice, then paternalism is indeed involved, even in cases that fall in category (3). In the domain of healthcare, an insistence on active choosing might well be paternalistic—and for some consumers and some patients, it is not justified on grounds of either welfare or autonomy.

Conclusion

Many people have insisted on an opposition between active choosing and paternalism, and in some cases, they are correct to do so. In the domain of healthcare, active choosing has an important and permanent place. But in many contexts, the opposition is illusory, even a logical error, because people do not want to choose actively. To be sure, the power to choose may well have intrinsic value, but people often exercise that power by delegating authority to others. Nanny states forbid people from choosing, but they also forbid people from choosing not to choose (Sunstein 2013). If and to the extent that hospitals and doctors forbid that choice, they are acting as nannies.

If choice architects are prohibiting people from choosing, they might well be acting paternalistically—and in the context of healthcare, paternalism runs into serious objections on the basis of both autonomy and welfare. But if choice architects *require* people to choose, they may also be acting paternalistically—at least if they are motivated by the belief that active choosing is good and important, notwithstanding the fact that people reject that belief. Insistence on active choosing may simultaneously reduce people's welfare and insult their autonomy—not least when people are vulnerable or aware of their own ignorance, and want some direction and help.

To be sure, active choosing has a central place in a free society, and I have emphasized that it needs to play a large role in the healthcare system. But for those involved in that system, as for everyone else, the same concerns that motivate objections to paternalism in general can be applied to paternalistic interferences with people's choice not to choose.

Notes

1. An important clarification: my focus throughout is not on "not choosing," which involves no choice at all, and which is different from choosing not to choose, in the sense of choosing someone else to choose on one's behalf. One might not choose because (for example) of procrastination or because one wants to retain option value (Carmon et al. 2003). There is, of course, an overlap between the two phenomena: people might decline to choose because they are busy, do not want to take responsibility, or think that they might err. But choosing

not to choose is a form of choice, and those who want to avoid choosing might be as adverse to that choice as any other.

2. I am understanding the term in a purely formal sense, to capture a response to a question about what one prefers. It would be possible to understand "choosing" in a more functional sense, to capture deciding for reasons, as distinguishing from simply "picking," which is akin to tossing a coin. Others have discussed this (Ullmann-Margalit and Morgenbesser 1977). As I understand it here, active choosing includes "picking," and can occur even when people lack an antecedent preference.

3. The basic idea is that if vote-selling were permitted, voting power could be concentrated in individuals or individual entitles, and while decisions to sell might be individually rational, the result would be bad from the standpoint of a large group of vote-sellers (Rieber 2001).

4. I am bracketing here the question whether markets can be seen as a kind of spontaneous order, or whether they should be seen as a product of conscious design. Others have discussed this issue at length (Ullmann-Margalit 1978).

References

Bartling, Bjorn, and Urs Fischbacher. 2012. "Shifting the Blame: On Delegation and Responsibility." *Review of Economic Studies* 79:67.

Batabyal, Amitrajeet. 2001. "On the Likelihood of Finding the Right Partner in an Arranged Marriage." *Journal of Sociology-Economics* 30:273.

Bernheim, B. Douglas, and Antonio Rangel. 2009. "Beyond Revealed Preference: Choice Theoretic Foundations for Behavioral Welfare Economics." *Quinnipiac Journal of Economics* 124:51.

Botti, Simona, and Christopher Hsee. 2010. "Dazed and Confused by Choice." *Organizational Behavior and Human Decision Processes* 112:161.

Bowal, Peter. 1999. "Reluctance to Regulate: The Case of Negative Option Marketing." *American Business Law Journal* 36:378–79.

Brown, Jeffrey R., Anne M. Farrell, and Scott J. Weisbenner. 2012. "The Downside of Defaults." National Bureau of Economic Research Working Paper 12-05. http://www.nber.org/aging/rrc/papers/onb12-05.pdf.

Bubb, Ryan, and Richard Pildes. 2014. "How Behavioral Economics Trims Its Sails and Why." *Harvard Law Review* 127:1594.

Camerer, Colin, Samuel Issacharoff, George Loewenstein, Ted O'Donoghue, and Matthey Rabin. 2003. "Regulation for Conservatives: Behavioral Economics and the Case for Asymmetric Paternalism." *University of Pennsylvania Law Review* 151:1211.

Carom, Ziv, Klaus Wertenbroch, and Marcel Zeelenberg. 2003. "Option Attachment: When Deliberating Makes Choosing Feel Like Losing." *Journal of Consumer Research* 30:15

Conly, Sarah. 2012. *Against Autonomy.* Cambridge University Press. New York.

Coons, Christian, and Michael Weber, eds. 2013. *Paternalism: Theory and Practice.* Cambridge University Press. New York.

Coupe, Tom, and Abdul Noury. 2004. " Choosing Not to Choose: On the Link Between Information and Abstention." *Economic Letters* 84:261.

Dickert-Conlin, Stacy, Todd Elder, and Brian Moore. 2011. "Donorcycles: Motorcycle Helmet Laws and the Supply of Organ Donors." *Journal of Law and Economics* 54:907.

Duflo, Esther. 2012. "Tanner Lectures on Human Values and the Design of the Fight Against Poverty" (May). http://economics.mit.edu/files/7904.

Dwengler, Nadja, Dorothea Kübler, and Georg Weizäcker. 2013. *Flipping a Coin: Theory and Evidence*. Unpublished manuscript.

Dworkin, Gerald. 1988. *The Theory and Practice of Autonomy*. Cambridge University Press. New York.

Glaeser, Edward. 2006. "Paternalism and Psychology." *The University of Chicago Law Review* 73:133.

Hayek, Friedrich. 2014. *The Market and Other Orders*. Edited by Bruce Caldwell. University of Chicago Press. Chicago. 384–86.

———. 1945. "The Uses of Knowledge in Society." *The American Economic Review* 35:519.

Hill, Lisa. 2006. "Low Voter Turnout in the United States: Is Compulsory Voting a Solution." *Journal of Theoretical Politics* 18:208.

Hirschmann, Albert O. 1997. *The Passions and the Interests*. Princeton University Press. Princeton, NJ.

Huffrage, Ulrich. 2004. "Overconfidence." In *Cognitive Illusions: A Handbook on Fallacies and Biases*, edited by R. F. Pohl. Psychology Press. Hove, UK. 235.

Johnson, Eric J., and Daniel G. Goldstein. 2013. "Decisions by Default." In *The Behavioral Foundations of Policy*, edited by Eldar Shafir. Princeton University Press. Princeton, NJ. 417.

Keller, Punam Anand, Bari Harlam, George Loewenstein, and Kevin G. Volpp. 2011. "Enhanced Active Choice: A New Method to Motivate Behavior Change." *Journal of Consumer Psychology* 21:377–78.

Loewenstein, George, Cindy Bryce, David Hagmann, and Sachin Rajpal. 2014. *Warning: You Are About to Be Nudged*. Unpublished manuscript.

Mill, John Stuart. 1859 [2002]. *On Liberty*. Edited by Kathy Casey. Dover. New York.

Mullainathan, Sendhil, and Eldar Shafir. 2013. *Scarcity: Why Having Too Little Means So Much*. Allen Lane. London. 39–66.

Rawls, John. 1993. *Political Liberalism*. Columbia University Press. New York.

Raz, Joseph. 1986. *The Morality of Freedom*. Oxford University Press. Oxford.

Reber, Rolf. 2001. "Availability." In *Cognitive Illusions: A Handbook on Fallacies and Biases*, edited by R. F. Pohl. Psychology Press. Hove, UK. 147.

Rebonato, Riccardo. 2012. "A Critical Assessment of Libertarian Paternalism." *Journal of Consumer Policy* 37:357.

Rieber, Steven. 2001. "Vote-Selling and Self-Interested Voting." *Public Affairs Quarterly* 15:35.

Sharot, Tali. 2011. *The Optimism Bias: A Tour of the Irrationally Positive Brain*. Random House. New York.

Singer, Natasha. 2014. "Listen to Pandora, and It Listens Back." *The New York Times*, January 5, BU3.

Sneddon, Andrew. 2001. "What's Wrong with Selling Yourself into Slavery? Paternalism and Deep Autonomy." *Crítica Revista Hispanoamericana de Filosofía* 73:97.

Sunstein, Cass R. 2013. "Deciding by Default." *University of Pennsylvania Law Review* 162:1.

———. 2014. *Why Nudge? The Politics of Libertarian Paternalism*. Yale University Press. New Haven, CT.

Sunstein, Cass R., and Richard H. Thaler. 2003. "Libertarian Paternalism Is Not an Oxymoron." *The University of Chicago Law Review* 70:1159.

Thaler, Richard. 2008. "Toward a Positive Theory of Consumer Choice." *Journal of Economic Behavior and Organization* 1:51–54.

Thaler, Richard H., and Cass R. Sunstein. 2008. *Nudge: Improving Decisions about Wealth, Health, and Happiness.* Yale University Press. New Haven, CT.

Ullmann-Margalit, Edna. 1978. "Invisible Hand Explanations." *Synthese* 39:263.

———. 2000. "On Not Wanting to Know." In *Reasoning Practically*, edited by Edna Ullmann-Margalit. Oxford University Press. New York. 72.

Ullmann-Margalit, Edna, and Sidney Morgenbesser. 1977. "Picking and Choosing." *Social Research* 44:757.

Waldfogel, Joel. 2009. *Scroogenomics: Why You Shouldn't Buy Presents for the Holidays.* Princeton University Press. Princeton, NJ.

Wright, Joshua D., and Douglas H. Ginsburg. 2012. "Behavioral Law and Economics: Its Origins, Fatal Flaws, and Implications for Liberty." *Northwestern University Law Review* 106:1033.

ACKNOWLEDGMENTS

A book like this could not have happened without the support and assistance of a number of people. We thank Cristine Hutchison-Jones for helping us mount the original conference that gave rise to this volume. Evelyn Blacklock, Thomas Blackmon, Noah Marks, and Jeffrey Zink helped us line edit and format the entire book, acting really as "deputy editors." We are always grateful to Harvard Law School and the Petrie-Flom Center for Health Law Policy, Biotechnology, and Bioethics for their support of our activities. Glenn Cohen also thanks the Greenwall Foundation Faculty Scholar in Bioethics program for its financial and intellectual support during the gestation of this book. And last, but certainly not least, we thank all of our contributors for their tremendous efforts.

SETTING THE STAGE

Introduction

Christopher T. Robertson, I. Glenn Cohen,
and Holly Fernandez Lynch

In the domain of health law and policy, there are many difficult problems. Doctors too often prescribe the wrong drugs, favoring expensive, patented ones, when cheaper generics would do just as well. There is a longstanding and severe shortage of organs for transplantation, even while we routinely destroy organs that could be transplanted from the cadavers of individuals who would not have objected to having their bodies used to save a life. Individuals also often fail to buy the optimal insurance plans for themselves, in part because they have unrealistic estimates of their own risks. And, of course, people consume too many calories and exercise too little, a pattern that worsens their health and imposes costs on insurers and taxpayers. These are merely the tip of the iceberg.

This book is about a particular aspect of these problems and a set of possible solutions. Law and policy have always been about manipulating behavior to avoid harms and promote social welfare. The traditional tools have been sticks and carrots—penalties and incentives. For example, we could use penalties to simply conscript organs as needed, denying patients and families any choice in the matter. Likewise, we could impose liability on physicians who prescribe suboptimally. Or we could use incentives, perhaps by opening a market for human organs, allowing those who need a kidney to pay those (or the families of those) who are willing to part with one, for example. (Cohen 2014; Robertson, Yokum, and Wright 2014). Similarly, there has been longstanding interest in paying physicians bonuses for optimal prescribing, or giving patients more "skin in the game" to deter costly consumption (Robertson 2013). Even if these policies were known to be effective, they would create their own profound normative problems, including infringement on liberty and commodification of the body in the organ example, as well as intrusion on physician professional discretion, potential conflicts of interests, and infringements on access to healthcare, in the prescribing example. These policy levers also activate particular political debates between libertarians and paternalists about the proper role of the state (Sunstein and Thaler 2003). For these reasons, although carrots and sticks have provided great fodder for scholars to debate and provide some clean theoretical lines, they have left many of the most trenchant problems unsolved.

Fortunately, in recent decades there has been an outpouring of research from psychologists, economists, and other social scientists, which provides a much more sophisticated, and frankly more interesting, set of tools to shape behavior. This field of work is sometimes called "behavioral economics," but it might be better described as "behavioral science" or, especially for our purposes, "behavioral law and policy." As Christine Jolls, Cass R. Sunstein, and Richard Thaler put it, "The unifying idea in our analysis is that behavioral economics allows us to model and predict behavior relevant to law with the tools of traditional economic analysis, but with more accurate assumptions about human behavior, and more accurate predictions and prescriptions about law" (1998, 1474).

As applied to health law and policy, this field has two distinctive insights to contribute. First, behavioral policy insists on being empirical and pragmatic about any proposed policy intervention. After all, if we are interested in manipulating behavior, the ultimate question is whether the intervention works to achieve the desired behaviors. Behavioral policy is often inspired by laboratory experiments with human subjects, using vignettes or economic games to identify foundational aspects of human behavior that may be predictive for how people will make health-related decisions in the real world. Ideally such research culminates in large-scale, randomized field experiments to confirm these findings in the clinic, the health insurance marketplace, or other realistic settings. If a particular policy fails to achieve its behavioral goal— whether it is increased organs transplanted or better prescriptions, and ultimately improving health at lower cost—it must be abandoned or further reformed. In this way, behavioral policymakers are empiricists, experimentalists, and, most importantly, fallibilists, subjecting their policy theories to the crucible of evidence and then innovating again as necessary. The behavioral policymaker recognizes that although such empirical testing can be costly and onerous, these costs are often dwarfed by the costs of making bad policy on the basis of sheer ideology.

Second, and relatedly, behavioral policy qualifies a particular theory of rationality that has historically dominated the field of economics (often referred to as "neoclassical economics")—the idea that individuals predictably behave in ways that maximize their own personal utilities, and by doing so create a market equilibrium that maximizes efficiency (Camerer and Loewenstein 2011). This constellation of ideas conceives human choice as a comparison of the costs versus benefits, where the chooser selects the behavior that will maximize net benefits to herself. For the purposes of theory-building, this conception has been useful, as Camerer and Loewenstein explain, "because it provides economists with a theoretical framework that can be applied to almost any form of economic (and even noneconomic) behavior, and it makes refutable predictions" (2011, 3). The dominance of this theory also explains why carrots and sticks have been our most obvious solutions in health law and policy: they simply manipulate the relative costs and benefits of any option, making good behavior less expensive than bad behavior to the actor. This is why scholars have been so quick to consider conscription and sale of organs, as well as penalties and bonuses for doctors. In theory, these are easy fixes. Even aside from their normative problems, however, the behavioral policymaker will insist on evidence that they work.

Of course, behavioral policy does "not imply a wholesale rejection of the neoclassical approach to economics" (Camerer and Loewenstein 2011, 3). The rational economic model is often a good starting point, as it roughly predicts how people will behave, at least when those costs and benefits are predictable, concrete, and salient to them when making the relevant decision. Behavioral policy does, however, subject this theory to the prior commitment of empiricism, and decades of scientific research have shown systematic departures from this model of human behavior (Thaler 2015; Kahneman 2013; Ariely 2008; Loewenstein 2007). People often have malleable notions of what is best for themselves, notions that are often constructed on the fly in a given situation. Even when such a conception of utility can be taken as given, decisions are often framed in ways that can dramatically change how costs and benefits (losses and gains) are perceived. The effort to actually weigh these costs and benefits against each other is also not straightforward, and is often not done even implicitly. Instead, people deploy various heuristics and biases to get around in the world. These mental shortcuts permit fast and instinctive reactions to most situations, such that people are forced only occasionally to slow down to weigh a decision carefully and consciously. Even then, there is evidence that such reasoning efforts are often matters of rationalization, or "motivated reasoning," which tend to track whatever intuitional view seems right in the first place. Even worse, people are often blind to their own biases and unrealistically optimistic about their abilities to function well in complex situations.

Thus, for certain aspects of health law and policy, simple economic models may fail us. It may turn out that paying for organs actually causes fewer people to contribute their organs overall, if it changes the social meaning of the transaction and "crowds out" the altruistic conception that currently drives donations. Similarly, too many carrots and sticks for doctors may cause them to focus too much on their incentives rather than patient health (aka "defensive medicine"), or cause patients to place less trust in their physicians, potentially reducing compliance with their best advice.

In sum, the carrot-and-stick model of regulation has two problems. First, in the most interesting cases, it raises cultural, normative, and epistemic problems, which also create difficulties for political implementation. Second, the carrot-and-stick model may actually backfire in implementation, if people do not in fact behave according to the predictions of economic rationality.

These shortcomings are general, but they are particularly interesting and important for health policy. The stakes are very high in this domain—for example, life and death for patients, and solvency or insolvency for healthcare systems. The behavioral dynamics are also sharpened in this domain, where decisions are distributed among millions of individual healthcare providers (rather than decided centrally by the government) and are highly indeterminate and discretionary, with no single right answer for every clinical presentation. If there were simply a mathematical formula that could be used to resolve whether organs should be donated, or whether a given patient should receive one drug or another, we would have little need for patient and physician decision-making. Instead, these decisions are often deeply ambiguous, mixing questions of value and fact, and are often future-looking, requiring individuals to make predictions about the future and to determine what sorts of risks are worth bearing. It is in precisely these sorts of complicated and ambiguous decisions that individuals are most likely to rely on heuristics and biases.

This book explores in detail many of the policy alternatives to carrots and sticks that may be utilized in the health sector. The general concept can be understood as constructing an "architecture" for choice. As Sunstein explains, those who make law and policy are "pervasively in the business of constructing procedures, descriptions, and contexts for choice" (Sunstein 1997, 1176). The behavioral policymaker can shape the social meaning of a decision, shape the salience of one choice over another, shape the outcome that occurs for those that do not make an active choice at all, or otherwise channel individuals into more desirable behaviors, all while preserving the freedom for any given individual to make the choice that she prefers. For the organ example, the choice architect may flip the default rule, structuring the decision in a way that makes it seem normal and routine to share organs upon death, and thereby increase donation rates, while nonetheless allowing those who feel most strongly to the contrary to opt out. Similarly, for physician prescribing, the choice architect can redesign the physician's electronic prescribing pad so that it is comparatively easier for him to allow generic substitution, and somewhat more onerous to find and specify an expensive patented drug instead. Alternatively, it may be that a small nonfinancial recognition has outsized effects for organ donor or physician behavior without crowding out altruism or the physician's focus on health as the ultimate goal.

Of course, behavioral policy is no panacea, and often simply raises more questions about how to make the optimal policy. There will be questions of efficacy, which are best answered through empirical investigation. There will also be legal and normative questions. Fundamentally, although behavioral policy often seeks to maintain some individual choice, it nonetheless seeks to manipulate those choices, and thus cannot avoid hard questions about the appropriate role of the government. There are often competing values at stake (for example, welfare, autonomy, efficiency, and transparency), and there are fair questions about whether a behavioral policy goes too far, or not far enough, to achieve the social planner's goal. There are questions about who should decide, and how decisions should be made. There are also epistemic questions, most pressingly about whether and how the policymaker knows what choice is likely to be best for the individual or best for society. These questions are at the heart of this book, which seeks to identify the most pressing and interesting problems in health law and policy, and explore the most tenable solutions inspired by behavioral science.

We begin with four pieces that frame the book, from leading voices in the field. Cass R. Sunstein, coauthor of the provocative book *Nudge*, perhaps the key work in explaining to a public audience what work behavioral economics can do for law and policy, opens the volume with a foreword. He situates the fundamental debate as between patient autonomy, choice, and paternalism. All other things being equal, policymakers prefer to preserve individual choices, but behavioral science has revealed a range of situations in which individuals predictably make very poor choices for themselves, which in the aggregate also undermines social welfare. Sunstein has famously argued for a conception of "libertarian paternalism," in which the policymaker can preserve choice but nonetheless shape those choices in ways that improve the likelihood of good outcomes. In the foreword, Sunstein advances the debate by suggesting that often individuals actually prefer not to choose for themselves, and there are prominent examples of this dynamic in healthcare. Where that is true, the case for policymakers to intervene is even stronger. If policymakers nonetheless insist on individuals choosing for themselves, Sunstein argues provocatively that this is itself a form of paternalism.

Russell Korobkin expands the debate beyond Sunstein's "libertarian paternalism" to also explore "libertarian welfarism"—in the service of aggregate social welfare, without preoccupation on the welfare of the individual chooser. Korobkin argues that just as carrots and sticks have been properly deployed to such social ends, behavioral policy should as well. Moreover, sticks should remain on the table too, which he calls "coercive paternalism" and "coercive welfarism." In the second half of his chapter, Korobkin also argues for "decision simplification" as a tool of behavioral policy and in particular reviews his proposal for "relative value health insurance." This model would create a menu of different insurance policies, each with its own breadth of coverage, priced accordingly, so that consumers would have a salient sense of how much insurance they are buying in any given plan. Like many of the issues in this volume, such reforms would require reconsideration of core legal doctrines, such as the idea that insurance must cover anything "medically necessary."

Alan M. Garber, a physician-economist and provost of Harvard University, seeks to apply behavioral economics to the Affordable Care Act (ACA). Garber reviews some promising evidence that smart policies could enhance health behaviors—such as exercise and diet, through small financial rewards, precommitment devices, and social contagion—to the ultimate benefit of aggregate healthcare costs savings. He also suggests places where the ACA is already using behavioral policy to solve market failures, including default rules and small but symbolic penalties that nudge people into health insurance plans. Garber closes with an agenda of additional opportunities for smarter health policy.

In the final chapter of this introductory part, Michael Hallsworth provides some perspective from across the pond, drawing on his experience with the United Kingdom's Behavioural Insights Team (BIT). Although it has often been called the "Nudge Unit," Hallsworth explains that the BIT's starting point is not necessarily searching for the right policy nudge, but rather addressing the foundational question of how to bring empirical evidence to bear on policy problems. Hallsworth utilizes a number of illustrative examples to outline seven ways to apply behavioral science to health policy: (1) stop or revise an existing action with unintended behavioral consequences; (2) decide not to try to change behavior but to shape policy around it; (3) prevent a counterproductive policy from being introduced; (4) address the flaws in policymaking process itself; (5) influence healthcare providers; (6) help people find new strategies for taking personal responsibility; and (7) prevent harm to others. He concludes that application of behavioral science to health policy can often result in approaches that enhance autonomy, rather than constrict it.

These introductory chapters identify a number of normative questions that are taken up in part I, "The Ethics of Nudges in Healthcare," with an introduction by I. Glenn Cohen. In the part's first chapter, David A. Hyman and Thomas S. Ulen turn the lens around to ask what the ACA can teach us about behavioral economics. They argue that "maybe we should be more skeptical about the utility of behaviorally informed regulation." After all, regulators may themselves be biased, and generally, there is only mixed evidence of behavioral policy successes in the field. Focusing on default choices in particular, Hyman and Ulen review literature from outside the healthcare sector, which shows that defaults sometimes backfire compared to either a more stringent policy intervention or no intervention at all. The authors also provide a useful explication of the insurance enrollment features of the ACA, showing that, with one partial exception, the defaults for five different aspects of the ACA were set to nonparticipation.

Next, Mark D. White turns from empirical to normative critique of the use of behavioral economics in health law and policy. If the goal of nudges in healthcare contexts is to help individuals make decisions that better align with their own "true" interests, White highlights the choice architect's epistemic problem: how to know people's true interests, which prove complex, multifaceted, and subjective. This gives rise to an ethical problem: even if well-intentioned, a nudge may press individuals to conform their behavior with choices that do not align with their own interest but instead with that of the choice architect. White then considers the application of these critiques to healthcare decision-making specifically, and argues that nudges are more not less normatively problematic in this as compared to other domains.

In his chapter, Nir Eyal examines a different ethical critique of the application of behavioral economics to health law and policy: that they are manipulative. On the one hand, contrary to Sunstein and others, he argues that genuine nudges are manipulative on a range of plausible definitions of manipulation. On the other hand, as illustrated by examples drawn from health law and policy, he does not find that determination to be ethically conclusive. He argues that there is a category of manipulative yet ethically benign nudges, and shows that many of the interventions in health law and policy fall comfortably into that category.

Closing this part, chapter 7 by Jonathan Gingerich shifts the normative terrain more starkly to the level of political theory. He argues against critiques of nudging focused on reducing the set of choices or eliciting behavior through means other than rational persuasion. What is problematic about nudges, he argues, is the way in which they hide the amount of social control, undermining democratic governance by making it more difficult to detect the social architect's pulling of the strings. This concern is particularly salient as to choices where it is important for people to directly engage with a certain set of values, "big personal decisions" (to use a simplifying phrase). He argues that many healthcare decisions are exactly these kinds of choices.

Holly Fernandez Lynch introduces part II, which explores "Nudging and Public Health Policy," and evaluates particular instantiations of public health nudges. First, chapter 8, by Jennifer Blumenthal-Barby, Zainab Shipchandler, and Julika Kaplan, addresses a nudge designed to improve childhood immunization rates in rural India. The intervention was somewhat successful in achieving its behavioral aims, but these authors argue that evaluating the nudge requires further analysis beyond that fact. They set forth an ethical framework to assess nudges via incentives (particularly in their design, implementation, and results), suggesting that questions must be asked about utility, justice, autonomy, legitimacy, transparency, and trust. On this analysis, the authors determined that the particular intervention in question had some potentially worrisome aspects, but was ultimately ethically appropriate given the stakes.

In the following chapter, Andrea Freeman asks whether nudges will really be able to push the needle forward on major issues in food policy and reaches a skeptical conclusion. She divides food policy into three categories—hard paternalism (the government actively makes the choice, or imposes penalties for a different one), aggressive soft paternalism (motivation through economic incentives), and gentle soft paternalism (information disclosure and other cognitive strategies)—with robust examples of each. She argues that financial concerns and industry interests result in the use or rejection (depending on goals) of strategies known to influence consumer behavior, whereas health concerns tend to be approached with policies less likely to have a genuine impact—for example, the gentle soft paternalism of nutrition labeling rather than soda taxes. Ultimately, Freeman argues that "[t]he high number of illnesses and deaths associated with poor nutrition . . . and dramatic racial health disparities point to the need for direct interventions in the form of hard paternalistic measures."

Matthew J. B. Lawrence introduces part III, "Behavioral Economics and Healthcare Costs." Chapter 10, by Christopher T. Robertson and David V. Yokum, suggests that familiar cost-sharing devices such as co-pays and deductibles create a "decisional burden," which has not heretofore been acknowledged. The authors review empirical evidence from the behavioral sciences, suggesting that patients' exposure to out-of-pocket costs may undermine their cognitive capacities to make good healthcare decisions. Further, although cost sharing can preserve additional choices for the patient (compared to a centralized rationing system), that plethora of choices may actually reduce patients' satisfaction with their healthcare and facilitate regret. Robertson and Yokum leave open the question of what the optimal rationing mechanism is, but argue that the disadvantages of cost sharing cannot be overlooked.

Ameet Sarpatwari, Niteesh K. Choudhry, Jerry Avorn, and Aaron S. Kesselheim shift the focus from the patient to the physician in chapter 11 to explore the ways in which behavioral economics could promote cheaper prescribing patterns, away from patented drugs toward generics. The authors review the law around generic substitution, and a similar pattern for biologic drugs, and discuss informational and financial interventions. Whether it is the subtle change to put information about generic drugs in a larger bolder font on packaging, or the overt effort to pay physicians bonuses to switch their patients over to generics, there is now a rich literature testing such interventions and exploring their legality and ethicality. The authors close with some guidelines to shape any such policy.

In chapter 12, Jim Hawkins focuses on how patients use consumer credit in the self-pay markets for healthcare, such as fertility care, plastic surgery, or dental care. Taking one major medical credit card company as a case study and drawing on the consumer finance literature, Hawkins identifies several cognitive biases that may prevent patients from making good choices about how to finance their healthcare (and, in marginal cases, perhaps whether to consume such healthcare at all). Of particular concern is the "halo effect" that imbues healthcare providers with special trust but can be exploited by creditors when the healthcare providers also peddle credit cards. Hawkins also highlights the ways in the healthcare setting may reduce the salience of important financial considerations. Although the empirical evidence is largely indirect, Hawkins suggests an agenda for future research and policymaking to protect patients.

Part IV focuses on the particular behavioral phenomenon of "crowding out," where increased incentives may actually reduce motivation, with an introduction by Neel Shah. In chapter 13, Kirsten Underhill surveys the literature, defines the crowding-out concept, and focuses on the instrumental question of whether incentives may actually be counterproductive for a policymaker seeking to encourage a behavior, such as organ donation, physician practice excellence, or participation in wellness programs implemented by insurers or workplaces. Underhill argues that there are in fact multiple psychological mechanisms that can create crowding-out phenomena and counsels caution in crafting policy accordingly to draw on the useful behavioral levers while avoiding those that are likely to undermine the goal.

In chapter 14, Aditi P. Sen leads a group of six coauthors to test a particular crowding-out hypothesis in the domain of weight loss incentives. Reporting two groundbreaking field experiments with workplace wellness programs, the team found no crowding-out effects, which is to say that individuals who received financial incentives to lose weight reported equally high levels of intrinsic motivation as those without financial incentives, and in fact lost as much or more weight as those not incentivized. Score this one as a win for neoclassical economics.

Aaron S. Kesselheim introduces part V, "Behavioral Economics and the Doctor-Patient Relationship," which focuses on the ways in which clinicians can improve their patients' decision-making, even without any specter of government intervention. In her chapter, Jennifer L. Zamzow acknowledges that patients are often called on to make decisions about their health without any real basis for evaluating how they are likely to feel with different possible outcomes. Their physicians, on the other hand, routinely watch patients make similar decisions and are able to witness patient satisfaction with various approaches over time. Thus, she calls on physicians to help their patients make more accurate affective forecasts—predictions about how an outcome will impact experiential quality of life, especially when the stakes are high and where patients typically have a poor understanding of what it is like to have a certain condition or undergo a certain treatment. Importantly, this is not a call for medical paternalism, but rather more empowered patient decision-making.

In chapter 16, Alexander M. Capron and Donna Spruijt-Metz address the potential for clinicians to conscientiously and creatively use mobile devices and wireless technologies (mHealth) and the "small data" they generate to learn what patients want out of treatment, guide them through decision-making, and behave in ways most likely to achieve those goals. They discuss the challenges for this approach, ranging from the clinicians' own possible biases to technical and legal problems associated with accessing and using mHealth data. Like Zamzow, Capron and Spruijt-Metz are careful to guard against paternalistic approaches, instead suggesting that mHealth can serve as a facilitator of a strong patient-centered relationship. They conclude that mHealth could ultimately render clinicians' nudges not only more effective, but also more ethical.

The final chapter in this part, by Ester Moher and Khaled El Emam, takes on the issue of concern about access to and secondary use of health information. The traditional response to these concerns—in law and practice—has been to engage in a lengthy consent process, with strong assurances of anonymity, privacy, or confidentiality. However, Moher and El Emam describe what they dub the "ironic effects" of anonymity and confidentiality—namely, rather than having the consistent effect of greater and more accurate disclosure, informing individuals that their responses will remain anonymous or confidential may sometimes result in less accurate or complete reports of their behavior. The authors report on their own studies to examine the role of anonymity and confidentiality assurances on disclosure rates of sensitive health information, which confirm these counterintuitive outcomes, and also find that when individuals pay closer attention to assurances in a consent form, they disclose less. The authors hypothesize that this effect may suggest that individuals see confidentiality statements as a warning, rather than a safeguard. These results have important implications for clinicians and researchers, who must find a middle ground between the need for accurate informed consent processes and their potentially negative impact.

Part VI, "Deciding for Patients and Letting Patients Decide for Themselves," addresses the tension between autonomy and manipulation in various health-related contexts, with an introduction by Christopher T. Robertson. In chapter 18, Matthew J. B. Lawrence describes the Medicare "backlog crisis," the three-year queue to appeal a Medicare coverage refusal, despite the statutory requirement for a decision within ninety days. Lawrence casts this as a design problem of a kind familiar to behavioral economics, in which the law provides the same procedural protections to all claimants, even though not all may want or need them, and many would prefer a speedier outcome. His solution: incentivize those claimants who care only about the outcome of the appeal and for whom the process itself has little inherent value (for example, nursing homes, hospitals, and other providers, suppliers, or payers) to opt in to a fast-track appeals process, freeing up the system for those who do value both the process and the result—usually individual patients.

Next, Manisha Padi and Abigail R. Moncrieff address some of the empirical controversy over one of ObamaCare's key provisions, the individual mandate requiring individuals to carry health insurance or pay a tax, in behavioral economics terms. Does the mandate correct a mistake of those who prefer to have insurance but would not otherwise secure it, or does it actually impede a purposeful preference to be uninsured—and in either case, is there welfare lost as a result of the mandate's inherent coerciveness, and if so, to what extent? Padi and Moncrieff do not themselves answer these questions, but they identify the various problems that plague attempts to empirically resolve them, and ultimately argue for an experiential approach, asking simply whether people are better off (or happier) now than they were before the mandate. This approach, they suggest, has the benefit of incorporating lost utility from lost autonomy, captures purely economic considerations that may have different effects on different people, and addresses biases the intervention fails to correct.

In chapter 20, Sarah Conly discusses something even more controversial than ObamaCare: how to best deal with individuals in permanent states of unconsciousness. She argues that our current default rule of continuing life-sustaining care for these individuals makes both them (and society) worse off because they would be "better off dead." Conly suggests that when people indicate a preference to continue such care (for their family members or future selves), it is a result of biases and irrational logic because "[w]hatever quality makes life valuable, . . . that element is not present when we are in a state of permanent and deep unconsciousness." At the same time, continuing life-sustaining care in these contexts is tremendously costly and wasteful. Thus, Conly concludes that we ought to be nudging people more forcefully toward the "rational decision" of declining or terminating such care when the situation of permanent unconsciousness arises.

Nina A. Kohn takes on a related topic in her chapter: what is the best way to select an appropriate surrogate decision-maker when someone has become incapacitated and is unable to make her own healthcare decisions? The current approach is to select a surrogate "based on their relationship to the patient, trustworthiness, and willingness to follow the patient's directions." However, available data suggest that this often fails to result in decisions that align with patient preferences. Thus, Kohn argues for a new default rule that can guide individuals, courts, and policymakers regarding surrogate selection: choosing surrogates based on the extent to which they personally share the patient's preferences and values, rather than simply agree to carry out the patient's own wishes. Kohn suggests that this approach can be encouraged by the relatively simple behavioral approach of providing individuals with information to challenge their existing assumptions about surrogate decision-making.

In the final chapter of this part, Barbara J. Evans explores current policies that aim to protect people from making bad medical decisions in response to uncertain genomic information, often by withholding such tests or information from them. The problem with this choice architecture, which applies the "brute force tactic of suppressing individual choice altogether," is that it casts patients as inept and dependent—a serious problem when trying to shift from a disease-oriented model of medicine, to a more prospective, wellness-oriented approach that requires active patient involvement. Evans questions the learned intermediary model that shaped twentieth-century medicine, and pushes for a new approach to help conquer the current uncertainty surrounding genomic information: allowing such information to flow and be shared, rather than suppressing it. She suggests that the "real challenge is to create choice architectures that encourage parties who know the clinical significance of specific gene variants to share their knowledge to facilitate high-quality . . . genomic interpretation for all."

Gregory Curfman introduces part VII, the final part of the book, on default rules. Anna D. Sinaiko and Richard J. Zeckhauser study the default rule that applies when healthcare plans are terminated. In the Medicare Advantage market in particular, they point out that even if individuals carefully chose to move out of traditional Medicare, and then very carefully chose an appropriate plan for themselves, when that plan closes, the individuals get shunted back into traditional Medicare. Instead, for those who fail to choose again at this second period, it may be more efficient to have a default that most closely reflects the individual's own original choices. In this sense, the notion that a default acts in lieu of a choice can be updated to recognize that sometimes a default can be "smart," and one mechanism is for it to simply replicate a prior choice. A default need not be uniform.

Finally, David Orentlicher wades into the problem of the cadaveric organ shortage, and asks whether the United States should adopt a donation default (aka "opt out" or "presumed consent"), as is used in several European countries, rather than the opt-in system that is now used in the United States. Provocatively, Orentlicher argues that a donation default would actually be a poor fit with traditional nudge theory since the nudge would be for social purposes rather than the benefit the donor himself (a theme raised in Sunstein's foreword and Korobkin's chapter in this volume). Orentlicher also questions whether a donation default would actually improve donation rates in the

United States, suggesting that other causes may explain the higher rates in European countries.

The wide-ranging chapters in this volume provide a mixed view of the prospects for "nudging health"—in some domains of health, there is strong evidence for the efficacy of behavioral interventions, which seem normatively unobjectionable. In other domains, there is much more work to be done. This contingent analysis is precisely what we should expect from a discipline that is self-avowedly empirical and fallibilist. The behavioral sciences provide a rich and interesting set of tools for modifying behaviors in the domain of healthcare, and a generation of scholars and policymakers will do the hard work of conceiving, testing, implementing, and evaluating each potential behavioral policy intervention.

References

Ariely, Dan. 2008. *Predictably Irrational: The Hidden Forces That Shape Our Decisions*. HarperCollins. New York.

Camerer, Colin F., and George Loewenstein. 2011. "Behavioral Economics: Past, Present, and Future." In *Advances in Behavioral Economics*, edited by Colin F. Camerer, George Loewenstein, and Matthew Rabin. Princeton University Press. Princeton, NJ.

Cohen, I. Glenn. 2014. "Regulating the Organ Market: Normative Foundations for Market Regulation." *Law and Contemporary Problems* 74:71.

Jolls, Christine, Cass R. Sunstein, and Richard Thaler. 1998. "A Behavioral Approach to Law and Economics." *Stanford Law Review* 50:1471.

Kahneman, Daniel. 2013. *Thinking, Fast and Slow*. Farrar, Straus and Giroux. New York.

Loewenstein, G. 2007. *Exotic Preferences: Behavioural Economics and Human Motivation*. Oxford University Press. Oxford.

Robertson, Christopher T. 2013. "The Split Benefit: The Painless Way to Put Skin Back in the Healthcare Game." *Cornell Law Review* 98:921.

Robertson, Christopher T., David V. Yokum, and Megan S. Wright. 2014. "Perceptions of Efficacy, Morality, and Politics of Potential Cadaveric Organ Transplantation Reforms." *Law and Contemporary Problems* 74:101.

Sunstein, Cass R. 1997. "Looking Forward: Behavioral Analysis of Law." *University of Chicago Law Review* 64:1175.

Sunstein, Cass R., and Richard H. Thaler. 2003. "Libertarian Paternalism Is Not an Oxymoron." *University of Chicago Law Review* 70:1159–1202.

Thaler, Richard H. 2015. *Misbehaving: The Making of Behavioral Economics*. Norton. New York.

CHAPTER 1

Three Choice Architecture Paradigms for Healthcare Policy

Russell Korobkin

Bounded Rationality and Choice Architecture

Information overload is ubiquitous in the twenty-first century. In nearly every realm of life, individuals and firms face constant pressure to make decisions that seem to require a literally superhuman ability to access, digest, and analyze information. Traditional, neoclassical economists tend to wish this problem away by assuming perfect rationality: that choices made maximize the subjective expected utility of the chooser given constraints. Or, put in a slightly different way, that our "revealed preferences," as determined by the choices we make, match our experienced utility or hedonic experience (Gul and Pesendorfer 2008). It does not take a social scientist to realize that this assumption is highly problematic. But the burgeoning body of social science research in the field, alternatively labeled "judgment and decision-making," "behavioral decision-making," or "behavioral economics," has provided a bumper crop of insights into the variety of ways in which our bounded rationality causes people to make decisions using heuristics that frequently lead to suboptimal outcomes (Gilovich, Griffin, and Kahneman 2002). The problem is a general one that cuts across decision-making contexts, but it is particularly acute in the realm of healthcare, both because the information relevant to decision-making is particularly dense and complex and because the stakes are notably high.

If healthcare decisions are often too difficult for boundedly rational individuals to make optimally, whether and how the government can aid in the decision-making process become important questions. One possibility is that the government consciously remove itself completely from the complicated markets for medical care, health insurance, and the like, with perhaps the minimal exception of policing fraud, and allow

Chris Robertson provided helpful comments on an earlier draft and Sam Pierce excellent research assistance.

admittedly boundedly rational actors to make unaided choices within those market environments. Individuals will no doubt make "mistakes," by which I mean decisions that fail to maximize their expected utility, but at least the mistakes will be their own. This option might appeal to a small cadre of hard-core libertarians who rate personal autonomy far above all other values, but it is unappealing to those who believe that the government has a role to play in promoting the welfare of its citizens as individuals and the public good more generally.

At the other end of the spectrum, the government could take over responsibility for making some or all healthcare decisions for individuals, directly providing medical care or dictating what care should be provided in what circumstances, under what conditions, and at what prices. A Stalinist command-and-control system, however, has even less appeal than does benign neglect. Not only does this approach ignore the value of individual autonomy for its own sake (Rachlinski 2003; Wright and Ginsburg 2012), it also implicitly relies on the problematic assumption that government decision-makers are not themselves subject to bounded rationality (Glaeser 2006, 134). Heavy-handed government regulation is also too rigid to respond to heterogeneity in values and preferences among the governed.

In the space between these opposite points on the continuum of government intervention rests all manner of partial government coercive control over healthcare decisions, from the requirement that physicians obtain a license from a state medical board before practicing (for example, California Business and Professions Code sec. 2052), thus effectively constraining consumer choice of providers, to the Affordable Care Act (ACA) requirement that individuals carry health insurance (sec. 1501(b) of the ACA, 26 U.S.C. §5000A(f)) but can choose their insurance provider and thus their doctors. This space also allows, however, for the government to regulate "choice architecture" (Thaler and Sunstein 2008), best understood as the prisms and structures through which individuals view and perceive decision options, rather than directly regulating the substantive choices themselves. Interventions in choice architecture seek to facilitate better private decision-making but, at the end of the day, leave the power of decision-making in the hands of those who will have to live with the consequences. There is not a monolithic approach to regulating choice architecture; this type of regulation can be informed by different paradigms. This chapter seeks to expand the conceptual menu of approaches to choice architecture available to policymakers by contrasting the best-known paradigm, "libertarian paternalism," with two alternatives, "libertarian welfarism" and "decision simplification," and illustrating how the relative desirability of each paradigm can depend on particular contextual features of the decision environment.

Libertarian Paternalism

The best known paradigm of government intervention in choice architecture is "libertarian paternalism," a concept first advanced by the behavioral economist Richard

Thaler and the legal scholar Cass Sunstein in the pages of academic journals (Sunstein and Thaler 2003; Thaler and Sunstein 2003) and then disseminated more widely in their justly popular book *Nudge: Improving Decisions about Health, Wealth, and Happiness* (Thaler and Sunstein 2008). Other scholars have advanced similar theories under labels like "asymmetric paternalism" (Camerer et al. 2003) or "light paternalism" (Loewenstein and Haisley 2008). The core idea of libertarian paternalism is that policymakers should encourage actors to act in a way that the policymakers think is in the actors' best interests, while still allowing the actors the opportunity to choose otherwise. The success of libertarian paternalism as a regulatory paradigm, at least among academic thinkers, is illustrated by the fact that the word "nudge" appears in the title of this edited volume, as well as by the plethora of references to the idea of "nudging" that can be found throughout its pages.

Libertarian paternalism has much to recommend it: it takes advantage of the knowledge policymakers sometimes have about what decisions are in the best interests of individual actors while simultaneously protecting personal autonomy. At the same time, this approach has several significant drawbacks that prevent it from being suitable in all contexts.

The most obvious problem with libertarian paternalism is that policymakers, of course, do not always know what is best for individuals (Mitchell 2005, 1268–69). So even when a nudge might be useful, sometimes it will be unclear, even to the policymakers themselves, which way to direct the nudge.

A second drawback is that, even though libertarian paternalism allocates the ultimate authority to choose to the subjects of the regulatory action rather than government decision-makers, nudges in the wrong direction—that is, in the direction of a choice that is suboptimal for the subject—will sometimes "succeed," with the result that the actor makes a decision that does not maximize his expected utility under the circumstances. Nudges in the wrong direction are thus not costless because individuals who are uncertain that they are being nudged in the wrong direction or are insufficiently motivated to determine what the optimal course of action for them actually is will yield to the nudge. After all, if all individuals were able to optimize to the extent that they could avoid the consequences of misplaced nudges, nudging would not be necessary in the first place.

A third problem is that the best choice for an individual is not always the best choice for a society generally. "Good-for-one" can be "bad-for-all" in many circumstances. There is no obvious normative justification for nudging individuals in a way that would maximize their private utility if doing so would reduce social welfare, which it sometimes might. Taking into account both the benefits and the drawbacks of libertarian paternalism leads to the conclusion that this paradigm provides a desirable regulatory approach (1) when policy-makers are highly confident about what choices and decisions will maximize the welfare of most actors; (2) when there is a high degree of homogeneity among the actors, so that nudging most people in the direction that is desirable for them will not have the side effect of nudging a large minority in a direction that is undesirable for them; and (3) when there are few negative externalities created by individual choices, such that behavior that is welfare maximizing for most individual decision-makers is also welfare maximizing for society. When one or more of these features is absent, the desirability of libertarian paternalism becomes much less clear.

The remainder of this chapter suggests two alternative paradigms of choice architecture regulation, thus expanding the menu of options available to policy-makers who seek noncoercive responses to the problems of bounded rationality.

Libertarian Welfarism

If the government's goal is to help boundedly rational individuals act in ways that serve their own best interests, the most straightforward policy option is to simply mandate behavior. In a nod to the "libertarian paternalism" label, we can call such command-and-control regulation "coercive paternalism." Helping citizens to maximize their individual utility, however, is not the only proper goal of government. Government power is often used to promote overall social welfare, even when this means that some individuals might be made worse off. Legal rules that force citizens to act in a way judged to be best for society as a whole can be called "coercive welfarism." The ACA's "individual mandate" is an example of this in the healthcare field: although some young and healthy individuals without employer-sponsored health insurance might maximize their own utility by forgoing insurance sold at community rates, betting on good luck and/or relying on charity care, the law now requires them to purchase health insurance in order to avoid adverse selection problems that might otherwise undermine a functioning insurance market (*Nat'l Federation of Independent Business v. Sebelius* 2012, 2585).

Just as libertarian paternalism seeks to achieve the goal of paternalism by nudge rather than by force, policy initiatives can seek the goal of maximizing social welfare by nudge rather than by force. I call strategies that fall into this regulatory paradigm "libertarian welfarism" (Korobkin 2009). The relationship between libertarian welfarism and both libertarian paternalism and coercive approaches to policy can be described in a 2 x 2 matrix (see fig. 1.1).

Establishing, or changing, legal default rules is a primary method of using choice architecture in a libertarian, rather than a coercive, way. The libertarian welfarism paradigm suggests that the government should choose default rules that are what I have called "policy forcing"—that is, that encourage individual actions that produce positive externalities (and thus increase social welfare) rather than encourage purely self-interested actions (Korobkin 2007). The debate over procuring solid organs for transplant illustrates the difference between the libertarian paternalist and libertarian welfarist approaches.

U.S. jurisdictions abide by a "no-donation" default rule (often called "opt-in") for the collection of solid organs for transplant after death; that is, the default is that ca-

Policy goal

	Paternalism	Welfarism
Coercive	Coercive paternalism	Coercive welfarism
Noncoercive	Libertarian paternalism	*Libertarian welfarism*

Means of implementation

FIGURE 1.1 Regulatory paradigms

daveric organs are not harvested for this purpose, and a potential donor (or the next of kin) must affirmatively elect donation in order to avoid application of the default (Orentlicher, this volume). At the time this chapter was written, more than 124,000 Americans were on the United Network for Organ Sharing's (UNOS) list of patients awaiting solid organ transplants (United Network for Organ Sharing 2014), and many of them will die before a suitable organ becomes available.

In what is perhaps the most famous article at the intersection of behavioral economics and healthcare, Eric Johnson and Daniel Goldstein (2003) provided evidence from Europe that suggests that the number of cadaveric donors would increase substantially in the United States if this country were to shift the default rule from one of no-donation to one of donation (often called a "presumed consent" rule because individuals are presumed to consent to donation unless they actively opt out). Other studies have demonstrated that countries that have shifted their default rule from opt in to presumed consent have experienced large increases in cadaveric donation rates (Rithalia et al. 2009), although there is currently some controversy over the extent to which the change in default rules is alone responsible for the increases (Orentlicher, this volume). A large number of people do not feel strongly about cadaveric donation one way or the other, and a combination of status quo bias (Samuelson and Zeckhauser 1988) and decision aversion (Beattie et al. 1994) suggests that most will probably not opt out of the default rule, whatever it is.

Implementing a presumed consent default, however, is almost certainly an example of libertarian welfarism rather than libertarian paternalism. It is difficult to make the case that cadaveric donation best serves the self-interest of the donor, who will, of course, be dead at the time of donation and will receive no tangible benefits. Even cadaveric donation brings with it some expected cost ex ante. There is some non-zero (albeit small) risk that a medical team could incorrectly pronounce a patient dead and attempt to remove organs for transplant, for example; regulators fined a New York hospital in 2009 for nearly committing just such a blunder (O'Brien and Mulder 2013). For some donors, the warm glow that comes from acting altruistically might make donation the option that maximizes individual utility, but members of this group are likely to opt into cadaveric donation under the current regime. Thus, a policymaker attempting to regulate consistently with the libertarian paternalism paradigm should probably favor the no-donation default. At a minimum, a true libertarian-paternalist policymaker could not confidently install a presumed consent rule.

From the perspective of libertarian welfarism, in contrast, it seems clear that presumed consent is the appropriate default rule (Korobkin 2009). It would be difficult to argue that an increase in available organs resulting from a switch from an opt-in to a presumed consent default would not increase net social welfare compared to the present regime. The ex ante expected cost to donors—who, remember, will be dead at the time of donation—might be real, but it would be quite small. In contrast, the positive utility experienced by recipients who receive a new lease on life or health would be enormous.

Where private behavior has few social consequences, positive or negative, libertarian paternalism and libertarian welfarism are functionally equivalent. But when individual choices carry with them significant positive or negative externalities, as is the case with cadaveric organ donation, libertarian welfarism is a normatively more defensible approach. Maximizing social welfare—rather than just the welfare of a subset of the population—is *the* commonly accepted policy goal of consequentialist legal traditions such as law and economics (Kaplow and Shavell 2002; Klick and Paresi 2005). There is a plausible argument, rooted in the value of autonomy, for why the government should not intervene at all in private behavior, even when that behavior has some negative social costs, but there is no obvious corresponding normative justification for the state to encourage individual actors to behave in a way that creates private benefits but reduces social welfare in the process.

If the policymaker's normative goal is to maximize social welfare, the difficult question will often not be whether to favor libertarian paternalism over libertarian welfarism, but whether to favor coercive welfarism. In this comparison, libertarian welfarism offers two advantages. First, by preserving the ultimate autonomy of actors, nudging has a social welfare advantage over mandating, to the extent that autonomy creates utility no matter how exercised, which it surely does. So when the negative externalities of selfish behavior exist but are relatively modest, libertarian welfarism can actually produce greater social welfare (including the welfare benefits of autonomy) than coercive welfarism. Second, when the positive externalities of private behavior are subject to declining marginal utility, nudges can be more efficient than mandates because they assure that the positive externalities will be created by individuals who can do so at the lowest private cost. The organ donation example demonstrates this point. A presumed consent default would allow individuals with the highest personal costs of donating to opt out, while procuring organs from individuals whose private preference is closer to indifference and thus would be most likely to accept the default. A mandate, in contrast, would procure the necessary organs without sensitivity to the utility consequences to the providers of those organs while they are still alive.

Decision Simplification

Policymakers can enhance the ability of individuals to make decisions that maximize their own subjective expected utility by combining and presenting information in ways that simplify the relevant choice. Thus, what I call "decision simplification" can be understood as a third paradigm of choice architecture, along with libertarian paternalism and libertarian welfarism, for responding to the problem of bounded rationality.

Choice architecture can never be entirely neutral—a choice must be presented in some context, and that context is likely to have an effect on outcomes (Johnson et al. 2012). To borrow a vivid example from *Nudge*, a cafeteria designer can place the fruit before the desserts (increasing the likelihood that any given customer will choose the fruit), or vice versa, but she cannot place both the fruit and the desserts first (Thaler and Sunstein 2008). But choice architecture can be relatively more or less neutral. If the buffet designer makes fruit and cake easy to see and to reach, the architecture will be much closer to neutrality than if she obscures the desserts from the diner's line of sight or places them out of reach. Decision simplification, as a general approach, seeks to facilitate choices that will maximize actors' subjective expected utility while avoiding, to the extent possible, placing a thumb on the scale.

In the world in which we live, decisions are many, time is scarce, and actors often have heterogeneous preferences, so decision simplification will often be an attractive approach to choice architecture. There are several features of healthcare decisions in general and medical treatment decisions specifically, however, that suggest that decision simplification can be a particularly useful strategy in this realm. Decisions that are very complex (Payne, Bettman, and Schkade 1999), that are novel (Payne, Bettman, and Schkade 1999), or that require tradeoffs that sacrifice deeply held moral values (Bettman, Luce, and Payne 1998) are particularly likely to result in individual actors' applying decision-making heuristics that are globally rational (in the sense that they help us to avoid unacceptably high personal costs of thorough and completely considered decision-making) but can result in suboptimal outcomes in individual cases. Medical care decisions are often complex for obvious reasons; other than those involving treatment of chronic conditions, most are novel for the patient; and when such decisions require trading off money against health, which most of us are instinctively reluctant to have to do, they can undermine rational cost-benefit analysis.

Virtually all private insurance in the United States purports to cover all "medically necessary" care, except to the extent that categories of treatment are explicitly excluded by contract (Morreim 2001, 47). State laws that give consumers expansive rights to appeal insurers' denial of care to medical committees essentially mandate that insurers pay for all treatments that offer some demonstrated, positive expected medical benefit compared to available alternatives, regardless of cost (Korobkin 2014a, 546–47). This implicit mandate can simplify difficult decision problems by eliminating the patient's need to balance price against the likely medical efficacy of available options at the point of treatment. But the consequence is that consumers are forced to buy more extensive ("deep") insurance than many might wish to purchase.

Supporters of proposals often called consumer-directed healthcare (CDHC) favor reducing the scope of insurance and increasing patient responsibility for medical expenses by significantly increasing patient cost sharing, often by substantially raising deductibles (Madison and Jacobson 2007). High-deductible plans, which are increasingly popular, enable patients to pay less for insurance ex ante than they would otherwise have to pay for a policy with little or no cost sharing, and then effectively requires them to balance their desire for medical services against its cost at the point of service—at least until they have spent the annual deductible amount and no longer face significant out-of-pocket costs. But this approach requires boundedly rational consumers to make difficult tradeoffs between cost and treatment that most will struggle to make optimally. When the choice is made in the shadow of illness, financial constraints, or both, evidence suggests making utility-maximizing choices will be even more difficult (Robertson and Yokum, this volume).

If the current insurance system mandates that actors purchase deep insurance, and the CDHC approach provides greater choice concerning the amount and types of healthcare services purchased but ignores the reality of consumer-bounded rationality, what are policymakers to do? I have proposed an approach that facilitates more consumer choice between cost and depth of treatment but simplifies the process of making the tradeoff between the two relative to the CDHC approach. I call this particular choice architecture, which requires consumers to balance cost against depth of treatment at the time of insurance purchase rather than at the point of service, "relative value health insurance" (RVHI) (Korobkin 2014b).

Facilitating the establishment of a system of RVHI would require two regulatory steps: first, a government body would rate treatments for different medical conditions on a scale of 1 to 10 based on the relative value of those treatments. A treatment that earns a score of 1 for a particular medical condition is one that meets a high cost-effectiveness threshold, providing substantial medical value for the cost. A treatment awarded a score of 10 is of marginal value: it provides some marginal health benefit, or it at least has the possibility of providing some benefit, but the low benefit coupled with a high cost makes it of questionable value. Ratings could be based on quality-adjusted life years (QALYs) per dollar of cost. Second, private insurers would be permitted to sell RVHI insurance—policies that provide coverage only for treatments that earn a particular relative value rating or better. This would require lifting legal requirements that effectively define "medical necessity" in health insurance policies expansively and easing ACA regulations that base minimum standards for policies marketable on health insurance exchanges on services provided by currently existing "benchmark plans" (45 C.F.R. 156.100).

These interventions would facilitate the creation of a market that offers health insurance policies that cover different depths of care at different prices. Customers would be able to choose, for example, between a shallow policy (perhaps one that covers only treatments that have earned relative value ratings of 1–4) and a deep policy (perhaps one that covers all treatments rated 1–9 or even 1–10). All policies would cover the most cost-effective medical treatments, but shallower policies would exclude coverage for treatments with worse cost-effectiveness profiles, either because the expected benefits are small, the costs are extremely high, or both. The exact point of demarcation would depend on the depth of coverage specified in the particular policy, as indicated by its relative value rating cutoff point. Of course, shallower policies will be much less expensive; since shallower policies will cover fewer benefits than deeper policies, they will cost insurers less to provide.

Due to income level, risk aversion, idiosyncratic preferences, or some combination of these factors, some people would prefer to spend relatively more money on medical care while others would prefer to spend relatively less and have more left over for other things. If health and safety were everyone's sole value concern, automobile manufacturers would not sell any cars that do not receive the Institute of Highway Safety's highest crash-safety rating. This is not, of course, what we observe in the automobile market, where some people choose greater safety and others opt for better performance, more luxurious styling, or lower prices. By consulting a current list of the relative value ratings of different treatments for different medical conditions, consumers could inform themselves, in a general way, of the consequences of choosing to purchase shallower or deeper insurance policies, and then make their insurance purchase decision accordingly. Just as government regulations establish a safety floor for automobile sales, regulations could establish a coverage floor for healthcare by requiring individuals to carry insurance that covers a specified depth of treatment. But that level need not be as deep as the current regulatory structure requires.

RVHI would help to simplify healthcare purchase decisions relative to a world of high-deductible health insurance plans that require patients to trade off cost against treatment options at the point of service by taking advantage of several mechanisms that have been demonstrated to facilitate decision-making: parsimony, linearity, and comparability (Johnson et al. 2012). First, RVHI would render the evaluation of the efficacy of treatment choices for different medical conditions parsimonious by collapsing extremely complex information about the quality of treatment options into a single numerical value that decision-makers can balance against price. Second, both the relative value rating and the price of insurance options would have a linear relationship to their relevant goals, either minimizing price or maximizing coverage. That is, as an insurance policy's relative value rating moves from 1 to 10, the depth of coverage associated with the product alternative decreases and, of course, as the price of the product increases, the cost of that alternative increases. Third, the depth of coverage provided by each insurance option available to consumers would be described using the same 1–10 scale, facilitating comparisons between alternative insurance policies. And by placing the decision choice temporally at the time customers must purchase insurance it avoids requiring difficult decisions be made at the emotionally charged moment when medical care is actually needed.

The decision problem faced by customers under this choice architecture would still be challenging, and the requirement of RVHI that the tradeoff between price and treatment choice be made before illness strikes could introduce its own biases: present-biased individuals who place exceedingly high value on immediate compared to future payoffs (O'Donoghue and Rabin 1999) and overly optimistic individuals who underestimate their actual risk of future ill health (Weinstein and Klein 1996) might be inclined to purchase shallower coverage than would actually maximize their subjective expected utility. But problems of choice architecture always require policymakers to choose between second-best options in a world in which perfection is elusive. Choice architecture in the decision simplification paradigm, such as RVHI, attempts to balance between the goals of maximizing choice and minimizing the complexity of exercising choice.

When private decisions have significant externalities, policymakers might use the libertarian welfarism paradigm to nudge actors toward the social optimum. When actors are homogeneous and policymakers believe they know what decision will be in their best interest, a libertarian-paternalist nudge toward the privately optimal choice might be indicated. But decision simplification will be relatively desirable, compared to both libertarian paternalism and libertarian welfarism, in circumstances in which private choices produce relatively modest externalities and either (a) policymakers are unsure what choice would maximize the expected utility of most actors or (b) there is substantial heterogeneity across actors (such that nudging even a majority in the optimal directions would mean nudging many in a suboptimal direction). Medical care decisions are a context in which the decision simplification paradigm arguably enjoys significant advantages. Preferences are likely to be highly heterogeneous, with some actors strongly preferring to spend a substantial portion of their income on medical care and other actors strongly preferring to spend less on medical care—especially care that comes at a relatively high cost and offers relatively modest expected benefits. And although greater individual investment of resources in medical care would have positive externalities—insurance pools might be more resistant to adverse selection and high research and development costs of pharmaceuticals and medical devices could be spread more broadly—the private utility consequences of those choices probably dwarf the social welfare implications, especially if the government mandates a minimal level of coverage and allows choice concerning coverage depth only beyond that point.

Conclusion

Regulating choice architecture, while leaving ultimate decision-making authority in the hands of individual actors, provides an alternative policy approach to both government withdrawal from markets and coercive mandates. But choice architecture regulation itself includes a variety of possibilities. This chapter describes and contrasts three competing paradigms. Libertarian paternalism, the best-known approach, is desirable when decisions that will maximize the expected utility of actors subject to regulation are well known to policymakers, are largely homogeneous, and have minimal externalities. Libertarian welfarism enjoys a comparative advantage when externalities are large and the policymakers have a better understanding of the social welfare function than the individual welfare functions of regulated actors. Decision simplification is preferable when decision externalities are small compared to their private significance but either policymakers cannot judge which decisions will maximize private utility or the utility consequences to the regulated actors are heterogeneous. Regulators who seek to employ principles of choice architecture in the healthcare context should be cognizant of these contextual features of the decision environment when choosing which paradigm to favor.

References

Beattie, Jane, Jonathan Baron, John C. Hershey, and Mark D. Spranca. 1994. "Psychological Determinants of Decision Attitude." *Journal of Behavioral Decision Making* 7:129–44.
Bettman, James R., Mary Frances Luce, and John W. Payne. 1998. "Constructive Consumer Choice Processes." *Journal of Consumer Resources* 25:187.
Camerer, Colin F., Samuel Issacharoff, George Loewenstein, Ted O'Donaghue, and Matthew Rabin. 2003. "Regulation for Conservatives: Behavioral Economics and the Case for 'Asymmetric Paternalism.'" *University of Pennsylvania Law Review* 151:1211.
Gilovich, Thomas, Dale Griffin, and Daniel Kahneman. 2002. *Heuristics and Biases: The Psychology of Intuitive Judgment.* Cambridge University Press. New York.
Glaeser, Edward L. 2006. "Paternalism and Psychology." *The University of Chicago Law Review* 73:133.
Gul, Faruk, and Wolfgang Pesendorfer. 2008. "The Case for Mindless Economics." In *The Foundations of Positive and Normative Economics: A Handbook*, edited by Andrew Caplin and Andrew Schotter. Oxford University Press. New York. 3.
Johnson, Eric J., and Daniel Goldstein. 2003. "Do Defaults Save Lives?" *Science* 302:1338.
Johnson, Eric J., Suzanne B. Shu, Benedict G. C. Dellaert, Craig Fox, Daniel G. Goldstein, Gerald Haubl, Richard P. Larrick, John W. Payne, Ellen Peters, David Schkade, Brian Wansink, and Elke U. Weber. 2012. "Beyond Nudges: Tools of a Choice Architecture." *Marketing Letters* 23:487–504.
Kaplow, Louis, and Steven Shavell. 2002. *Fairness versus Welfare.* Harvard University Press. Cambridge, MA.
Klick, Jonathan, and Francesco Paresi. 2005. "Wealth, Utility, and the Human Dimension." *New York University Journal of Law & Liberty* 1:590.

Korobkin, Russell. 2014a. "Comparative Effectiveness Research as Choice Architecture." *Michigan Law Review* 112:523–74.

———. 2009. "Libertarian Welfarism." *California Law Review* 97:1651.

———. 2007. "'No Compensation' or 'Pro Compensation': *Moore v. Regents* and Default Rules for Human Tissue Donations." *Journal of Health Law* 40:1.

———. 2014b. "Relative Value Health Insurance." *Journal of Health Politics, Policy and Law.* 39:417–40.

Loewenstein, George, and Emily Haisley. 2008. "The Economist as Therapist: Methodological Ramifications of Light Paternalism." In *The Foundations of Positive and Normative Economics: A Handbook*, edited by Andrew Caplin and Andrew Schatter. Oxford University Press. New York. 210.

Madison, Kristen, and Peter D. Jacobson. 2007. "Consumer-Directed Health Care." *University of Pennsylvania Law Review* 156:107.

Mitchell, Gregory. 2005. "Libertarian Paternalism Is an Oxymoron." *Northwestern University Law Review* 99:1245.

Morreim, E. Haavi. 2001 *Holding Health Care Accountable*. Oxford University Press. New York.

Nat'l Federation of Independent Business v. Sebelius, 132 S.Ct. 2566 (2012).

O'Brien, John, and James T. Mulder. 2013. "St Joe's 'Dead' Patient Awoke as Docs Prepared to Remove Organs." *Syracuse Post-Standard*, July 7. http://www.syracuse.com/news/index.ssf /2013/07/st_joes_fined_over_dead_patien.html.

O'Donoghue, Ted, and Matthew Rabin. 1999. "Doing It Now or Later." *The American Economic Review* 89:103.

Payne, John W., James R. Bettman, and David A. Schkade. 1999. "Measuring Constructed Preferences: Toward a Building Code." *Journal of Risk and Uncertainty* 19:243.

Rachlinski, Jeffrey J. 2003. "The Uncertain Psychological Case for Paternalism." *Northwestern University Law Review* 97:1165.

Rithalia, Amber, Catriona McDaid, Sara Suekarran, Lindsey Myers, and Amanda Sowden. 2009. "Impact of Presumed Consent for Organ Donation on Donation Rates: A Systematic Review." *British Medical Journal* 338:a3162.

Samuelson, William, and Richard Zeckhauser. 1988. "Status Quo Bias in Decision Making." *Journal of Risk and Uncertainty* 1:7.

Sunstein, Cass R., and Richard H. Thaler. 2003 "Libertarian Paternalism Is Not an Oxymoron." *The University of Chicago Law Review* 70:1159.

Thaler, Richard H., and Cass R. Sunstein. 2003. "Libertarian Paternalism." *The American Economic Review* 93:175.

———. 2008. *Nudge: Improving Decisions about Health, Wealth, and Happiness*. Yale University Press. New Haven, CT.

United Network for Organ Sharing. 2014. "Organ Procurement and Transplantation Network Data." http://optn.transplant.hrsa.gov/converge/data/.

Weinstein, Neil D., and William M. Klein. 1996. "Unrealistic Optimism: Present and Future." *Journal of Clinical Psychology* 15:1.

Wright, Joshua D., and Douglas H. Ginsburg. 2012. "Behavioral Law and Economics: Its Origins, Fatal Flaws, and Implications for Liberty." *Northwestern University Law Review* 106:1033.

CHAPTER 2

Can Behavioral Economics Save Healthcare Reform?

Alan M. Garber

The Affordable Care Act (ACA), like many earlier proposals for reform of the U.S. healthcare system, seeks to improve health by making health insurance more widely available. Some nations offer access to healthcare by providing it directly, often in government-run clinics and hospitals. In contrast, in the United States, and in many other nations, health insurance serves as the gateway to healthcare, most of it provided privately. Patients with adequate insurance can be admitted to hospitals and receive expensive procedures and drugs knowing that insurance payments will offset much of the financial impact of the care, so access to health insurance can mean access to healthcare.

The cost of health insurance expansion is directly tied to the cost of care, so the extraordinarily high level of medical expenditures poses daunting challenges to health reform in the United States. If a health insurance expansion were implemented by perhaps the most direct means—subsidizing the purchase of existing private health insurance plans and broadening enrollment in existing government programs—the program would be prohibitively expensive. For example, in 2014, the average premium cost for employer-sponsored insurance for an individual was $6,025 (Claxton et al. 2014). And seldom can policies that expand coverage by subsidizing health insurance premiums be narrowly targeted to people who would not otherwise purchase insurance. Consequently, the subsidies often go to people who would have been covered by insurance anyway, adding greatly to the cost of expansion. The high cost was among the principal criticisms of the ACA (Holtz-Eakin and Ramlet 2010) and is a threat to the long-term viability of the legislation. The ACA faces a series of political threats, but the challenges are not exclusively political. To save healthcare reform, it will be necessary to find savings to offset the costs of the insurance expansion.

Concerns over the costs of healthcare did not originate with the ACA. The decades-long discussion about how to control health costs and to deliver care efficiently has led to a better understanding of the capabilities and limitations of conventional economic incentives. The body of evidence addressing the effectiveness of cost sharing, for example, is extensive. It shows that individuals who pay a larger fraction of the cost of the care they receive generally use less care (Newhouse et al. 1981). But critics argue that patient cost sharing is not a complete solution (Baicker and Goldman 2011). A largely observational literature suggests that an increase in out-of-pocket costs can lead to underutilization of effective, cost-effective drugs. Furthermore, financial risks to patients rise as their responsibility for out-of-pocket expenses increases, so overly aggressive cost sharing can defeat much of the purpose of health insurance. That is why newer health insurance designs that expose patients to more of the costs of the care they use, such as high-deductible health plans, limit cost sharing and preserve many features of traditional health insurance. When a patient with a high-deductible health plan is hospitalized, her expenses will usually exceed the deductible threshold, and at that point, most high-deductible plans look much like conventional health insurance—they have similar limits on out-of-pocket expenses, and their incentives to discourage the use of additional care are generally no stronger.

The search for additional approaches to manage costs and improve the efficiency of care has piqued the interest of health reformers in behavioral economics. They have been impressed by evidence from behavioral economists and psychologists that non-financial incentives have powerful effects, and that financial incentives can, in some circumstances, have unexpected consequences (Gneezy, Meier, and Rey-Biel 2011; Gneezy and Rustichini 2000). Some of the architects of President Barack Obama's health reform plan, notably Peter Orszag, who was the director of the Office of Management and Budget when the legislation was crafted and signed into law, explored ways that behavioral economics–based interventions might be incorporated into the ACA. Now that enough time has elapsed to implement some of the most ambitious features of the act, it is timely to ask, how can behavioral economics help solve the challenges that health reform faces? Can behavioral economics be used to craft and implement policies that will lower costs, enable health insurance to function as intended, and improve health outcomes?

Better Health Behaviors

For politicians eager to offer solutions that will improve health while reducing expenditures, disease prevention holds great appeal. Some preventive strategies are either cost-saving or, even when they increase health expenditures, highly cost-effective. Examples of high-value preventive strategies include immunization to prevent influenza in high-risk groups, cholesterol reduction following a heart attack, and blood pressure reduction among patients whose blood pressure is moderately or severely elevated. Avoidance of high-risk behaviors, such as cigarette smoking, can also reduce health expenditures by preventing injury and disease (Goldman et al. 2009).

Despite their obvious appeal—they are generally safe and often highly effective—these preventive approaches have had mixed success. Prevention often increases health expenditures, in part because people live longer (Russell 2009). Many people who stand to benefit do not, often because they fail to comply with recommendations to take the necessary medications or to change their behavior. Recognition of the need for compliance has prompted interest in behaviorally informed strategies for health promotion and disease prevention (Livingood et al. 2011).

Rising obesity rates in the United States and abroad, along with recognition that obesity is associated with extensive morbidity and mortality, has made weight loss one of the most prominent targets for behavioral interventions. Apart from anti-obesity (bariatric) surgery, medical interventions have fallen short of producing sustained, substantial weight loss (Buchwald et al. 2004; Maggard et al. 2005; Douketis et al. 2005). Exercise and diet can lead to weight loss when negative caloric balance is maintained, and their costs and adverse effects are predominantly opportunity costs and self-denial. These disadvantages are not to be dismissed—they are daunting barriers that frustrate even fervent plans to trim down and shape up. But they are, or seem to be, amenable to interventions whose purpose is to change behavior. If exercise could be made pleasurable, or if dieting could be pursued as part of a group activity, creating social bonding rather than isolation, behavioral interventions might accomplish more than a drug or surgical procedure.

Psychologists and behavioral economists have tested a variety of strategies to alter the balance of cost and reward in pursuing better health behaviors. Some involve financial rewards, but in novel ways. They explore the possibility that different ways of administering the rewards (for example, lotteries versus fixed payments as the reward for behavioral change) can have different effects on behavior, even if the alternatives have identical financial value (Volpp et al. 2011; Volpp et al. 2009). Others make use of precommitment devices such as commitment contracts, as a self-control technique for overcoming the effects of hyperbolic discounting (Giné, Karlan, and Zinman 2010; Goldhaber-Fiebert, Blumenkranz, and Garber 2010; Bryan, Karlan, and Nelson 2010). And the finding that health behaviors appear to be contagious within social networks, even when those networks are geographically dispersed, offers the hope that group-targeted interventions might succeed when individual interventions do not (Christakis and Fowler 2007, 2008).

Why highlight behavioral approaches to disease prevention as part of health reform? Behavioral interventions can substitute for the forms of medical care that health insurance pays for, and without their own subsidies behavioral interventions will be underused, especially when compared to generously reimbursed medical services. Furthermore, drugs and surgical procedures can cause adverse effects that may be more consequential than the drawbacks of behavioral interventions. Small wonder that be-havioral economics findings, when they can be put to use in a practical and effective way, hold so much appeal for reform advocates.

Mitigating Market Failure

By improving health and averting the healthcare costs that accompany disease, be-havioral interventions can enhance the prospects that a health insurance expansion will succeed. The insights of behavioral economics can also facilitate reforms based on health insurance expansions via two additional mechanisms: improving the func-tion of health insurance and markets for health insurance, and addressing imperfec-tions in markets for health services.

Behavioral economics is motivated by findings that people often display behavior that is inconsistent with the strict forms of rationality that are assumed in the most basic versions of neoclassical economic theory. This irrationality, especially when it is manifest in self-contradictory behavior such as time-inconsistent preferences, under-mines attempts by an individual to determine whether the actions taken are in his best interest. And more worryingly for the notion that personal autonomy is sacro-sanct, it leads to a presumption that their irrationality will lead people to make poor decisions. For example, they will overweight near-term costs and benefits while un-derweighting delayed costs and benefits, so some will choose to smoke cigarettes even though they know that their "future selves" will regret the decision. Such "errors" can occur even if markets conform to the textbook model of perfect competition.

But the role of behavioral economics is not simply to respond to or correct irratio-nal behavior. Markets for healthcare and health insurance do not conform to the text-book model, so market failure occurs even when, and sometimes especially when, individuals behave perfectly rationally. In Kenneth Arrow's classic formulation (Arrow 1963), pervasive uncertainty in health and in healthcare is responsible for the unique characteristics of the economics of healthcare. The onset of illness and injury is largely unpredictable; patients often do not know which treatments work; and al-though a patient may have definite opinions on the matter, she is not sure whether the surgeon planning to repair her leaky heart valve is among the best, or worse than mediocre. In our attempts to mitigate these risks, we abandon many of the features of markets that would under other circumstances give rise to more efficient allocations of resources.

Although irrational behavior is not a cause of this uncertainty nor, for the most part, is it necessary for any of the market failures that characterize healthcare mar-kets, knowledge of deviations from rational behavior can lead to interventions that will reduce or even overcome some of the inefficiencies of health markets. In this con-text, "irrationality" introduces not only complexity but also opportunity since inter-ventions can be designed to take advantage of the apparently irrational ways that people behave.

Adverse Selection

Fundamental to the ACA, and indeed to mainstream health reform plans ("single payer" in most of its incarnations avoids this problem, insofar as everyone is in the same health insurance plan), is choice among different health insurance plans. Especially if competing health plans have substantially different features—for example, a broader physician and hospital network, or markedly different cost-sharing features—they will appeal to different market segments. If they cannot perfectly price for differences in expected healthcare consumption, or if the purchasers of health insurance know more about their likely utilization than insurers do, the plans are subject to adverse selection, one of the causes of market failure that Arrow identified. Among the most dramatic consequences of adverse selection is the "death spiral," or, in the less colorful terms of economic theory, the Rothschild-Stiglitz equilibrium (Rothschild and Stiglitz 1976) in which the health insurance market can collapse. This equilibrium results from informational asymmetry: individuals who know that they will use more healthcare than others are able to select health plans with more generous coverage. These high utilizers raise the average cost of coverage. This leads to a rise in premiums, making the plan only attractive to even more costly enrollees. Subsequent costs rise higher still, leading to yet higher premiums, leading to more adverse risk selection, and so on, in a spiral that ends in collapse of the market.

Adverse selection weakens risk pooling, one of the most important goals of health insurance, even when it does not result in a death spiral. Markets that have multiple health insurance plans tailored to different preferences and risk characteristics make it possible for individuals to find plans that closely match their preferences. But when they separate the sick and the well, they undercut the subsidy from the well to the sick that is usually necessary to provide comprehensive insurance for the sick.

Adverse selection can be avoided by denying choice. Medicare's hospital insurance program (Part A) is not subject to risk selection, at least among the elderly, because all U.S. citizens 65 years of age and older are covered by the plan (in contrast, the private plans that are part of Medicare Advantage compete with one another and are at least potentially subject to risk selection). The ACA builds on plan competition, albeit in a form that limits the range of variation among plans. It accepts the drawbacks of adverse selection in order to gain the advantages of plan choice, including price competition among plans and the possibility of more rapid and dramatic innovation than is typical of government plans like Medicare and Medicaid.

The ACA includes features intended to reduce the effects of adverse selection. For the most part, this means that it is necessary to ensure that the health insurance expansions (through exchanges as well as Medicaid expansions) attract people who do not have extraordinarily high health expenses; at a minimum, unfavorable risk selection would raise the costs of providing health insurance, increasing government contributions and enrollee contributions to health plans purchased on the exchanges.

The ACA draws on findings of the literature on default choices (Choi et al. 2003) to encourage employers to structure health insurance plans so that, by default, their employees will be enrolled in an employment-based health plan (29 U.S.C. §218a). The requirement to opt out in order not to be covered by the employer can be expected to increase the proportion of employees who enroll in a plan. Insofar as the marginal workers who are influenced by the choice of default (they enroll in an insurance plan simply because declining insurance would require an active choice) are healthier than the employees who would actively choose to be covered by health insurance, structuring health plan choice this way lowers the average premium cost by including more low-cost enrollees.

Employer and individual mandates for health insurance purchase provide financial incentives to improve the risk pool. The rationale for the individual mandate, which is particularly controversial, includes the following. A young man or woman, with modest expected utilization of healthcare, might find the premiums for health insurance plans offered on exchanges to be too high for the value they offer, so it is necessary to impose a financial penalty if they do not enroll in a health plan. This stick is a complement to the carrots—in the form of subsidies for insurance purchase that are available to lower-income individuals.

The individual mandate is a straightforward response to the (arguably) rational decision of a low-risk individual to forgo expensive insurance. The mandate seemingly has little to do with the insights of behavioral economics. But at the national level, the political support for imposition of a penalty for the non-purchase of health insurance is, at best, soft. In its March 2013 tracking poll, the Henry J. Kaiser Family Foundation reported that 40% of respondents supported an individual mandate, whereas 80% supported creating health insurance exchanges (Henry J. Kaiser Family Foundation 2013). Support for an individual mandate was likely stronger in the Commonwealth of Massachusetts, whose health reform scheme had included a mandate. For many low-risk individuals, neither the Massachusetts penalty nor the national penalty for failure to purchase health insurance was large enough to make insurance purchase attractive to a sizable number of low-risk individuals. During the first year of the Massachusetts health reform effort, the penalty for non-purchase of insurance was only $219 (though it later rose to $900), a number that is very small compared to the insurance premium (Steinbrook 2008). Yet few people ended up paying the penalty.

Why would small penalties have outsized effects? Noting that Massachusetts had rolled out its health reform plan with a campaign to encourage participation, some analysts cited the power of the nonfinancial incentives to purchase insurance. Both the employer and the individual mandates in Massachusetts seemed to have much greater effects on insurance purchase than could be explained by financial incentives (Chandra, Gruber, and McKnight 2011); in fact, the percentage of employees obtaining insurance through the workplace rose even though employers had incentives to stop offering coverage (Gruber 2011). According to this view,

Massachusetts had succeeded in making insurance purchase not only a financial decision, but also a social obligation. The health reform rollout advanced the theme of "shared responsibility," intending to create a social more that good citizenship required purchase of health insurance (Kingsdale 2009). There was also an extensive political campaign to drive public acceptance of the health reforms. Perhaps the designers of the mandate were inspired by the often-challenging experience of parking a car in Boston. Even when the benefits—in saved time, if nothing else—of parking in a no-parking zone exceed the costs of either the risk or the certainty of a parking ticket, most people will not park illegally. That is, they would rather comply with the law. Similarly, the power of the individual mandate derives not only from the size of the financial penalty, but also from the desire to satisfy legal and social norms.

Baicker and colleagues suggest several ways in which the insights of behavioral economics might be used specifically to increase the uptake of health insurance, thereby blunting adverse selection (Baicker, Congdon, and Mullainathan 2012). They note the cognitive burden of choice and the importance of channels by which both advice and insurance are obtained, reinforcing the importance of recognizing psychological and social factors in addressing adverse selection.

Moral Hazard

Moral hazard—the tendency to overconsume subsidized services—is another long-recognized challenge to health insurance identified by Arrow and others (Arrow 1963; Pauly 1968). Overconsumption can result both from consumer behavior (the demand increase from a price subsidy) and producer behavior (typically through induced demand—providers can gain financially by offering more expensive or simply more care). Because the mismatch between producer incentives and patient or societal welfare can be viewed as a principal-agent problem, typical economic solutions adopt a principal-agent perspective.

In a sense, both adverse selection and moral hazard could be addressed by a combination of symmetric information and monitoring—adverse selection would be removed if premium costs were appropriately adjusted for expected utilization, while moral hazard could be eliminated by providing care for which marginal benefits equated to marginal costs. But if the informational needs could have been met and the information used effectively, they would have been.

The ACA includes financial incentives designed to mitigate the effects of moral hazard. For example, the features designed to promote bundled payments and the creation of Accountable Care Organizations in Medicare give providers incentives to avoid overprovision of services, much as capitated payment does. High-deductible health plans also increase the share of healthcare costs borne by patients, offsetting (at least for expenditures that cumulatively fall below the deductible level) the subsidy effects on healthcare utilization.

The strengths and weaknesses of financial incentives targeted toward both patients and providers are well understood, having been studied for many years. Attempts to moderate the effects of moral hazard by increasing patient cost sharing expose the patient to greater financial risk from illness, and that is among the reasons why cost-sharing features are invariably limited. Furthermore, cost sharing is an imperfect solution to some problems. For example, the production of many drugs is characterized by large economies of scale; with a marginal cost near zero, usual rules for competitive pricing would result in losses for manufacturers. Thus, the usual welfare criterion for Pareto optimality—equating marginal benefit to marginal cost—is infeasible.

Some studies have pointed to the possibility of underconsumption that is exacerbated by poorly targeted cost sharing (Goldman, Joyce, and Zheng 2007; Selby, Fireman, and Swain 1996). Value-based insurance design is a general approach that adjusts patient cost sharing to reflect the benefits of the care received; co-payments can be low or even negative (that is, the patients receive subsidies) for care that is sufficiently high-value, or cost-saving (Chernew, Rosen, and Fendrick 2007). Patients whose health can improve dramatically when they take their medications for conditions like high blood pressure, diabetes, and high blood cholesterol often fail to adhere to their prescribed drug regimens, even when their out-of-pocket costs are low. The quandary is why, even for those who can easily afford the co-payments or for whom the treatment is free and who are not deterred by side effects, compliance is poor when the benefits greatly exceed the costs. Value-based insurance design uses financial incentives to overcome apparently irrational behavior.

What Can Behavioral Economics Offer?

These approaches to market imperfections in healthcare may only represent the first steps toward the use of a much broader set of tools to improve the function of health insurance and healthcare markets, as well as health itself. Doing so would improve the prospects for the success of health reform and much else.

The ACA was passed with the support of only one political party and has been under intense scrutiny since before it was signed into law. But opposition to any substantial health reform effort should be expected. Health reform has substantial costs—to individuals, employers, and the government—in addition to the benefits of widened availability of appropriate care. It is almost impossible to produce major legislation that does not disadvantage some people as it addresses the problems of others, and comprehensive health reform is not an exception. Many of the challenges faced by the ACA are those that would be faced by any ambitious attempt to expand access to healthcare.

How can the insights of behavioral economics and psychology be used to address problems that are intrinsic to health insurance, such as adverse selection and moral hazard, as well as the other challenges to the future of healthcare? The major contribution of behavioral economics may be its expansion of the tools that we use to achieve social goals. The behavioral economics literature suggests that novel nonfinancial incentives can complement financial incentives, not only to reduce healthcare costs but also to improve the function of markets for health insurance and for healthcare. Experience and well-designed studies point to areas in which such efforts hold particular promise: use of social norms, recognition of cognitive behavior, and choice architecture.

Use of Social Norms

Just as individual mandates have been more successful than could have been predicted from the size of the penalties, it may be possible to establish standards of behavior that will reduce the impact of counterproductive financial incentives. One example is recognition of prosocial behavior; acts of generosity can sometimes be rewarded most effectively by forms of public recognition, while prosocial behavior that cannot be publicly observed might be better rewarded by financial incentives (Ariely, Bracha, and Meier 2009). Professional norms can offset strong financial incentives to provide more or more expensive care than is necessary. Social norms could enhance the feeling that patients have a responsibility to others to avoid overusing care, and to improve their compliance with high-value care.

Recognition of Cognitive Burden

When an individual is newly diagnosed with advanced cancer, and asked to consider potentially effective but highly toxic treatment, he must weigh difficult choices when he is suffering from the shock of receiving dreaded news and is anxious about the future. The hardest choices often arise in the context of illness or severe injury, where the stakes and emotional distress are high. Thus, the cognitive burden associated with healthcare decisions can be great at a time when the capacity to process the information is impaired. Any health reform plan must take into account the limits of rational choice in such settings and provide appropriate support for decision-making.

Cognitive burden is also elevated in less emotion-laden circumstances, such as the choice of a health plan or a healthcare provider. Here too approaches such as default choices or direction toward choices that are consistent with the individual's preferences can improve the decisions that are made. The use of healthcare proxies and norms, and the judicious use of appropriate default choices, may hold promise for improving decisions and thereby the allocation of healthcare.

Choice Architecture

As Cass Sunstein and Richard Thaler have argued in their bestselling book *Nudge: Improving Decisions about Health, Wealth, and Happiness*, there is a role for gently pushing people toward choices that we believe to be in their best interests (Thaler and

Sunstein 2008). Such an approach is not without controversy, but in healthcare, overt paternalism—not the softer libertarian paternalism of Sunstein and Thaler—has a long history. More directive approaches toward health decisions, and insurance decisions, may play an important role in the success of health reform, especially if the paternalism reflects the interests of individuals, rather than the needs and desires of healthcare providers, insurers, or the government. Perhaps the most important contribution will be the ability to demonstrate that health reform leads to better decisions and care that benefits the public more. That goal is not new, but the availability of more and better tools offers the hope that success will become more likely.

Conclusion

Undoubtedly, many more aspects of psychology and social relationships will be explored in the effort to improve policies intended to promote health and make healthcare more efficient and effective. The problem is important, and financial incentives alone are unlikely to be fully successful. Financial incentives, if large enough, will change behavior, but at the cost of increasing financial risk.

The tools of behavioral economics can be applied to both physicians and patients since both of them have a direct influence on the care received and its costs, as well as its success. Subtle and not-so-subtle approaches to making the "right" decision easier may be especially suitable. Many patients, in many circumstances, are happy to delegate major decisions to their physicians. Defaults and guideline-based care might be attractive if endorsed by trusted parties. Behavior change—whether on the part of physicians or patients—is more likely to occur if it is easier, and especially if it is automatic. That is one of the powerful attractions of a tool as simple as the use of checklists for surgery and other forms of care (Haynes et al. 2009; Gawande 2010), although the success of checklists depends greatly on the setting in which they are applied and on their specific features (Urbach et al. 2014). Similarly, the easier it is to follow a diet or exercise regimen, the more likely an individual will follow it.

The strength of political opposition will determine the future of the ACA, but successful implementation also matters, if only because it will influence political support. From a pragmatic perspective, whether one fundamentally agrees or disagrees with the ACA, we all share an interest in enabling health insurance markets to work well and in efforts to ensure that healthcare is both effective and efficient. Cost reduction and health improvement remain crucial challenges. Too much is at stake to overlook the promise of approaches based on the findings of behavioral economics.

References

Ariely, Dan, Anat Bracha, and Stephan Meier. 2009. "Doing Good or Doing Well? Image Motivation and Monetary Incentives in Behaving Prosocially." *The American Economic Review* 99(1):544–55.

Arrow, Kenneth J. 1963. "Uncertainty and the Welfare Economics of Medical Care." *The American Economic Review* 53(5):941–73.

Baicker, Katherine, William J. Congdon, and Sendhil Mullainathan. 2012. "Health Insurance Coverage and Take-Up: Lessons from Behavioral Economics." *Milbank Quarterly* 90(1):107–34.

Baicker, Katherine, and Dana Goldman. 2011. "Patient Cost-Sharing and Healthcare Spending Growth." *Journal of Economic Perspectives* 25(2):47–68.

Bryan, Gharad, Dean Karlan, and Scott Nelson. 2010. "Commitment Devices." *Annual Review of Economics* 2(1):671–98.

Buchwald, Henry, Yoav Avidor, Eugene Braunwald, Michael D. Jensen, Walter Pories, Kyle Fahrbach, and Karen Schoelles. 2004. "Bariatric Surgery: A Systematic Review and Meta-Analysis." *Journal of the American Medical Association* 292(14): 1724–37.

Chandra, Amitabh, Jonathan Gruber, and Robin McKnight. 2011. "The Importance of the Individual Mandate—Evidence from Massachusetts." *New England Journal of Medicine* 364(4):293–95.

Chernew, M. E., A. B. Rosen, and A. M. Fendrick. 2007. "Value-Based Insurance Design." *Health Affairs* 26(2):w195–203.

Choi, James J., David Laibson, Brigitte C. Madrian, and Andrew Metrick. 2003. "Optimal Defaults." *The American Economic Review* 93(2):180–85.

Christakis, N. A., and J. H. Fowler. 2007. "The Spread of Obesity in a Large Social Network over 32 Years." *New England Journal of Medicine* 357(4):370–79.

———. 2008. "The Collective Dynamics of Smoking in a Large Social Network." *New England Journal of Medicine* 358(21):2249–58.

Claxton, Gary, Matthew Rae, Nirmita Panchal, Heidi Whitmore, Anthony Damico, and Kevin Kenward. 2014. "Health Benefits in 2014: Stability in Premiums and Coverage for Employer-Sponsored Plans." *Health Affairs* 33(10):1851–60.

Douketis, J. D., C. Macie, L. Thabane, and D. F. Williamson. 2005. "Systematic Review of Long-Term Weight Loss Studies in Obese Adults: Clinical Significance and Applicability to Clinical Practice." *International Journal of Obesity* 29(10):1153–67.

Gawande, Atul. 2010. *The Checklist Manifesto: How to Get Things Right*. Metropolitan Books. New York.

Giné, Xavier, Dean Karlan, and Jonathan Zinman. 2010. "Put Your Money Where Your Butt Is: A Commitment Contract for Smoking Cessation." *American Economic Journal: Applied Economics* 2(4):213–35.

Gneezy, Uri, Stephan Meier, and Pedro Rey-Biel. 2011. "When and Why Incentives (Don't) Work to Modify Behavior." *Journal of Economic Perspectives* 25(4):191–209.

Gneezy, Uri, and Aldo Rustichini. 2000. "Pay Enough or Don't Pay at All." *The Quarterly Journal of Economics* 115(3):791–810.

Goldhaber-Fiebert, Jeremy D., Erik Blumenkranz, and Alan M. Garber. 2010. "Committing to Exercise: Contract Design for Virtuous Habit Formation." National Bureau of Economic Research Working Paper 16624. http://www.nber.org/papers/w16624 .pdf.

Goldman, Dana P., Geoffrey F. Joyce, and Yuhui Zheng. 2007. "Prescription Drug Cost Sharing: Associations with Medication and Medical Utilization and Spending and Health." *Journal of the American Medical Association* 298(1):61–69.

Goldman, Dana P., Yuhui Zheng, Federico Girosi, Pierre-Carl Michaud, S. Jay Olshansky, David Cutler, and John W. Rowe. 2009. "The Benefits of Risk Factor Prevention in Americans Aged 51 Years and Older." *American Journal of Public Health* 99(11):2096.

Gruber, Jonathan. 2011. "The Impacts of the Affordable Care Act: How Reasonable Are the Projections?" National Bureau of Economic Research Working Paper 17168. http://www.nber.org/papers/w17168.pdf.

Haynes, Alex B., Thomas G. Weiser, William R. Berry, Stuart R. Lipsitz, Abdel-Hadi S. Breizat, E. Patchen Dellinger, Teodoro Herbosa, Sudhir Joseph, Pascience L. Kibatala, Marie Carmela M. Lapitan, Alan F. Merry, Krishna Moorthy, Richard K. Reznick, Bryce Taylor, and Atul A. Gawande. 2009. "A Surgical Safety Checklist to Reduce Morbidity and Mortality in a Global Population." *New England Journal of Medicine* 360(5):491–99.

Henry J. Kaiser Family Foundation. 2013. "Kaiser Health Tracking Poll: March 2013." March 20. www.kff.org/health-reform/poll-finding/march-2013-tracking-poll/.

Holtz-Eakin, D., and M. J. Ramlet. 2010. "Health Care Reform Is Likely to Widen Federal Budget Deficits, Not Reduce Them." *Health Affairs* 29(6):1136–41.

Kingsdale, J. 2009. "Implementing Health Care Reform in Massachusetts: Strategic Lessons Learned." *Health Affairs* 28(4):w588–w594.

Livingood, William C., John P. Allegrante, Collins O. Airhihenbuwa, Noreen M. Clark, Richard C. Windsor, Marc A. Zimmerman, and Lawrence W. Green. 2011. "Applied Social and Behavioral Science to Address Complex Health Problems." *American Journal of Preventative Medicine* 41(5):525–31.

Maggard, Melinda A., Lisa R. Shugarman, Marika Suttorp, Margaret Maglione, Harvey J. Sugerman, Edward H. Livingston, Ninh T. Nguyen, Zhaoping Li, Walter A. Mojica, and Lara Hilton. 2005. "Meta-Analysis: Surgical Treatment of Obesity." *Annals of Internal Medicine* 142(7):547–59.

Newhouse, J. P., W. G. Manning, C. N. Morris, L. L. Orr, N. Duan, E. B. Keeler, A. Leibowitz, K. H. Marquis, M. S. Marquis, and C. E. Phelps. 1981. "Some Interim Results from a Controlled Trial of Cost Sharing in Health Insurance." *New England Journal of Medicine* 305(25):1501–7.

Pauly, Mark V. 1968. "The Economics of Moral Hazard: Comment." *The American Economic Review* 58(3):531–37.

Rothschild, Michael, and Joseph Stiglitz. 1976. "Equilibrium in Competitive Insurance Markets: An Essay on the Economics of Imperfect Information." *The Quarterly Journal of Economics* 90(4):629–49.

Russell, Louise B. 2009. "Preventing Chronic Disease: An Important Investment, But Don't Count on Cost Savings." *Health Affairs* 28(1):42–45.

Selby, Joe V., Bruce H. Fireman, and Bix E. Swain. 1996. "Effect of a Copayment on Use of the Emergency Department in a Health Maintenance Organization." *New England Journal of Medicine* 334(10):635–42.

Steinbrook, R. 2008. "Health Care Reform in Massachusetts—Expanding Coverage, Escalating Costs." *New England Journal of Medicine* 358(26):2757–60.

Thaler, Richard H., and Cass R. Sunstein. 2008. *Nudge: Improving Decisions about Health, Wealth, and Happiness.* Yale University Press. New Haven, CT.

Urbach, David R., Anand Govindarajan, Refik Saskin, Andrew S. Wilton, and Nancy N. Baxter. 2014. "Introduction of Surgical Safety Checklists in Ontario, Canada." *New England Journal of Medicine* 370(11):1029–38.

Volpp, Kevin G., David A. Asch, Robert Galvin, and George Loewenstein. 2011. "Redesigning Employee Health Incentives—Lessons from Behavioral Economics." *New England Journal of Medicine* 365(5):388–90.

Volpp, Kevin G., Andrea B. Troxel, Mark V. Pauly, Henry A. Glick, Andrea Puig, David A. Asch, Robert Galvin, Jingsan Zhu, Fei Wan, and Jill DeGuzman. 2009. "A Randomized, Controlled Trial of Financial Incentives for Smoking Cessation." *New England Journal of Medicine* 360(7):699–709.

CHAPTER 3

Seven Ways of Applying Behavioral Science to Health Policy

Michael Hallsworth

This chapter sets out seven ways of applying behavioral science to policy that are not subject to many of the key criticisms leveled at nudging—most notably, that nudges are manipulative and disempowering. In doing so, I draw on my experience of working for the U.K. Behavioural Insights Team (BIT), and therefore start with a brief outline of BIT's creation and development.

The Behavioural Insights Team

BIT was set up in 2010 to apply insights from behavioral economics and social psychology to public policy. This mission drew on the explicit commitment in the U.K. government's Coalition Agreement (an official five-year plan for government) to "harnessing the insights from behavioural economics and social psychology" (HM Government 2010). As a result, BIT members were a mix of economists, psychologists, and policy experts, headed by Dr. David Halpern, who had been an academic at the University of Cambridge before moving into government. BIT was established in the Cabinet Office (the central coordinating department for the U.K. government) and reported to the Prime Minister and to the Head of the Civil Service (the most senior public official) (Cabinet Office 2011).

Despite this high-level support, the initial reaction from public officials was fairly skeptical. This is quite understandable: creating the team could have easily been seen as a case of the government "buying the hype" and adopting the latest fashionable idea, at the expense of more reliable approaches (Lang and Rayner 2011). In addition, there were justifiable concerns that many of the findings BIT would be using were derived from laboratory experiments, and thus might not be replicated in real-world settings (Dolan et al. 2012). Given this context, the team was deliberately kept small (just eight people) and had a "sunset clause": it had to "transform two major areas of policy" and "achieve at least a ten-fold return on the cost of the team," or it would be closed down (Cabinet Office 2011).

This push for results had a significant consequence: in addition to applying behavioral insights, BIT directed its energies toward conducting robust evaluations of its interventions (as well as appointing a distinguished Academic Advisory Panel) (Cabinet Office 2011). In particular, BIT focused on setting up Randomized Controlled Trials—usually seen as the "gold standard" of evidence—as well as promoting the wider use of such trials in the public sector (which remains limited) (Haynes et al. 2012). This focus on robust evaluation meant that, before long, BIT could point to convincing evidence of its impact on policy outcomes—evidence that meant policymakers became increasingly convinced of the value of these approaches (Wright 2012). Gradually, more and more departments began approaching the team with potential collaborations, rather than the other way around (Bennhold 2013). This perception of BIT's success spread, leading to other countries setting up organizations modeled on BIT (to a greater or lesser extent), including a Social and Behavioral Sciences Team in the U.S. government (Thaler 2013).

Although BIT had prompted increased demand for its services, this demand could not be met because of official headcount restrictions (linked to austerity measures). Therefore, in order to meet the increased demand, senior officials worked with BIT members to separate the organization from government and give it greater freedom to hire new employees. Since 2014, BIT has been a social purpose company that is owned partly by the government, partly by the employees, and partly by Nesta, an innovation charity (Behavioural Insights Team 2014). Therefore, the views I express in this chapter should not be taken as representing those of the U.K. government.

Behavioral Science and Policy: More Than Nudging

Examining BIT's approach can help advance discussions about the policy applications of behavioral science, which have tended to focus heavily on the pros and cons of nudging. BIT has been referred to widely and informally as the "Nudge Unit," and has the privilege of being advised by Richard Thaler (Benedictus 2013). Many of the team's initiatives would qualify as nudges if Thaler and Sunstein's criteria were applied (Thaler and Sunstein 2008). However, much of BIT's work differs from the generally accepted definition of nudging.

BIT attempts to ensure that policymakers know and use empirical findings about how people actually behave (and why). Rather than starting with the question "How can we nudge?" we take the perspective of policy analysts and ask, "We have a policy problem here—what do we know? What evidence can we bring to bear?" We try to understand the policy issue in the round and assess all policy options, whether they are nudges or not. We take this fuller view because the fundamental truth is that *most government policy intends to influence behavior*, from murder laws and tax breaks to drinking water standards and guidelines for financial products.

Governments have traditionally relied mainly on tools such as regulation, taxation, and information provision to achieve this influence. Thaler and Sunstein effectively present nudges as an alternative to these traditional tools. As they state, a nudge "alters people's behavior in a predictable way without forbidding any options or significantly changing their economic incentives" (Thaler and Sunstein 2008, 6). However, there is much that behavioral science can say about how legislation is constructed and economic incentives are structured (for example, to take into account loss aversion or hyperbolic discounting). There is therefore much scope for behavioral science to help us enhance or reassess the use of more traditional policy options, in addition to offering new options to sit alongside them (the main focus of *Nudge*).

Unfortunately, this point often gets lost when people discuss behavioral science and policy, and this is partly because of the focus on nudging.[1] At worst, I have heard policymakers talk as if they could either do "normal policy" or try something "behavioral"—a nudge, for example—as if they were totally separate things. To reiterate: most policies influence behavior and therefore behavioral science has something to say about most policies. The work of BIT has shown the value of using behavioral science to improve *the way in which policies are applied*, rather than simply suggesting particular policy interventions. In sum, it is more useful to see behavioral science as a lens through which to see all government action, rather than simply offering new tools in the policy toolbox (although it does that as well).

This wider perspective allows us to see that there are many different ways of applying behavioral science to policy that avoid the objections generally raised against this move. Many of these objections are presented elsewhere in this volume, especially in part II, but to sum them up briefly: applying behavioral science to policymaking results in actions that are "paternalistic (in a negative sense), manipulative, disempowering, or some combination of the above" (Hallsworth and Sanders 2016, 121).[2] The thrust of the paternalist critique is that the language of "irrationality," "biases," and "internalities" helps to justify government interventions to "correct" these biases and help people fulfill (what the government believes to be) their real intentions.[3] The manipulation critique is that interventions based on behavioral science are problematic because they often target automatic drivers of behavior, which operate outside conscious awareness and thus may not alert a citizen to the fact that her behavior is being influenced (Rebonato 2012). The disempowerment critique is that focusing on automatic drivers of behavior is infantilizing since it does not encourage people to learn from their actions and take personal responsibility (Bovens 2009). The disempowerment critique thus has similarities to the manipulation critique, but its concerns are consequentialist in nature rather than deontological.

I believe there are valid responses to all three of these critiques, but I do not intend to rehearse them in this chapter because I have done so elsewhere (Hallsworth and Sanders 2016). One general defense is worth noting quickly, however, and that is what might be called the technocratic defense of applying behavioral science to policy. The essence of this defense is as follows: "the government has decided to address certain policy issues, and it should do that as effectively as possible, applying the best available evidence." In other words, if there is new evidence (for example, from behavioral science) about the effects of a policy (for example, how people will actually react in practice), then this evidence should be used to enhance the policy's effectiveness. Some people would say that you have a duty—even a moral duty—to maximize effectiveness in this way since it means you are spending limited resources wisely. For example, the U.K. Civil Service Code requires officials to make decisions and provide advice on "rigorous analysis of the evidence" (Civil Service 2015).

The reason I mention this defense is that I think it has particular resonance in the field of healthcare. A common goal of health policymakers is to reduce the number of disability-adjusted life years lost due to ill-health as cost-effectively as possible. Research shows that a large proportion of the loss of life arises from our own behaviors, such as how much we eat, how much we smoke, how much we move, or how much alcohol we drink (Institute for Health Metrics and Evaluation 2013). Therefore, one reasonable conclusion from this research is that "rigorous analysis of the evidence" for healthcare means understanding how to change behavior.[4] A diligent policymaker should be obtaining or commissioning the best empirical evidence on influencing behavior and applying it. Since this is a technocratic argument, it does not address the philosophical critiques outlined above. However, I would suggest that the sheer burden of disease arising from behavioral factors means that this defense should not be dismissed lightly.

Seven Ways of Applying Behavioral Science to Health Policy

Seeing behavioral science as a lens through which government action is perceived, rather than just suggesting a particular set of actions, reveals several potential approaches that are not subject to the critiques outlined above. Taking the case of health policies, applying behavioral science may show that the best policy option is to:

1. Stop or revise an existing action that has unintended behavioral consequences
2. Decide not to try to change behavior, but shape policy around it
3. Prevent a counterproductive policy from being introduced
4. Address the flaws in the policymaking process itself
5. Influence healthcare providers
6. Help people find new strategies for taking personal responsibility
7. Prevent harm to others

I discuss each of these in turn below.

Stop or Revise an Existing Action That Has Unintended Behavioral Consequences

Applying behavioral science can lead the government to reassess the impact of its current actions. We can distinguish between two different situations here. In the first, the government is intentionally trying to influence behavior through a program or initiative that seems to make sense—but which behavioral science reveals to be counterproductive. A famous example here is the "Scared Straight" initiative, which involved sending juvenile delinquents on a visit to adult prisons in order to deter them from crime. This initiative seems to be "common sense," and initial small-scale narrative studies seemed to support its effectiveness—leading to the widespread adoption of the program. However, a behavioral analysis suggests that the visits (and ensuing contact with prisoners) may make it easier for recipients to imagine a viable life in prison, and thus lead to more offending behavior. Indeed, a meta-analysis of randomized controlled trials shows that the program is actually more harmful than doing nothing at all (Petrosino, Turpin-Petrosino, and Beuhler 2003).

The other situation is where the government is not trying to influence behavior, but is doing so nonetheless. In other words, policies may be having unnoticed and unintended effects on behavior. Perhaps the best example here is the design work that has been done in hospital emergency departments in the United Kingdom. Violence and aggression against hospital staff costs the National Health Service (NHS) at least £69 million a year in staff absence and additional security (House of Commons Committee of Public Accounts 2003). It turns out that one factor contributing to these levels of violence is poor design in emergency departments—for example, unclear signage, obscured lines of sight, and lack of feedback on a patient's progress through the system. This inadequate design may have come about from lack of understanding of effects on behavior, carelessness, failure to adopt the perspective of the patient, and so on. When the United Kingdom's Design Council ran a project to identify and address these issues in two hospitals, they found a reduction in aggressive behavior and reported frustration (The Design Council 2015). It could be argued that this violence represents a case of unintentional harm that it would be unethical not to address.

Decide Not to Try to Change Behavior, But Shape Policy Around It

Hospital emergency departments can also illustrate the second option. The United Kingdom is dealing with major pressure on its emergency departments, with the problem partly caused by attending with only minor ailments.[5] Policymakers could try to nudge people by informing them of alternative options when or just after they make an unnecessary visit. However, adopting the position of health system users reveals that attending emergency departments in this way is entirely reasonable behavior. A behavioral analysis of this kind can actually show that it is difficult to change behavior in this instance because people are using a heuristic—"go to hospital"—that is working for them. The best policy may actually be to adapt the service so people do not have to change their behavior—perhaps by co-locating emergency and nonemergency care. The policy problem is resolved without individuals having to change their behavior.

Prevent a Counterproductive Policy from Being Introduced

The application of behavioral science may help prevent the introduction of a policy by showing that it may have a counterproductive effect on behavior. BIT has highlighted the potentially enormous impact of electronic cigarettes to save lives through substitution, which data are now beginning to show (King 2011). This analysis is based on evidence that a successful way to reduce the harm caused by habits is to keep the existing cues and routines the same, but change the target of the behavior (Verplanken and Wood 2006). Therefore, we have argued against measures (like overzealous regulation) that may significantly affect take-up. Of course, we need to monitor how this situation develops and, if it looks like electronic cigarettes are leading to smoking, consider further action. But we do not have that evidence yet, and a behavioral analysis argues that we may cause harm by starting with those measures.

Address the Flaws in the Policymaking Process Itself

As these examples show, applying behavioral insights does not necessitate new government action. But neither does it rule out more traditional policy options, such as regulation and taxation. It is more concerned with improving the effectiveness of government action, whatever that may be. These actions include improving the way policy is made. As many others have pointed out, government itself is affected by the biases that behavioral science highlights—policymakers do not have some special immunity (Glaeser 2006). I agree. But I see this as a strong reason for applying behavioral science to governance itself, rather than abandoning it altogether.

Take availability bias and confirmation bias.[6] Anecdotally, there are many examples where a policy has come about from a single story or observation that a policymaker encounters, even though it may not be the best course of action—or even an effective one. Confirmation bias takes hold, and evidence is sought out to confirm the initial impression. For example, many U.K. hospitals have a policy that healthcare professionals should be "bare below the elbow" (that is, wear sleeveless clothes or roll up sleeves) in order to reduce the rate of patient infection (Department of Health 2007). It is said that the introduction of this policy, controversial at the time, was prompted by a specific conversation between a minister and a clinician during a hospital visit. The evidence for such a policy is still contested, however.[7] We can and should use behavioral science to suggest ways of adjusting policymaking processes to ensure that government officials do not produce biased, ineffective, or ill-considered policies.

Influencing Actors in the Healthcare System

We can focus on influencing actors in the healthcare system. In 1999, the Institute of Medicine found that in the United States 100,000 deaths a year came from avoidable medical errors (Institute of Medicine 1999). In the United Kingdom, half of

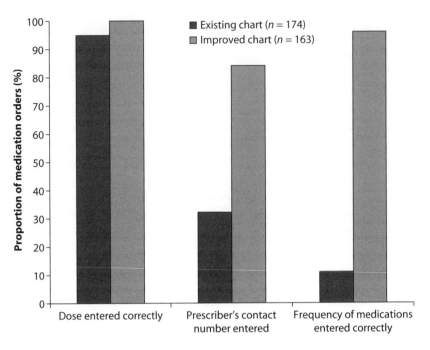

FIGURE 3.1 Impact of simplified prescription chart on correct completion of medication orders. *Adapted from King et al. (2014).*

hospital admissions suffer prescribing errors where paper-based charts are used (Lewis et al. 2009). The concern is that these charts hinder clear communication between professionals. It can be difficult to distinguish between milligrams and micrograms when written out by hand in a hurry. If a lack of attention to the behavioral impact of such forms is actively harming patient health, then I believe we have a duty to apply behavioral science to reduce this harm.

Indeed, a study by Imperial College London, funded by BIT, tried to reduce these errors by redesigning prescription charts (King et al. 2014). The microgram/milligram problem was addressed by creating options that just had to be circled. In simulation testing, the new charts significantly improved correct dose entries (fig. 3.1). Improvements like these are likely to mean fewer medical errors and better patient outcomes with little cost and no additional burden.

Help People Find New Strategies for Taking Personal Responsibility

We may also try to influence health system users directly. But, again, there are ways of doing this that do not impede autonomy, learning, or flourishing. In fact, behavioral science can be used in the service of these principles. Take obesity, for example. There is much evidence that our eating is "mindless"—we eat what is put in front of us, with little regard to portion size (Levitsky and Pacanowski. 2012). One response to this may be to change the choice environment (reduce plate sizes, reformulate food, insert "break points" into food packaging). However, another legitimate use of behavioral science is to tell people about how eating works, and help people adopt pragmatic and effective "rules of thumb" that address our tendency to eat mindlessly (Wansink 2014).

For example, if we become more aware that we usually overestimate our ability to resist temptation (and there is good evidence we do), we can use simple strategies to ensure in advance that we will not be exposed to tempting food at a particular time. The point of these strategies is not to try to change the hard-wired aspects of how we eat: this will fail. Rather, the idea is to allow us to bring them under control—by using our capacity for conscious planning to manage the effects of our unconscious and automatic behavioral responses. This is exactly what Brian Wansink's Mindless Eating Challenge is doing in the United States (Wansink 2015). Similarly, behavioral science would point toward the large literature on how creating "implementation intentions" means that people are more likely to follow through on their goals (Gollwitzer and Sheeran 2006). These approaches are not about reducing autonomy; they are about giving us better ways of realizing autonomy.

Prevent Harm to Others

As usually conceived, nudges are only concerned with decisions that benefit individuals themselves (Thaler and Sunstein 2008). Therefore, they are often subjected to the paternalist critique mentioned above (how can the government know our "real" intentions?). However, from a policymaker's point of view, there are many instances where benefit to one individual means harm to others. It is generally accepted that government involvement is more legitimate in these situations than if you are purely considering harms to the self.[8] One consequence of the focus on nudging is that these kinds of policy questions are often neglected. Therefore, to most policymakers Russell Korobkin's discussion of "libertarian welfarism" in chapter 1 of this volume may seem puzzling: talking about applying nudging to questions of general welfare only seems like a new debate if the previous one has been limited. For a policymaker dealing with crime (for example), this kind of application would be the obvious starting point.

Nevertheless, the line between harms to self and harms to others is often unclear. Not turning up to your hospital outpatient appointment harms others by creating unnecessary delays and waste in the system. But it may also harm your own health because you are not getting the care you need. I think we would also agree that it is justified to impose some small costs on people to prevent harms elsewhere, even if they are not causing the harms themselves. For example, a fascinating recent study examines the effect of a 1998 law relating to paracetamol (acetaminophen) packaging.[9] The law limited how much of the painkiller could be bought from one shop. The study shows that this law reversed the upward trend of suicides and accidental poisonings; the authors estimate that 765 lives were saved in the following decade.

I suggest that most people would agree that there are substantial benefits to this policy. It does not reduce choice—consumers can still obtain the same amount of paracetamol. Does it, however, disrespect people's "true intentions" to commit suicide? Perhaps, but given that the realization of this intention seems to hinge on the additional effort of going to a second shop, this intention may be fairly weak (which is surely a relevant criterion for whether it is "true"). Of course, it may be that there are spillovers that we cannot see, and that people are finding other ways to kill themselves. But, on this evidence, those alternative options have got to be easy as well.[10]

Is this law different from the "Big Gulp ban" and, if so, how (Bittman 2013)? One stops people from buying large cups of soda in one go to reduce the likelihood of obesity; the other stops people from buying large bottles of painkillers in one go to stop the likelihood of suicide and accidental poisoning. In both cases you can still obtain the product. I would say that the harms involved and the strength of the evidence make them quite different; and I think most people would agree they seem different in important ways. But these are more technical points; if you deal purely in abstractions, then you could argue they operate on the same principles. (I am not advocating for the soda ban; I am just using it as a point of contrast.) Case by case is a better way of assessing these issues, and this is how policymakers deal with them in practice. We cannot dismiss options out of hand; nudging and behavioral science should be part of the policy mix.

Conclusion

Taking a broader view of the relationship between behavioral science and policy shows that it offers approaches that are not about changing behavior; that are directed at those with a professional responsibility; and that can help strengthen autonomy, not reduce it. Of course, it could be argued that just presenting examples where "behavioral" policies allowed learning and autonomy does not mean that these kinds of policies can never be manipulative. But addressing this criticism was not the main purpose of this chapter. Rather, I hope that these examples of how behavioral science can be used in health policy help broaden the debate about if, when, and how its use is justified.

Notes

1. I should point out that this is in no way a criticism of Thaler and Sunstein. It is a testament to the strength of their work that nudging has been discussed so extensively.
2. The following paragraphs draw on Hallsworth and Sanders 2016.
3. See White's discussion of "epistemic problems" in this volume.
4. There is an argument that research systems are not doing enough to help answer these questions. Although structural factors obviously play a big role in determining behavior, it is remarkable that only around 4% of total U.K. health research spending considers

psychological or behavioral factors (U.K. Clinical Research Collaboration 2012). The United Kingdom spends around £2.7 billion a year treating smoking-related diseases, but only £150 million on helping people quit (Department of Health 2010).

5. The extent to which unnecessary attendances contributes to the overall pressure is disputed (Blunt, Edwards, and Merry 2015).

6. Availability bias: the tendency to place unjustified weight on ideas just because they are particularly novel or salient. Confirmation bias: the tendency to interpret new information in a manner that confirms existing beliefs or attitudes.

7. For a short overview, see Clement 2012.

8. This question has been examined from various perspectives. John Stuart Mill's work is perhaps the best known philosophical discussion; the concept of negative externalities is core to modern economic analysis.

9. Paracetamol is the name for acetaminophen used in the United Kingdom and many other countries; in the United States, this painkiller is marketed under the names Tylenol and Panadol (Hawton, et al. 2013).

10. There is other evidence that restricting opportunities for suicide reduces suicides (that is, that there is a strong opportunistic element) (Clarke and Mayhew 1989).

References

Behavioural Insights Team. 2014. "EAST: Four Simple Ways to Apply Behavioural Insights." http://www.behaviouralinsights.co.uk/sites/default/files/BIT%20Publication%20EAST_FA_WEB.pdf.

Benedictus, Leo. 2013. "The Nudge Unit—Has It Worked So Far?" *The Guardian*, May 2. http://www.theguardian.com/politics/2013/may/02/nudge-unit-has-it-worked.

Bennhold, Katrin. 2013. "Britain's Ministry of Nudges." *The New York Times*, December 7, International Business sec. http://www.nytimes.com/2013/12/08/business/international/britains-ministry-of-nudges.html?pagewanted=all&_r=1.

Bittman, Mark. 2013. "Banning the Big Gulp Ban." *The New York Times*, March 19, Opinion Pages sec. http://opinionator.blogs.nytimes.com/2013/03/19/banning-the-big-gulp-ban/.

Blunt, Ian, Nigel Edwards, and Leonora Merry. 2015. "What's Behind the A&E 'Crisis'?" *Nuffield Trust*. http://www.nuffieldtrust.org.uk/sites/files/nuffield/publication/election_briefing_urgent_care_in_crisis_final_web.pdf.

Bovens, Luc. 2009. "The Ethics of Nudge." In *Preference Change*, edited by Till Yanoff and Sven Ove Hansson. Springer. New York.

Cabinet Office. 2011. "Behavioural Insights Team Annual Update 2010–11." Cabinet Office Behavioural Insights Team. September. https://www.gov.uk/government/uploads/system/uploads/attachment_data/file/60537/Behaviour-Change-Insight-Team-Annual-Update_acc.pdf.

Civil Service. 2015. "Civil Service Values." *The Civil Service Code*. March 16. https://www.gov.uk/government/publications/civil-service-code/the-civil-service-code.

Clarke, R. V., and P. Mayhew. 1989. "Crime as Opportunity: A Note on Domestic Gas Suicide in Britain and the Netherlands." *British Journal of Criminology* 29(1):35–46.

Clement, Rhys. 2012. "Is It Time for an Evidence Based Uniform for Doctors?" *British Medical Journal* 345:e8286.

Department of Health. 2010. "Healthy Lives, Healthy People: Our Strategy for Public Health in England." November 30. https://www.gov.uk/government/uploads/system/uploads/attachment_data/file/216096/dh_127424.pdf.

———. 2007. "Uniforms and Workwear: An Evidence Base for Developing Local Policy." September 17. http://webarchive.nationalarchives.gov.uk/+/www.dh.gov.uk/en/publicationsandstatistics/publications/publicationspolicyandguidance/dh_078433.

The Design Council. 2015. "Reducing Violence and Aggression in A&E through a Better Experience: Impact Evaluation Findings Summary." http://www.designcouncil.org.uk/sites/default/files/asset/document/AE_evaluation_summary_1_0.pdf.

Dolan, P., M. Hallsworth, D. Halpern, D. King, R. Metcalfe, and I. Vlaev. 2012. "Influencing Behaviour: The Mindspace Way." *Journal of Economic Psychology* 33(1):264–77.

Glaeser, Edward L. 2006. "Paternalism and Psychology." *The University of Chicago Law Review* 73(1):133–56.

Gollwitzer, Peter M., and Paschal Sheeran. 2006. "Implementation Intentions and Goal Achievement: A Meta-Analysis of Effects and Processes." *Advances in Experimental Social Psychology* 38:69–119.

Hallsworth, Michael, and Michael Sanders. 2016. "Nudge: Recent Developments in Behavioural Science and Public Policy." In *Beyond Behaviour Change: Key Issues, Interdisciplinary Approaches and Future Directions*, edited by Fiona Spotswood. Bristol: Policy Press.

Hawton, Keith, et al. 2013. "Long Term Effect of Reduced Pack Sizes of Paracetamol on Poisoning Deaths and Liver Transplant Activity in England and Wales: Interrupted Time Series Analyses." *British Medical Journal* 346:f403.

Haynes, Laura, Owain Service, Ben Goldacre, and David Torgerson. 2012. "Test, Learn, Adapt: Developing Public Policy with Randomised Controlled Trials." Cabinet Office Behavioural Insights Team. June. https://www.gov.uk/government/uploads/system/uploads/attachment_data/file/62529/TLA-1906126.pdf.

HM Government. 2010. "The Coalition: Our Programme For Government." https://www.gov.uk/government/uploads/system/uploads/attachment_data/file/78977/coalition_programme_for_government.pdf.

House of Commons Committee of Public Accounts. 2003. "A Safer Place to Work: Protecting NHS Hospital and Ambulance Staff from Violence and Aggression." http://www.publications.parliament.uk/pa/cm200203/cmselect/cmpubacc/641/641.pdf.

Institute for Health Metrics and Evaluation. 2013. "The State of US Health." http://www.healthdata.org/sites/default/files/files/country_profiles/GBD/ihme_gbd_country_report_united_states.pdf.

Institute of Medicine. 1999. "To Err Is Human: Building a Safer Health System." November. https://www.iom.edu/~/media/Files/Report%20Files/1999/To-Err-is-Human/To%20Err%20is%20Human%201999%20%20report%20brief.pdf.

King, Dominic, et al. 2014. "Redesigning the 'Choice Architecture' of Hospital Prescription Charts: A Mixed Methods Study Incorporating in Situ Simulation Testing." *British Medical Journal Open* 4:e005473.

King, Victoria. 2011. "'Nudge Unit' Urges Use of Smokeless Cigarettes." *BBC News Online*. September 15. http://www.bbc.com/news/uk-politics-14927871.

Lang, Tim, and Geof Rayner. 2011. "Is Nudge an Effective Public Health Strategy to Tackle Obesity? No." *British Medical Journal* 432.

Levitsky, D. A., and C. R. Pacanowski. 2012. "Free Will and the Obesity Epidemic." *Public Health Nutrition* 15(1):126–41.

Lewis, P. J., et al. 2009. "Prevalence, Incidence and Nature of Prescribing Errors in Hospital Inpatients: A Systematic Review." *Drug Safety* 32(5):379–89.

Petrosino, Anthony, Carolyn Turpin-Petrosino, and John Beuhler. 2003. "Scared Straight and Other Juvenile Awareness Programs for Preventing Juvenile Delinquency: A Systematic Review of the Randomized Experimental Evidence." *The Annals of the American Academy of Political and Social Science* 589(1):41–62.

Rebonato, Riccardo. 2012. *Taking Liberties: A Critical Examination of Libertarian Paternalism.* Palgrave Macmillan. New York.

Thaler, Richard H. 2013. "Public Policies, Made to Fit People." *The New York Times*, August 24, Business Day sec. http://www.nytimes.com/2013/08/25/business/public-policies-made-to-fit -people.html.

Thaler, Richard H., and Cass R. Sunstein. 2008. *Nudge: Improving Decisions about Health, Wealth, and Happiness.* Yale University Press. New Haven, CT. 6.

U.K. Clinical Research Collaboration. 2012. "UK Health Research Analysis 2009/10." http://www.ukcrc.org/wp-content/uploads/2014/03/2UKHealthResearchAnalysis-1.pdf.

Verplanken, Bas, and Wendy Wood. 2006. "Interventions to Break and Create Consumer Habits." *Journal of Public Policy & Marketing* 25(1):90–103.

Wansink, Brian. 2015. "A Personal Note from Dr. Wansink." Mindless Eating. http://mindlesseating.org/letter.php.

———. 2014. *Slim by Design: Mindless Eating Solutions for Everyday Life.* HarperCollins. New York.

Wright, Oliver. 2012. "Has Steve Hilton's Blue-Sky Thinking Finally Come Good?" *The Independent*, February 8. http://www.independent.co.uk/news/uk/politics/has-steve-hiltons -bluesky-thinking-finally-come-good-6661001.html.

PART I **THE ETHICS OF NUDGES IN HEALTHCARE**

Introduction

I. Glenn Cohen

In the film trilogy that begins with *The Matrix*, midway through the saga the designer of the computer network that has enslaved mankind makes an appearance. The designer is itself a computer program, but within the Matrix it is anthropomorphized as a man, "the Architect." The Architect at one point explains to the rebellious protagonist of the films that the system has been designed to take into account the randomness of human will, by making room for an anomaly (the protagonist) to liberate the system every so often only to later be subjugated (Wachowski et al. 2003). Every variable has been controlled for, even the random ones.

In the world of health nudges instead of a nefarious computer architect we have a vaguer choice architect. The chapters in this part of the book all try, in one way or another, to resist the grip of this architect.

The choice architect, of course, is supposed to be an improvement over the regulator, his more dictatorial brother. Nudges are supposed to be an advantageous innovation over "old school" regulation, in healthcare or elsewhere. In their more philosophical description of the nudge, Thaler and Sunstein purposefully choose to call this "libertarian paternalism" and present it as a form of regulation that can achieve some of the goals of paternalism without being too offensive to libertarians (Sunstein and Thaler 2003).

The chapters in this part of the book challenge at a more ten-thousand-foot level the success of the nudge strategy as it applies to health. What makes them compelling as a unit is their demonstration of the old adage "there is more than one way to skin a cat." The points of attack vary—data-driven analysis of how nudge strategies have played out so far, internal critique that the nudge cannot achieve what it sets out as its goals on its own terms, and external critique of its methods of achieving its goals—all as applied to healthcare.

David A. Hyman and Thomas S. Ulen's "What Can PPACA Teach Us about Behavioral Law and Economics?" critiques Sunstein and Thaler's attempts to achieve a middle ground and use the Patient Protection and Affordable Care Act (colloquially, "Obama-Care") as their test case. They adopt a common strategy to nudge skeptics outside the healthcare context of demonstrating the ways in which nudges have underperformed in real-world settings and how frequently more coercive direct regulation would be superior. While acknowledging that "the fact that a nudge might fall short of the results of a more coercive strategy does not necessarily constitute a basis for condemnation of nudges or a reason for paternalistic interventions"—because avoiding coercive regulation is, on the normative picture of nudge enthusiasts, a good that counts for something—they also argue that enthusiasm for the nudge has far outstripped realism about its potential for implementation. Using data on several ObamaCare elements designed to take advantage of default choice architecture, they demonstrate that the data show that nudges have had a mixed (at best) record of success. They see this as a critique of the simplicity with which implementing choice architecture is sometimes presented; as they put it, "defaults matter, but so do lots of other things," and "[w]e do not know nearly enough about the circumstances in which defaults" work to engage in wise design.

Mark D. White's "Bad Medicine: Does the Unique Nature of Healthcare Decisions Justify Nudges?" examines whether general philosophical critiques of nudges have more or less purchase when choice architecture is deployed in the healthcare setting. Like Hyman and Ulen he is skeptical that the architect has enough knowledge to set and implement defaults wisely. But he engrafts on this critique a more philosophical one: "Traditional conceptions of autonomy and liberal neutrality maintain that people should have the right to live their lives as they choose, free from judgment from their government, provided they do not infringe on the similar rights of others" while "policymakers use nudges to steer people's decisions in interests that are not necessarily their own, but rather the policymakers' idea of those interests." He then considers two arguments that nudges should be more palatable in health as opposed to other domains—that individuals' interest in health is so high and universal that nudges promoting health are less likely to impose external interests on them, and that health decisions are so complex and emotional that nudges are more justified to help overcome cognitive biases. Not only does White reject these arguments, but he actually finds the case against nudges stronger in the health domain. He views nudges for health as being at greater risk of "subverting and manipulat[ing]" the integrity and autonomy of personal decision-making because the architect has "no way to know how any person values or conceptualizes health." Of course, one might press "as compared to what." The same deficit is true for good old-fashioned paternalism in the health sphere, though one imagines that White might find some elements of that troublesome as well.

Nir Eyal's chapter, "Nudging and Benign Manipulation for Health," locates the problem with nudging in a slightly different place related to its mechanism. Nudges are supposed to be morally superior to coercive threats, but Eyal argues that they affect choice through another ethically dubious mechanism—manipulation. At the threshold he disagrees with Sunstein's contention that nudges are not manipulative, adopting instead a definition of Ruth Faden and Tom Beauchamp wherein manipulation is "a catch all category for any intentional and successful influence of a person by non-coercively altering the actual choices available to the person or by non-persuasively altering the person's perception of those choices" (Faden and Beauchamp 1986, 261). Indeed, Eyal goes on to suggest that nudges might necessarily be manipulative (and indeed purported examples of non-manipulative nudges might not be nudges at all). But, contrary to some of Sunstein's philosophical critics, Eyal concludes that the mere fact that nudging involves manipulation is not sufficient to make nudges wrongful, that there is a category of "benign" manipulative nudges. He finds examples of the use of nudges in healthcare to be a prominent example of these kinds of benign manipulative nudges, and defends their permissibility against critics. In this way his take is the opposite of White's—Eyal finds nudges more defensible in health contexts, while White finds them less defensible.

Finally, Jonathan Gingerich's chapter focuses on the political philosophical critique of nudges, and the fact that they are not merely anyone's attempt to influence behavior but the state's attempts. He argues that on this critique "nudges are morally worrisome insofar as they undermine democratic control of default rules by making it more difficult for people to detect that the choice architecture in which they operate has been actively shaped by policymakers." That is, while old-fashioned paternalism is highly visible, nudges fly under the radar. This generates not a blanket condemnation of governmental use of nudges but (like Eyal) a critique of only a subset of nudges—in Gingerich's case only those nudges that "prevent people from directly engaging with the reasons and values that bear on a decision that it is morally important for them to make for themselves." He then applies this approach to health nudges—a city's choice of what health insurance plan to make the default it offers to employees, attempts to influence a patient deciding between aggressive chemotherapy and palliative treatment—and asks whether nudging here is more or less of a concern.

In the shadow of all of these chapters is the "as against what" question, though few address it head on. The argumentative burden of Sunstein and other nudge proponents is not that nudges are a panacea, but that they may be superior to other forms of regulation, particularly more direct old-fashioned paternalism. At a deeper level all of these chapters seem to wrestle with this underlying premise. Hyman and Ulen attack it implicitly on the grounds that traditional nudges are less effective, harder to predict, and harder to implement than direct regulation. Gingerich finds the visibility of direct regulation to be a point in its favor that allows a direct democratic engagement with the policy in a way that nudges do not. For Eyal, the key category does not seem to be nudge versus direct regulation but benign versus malign, such that in the end he is willing to countenance manipulation if benign, but presumably also direct regulation. In his closing paragraph White emphasizes hostility to nudges as non-neutral and transparent ways of helping people "make the best choices they can," but on at least some of these criteria it seems to me that direct regulation would fare still worse. On the other hand, one might think that from a political economy perspective direct regulation is less likely to be enacted than nudge solutions, such that for the libertarian the choice may be a world with more frequent nudges or more paternalistic but less frequent instances of direct regulation.

These chapters also leave one with an ambivalent picture of the choice architect. Is he well intentioned if inevitably under-informed? A tired clockmaker who designs her system and lets it run without correction, even if at some point it begins to lose time? Or is he an evil genius along the lines sketched by Descartes, who is subtly pulling the strings of his subject, all the while deluding her into believing herself to be acting in accord with her own values? The authors in this part do not converge on a common vision.

Finally, can the critiques of nudging be reduced or eliminated when these techniques are used for healthcare? Again, there is not convergence. All take as common ground the idea that healthcare decision-making has features—the special importance of health (Daniels 2008), our poor performance in healthcare decision-making, the emotional nature of the questions—that distinguish the health context. But they disagree on whether this makes healthcare a more or less appealing case for nudging, as no doubt will many readers of this book.

References

Daniels, Norman. 2008. *Just Health*. Cambridge University Press. Cambridge.

Faden, Ruth R., and Tom L. Beauchamp. 1986. *A History and Theory of Informed Consent*. Oxford University Press. New York.

Sunstein, Cass R., and Richard H. Thaler. 2003. "Libertarian Paternalism Is Not an Oxymoron." *The University of Chicago Law Review* 70:1159.

Wachowski, Andy, Lana Wachowski, Joel Silver, Keanu Reeves, Laurence Fishburne, Carrie-Anne Moss, Hugo Weaving, et al. 2003. *The Matrix Reloaded*. Warner Bros. Pictures. Burbank, CA.

CHAPTER 4

What Can PPACA Teach Us about Behavioral Law and Economics?

David A. Hyman and Thomas S. Ulen

The insights of behavioral economics have been applied to a diverse array of issues in law and policy. The thrust of those efforts has been to identify "behavioral market failures"—systematic and predictable errors in judgment and decision-making. These behavioral market failures, in combination with (or in addition to) the traditional sources of market failure, lead to suboptimal decisions by individuals. Based on the findings of this research, prominent scholars have argued in favor of "nudges" as the best (that is, most effective and least disruptive of personal autonomy) corrective (White 2013; Rebonato 2014).

In this essay, we analyze several aspects of the Patient Protection and Affordable Care Act (PPACA) through a behavioral lens. The basic problem is simple. Behavioral economics promises "better" (that is, less heavy-handed and more choice-preserving) regulation than traditional command-and-control regulatory strategies (Thaler and Sunstein 2008). The Obama administration came into office in 2009 trumpeting its expertise in behavioral economics and promising to avoid behavioral biases of the sort that had beset previous administrations.

But some recent literature suggests that nudges may turn out to be useful in a far more limited set of circumstances than previously believed. Also, those responsible for the development and implementation of regulations are subject to their own behavioral biases. Maybe we should be more skeptical about the utility of behaviorally informed regulation. As Richard Epstein has noted, "it would be easy to assume that collective responses are preferred when markets are corrupt and governments virtuous. It is far harder to reach that conclusion when self-interest and corruption creates difficulties from both quarters" (Epstein 1992, 311). To put the matter bluntly, maybe the enthusiasm for nudges is just another behavioral bias.

We appreciate the helpful comments we received from Peter Molk and Kathy Zeiler.

The Behavioral Economics of Defaults

The findings of behavioral economics fill numerous books and articles. In what follows, we focus on the findings relating to default choices. The behavioral literature finds that defaults are likely to prove "sticky," virtually independent of their substantive content. Thus, whether one frames the default as "opt-in" or "opt-out" has a profound impact on the choices that are made—even in high-stakes settings. Based on such research, proponents of behavioral economics concluded that "choice architecture," including the careful choice of defaults, can "nudge" people to make "better" decisions while preserving the individual's option to choose among alternatives (Thaler and Sunstein 2008).

These claims have not gone unanswered. Critics have pointed out the ad hoc nature of many behavioralist claims; the assumption that only those being regulated are subject to such behavioral biases; the benefits of allowing people to learn from their mistakes; the implausibility of nudges for dealing with many issues; the paternalistic assumptions that lie behind most nudging; and various other problems (Wright and Ginsburg 2012).

Others have argued that behavioral findings actually strengthen the case for mandatory regulation (Bubb and Pildes 2014). Consider retirement savings. Consumers, left to their own devices, do not save "enough" for their retirement. The behavioralist recommendation is to change the default rule from opt-in to automatic enrollment, with the right to opt out. However, "the adoption of automatic enrollment has in practice *lowered* retirement savings for many workers and on net likely lowered average retirement savings" (Bubb and Pildes 2014, 1593). Bubb and Pildes also identify various shortcomings of the automatic enrollment policy, including the difficulty in setting the "right" default rate; failing to devote sufficient attention to those who do opt out; failing to analyze the efficacy of existing tax incentives; and the systematic bias in favor of voluntary strategies (Bubb and Pildes 2014).

In a similar vein, Willis reports on the effects of legislation that changed the default option for checking-account overdraft fees (Willis 2013). Until 2010, the default rule with respect to overdrafts was one in which customers could, at the bank's discretion and for a fee, overdraw their accounts. After that, new banking regulations changed the default rule to one in which banks could not charge customers for overdrafts unless account holders opted out of the default. Those who did not opt out had no liability for overdrafts but might find themselves unable to obtain funds when they needed them. In order to opt out, consumers had to speak to a bank representative, click a box on an online banking form, or send the bank a written request (Willis 2013). Subsequent research found that heavy users of overdraft privileges—the supposed beneficiaries of the nudge—were the quickest to opt out of the default (Willis 2013). Within a few years, almost half of those studied had opted out (Willis 2013).

Why was the nudge so ineffective? Willis suggests the nudge did not work because banks had an economic incentive to make the default slippery. Indeed, banks made considerable effort to lower the cost of opting out; in a survey of customers, almost half "reported they had opted out of the default . . . at least in part to stop receiving overdraft marketing" (Willis 2013, 1188). The vast majority of customers—even those who had been heavy users of overdraft privileges in the past—did not think that they would use the privilege in the future.

Thus, the default turned out to be slippery rather than sticky—and those who opted out were disproportionately likely to pay overdraft fees. Willis identifies four factors that helped make the 2010 default slippery and considers policy alternatives that would make the default more sticky. Most of her alternatives involve making the opt-out more costly or the consequences more transparent. But the most obvious alternative—as in the instances considered by Bubb and Pildes—is simply to abandon the behavioral commitment to a nudge in favor of a mandatory rule (hard paternalism). That would, of course, be a difficult sell to banks and to many consumers. But at least for the instance studied by Willis, and perhaps in a much wider set of instances, the soft paternalism of setting the default to serve the desired corrective function has not worked and cannot plausibly be made to work.

However, the fact that a nudge might fall short of the results of a more coercive strategy does not necessarily constitute a basis for condemnation of nudges or a reason for paternalistic interventions. Indeed, if we are to take the libertarian assumptions behind nudging seriously, it is not meaningful to speak of a "failed" nudge (other chapters in this book provide more philosophical critiques of nudging). Nonetheless, these examples indicate that nudges, as prescriptions for behavioral and traditional market failures, may not be as seamlessly effective as previous advocates have suggested, nor as universally applicable, nor as obviously superior to traditional command-and-control regulation. To say the very least, nudging (and the use of defaults) raises interesting and complicated questions, irrespective of whether the target for intervention is healthcare or any other domain of human enterprise.

We now turn to the use of nudges (in the form of defaults) in PPACA.

Application to PPACA

The effectiveness of nudges and defaults is ultimately an empirical question. The whole issue of the advisability of nudging is far more complicated than its proponents have suggested; there are many open questions about nudging about which we simply do not have evidence, such as whether it is likely to be less or more effective for healthcare decisions than for other matters (Johnson et al. 2013). But we do have some ideas, mentioned in the previous section, about what factors might help to explain when nudges are likely to be successful. What insights can we glean about this subject from PPACA? As it happens, the coverage expansions at the heart of PPACA are built around five provisions, each structured on an opt-in basis (Henry J. Kaiser Family Foundation 2013). The five provisions are:

- Exchanges
- Medicaid expansion
- Community Living Assistance Services and Supports Act (CLASS)
- Employer mandate
- Coverage of those under 26 on their parents' plans

The first two provisions were structured as two-level opt-ins. States first decide whether to create an exchange and/or participate in the Medicaid expansion. Individuals then decide whether to enroll in the specified coverage. The third and fourth provisions are structured as two-level opt-in/opt-outs. For CLASS, workers can opt in. If employers opt in, their employees are automatically opted in unless they opt out. For the employer mandate, employers with more than fifty employees can opt in to offering coverage and employees can then opt in to coverage if they choose to do so. Employers with more than two hundred employees can opt in to offering coverage, and if they do so, employees will be auto-enrolled but are able to opt out. The final provision is a pure single-level opt-in. Individuals decide whether to enroll/continue dependents who are under 26 in their existing coverage. Obviously, the impact of these five nudges is affected by the mix of carrots (subsidies) and sticks (taxes/penalties) in PPACA for those individuals/employers who do not offer/secure coverage and for those states that do not create a state-level exchange or expand their Medicaid program.

Thus, with the partial exception of CLASS and the employer mandate for employers with more than two hundred employees, the default for each of these five policies was set to nonparticipation. States, whose decisions might well be subject to a different set of calculations than those of individuals, had to voluntarily opt in to the exchanges and the Medicaid expansion. Workers and employers had to voluntarily opt in to CLASS, although if employers opted in, workers had to opt out if they did not want to participate. The employer mandate was structured as an opt-in as well. Finally, individuals had to voluntarily enroll themselves and/or their dependents in coverage (exchange, Medicaid, and dependents under 26) unless they worked for an employer with more than two hundred employees who provided coverage, in which case they had to opt out.

Because all five of these policies are structured as opt-in arrangements, one would expect the default to dominate (that is, relatively few states create exchanges and opt in to Medicaid; relatively few employers offer coverage; and relatively few people enroll in exchanges, CLASS, and employer-based coverage). If defaults have a consistent impact, then one would expect similar results across all five of these domains, with the possible exception of CLASS and the employer mandate for employers with more than two hundred employees—because of the peculiar opt-in/opt-out strategy for these two provisions. But if not, then other factors must play a role in the success or failure of any given nudge—some of which might be specific to the decision-maker (which, depending on the context, is either a state, an employer, or an individual) while other factors might be generalizable. If there are factors other than the framing of the default matter, then nudges (and defaults) once again turn out to be a far more complex policy undertaking than previously believed. So, what actually happened?

The results were decidedly mixed. As of January 2016 , there were 13 pure state exchanges, 4 federally supported exchanges, 7 state partnership exchanges, and 27 pure federal marketplaces (Henry J. Kaiser Family Foundation 2016). Thirty-one states and the District of Columbia decided to expand Medicaid (Henry J. Kaiser Family Foundation 2016). CLASS was killed in 2011, before a single person enrolled, because of concerns about adverse selection—meaning that everyone involved believed the opt-in approach would be too successful in disproportionately enrolling high-risk beneficiaries and comparatively unsuccessful in enrolling low-risk beneficiaries (Kane 2011).

Pre-PPACA, large employers almost invariably offered coverage to employees while small employers were much less likely to do so. There was also significant variation based on industry sector, with retail and agricultural employers much less likely to offer coverage. Finally, employee uptake varied significantly as well by income and age. Post-PPACA, the employer mandate was postponed to 2015 (large employers) or 2016 (medium-sized employers), so it has not yet had any effect.

It is difficult to get reliable figures for the actual impact of PPACA on net coverage. Estimates have ranged from 7 million to 16.4 million (Blumenthal et al. 2015). Gross enrollment figures are much higher: in 2015, 11.7 million individuals obtained coverage through the exchanges; 10.8 million obtained coverage through Medicaid; and 3 million obtained coverage by staying on their parents' policies. The large differences between the gross and net effect is due to differences in sampling methodology, as well as the fact that some of these individuals were insured pre-PPACA, and simply switched their source of coverage (either voluntarily or because their coverage was terminated as a result of PPACA). In addition, there is considerable "churn" in Medicaid, and some of the "new" enrollees qualified for Medicaid pre-PPACA. Strictly speaking, PPACA should only get credit for net new enrollments in states that expanded Medicaid—that is, for enrollments that would not have occurred but for PPACA. Even in states that expanded Medicaid, it was not clear how many were able to secure coverage because of the Medicaid expansion (as opposed to better outreach, greater public visibility, and the like). Finally, some have argued that far fewer than 3 million individuals obtained coverage by staying on their parents' policies That said, the most striking thing about the under-26 coverage provision is the extent to which it was implemented without any significant attention or controversy—unlike the exchanges and the Medicaid expansion. All of these factors complicate any assessment of the impact of PPACA on net coverage.

It is clear that setting the default against enrollment (by requiring opt-in) had quite variable effects, depending on the specific policy initiative. To be sure, the "compared to what" counterfactual is hard to answer: by 2016, 25% of the states had their own pure exchange, and 63% expanded their Medicaid programs. Is that a success or failure, compared to what would have happened had the default been flipped (assuming away the political and constitutional difficulties with doing so)? We do not (yet) have sufficient information to compute similar percentages for the enrollment in exchange-based coverage, Medicaid, and those under 26 who remained on their parents' policies.

It also remains to be seen how many of those who opted in already had insurance coverage as opposed to those without such coverage—since it was the latter group that was the target of PPACA. Ironically, the default may have operated to discourage those whom PPACA was intended to reach (that is, the currently uninsured). Further analysis will be necessary to fully understand the distributional consequences of PPACA enrollment and the way in which various factors, including the defaults, affected those patterns.

Discussion

In this section we build on the analysis in the previous sections, and also propose some empirical investigations to evaluate the impact of nudges—both those included in PPACA and more broadly.

The Behavioral Economics of Defaults

A naïve interpretation of behavioral economics is that all one has to do is structure the defaults in an appropriate way and everything else—including any behavioral market failures—will take care of themselves. Conversely, if the defaults are set up incorrectly, it really does not matter what else you do—things will not work out well. Obviously, life is substantially more complicated than that.

Consider Sunstein's treatment of the default with regard to last names after one gets married:

Both men and women retain their premarital names when they get married. Note that we could easily imagine a large number of default rules:
- The husband's name stays the same, but the wife's name changes to that of her husband. Indeed, that approach, however discriminatory, would mimic people's behavior, at least in the United States.
- The husband's name changes to that of his wife, and the wife's name stays the same.
- The spouses' names are hyphenated.
- Unless you opt out, your marital name is Smith (or Dylan, or Kennedy, or Pie, or Simpler, or Australia; you get the idea).
  So, there is nothing inevitable about the current default rule. What are its effects? In the overwhelming majority of cases, men stick with the default. A very small percentage

of men change their names. By contrast, the overwhelming majority of women do so (probably more than 80 percent). In that respect, the default rule does not seem to have a large effect on women (though admittedly, the percentage of women with their husband's names would probably be even higher if that were the default). (Sunstein 2013, 116)

Sunstein suggests that these results are observed because those involved have clear preferences, clear timing, and positive feelings about opting in. Unfortunately, Sunstein's criteria are little more than a list of three observable attributes of the circumstances associated with getting married. He provides no evidence of causality, comparative significance, or representativeness. Should we infer that these attributes (and only these attributes) govern whether all defaults will be effective? This is still an open question, one that cannot simply be asserted but must be backed with convincing empirical evidence. Similar difficulties apply to the attributes identified by Willis that characterize a slippery default.

In our view, defaults matter, but so do lots of other things. We do not know nearly enough about the circumstances in which defaults are sticky and when they are not. Although a few case studies have been conducted, post hoc rationalization and just-so stories are dominant. Ironically enough, this is just what a behavioralist would predict!

Improving the Knowledge Base

If we do not know nearly enough about the performance of defaults and nudging, the obvious solution is to improve our knowledge base on the subject. (As is widely known, the first result of all research is the need for further [funded] research.) Accordingly, we offer several pathways for further research on these issues, focusing on healthcare.

One obvious path of empirical research regarding the suitability of nudges in PPACA would be to take the factors that Willis and Sunstein identified as being likely to make defaults slippery and examine the extent to which those factors are likely to influence the effectiveness of PPACA. For example, there can be little doubt that consumer confusion and a lack of preexisting preferences are likely to be significant—particularly when we analyze selection among the various policies available through the exchanges. An additional complication is that all five of the relevant provisions were set as either one-stage or two-stage opt-ins (with CLASS and the employer mandate partial exceptions to that approach).

We are unaware of any experiments that were done to evaluate how consumers processed the information provided on the exchanges—let alone whether several variations were tested. Even if such research exists, the catastrophic launch of the federal and various state exchanges would make us skeptical of the value of such research. But it certainly makes sense to try out several alternative means of presentation to discover which strategies minimize consumer confusion and evaluate the best way to "prime" consumers so as to compensate for the absence of strong preexisting preferences. The heterogeneity of presentation strategies of state exchanges provides an obvious test bed for evaluating such matters.

The ability of parents to extend coverage for those under age 26 presents a similar test bed for evaluating nudging. As we have noted already, that provision was implemented smoothly and without drama. It is not entirely clear how many individuals obtained coverage through this provision (which is itself an indication of our point), but why did things work so smoothly? Is it because parents were making decisions for their children? Or because it seamlessly integrated with existing coverage arrangements? Do some employers have a much higher enrollment rate among their employees than others? What do we know about employees who opted in versus those who did not? How long do people maintain such coverage, and where do they go once they drop it? And so on.

Another path of empirical research would be to analyze the information that resulted from the initial sign-up periods for obtaining coverage through the state and federal exchanges and through Medicaid—in both states that have and states that have not opted in to the PPACA expansion of Medicaid. Certainly, there are those who are doing their best to analyze these issues now. Such efforts have been handicapped by the limited information that is made available by the administration—and the superheated political environment in which such analyses are being conducted. It is unfortunate that PPACA did not provide for the collection and dissemination of standardized data in a specified format—or that some respected, disinterested independent body was not given authority to secure that data, analyze it, and disseminate information.

In the absence of either of those alternatives, we are now being treated to a disheartening spectacle of warring claims and counterclaims of success and failure. Anyone who hopes for a clear set of answers to the important questions (How many people who were previously uninsured have obtained insurance? At what cost? How good is the coverage that is provided? To what extent is PPACA bending the cost curve downward?) is surely mystified by the swirling controversy about PPACA and its effects. The environment is dominated by grandiose claims, "spinning," and pseudo-statistics, rather than useful information and analysis.

It is still not too late to require the collection, analysis, and dissemination of relevant information—for both those who obtain coverage through the exchanges and those who decline to do so. Democrats and Republicans seem incapable of agreeing on much of anything regarding PPACA—and matters seem likely to get worse in the run-up to the 2016 election. But the warring parties might be able to agree on data collection mechanisms and descriptive statistics with which to assess the experience of those participating in the exchanges.

Although we generally favor a multitude of independent researchers working independently on these issues (on the ground that competition and multiple points-of-view would provide a more complete and nuanced view), a bipartisan, authoritative analysis of PPACA's effects has social benefits as well. We should "hope for the best, but plan for the worst" in these matters.

Crafting public policy is an extremely difficult matter, and PPACA was extraordinarily politically divisive. Even so, in sensitive high-stakes areas like healthcare, it is critical to gather the necessary information to assess performance—and to revisit statutory design and implementation decisions that do not measure up. Many people view PPACA as a moral crusade—but we view it as just another government program. The coverage nudges it contains will either work, or they will not. Given the amount of money being spent, it would be nice if we gathered sufficient information to evaluate the matter—particularly if the resulting insights were applied going forward. Until we strengthen our knowledge base, we simply do not know enough to assess when nudges will (and will not) correct behavioral market failures more effectively than alternative public policies.

Modesty, Judgment, and the Utility of Behavioral Economics

Improving our knowledge base as to the performance of defaults and nudging is important but will make little (if any) difference if those responsible for designing and implementing such matters lack modesty and judgment about the utility of this latest addition to the regulatory tool-kit. We flag two distinct reasons for caution.

First, many law professors seem to be enthusiastic about behavioral economics because it appears to provide an escape hatch from the strictures otherwise imposed by neoclassical law and economics. Many law professors like telling other people how they should live their lives. Neoclassical law and economics makes it harder for them to do so while behavioral economics gives them considerably more running room (Ulen 2014).

The short version is that if you turn law professors and regulators loose with a behavioral economics hammer, you should not be surprised that some of them will see nails everywhere they look (Rizzo and Whitman 2009; Wright and Ginsburg 2012). As Kate Litvak cuttingly described matters:

> I remember the times when legal academics discovered "cognitive biases." This was huge! Now, you don't have to know anything about the [field] you are proposing to regulate, or [the] economics behind regulation. All you had to do is list a couple of random "cognitive biases" that you found in law reviews or in popular magazines . . . Sometimes the same article would list a set of conflicting "biases" and then, in all seriousness, propose to simultaneously counteract all of them.
>
> This started in consumer protection and borrowing. But now, it has metastasized into health law! Did you know that we need Obamacare because people underestimate their future demand for health services . . . and they also overestimate their future demand for health services . . . and they are too worried they will not receive the right services . . . and they are not worried enough. (Litvak 2013)

Similarly, Joshua Wright noted, "I've been fairly critical of those, especially in the law review literature, who invoke terms like irrationality and endowment effect willy-nilly, wave their hands around quickly while saying something about market failure (usually this section of the paper also has the term "orthodox neoclassical theory" in it somewhere), and move on to discuss regulatory proposals on the assumption that they will be costless" (Wright 2010).

Second, merely because an analyst can identify one or more behavioral "biases" does not mean that she has made the case for regulatory intervention—let alone identified the form that intervention should take. Biases can be heterogeneous in their impact, and often point in different directions. The overall effect is often hard to predict. Regulatory intervention is never costless, and regulators have their own biases and other shortcomings. As one of us has noted, "platonic guardians are in short supply, no matter how high the demand" (Hyman and Franklyn 2015, 377).

There is no replacement for modesty and judgment in the implementation of regulatory initiatives. Regrettably, we seem to select systematically against those attributes, preferring those who offer moral and physical salvation to those who more realistically offer "a few modest suggestions that may make a small difference" (Wilson 1989, 369–76).

Taking No for an Answer

Nudges were sold by Thaler and Sunstein as a form of libertarian paternalism. Choice architecture would allow individuals to opt out if they did not like the default, while protecting the rest of the population from bad decisions, with "bad" defined by reference to what those individuals would prefer (chap. 5 by Mark D. White in this volume further discusses these issues). But what happens when people stubbornly insist on opting out of the default, or resist the nudge? If there were truly a libertarian component to libertarian paternalism, the choice architect should be more than willing to take no for an answer. But it turns out that many of them are not—and when people ignore the default or resist the nudge, it is taken as evidence of a problem with the design of the default/nudge (Willis 2013; Bubb and Pildes 2014). For those who take this approach, choice architecture turns out to be about rebranding and repackaging paternalism—and not about respecting the autonomous choices of individuals about how they should live their own lives (Teles 2014).

Maybe shove is the new nudge (Wright 2010). If that is the case, maybe a little truth in advertising is in order. We should drop the pretense that all of this activity has anything to do with behavioral economics, or is much more than pure paternalism, leavened by a rhetorical patina of pseudo-choice. Maybe those using nudges and defaults should be required to provide a mandatory disclosure statement about their intentions, preferences, and priorities. We leave the drafting of the disclosure statement for another day, but we think it would be unfortunate if it had to read as follows: "Chump: if you choose what I think is best for you, then I will respect your choice. Otherwise,

I will figure out a way to get you to choose what I want you to choose. Aren't you glad I am respecting your right to choose?"

Truth Is Stranger Than Fiction

Science fiction typically posits worlds that are barely recognizable as having developed from the here and now. Part of that genre's charm lies in trying to detail the dimly discernible connection between today and the far future that its creators imagine. Political satire shares some of the same values—imagining a world so far removed from the current state of affairs that its outrageousness causes smiles and thoughts of "There but for the grace of God . . ."

Imagine then our surprise when a prescient bit of satire from *The Onion* of November 5, 2003, seems to come far too close to describing the world that we describe in this chapter. The article is entitled "Americans Demand Increased Governmental Protection from Selves" and explains that Americans are deeply concerned about the "unhealthy choices they make every day" (*The Onion* 2003). Unable to correct those choices on their own, they seek help from the government. One (fictional) enthusiast reports that the "Government is finally starting to take some responsibility for the effect my behavior has on others." Another laments that it is "not just about Americans eating too many fries or cracking heads open when they fall off their bicycles . . . It's a financial issue, too. I spend all my money on trendy clothes and a nightlife that I can't afford. I'm $23,000 in debt, but the credit-card companies keep letting me spend. It's obscene that the government allows those companies to allow me to do this to myself. Why do I pay taxes?" Who knew we could go from the pages of *The Onion* to the preferred policy strategy of elite academics in under a decade? Truth really is stranger than fiction.

Conclusion

Popular enthusiasm for behavioral economics and legal interest in nudges has led many to believe they are a cure-all for every regulatory problem. But even our abbreviated treatment of the impact of PPACA's five opt-in coverage provisions makes it clear that matters are substantially more complicated. Defaults appear to be effective— except when they are not—which is not the kind of theory (or tool) that lends itself to general application. Sometimes we can use nudges. Sometimes we will need to use hard paternalism. And sometimes (perhaps often, given the baseline rate of regulatory intervention and the frequency of government failure) we probably should not do anything at all, other than deregulating and leaving well enough alone. Deciding when each of these strategies should be used (and the authors themselves disagree on such matters) is where the rubber hits the road—and no amount of "happy talk" about the virtues of choice architecture, nudging, and defaults will change that fact.

References

Blumenthal, David, Melinda Abrams, and Rachel Nuzum. 2015. "The Affordable Care Act at 5 Years." *New England Journal of Medicine* 372:2451.

Bubb, Ryan, and Richard H. Pildes. 2014. "How Behavioral Economics Trims Its Sails and Why." *Harvard Law Review* 127:1593.

Epstein, Richard A. 1992. "Why Is Health Care Special?" *Kansas Law Review* 40:307, 311.

Henry J. Kaiser Family Foundation. 2016. "State Decisions on Health Insurance Marketplaces and the Medicaid Expansion." Accessed February 26, 2016. http://kff.org/health-reform /state-indicator/state-decisions-for-creating-health-insurance-exchanges-and-expanding -medicaid/#note-4.

———. 2013. "Summary of the Affordable Care Act." Accessed January 25, 2015. http://kff.org /health-reform/fact-sheet/summary-of-the-affordable-care-act/.

Hyman, David A., and David Franklyn. 2015. "Search Bias and the Limits of Antitrust: An Empirical Perspective on Remedies." *Jurimetrics* 55:339.

Johnson, Eric J., Ran Hassin, Tom Baker, Allison T. Bajger, and Galen Treuer. 2013. "Can Consumers Make Affordable Care Affordable?: The Value of Choice Architecture." *PLOS One* 8:12:e81521.

Kane, Jason. 2011. "What the Death of the CLASS Act Means for Long-Term Disability Care." *PBS NewsHour*. October 14. http://www.pbs.org/newshour/rundown/what-the-death-of-the -class-act-means-for-long-term-disability-care/.

Litvak, Kate. 2013. Facebook posting. November 19. Facebook, Inc.

The Onion. 2003. "Americans Demand Increased Government Protection from Selves." *The Onion* 39(43). http://www.theonion.com/articles/americans-demand-increased -governmental-protection-1652/.

Rebonato, Riccardo. 2014. "A Critical Examination of Libertarian Paternalism." *Journal of Consumer Policy* 37:357.

Rizzo, Mario, and Douglas Glen Whitman. 2009. "The Knowledge Problem of the New Paternalism." *Brigham Young University Law Review*:905.

Roy, Avik. 2014. "Census Data: Since 2008, There's Been No Net Change in the Proportion of Young Adults with Health Coverage." *Forbes*. http://www.forbes.com/sites/theapothecary /2014/04/03/census-data-since-2008-theres-been-no-net-change-in-the-proportion-of-young -adults-with-health-coverage/.

Sunstein, Cass R. 2013. *Simpler: The Future of Government.* Simon and Schuster. New York.

Teles, Steven. 2014. "Nudge or Shove?" *American Interest* 10(3).

Thaler, Richard H., and Cass R. Sunstein. 2008. *Nudge: Improving Decisions about Health, Wealth, and Happiness.* Yale University Press. New Haven, CT.

Ulen, Thomas S. 2014. "The Importance of Behavioral Law." In *The Oxford Handbook of Behavioral Law and Economics*, edited by Doron Teichman and Eyal Zamir. Oxford University Press. Oxford.

White, Mark D. 2013. *The Manipulation of Choice: Ethics and Libertarian Paternalism.* Palgrave Macmillan. New York.

Willis, Lauren E. 2013. "When Nudges Fail: Slippery Defaults." *The University of Chicago Law Review* 80:1155.

Wilson, James Q. 1989. *Bureaucracy: What Government Agencies Do and Why They Do It.* Basic Books. New York.

Wright, Joshua. 2010. "Has the Obama Administration Retreated from Behavioral Economics?" http://truthonthemarket.com/2010/03/09/has-the-obama-administration-retreated-from-behavioral-economics/.

Wright, Joshua D., and Douglas H. Ginsburg. 2012. "Behavioral Law and Economics: Its Origins, Fatal Flaws, and Implications for Liberty." *Northwestern University Law Review* 106:1033.

CHAPTER 5

Bad Medicine
Does the Unique Nature of Healthcare Decisions Justify Nudges?

Mark D. White

Behavioral economics, based on the work of Daniel Kahneman, Amos Tversky, and others, has led scholars and policymakers to reconsider their theories of how people make choices and react to incentives.[1] Individuals can no longer be assumed to follow textbook models of perfect rationality, knowledge, and willpower after weaknesses in all three areas were identified experimentally. Soon thereafter, economists and legal scholars incorporated behavioral economics into their own work, designing policies to help people overcome their cognitive imperfections and make better decisions.[2] After publishing influential academic work in the area (Sunstein and Thaler 2001), the behavioral economist Richard Thaler and the legal scholar Cass Sunstein released their 2008 book, *Nudge*, which in turn launched a revolution in the way governments on both sides of the Atlantic look at policymaking.[3]

In Thaler and Sunstein's conception, nudges are directed changes in the circumstances of a choice situation (or the "choice architecture") designed to steer individuals' decisions in their best interest, often by making use of the same cognitive biases and dysfunctions that motivated their use. For example, they endorse the automatic enrollment of new employees in retirement plans, with the option to withdraw, reasoning that many new employees neglect to enroll out of procrastination or default bias (Thaler and Sunstein 2008, chap. 6). Advocates of nudging refer to it as "libertarian paternalism" because it does not mandate and prohibit any options, but critics argue nonetheless that nudges are coercive and manipulative, albeit in a subtler way than traditional paternalism, and threaten autonomy without necessarily improving the quality of choices.[4]

One area of individual decision-making that has received particular attention in this context is health, such as decisions regarding diet and exercise. The importance, complexity, and emotionality of decisions regarding health suggest that nudges can be effective in improving such decisions, which raises the question of whether the problems with nudges are lessened or negated in the context of health and healthcare. In this chapter, I begin by discussing the ethical and practical problems with nudges in general, and then suggest several ways in which the unique nature of health may justify the uses of nudges despite any concerns in general. After considering these factors, I conclude nonetheless that the unique aspects of healthcare decision-making are not sufficient to justify the use of nudges. Rather, given the inherently personal nature of health choices, even greater care should be taken than in cases of ordinary consumer decisions to ensure that patients are as involved in decision-making as possible without having their autonomy compromised by any kind of paternalistic intervention.

The Problems with Nudges

The problems with nudges in general can be split into three interrelated categories—epistemic, ethical, and practical—with the first problem being primary and leading to the other two.[5]

The first problem deals with the information available when designing nudges. Scholars and policymakers claim that they are steering people to make better decisions that advance their own interests. But they have no way to know people's true interests, which are complex, multifaceted, and subjective. Instead, they impose their own idea of people's interests on them and then use nudges to guide their choices toward these imposed interests. For example, when policymakers recommend automatic enrollment in retirement programs for new employees, they are implicitly assuming a singular overriding interest in retirement savings. While retirement savings may be an interest of many if not most people, there is no reason to maintain that it is the only or predominant interest, even solely in the narrow area of home finance. New employees who do not sign up for a retirement program may have fallen prey to the irrational pull of laziness or procrastination, but they also may have other uses for the extra money, such as making a down payment on a new home, saving for the arrival of a new child, or maybe just enjoying a spending spree in Paris. It is not relevant how others would judge their interests; the issue is that people have their own interests that policymakers override with their (often narrow and simplistic) idea of those interests.

This epistemic problem is also the basis of an ethical problem with nudges: they deny individuals the right to make choices in their own interests. Traditional conceptions of autonomy and liberal neutrality maintain that people should have the right to live their lives as they choose, free from judgment from their government, provided they do not infringe on the similar rights of others. But as we saw above, policymakers use nudges to steer people's decisions in interests that are not necessarily their own, but rather the policymakers' idea of those interests. Furthermore, because nudges often rely on the same cognitive biases and dysfunctions that motivated their use, the decision indicated by a nudge is no easier to avoid than the one the nudge is designed to change. Therefore, however beneficent the intention behind a nudge, it limits the ability of individuals to make choices in their own interests; instead, they are to led to select an option (such as enrollment in a retirement plan) that was chosen for them based on interests that are not their own.

This criticism does not deny that people sometimes make bad decisions that do not serve their interests well. By their own judgments, many people eat too much and exercise too little; they spend too much and save too little. But this does not mean that any person who eats a muffin instead of a carrot, or spends money on a big-screen TV instead of putting it in the bank, is making a bad decision according to his interests. Since there is no way for outside observers to know people's true interests, no one knows whether a decision was a bad one except the decision-makers themselves. Policymakers must resist the temptation to judge the wisdom of other people's decisions based on their own preferences and interests and instead give people the benefit of the doubt that their choices generally advance their interests. Rather than presume to know people's real interests and help them make decisions toward them, policymakers should find less invasive ways to help people make better decisions in their own true interests.

The epistemic problem also leads to practical problems in terms of nudges doing what supporters claim: helping people make better decisions in their own interests. Because policymakers do not know people's true interests, they cannot help to advance them; instead, they steer people's decisions toward interests that were imposed on them. For example, the interests of a new employee who needs money for a down payment on a house—but who forgets to opt out of automatic enrollment in a retirement program—are frustrated by being nudged into the program, even though the nudge "worked" from the policymakers' point of view. As Sunstein and Thaler (2001, 1172) point out, most employees who receive matching contributions from their employers sign up for the savings program eventually, but automatic enrollment results in more signing up sooner. They interpret this as a success of the program, but the success can only be attributed to the ability of the nudge itself to change behavior, not to the advancement of employees' true interests.

Note that I did not criticize nudges along the lines of their manipulative effect aside from the fact that they steer people's choices away from their true interests. This manipulative effect is a significant but secondary concern here; the more immediate concern is in which interests people are being manipulated. Businesses, especially marketers and advertisers, also manipulate, but this is done in their own interests; they do not presume to know their customers' true interests and manipulate their choices for their own good. Furthermore, most people expect businesses to use manipulative tactics to get their business, but they do not expect the same from their government. To me, concerns about manipulation derive from epistemic and ethical issues regarding interests, and for that reason I have little reason to mention them further in this chapter.[6]

Specific Issues with Health-Promoting Nudges

From the point of view of proponents of nudges, one of their most promising applications is in the area of health, including policies that promote better diet and exercise and improve adherence to medical protocols such as physician appointments and prescription drug regimens. There are (at least) two significant arguments that suggest that nudges are less problematic in the case of health than in other areas of individual choice. First, health is an interest of high importance to everyone, so nudges designed to promote health do not impose an external interest on anybody. Second, decisions regarding health are more complex and emotional than most and so may justify the use of nudges to help overcome cognitive biases and dysfunctions. They often involve advanced medical science, which develops and changes rapidly, requiring outside expertise to intervene in the process of decision-making. They are intensely personal and emotional, further complicating the processing of the complex medical information involved; for example, this can affect the comparison and weighing of probabilities of surgical outcomes, which people are notoriously bad at doing properly under ideal conditions but even worse when in an emotionally "hot" state. They also often involve the performance of tasks over time (such as exercise or drug regimens), which requires self-control, a faculty that is lacking in many (if not most) people.[7]

In what follows, I argue that neither of these reasons justifies the use of nudges in healthcare and may actually make the arguments against nudges even stronger in the case of health.[8]

Interests

For the most part, scholars working in health policy take for granted that health is an important if not *the most* important interest relevant to individuals' decision-making processes, so much so that this is rarely stated or defended explicitly. Of course, health is an important interest of almost all people, if only instrumentally, enhancing a person's capacity to pursue interests of more intrinsic value. Nonetheless, it is not necessarily the most important interest of all, nor is it a simplistic, monolithic interest that can be stated and measured easily. Both of these realizations raise questions about the use of nudges to improve people's decisions solely in their health interests.

It is the rare person who makes every choice in her life by first weighing the effect on health, even in terms of choices with a direct impact on health outcomes. Even the professed "health nut" does not try to optimize every single decision according to his idea of health. Most of us who do take our health seriously make tradeoffs with other values important to us. Compared to ideally healthy behavior, we sometimes drink more than we should, eat more than we should, and lie around more than we should, for various reasons, including celebration, sociality, or simple relaxation. We value our health but also our happiness, relationships, work, and other elements of what we might see as the good life, elements that each of us balances in a unique and constantly changing way to make up our general interests.

But policymakers who design nudges in the interest of health do not, and indeed cannot, balance this one interest against the countless others of which they can have no definite knowledge. They are acting primarily to increase health, in the same way that nudges to encourage savings are intended primarily to increase savings. Policymakers who focus on one area of behavior are naturally going to recommend choice interventions to steer decisions in that area, normally with little thought to other areas of choice, action, and interests (although the intervention of other policymakers and agencies may broaden and temper this focus by the time a nudge is implemented).[9] Even when they do try to account for other aspects and goals of decision-making, policymakers cannot steer decisions in people's true interests due to their complex, multifaceted, and subjective nature. Therefore, nudges designed to improve health may interfere with interests representing other aspects of the good life, such as finances, career, and family, overriding the way people balance the many interests in their lives (Holm and Ploug 2013).

Even if health could be assumed to be people's predominant interest, however, each person's conception of health might vary. As with "happiness," "health" itself is an essentially vague term and represents something different for each person. While many people are concerned with their health and place a high value on improving it, some focus on their weight, others on cardiovascular fitness, yet others on strength or endurance—or any combination of the various elements of personal health. Furthermore, others may have specific or urgent health concerns, such as pregnancy, recovery from surgery, or treatment for cancer, that distract them from these more general concerns or shift the priorities given to them. Health nudges, by their nature, are specific, influencing decisions that focus on specific areas of health such as sugar intake and exercise frequency. As a result, a nudge designed to change decision-making in one particular area of health will not necessarily promote the interests of even very health-conscious persons who nonetheless have different personal health maintenance priorities.

In sum, health is undoubtedly a significant concern for almost all people, but policymakers do not have information regarding how individuals balance their interests in health with other important interests to form their overall idea of the good life, or how each person conceptualizes "health" itself and balances the various components of it. Any nudge designed to promote a particular aspect of health will most likely fail to correspond to how any given person incorporates health into her overall interests as well as that person's particular health goals. Furthermore, decisions regarding health are more personal and intimate compared with ordinary consumer choices, reflecting how a person chooses to maintain her body and mind. The personal nature of health interests represents an additional argument against nudges in this area: the integrity and autonomy of personal health decisions should be preserved and protected against any chance of subversion and manipulation, especially given that policymakers have no way to know how any person values or conceptualizes health.[10]

Decision-Making

Advocates for the use of nudges in healthcare rightly emphasize the difficulty consumers and patients have making decisions in the face of complicated, ever-changing science, comparing numerous options with imprecise probabilities and uncertain consequences, and exerting self-control to maintain a healthy lifestyle, all while in an emotionally fraught state. Obviously, people with no medical background cannot make most decisions regarding their health without help from medical experts. Doctors, nutritionists, pharmacists, and other medical professionals have specialized expertise in their specific areas of health maintenance and provide invaluable assistance to patients and their loved ones. This applies both in and out of the hospital, in terms of preventive care, treatment, and recovery, as well as basic and essential lifestyle choices regarding diet, exercise, and sleep. Medical professionals also provide invaluable assistance to people in understanding the implications of options, assessing the risk correctly, and trying to manage the emotions involved in making what are often life-and-death decisions.

However, medical professionals and policymakers cannot make these decisions for people and normally would not presume to do so, based on a traditional adherence to the principle of patient autonomy.[11] Medical experts and professionals can and should help people be aware of their options; weigh the advantages, disadvantages, and risks of each one; and consider how these choices affect the rest of their lives. However, even the most knowledgeable professionals and policymakers cannot know the true nature of people's interests and how each person chooses to balance health concerns with the other important things in his life. Decisions regarding health issues are complicated not only because of the advanced science involved and the emotional nature of the decision-making contexts, as behavioral economists are correct to emphasize, but also because so many others factors and concerns must be balanced, resulting in a nuanced complexity that can be lost when the wide range of personal interests is narrowed down to the several on which medical professionals have knowledge and expertise. Any medical decisions must be made in the broader context of family, career, and resources, and medical professionals can offer expert advice and input on only some aspects of this choice.[12]

In medical ethics, particularly with regard to the relationship between physician and patient, autonomy and beneficence are foundational principles that are often set at odds (Beauchamp and Childress 2012).[13] Medical professionals are instructed to respect their patients' wishes while at the same time providing care in the best way they can, which often results in a dilemma when doctors disagree with their patients' declared preferences.[14] One implication of the preceding discussion of interests is that the capacity for informed beneficence is necessarily limited because medical professionals do not have sufficient insight into their patients' interests and how they choose to balance them.[15] Even if autonomy and beneficence are equally important principles in theory, the difficulty of informed beneficence tilts the scale in favor of autonomy: medical professionals should provide information and guidance while allowing patients to make a decision in as neutral a choice environment as possible, according to the ideal of shared decision-making (Miller and Gelinas 2013; White 2013, 96–101). As Charles Douglas and Emily Proudfoot write, acknowledging the difficulty of the physician knowing the best things to do in any given circumstance, "it would be ridiculous to be too self-consciously committed to nudging the patient one way or another" (2013, 17). Furthermore, it is difficult for anyone, even an experienced physician, to know when patients are making decisions against their best interests, given the subjective and complex nature of personal interests. As Emily Bell and her coauthors emphasize, "the suggestion that health care providers can easily deduce when individual patient preferences have been subverted by irrational cognitive reasoning is debatable" (2013, 18). Given such limitations, respect for individual choice should be privileged over even the expert medical opinion of the physician (or, in a more distant setting, the policymaker).

Paralleling what we said above in the context of interests, while the emotionalism of health decisions complicates and seems to endanger rational choice, it also reflects how intensely personal these decisions are. While medical professionals play an indisputably essential role in helping people make these decisions, an even stronger presumption of autonomy is warranted given the personal nature of health. It is in the nature of nudges to subvert people's rational deliberative processes—and leverage the very cognitive biases and dysfunction that inspired their use—to steer decision-making in a certain direction. Given the personal importance of health, extra care must be taken to ensure that people are as engaged as possible in their health choices and that advice be provided as transparently as possible. While perfect deliberative rationality is impossible, significant efforts should be made to enhance this aspect of decision-making in health consumers and patients, rather than consciously compromising it to generate behavior that the expert or the policymaker thinks is best (Cohen 2013, 6–9; Blumenthal-Barby 2013).

Summary

In this chapter I argued that nudges are not justified in healthcare contexts, despite the complexity of such decisions, primarily because external values are substituted for persons' own true interests. Medical professionals and policymakers should focus on giving patients and consumers expert guidance in the most neutral terms possible. If consumers or patients make decisions that go against best medical advice, medical experts and policymakers should give them the benefit of the doubt that these decisions are in their best personal interests.

While it perhaps comes as no surprise that the subjective and complex nature of interests places nudges in conflict with deontological concerns about autonomy and respect, it also implies that meaningful consequentialist evaluation of nudges is impossible.[16] Scholars and policymakers often recommend cost-benefit analysis of specific behavioral initiatives, but this process begs the question, given that benefits will often be measured according to the behavior or outcomes the nudges were designed to produce, not whether people's actual interests were furthered (or to what extent others were frustrated).[17] Cost-benefit analysis can provide evidence regarding the effectiveness of a nudge in producing the outcomes it was meant to produce, which can be particularly valuable when comparing a nudge to other policy or regulatory methods. But it cannot assess how well nudges do what they ostensibly claim: to help people make choices to better further their true interests.[18]

Conclusion

Health decisions are tremendously important to people's interests, as well as incredibly complicated and emotional, and most of the time should not be made alone. But these factors do not justify the use of nudges that impose simplistic, external conceptions of people's interests on them and then steer decisions in those interests. If anything, the personal nature and importance of health implies that respect for individuals' autonomy is more essential in this area than with respect to ordinary consumer decisions. Medical professionals and policymakers must be particularly wary of making judgments based on their own idea of people's interests and how they should be balanced, as well as of taking steps to steer people's behavior in that direction. As long as the traditional emphasis on autonomy in medical ethics is retained, nudges in the field of health should be avoided. In healthcare even more so than in other areas, choice architectures should be designed as transparently and neutrally as possible to ensure that people make the best choices they can, in their own true interests, and with the invaluable assistance and advice of medical professionals.

Notes

1. See, for instance, Kahneman, Tversky, and Slovic (1982). For a recent overview of behavioral economics, see Angner (2012).
2. This is the emphasis primarily of *behavioral law and economics*; for seminal work, see Jolls, Sunstein, and Thaler (1998), Korobkin and Ulen (2000), and Sunstein (2000).
3. For a recent elaboration and defense, see Sunstein (2014).
4. See Rebonato (2012) and White (2013) and references therein.
5. These critiques are based on White (2013).
6. See Klick and Mitchell (2006) and White (2013, 119–25) on the longer-term effects of manipulation on choice capabilities, another problem deriving from the manipulative aspect of nudges. Sanghai (2013) considers the degree of manipulation of various nudges in the context of healthcare, but explicitly does not deal with their paternalistic aspects.

7. For a survey of these problems with medical decision-making among patients, see Schneider and Hall (2009).

8. Another general argument for nudges in healthcare is that health is not simply a matter of individual well-being but is also a social and political concern, which justifies some degree of government regulation (including nudges when effective); see, for instance, Daniels (1985; 2008) and Coggon (2012). On behavioral interventions designed to promote general welfare rather than individual well-being, see Korobkin (2009). Because this argument negates the paternalism concern with nudges, however, it is beyond the purview of this chapter.

9. The focus on a singular interest might be attributed to traditional economic models of decision-making that assume a unitary goal of utility or preference satisfaction. Ideally, this goal can encompass many disparate aspects of life, but normally it is understood to represent wealth alone, a problem that behavioral economics inherited. For more, see White (2013, chaps. 1–2).

10. Sanghai (2013, 7) suggests that not all health decisions are central enough to the pursuit of a good life as to warrant such unquestionable respect; see also Powers, Faden, and Sanghai (2012). It is difficult, however, to make this determination absent more knowledge about a person's interests or an outside judgment regarding which decisions promote which interests in a significant way. For more on the critical importance of interests to discussions of libertarian paternalism, see White (2016).

11. This adherence is being increasingly questioned, however, in light of the behavioral research into cognitive limitations of patients; see, for instance, Levy, who celebrates the decline of old-fashioned medical paternalism but argues that "the pendulum has swung too far" in the direction of unfettered patient autonomy (2014, 293).

12. Misreading patients' preferences is a danger in medical practice more generally, of course; see Mulley, Trimble, and Elwyn (2012). On the issue of paternalism and trust in the doctor-patient relationship, see Sagoff (2013) and, more generally, O'Neill (2002).

13. Beneficence is a less appropriate concern with respect to policy actions because the government is not close enough to its citizens to take a position of care toward them; on this, see White (2014).

14. Cohen (2013) sees nudging as a way to solve this dilemma by steering patients away from "unhealthy preferences" before they are formed. In part, this reflects behavioral economists' emphasis on "unformed preferences" to the exclusion of the firmer but more general interests that support them (White 2013, 111–13). In effect, because preferences are revealed in choice, guiding preferences is no different from steering the patient's choices in the physician's idea of the patient's interests. On this point, see Miller and Gelinas (2013) and Blumenthal-Barby (2013).

15. There is much evidence that we do not know our own selves and interests as well as we think we do; see, for instance, Wilson (2004). The fact remains that, with the likely exception of close friends and family, we know our own interests better than anyone else—certainly better than strangers or casual acquaintances—and are therefore best situated to promote those interests with the assistance and advisement of those with expertise (such as medical professionals in the case of healthcare).

16. White (2014) makes this point with reference to all policymaking that relies on measures of welfare, particularly those based on happiness or subjective well-being.

17. Blumenthal-Barby and Burroughs (2012, 3) endorse consequentialist analysis of nudges but using a much broader measure of effects that include unanticipated consequences, such as

the psychological impact of learning one has HIV when considering automatic testing. Nonetheless, their frequent call for evidence-based testing does not—and cannot—include the impact on subjective interests.

18. This problem could be easily solved if supporters of nudges abandoned the pretense of acting in people's best interests as they judge them and embraced an objective theory of value based on health, wealth, or whatever value the nudge is promoting (White 2016). This would not avoid the problem of plural values, but would make assessment and justification of nudges much more straightforward.

References

Angner, Erik. 2012. *A Course in Behavioral Economics*. Palgrave Macmillan. New York.

Beauchamp, Tom L., and James F. Childress. 2012. *Principles of Biomedical Ethics*. 7th ed. Oxford University Press. Oxford.

Bell, Emily, Veljko Dubljevic, and Eric Racine. 2013. "Nudging without Ethical Fudging: Clarifying Physician Obligations to Avoid Ethical Compromise." *The American Journal of Bioethics* 13:18–19.

Blumenthal-Barby, J. S. 2013. "On Nudging and Informed Consent—Four Key Undefended Premises." *The American Journal of Bioethics* 13:31–33.

Blumenthal-Barby, J. S., and Hadley Burroughs. 2012. "Seeking Better Health Care Outcomes: The Ethics of Using the 'Nudge.'" *The American Journal of Bioethics* 12:1–10.

Coggon, John. 2012. *What Makes Health Public? A Critical Evaluation of Moral, Legal, and Political Claims in Public Health*. Cambridge University Press. Cambridge.

Cohen, Shlomo. 2013. "Nudging and Informed Consent." *The American Journal of Bioethics* 13:3–11.

Daniels, Norman. 2008. *Just Health*. Cambridge University Press. Cambridge.

———. 1985. *Just Health Care*. Cambridge University Press. Cambridge.

Douglas, Charles, and Emily Proudfoot. 2013. "Nudging and the Complicated Real Life of 'Informed Consent.'" *The American Journal of Bioethics* 13:16–17.

Holm, Søren, and Thomas Ploug. 2013. "'Nudging' and Informed Consent Revisited: Why 'Nudging' Fails in the Clinical Context." *The American Journal of Bioethics* 13:29–31.

Jolls, Christine, Cass R. Sunstein, and Richard Thaler. 1998. "A Behavioral Approach to Law and Economics." *Stanford Law Review* 50:1471–1550.

Kahneman, Daniel, Paul Slovic, and Amos Tversky, eds. 1982. *Judgment under Uncertainty: Heuristics and Biases*. Cambridge University Press. Cambridge.

Klick, Jonathan, and Gregory Mitchell. 2006. "Government Regulation of Irrationality: Moral and Cognitive Hazards." *Minnesota Law Review* 90:1620–63.

Korobkin, Russell B. 2009. "Libertarian Welfarism." *California Law Review* 97:1651–85.

Korobkin, Russell B., and Thomas S. Ulen. 2000. "Law and Behavioral Science: Removing the Rationality Assumption from Law and Economics." *California Law Review* 88:1051–1144.

Levy, Neil. 2014. "Forced to Be Free? Increasing Patient Autonomy by Constraining It." *Journal of Medical Ethics* 40:293–300.

Miller, Franklin G., and Luke Gelinas. 2013. "Nudging, Autonomy, and Valid Consent: Context Matters." *The American Journal of Bioethics* 13:12–13.

Mulley, Albert G., Chris Trimble, and Glyn Elwyn. 2012. "Stop the Silent Misdiagnosis: Patients' Preferences Matter." *British Medical Journal* 345:1–6.

O'Neill, Onora. 2002. *Autonomy and Trust in Bioethics.* Cambridge University Press. Cambridge.

Powers, Madison, Ruth Faden, and Yashar Sanghai. 2012. "Liberty, Mill and the Framework of Public Health Ethics." *Public Health Ethics* 5:6–15.

Rebonato, Riccardo. 2012. *Taking Liberties: A Critical Examination of Libertarian Paternalism.* Palgrave Macmillan. New York.

Sagoff, Mark. 2013. "Trust versus Paternalism." *The American Journal of Bioethics* 13:20–21.

Sanghai, Yashar. 2013. "Salvaging the Concept of Nudge." *Journal of Medical Ethics* 39:487–93.

Schneider, Carl E., and Mark A. Hall. 2009. "The Patient Life: Can Consumers Direct Health Care?" *American Journal of Law and Medicine* 35:7–65.

Simon, Herbert A. 1955. "A Behavioral Model of Rational Choice." *Quarterly Journal of Economics* 69:99–118.

Sunstein, Cass R. 2014. *Why Nudge? The Politics of Libertarian Paternalism.* Yale University Press. New Haven, CT.

———, ed. 2000. *Behavioral Law and Economics.* Cambridge University Press. Cambridge.

Sunstein, Cass R., and Richard H. Thaler. 2001. "Libertarian Paternalism Is Not an Oxymoron." *The University of Chicago Law Review* 70:1159–1202.

Thaler, Richard H., and Cass R. Sunstein. 2008. *Nudge: Improving Decisions about Health, Wealth, and Happiness.* Yale University Press. New Haven, CT.

White, Mark D. 2014. *The Illusion of Well-Being: Economic Policymaking Based on Respect and Responsiveness.* Palgrave Macmillan. New York.

———. 2013. *The Manipulation of Choice: Ethics and Libertarian Paternalism.* Palgrave Macmillan. New York.

———. 2016. "The Crucial Importance of Interests in Libertarian Paternalism." In press. In *Nudging: Possibilities, Limitations and Applications in European Law and Economics*, edited by Klaus Mathis and Avishalom Tor. Springer. New York.

Wilson, Timothy D. 2004. *Strangers to Ourselves: Discovering the Adaptive Unconscious.* Belknap. Cambridge, MA.

CHAPTER 6

Nudging and Benign Manipulation for Health

Nir Eyal

Dan Hausman and Brynn Welch, Mark White, Riccardo Rebonato, T. M. Wilkinson, and other critics of Cass Sunstein and Richard Thaler's *Nudge* oppose the use of some nudges, which I call "genuine nudges." These nudges differ from coercive threats, but they affect our choice through another route that ethicists tend to frown on: manipulation. As elaborated below, these critics claim:

    I. Genuine nudges are manipulative.
    II. As such there are (nearly) always weighty reasons against their use, even for good causes like health and welfare.

The first section of this chapter argues that claim I is true and the second section, that claim II is false.

My basic thought can be demonstrated using the most famous nudge discussed by Sunstein and Thaler:

> *Cafeteria*: Nutritious food items are placed at the beginning of a cafeteria's long, single serving counter so that diners make healthier food choices (Sunstein and Thaler 2008, 1–3).

Intuitively, there simply is nothing too worrying about locating salad at the cafeteria entrance or at eye level, while keeping pizza a few steps away, when that helps customers live longer, healthier lives. Many other genuine nudges intuitively seem quite benign, in the following sense: when they work and promote health and welfare then,

---

For helpful comments, I thank Anne Barnhill, I. Glenn Cohen, Moti Gorin, Judith Lichtenberg, Noah Marks, Leah Price, Regina Rini, the editors, and audiences at NYU, Harvard's T. H. Chan School of Public Health, and ACPM 2016.

intuitively, not only is it permissible to use them; there is (virtually) nothing wrong about using them. In philosophical parlance, there is no (weighty) *pro tanto* reason against their use. To be legitimate, they need not be crucial for saving a life or the like, just helpful on balance. At the same time, there remains something manipulative about them.

Additional examples of "genuine nudges" include:

- *Save More Tomorrow*: Schemes that offer employees to commit now to saving later more for retirement (Sunstein and Thaler 2008, 114–19).
- *Dollar a Day*: Schemes that offer teen moms a dollar for each day they are not pregnant again. These schemes are successful simply because "the small recurring payment is salient enough to encourage teenage mothers to take steps to avoid getting pregnant again" (Sunstein and Thaler 2008, 236).
- *Don't Mess with Texas*: An ad campaign that helped sway Texans to throw less litter on the highway by associating the identity of being a proud Texan with not littering (Sunstein and Thaler 2008, 60).
- *Framing*: Describing a product as 10% fat, and not as 90% fat-free (Sunstein, forthcoming, §V.E.1).

By contrast with genuine nudges, some things that Sunstein and Thaler call "nudges" seem incompatible with their definition of nudges: first, "the intervention must be easy and cheap to avoid. Nudges are not mandates"; and second, "any factor that significantly alters the behavior of Humans, even though it would be ignored by Econs." "Humans" means real people with bounded rationality, and "Econs" means fully rational choosers (Sunstein and Thaler 2008, 6–7, 8; Sunstein 2014b, 8).

Both definitional features seem to fail for some alleged "nudges". For instance, self-bans on gambling, in which gambling addicts ask casinos to deny them future admission, and other "Ulysses contracts" (for example, Sunstein and Thaler 2008, 231, 233–34, 247, 264), influence people by using (self-imposed) mandates. Moreover, Econs would not ignore such mandates: they come with real sanctions. Red warning lights that blink as air conditioners begin to clog (Sunstein and Thaler 2008, 236–37), and full disclosure of calorie counts and of the annual fuel costs of cars for sale (Sunstein and Thaler 2008, 260, 262–63; Sunstein 2014b, 8) would not be ignored by Econs either: Econs also need information.

Genuine Nudges Are Manipulative

Several critics have claimed that genuine nudges are manipulative (Hausman and Welch 2010; Rebonato 2012; White 2013; Wilkinson 2013). Sunstein and Thaler usually respond by distinguishing nudges from manipulation (Sunstein and Thaler 2008, 236; Sunstein 2014a, chap. 5, §II; WIP; forthcoming, §V.E).[1] This section shows that Sunstein and Thaler are wrong.

Many definitions of manipulation would confirm that genuine nudges are manipulative. For Ruth Faden and Tom Beauchamp, manipulation is "a catch all category for any intentional and successful influence of a person by non-coercively altering the actual choices available to the person or by non-persuasively altering the person's perception of those choices" (Faden and Beauchamp 1986, 261; see also Raz 1986, 378; Cave 2007, 131; Mandava and Millum 2013, 41). Since nudges purportedly influence us neither coercively nor persuasively, on this definition they would be manipulative. Moti Gorin defines manipulation as a "process of interpersonal influence that deliberately fails to track reasons" (Gorin 2014, 97). Genuine nudges work not by providing us with what are taken to be good reasons, but by other means. For Thomas Hill, manipulation means "intentionally causing or encouraging people to make the decisions one wants them to make by actively promoting their making the decisions in ways that rational persons would not want to make their decisions" (Hill 1984, 251). Rational persons usually do not want to use genuine nudges to overcome weak will because (usually they know that) their will is not weak. Admittedly, Hill might mean that rational persons would want not to make decisions subject to manipulation. But Hill gives no ground for assuming that rational persons would always want not to make decisions subject to manipulation. For example, nothing in their definition as rational entails that.

"Manipulation" has many uses in English, perhaps connected by family resemblance alone (Coons and Weber 2014, 4). But the above definitions are most functional to our inquiry. For example, some authors use "manipulation" to include coercion, but a narrower definition helps us focus on the category that is of interest to us in this chapter—the notion of nudge, which excludes coercion. Likewise, some notions of manipulation are moralized. They would call nudges manipulative only if it is wrong to nudge. But when our aim is to ascertain whether something manipulative (for example genuine nudging) is moral, we do better using a non-moralized definition. On the moralized notion, you cannot call anything manipulative before you decide that it is immoral (Hausman and Welch 2010, 128–29; Buss 2005, 209n19; Wood 2014, 20; Coons and Weber 2014, 28ff.).

Sunstein denies that nudges are manipulative on several grounds. First, he defines "manipulative" as attempting "to influence people subconsciously or unconsciously, in a way that undermines their capacity for conscious choice" (Sunstein forthcoming, §109); since Sunstein endorses only public and transparent nudges (Sunstein and Thaler 2008), this definition would prevent the nudges he endorses from being manipulative. However, it is usually agreed that manipulation need not be subconscious or unconscious (for example, Coons and Weber 2014, 10).

Sunstein also denies that nudges are manipulative because "information disclosure, reminders, and warnings [are not] plausibly treated as manipulative" (Sunstein, WIP; forthcoming, §46, 119). That may be true. But it cannot show that other nudges are non-manipulative, and Sunstein concedes that other nudges, which he calls non-educative, usually "target System 1," our more impulsive and less deliberative psychological system (Sunstein, forthcoming, §159). In fact, since, as noted earlier, educative "nudges" are not genuine nudges, it may turn out that all genuine nudges are manipulative.

But Sunstein usually[2] denies that genuine nudges (that he or others have espoused) count as manipulation (Sunstein, forthcoming, §159). Sometimes his basis for that denial seems to be that we "cannot avoid influences on System 1" because any "cafeteria or grocery system has to have a design; any list of items has to have an order; [and] any food wrapper has to have a color" (Sunstein 2014a, 150–51; forthcoming, II.B). Since "there is no such thing as a 'neutral' design" (Sunstein and Thaler 2008, 3, 10–11), why not make that first item on the counter at least a nutritious one?

In other words, in order to deny that nudging for health and welfare is manipulative, Sunstein denies that it is avoidable and (by implication) morally wrong. To me, that suggests that Sunstein's background notion of manipulation may be moralized: that, for him, to show that an intervention is not wrong or blamable would also show that it cannot be manipulative. For the reasons stated above, I prefer a thin definition of manipulation. More fundamentally, it is not true that we have only the two options:

1. Definitely (that is, not depending on lottery results) placing salad at the beginning of the counter and pizza at the end
2. Definitely placing pizza at the beginning of the counter and salad at the end

There are additional, more neutral options, such as:

3. Letting the matter hang on a lottery.

Of course, to let the matter hang on a lottery would be a grave mistake. But that is beside the present point, which is simply that alternatives to option 1 and option 2 exist, and that some (like the gravely mistaken option 3) are more neutral than either.[3] Since Sunstein's assumption that there are no neutral alternatives to nudging for health and welfare is false, then his denial that genuine nudging is manipulative is false.

When *Nudge*-like cafeteria tricks are used by commercial grocers for profit (Shanker 2014; Kawachi 2014, 489), we readily call them manipulative. Shouldn't we call the same tricks "manipulative" when we approve of their aim?[4] Sunstein concedes that using nudges commercially or to promote evil causes is manipulative (Sunstein, WIP). But he insists that when the goal is to promote a person's own good, then the same trick can be non-manipulative. His argument seems to rest on his latest definition of manipulation: "an effort to influence people's choices counts as manipulative to the extent that it does not *sufficiently* engage or appeal to their capacity for reflection and deliberation" (Sunstein, WIP, emphasis added). He holds that when the levels of effort to influence and of failure to engage deliberative capacities are exactly the same, an intentionally beneficial effort remains non-manipulative; presumably, the reason is that when an effort is intentionally beneficial, partially deliberative engagement is sufficient.

But it is arbitrary to assume that partially deliberative engagement is sufficient for avoiding manipulation, just because the intentions behind it are beneficial. For instance, one might have answered that that is because the notion of manipulation includes a moral judgment: all things considered, it obviously takes less to justify a beneficial influence than a harmful one. This is why failure to engage deliberation can remain justified and non-manipulative when beneficial, and unjustified and manipulative otherwise. But above we decided not to use moralized definitions of manipulation.[5]

Genuine Nudges Usually Remain Ethically Benign
The Position That There Are Usually Weighty Reasons against Manipulative Nudges

Authors who claim that genuine nudges are manipulative typically argue that therefore there are (nearly) always weighty reasons against their use, even for good causes like health and welfare. For example, Mark White writes, "because [nudges] are designed with the express purpose of *manipulating* people's decision-making processes to change their behaviour in pursuit of interests that are not their own, I argue that nudges are coercive [and wrong]" (White 2013, 91, emphasis added; see also White, chapter 5 in this volume). Other economic conservatives, skeptical that a free market is reconcilable with libertarian paternalism, similarly protest nudges' manipulative nature (Mitchell 2005; Rebonato 2008, 139, 195, 196, 215). Hausman and Welch add: manipulating "people's choices for their own benefit seems to us to be alarmingly intrusive . . . such nudges on the part of the government may be inconsistent with the respect toward citizens that a representative government ought to show" (Hausman and Welch 2010, 130, 134). This terminology of respect suggests strong reasons against genuine nudging. And, because their account of what is wrong with manipulation is that, *just* like paternalistic coercion, paternalistic manipulation "attempt[s] to substitute the policymakers' judgment of what is good for the agent for that of the agent" (Hausman and Welch 2010, 129), these reasons could not be much weaker than the ones against paternalistic coercion. In fact, they argue that "there may be something more insidious about [manipulating] choices than about open constraint" (Hausman and Welch 2010, 130f.; and see likewise Coons and Weber 2014, 16; Wood 2014, 42). They conclude that there are strong *pro tanto* reasons against any manipulative use of nudges that is avoidable and does not simply facilitate rational choice (Hausman and Welch 2010, 134).[6]

T. M. Wilkinson likewise describes a subset of nudges akin to what I call "genuine nudges" as "manipulative, and thus objectionable" (Wilkinson 2013, 342). Many more writers who do not write on nudges accept weighty reasons against using manipulation in nearly all circumstances (Korsgaard 1986 [for example, 336n13, on deceitful manipulation]; Christman 1988; Cave 2007; Mandava and Millum 2013; Wood 2014). We can speculate that if they accepted that genuine nudges are manipulative (claim I), they would deny that genuine nudges remain benign (claim II). Take Allen Wood. For him, manipulative advertising is not just harmful but it also "corrupts the root of rational communication [and] precludes the possibility of any free human community." Importantly, Wood targets not only commercial advertising but also ads that influence people to quit smoking. All advertising manipulates people into acting on impulses "arising from what is most contemptible in their nature" (Wood 2014, 38). Wood's strong words suggest weighty reasons against manipulation, nudging manipulation potentially included.

Concrete Nudges

In my view, some genuine nudges are benign even though they are manipulative. Consider two concrete nudges.

First, the *Cafeteria* nudge. Let us compare again options 1 and 3 above:

1. Definitely placing salad at the beginning of a cafeteria counter and pizza at the end
3. Letting the matter hang on a lottery

Intuitively, option 1 seems preferable. Placing nutritious food at the cafeteria entrance is a nudge that is now widely implemented with beneficial results and has not generated widespread complaints. But not only is it right to use it on balance. There are simply no serious *pro tanto* reasons against it. (Compare the position that nudging for health is permissible only because the enormous value of health overrides what are strong reasons against manipulation [Scoccia 2014; Mandava and Millum 2013].) There is no weighty reason against it. To illustrate the absence of serious *pro tanto* reasons against option 1, note that other things being equal, option is also intuitively preferable to:

4. Not selling pizza most days
5. Force-feeding salad

By contrast with options 4 and 5, intuitively there is little if anything weighing against option 1. And so I am drawn to saying that genuine nudges, despite being manipulative, often remain ethically benign.

Someone might respond that option 1 may be more benign than options 4 and 5, and yet that it is far from benign. But consider now *Save More Tomorrow*, whereby people commit to start saving large amounts later. That is another nudge that intuitively feels wholly benign. *Save More Tomorrow* is just fine, whether understood as non-manipulative or as somewhat manipulative. On a non-manipulation account, what *Save More Tomorrow* does is to preempt any bias that hyperbolic discounting might have introduced. Hyperbolic discounting would have made us too averse to saving now, and what the program does is only to prevent that bias against spending money now from influencing our savings. On a manipulation account, *Save More Tomorrow* introduces a bias, of indifference to setting money aside in the (nearer) future, and that bias counters the one coming from hyperbolic discounting—with the net effect that we can make decisions free from any net bias.

My point is that it does not matter which of these two accounts holds. Either way, the intuition is that the second account has the program create bias and, in that way, manipulate us.

It may be objected that countering one bias with another does not count as manipulation. But sometimes what counters bias is manipulation. Sunstein himself may agree that countering bias and even outright manipulation permits (wrongfully) remaining manipulative.[7]

A Different Picture: Benign Manipulation for Health

Not all manipulative acts are morally problematic as such. Many wrongful manipulative acts are wrong not simply for being manipulative. They are only wrongful because of aspects wholly separate from manipulation, or because confluence of manipulation with a special context gives rise to wrongs locally, without making manipulation generally wrong (compare Buss 2005, 226–27).

As an example of the former, consider lies and deceit. Officials have good reasons not to lie to the public, not even to promote public health. For example, lying risks loss of credibility, which could have dire consequences for public health and in general. Manipulation need not involve any of that. "Sometimes there is manipulation without any deception" (Coons and Weber 2014, 10). Clearly, *Cafeteria* can work without misleading diners into thinking that there is no pizza today and without any other deceit (but rather, for example, by eliciting a craving for fresh, crunchy vegetables).

An example of wrongful confluence of manipulation with local context is when manipulation subverts a defining feature of one's plans and intrudes into an exquisitely private sphere. A classical discussion is of a dentist who, in order to pull out his patient's teeth, as is medically indicated, has not informed her that, once she becomes sedated, he will do so (Donagan 1977). This violation of the person's rights to bodily integrity, a freestanding moral problem with such behavior, is absent from the *Cafeteria* and *Save More Tomorrow* nudges. This violation is not simply a matter of manipulation. It is about manipulation on *this* matter.

Dan Hausman and Brynn Welch write as though, since both transgress autonomy, there is no real advantage in manipulating instead of coercing. But there are big differences, at least between manipulative nudging and extreme instances of coercion like force-feeding. Physical coercion is also coded in our society as a mark of extreme disrespect in a way that is simply not present in nudges such as *Cafeteria*. Coercive threats tend to wind up harming people when (as is often the case) some people do not comply.

Let me propose an alternative picture. What if the autonomy of choice is not always very important, and commonly cited examples of horrific manipulation display problems that arise only locally, and not in every instance of manipulation. On this picture, there is no general moral ban on manipulation because there is no general moral problem with manipulation. In a wide range of circumstances, there is nothing, or almost nothing, wrong with manipulating for health. Genuine nudges remain benign except when something special obtains. When an act that is manipulative is seriously wrong, there is an independent local problem or local confluence of benign factors that is what made it problematic. On such occasions, the manipulative act takes the form of a lie that jeopardizes public trust, or makes a person betray a deep personal value, causes a person appear publicly like a ridiculous puppet, and so forth. But manipulation itself remains ethically benign. That is not to say that manipulative nudging is ethically optimal and precisely as good as rational persuasion, just to say that it is not substantially worse; the *pro tanto* reasons against manipulation as such, including manipulative nudging, are either nil or weak.

Nudge-Focused Answers to Arguments against Manipulation

I cannot take on a full-blown defense of manipulation, but let me put forth a pertinent, partial one. Applying prevalent arguments against manipulation to manipulative nudges like *Cafeteria* makes some of these arguments appear hyperbolic. Take a few examples:

Disrespect toward Autonomy

It is standard to say that manipulation is *pro tanto* seriously wrong because it violates or disrespects the manipulee's personal autonomy or liberty (Hausman and Welch 2010, 128; Berofsky 1983, 311; Raz 1986, 378, 420; Christman 1988, 19; Cave 2007; Bovens 2012; Mandava and Millum 2013, 41; Wilkinson 2013, 354; Wood 2014, 42; but see Gorin 2014, 84, 85).

Consider, however, of what exactly such a violation would consist. If manipulative acts always destroyed the manipulee's autonomy (as murder and brainwashing do), then obviously there would have been a weighty reason against manipulative acts; but most manipulation (genuine nudges included) does not do so (Buss 2005, 197, 216). At worst, manipulation thwarts a single instance of the mere enactment of that capacity (or that enactment's mere efficacy in the world), or it bypasses its enactment just once. But that crime is typically far less serious. Such single thwarting or bypassing is what the manipulation in *Cafeteria* does. States of nature regularly thwart such enactments and we think nothing of it (compare Buss 2005, 212). If another human took over permanently, that might have been creepy—but this is precisely what is not going on in one-time manipulation. So while such thwarting is a more realistic description of what manipulation does to the manipulee, it does not seem weighty enough on most occasions to substantiate weighty reasons against manipulating.[8]

Bovens worries that nudges, by deciding "for the manipulee," may lead to hindrance of her moral development (Bovens 2012). Sunstein shares these worries about choice delegation (Sunstein 2014c). But Sunstein also wisely counsels a sense of proportion: nudging also achieves great things, including autonomy enhancement (see below), and one tiny step toward destruction is very different from destruction.

An opponent might alternatively explain that even trifles like thwarting a single fulfillment of an exalted capacity matter—as symbols of disrespect toward that capacity. Symbolizing disrespect for autonomy, she could add, is seriously wrong. Indeed, several authors use "disrespect" to describe what is supposedly wrong with (nudging) manipulation (for example, Hausman and Welch 2010, 134; Coons and Weber 2014, 16; Baron 2014, 113–14).

But how can an act symbolize disrespect when otherwise it constitutes only a minor transgression, or none at all? How can it symbolize true disrespect for autonomy, especially when in some ways it promotes autonomy—and nudges do, by helping us fulfill our autonomous goals and otherwise?[9] Disrespectfulness could simply be conventional, but philosophical foes of manipulation seem to hold that the problem with manipulation is deeper. And none have conducted the cultural and anthropological studies to show that every instance of manipulation (genuine nudges included conventionally) symbolizes disrespect. It is also open to the opponent to insist that manipulation "disrespects" us or our autonomy in a nonsymbolic sense. But in that case she owes us an account of what such disrespect means, and why it matters.

Domination

The value underlying Allen Wood's objection to manipulation is "freedom as non-domination. This can be distinguished from freedom merely as non-interference . . . Freedom as non-domination is what . . . Philip Pettit and Quentin Skinner . . . have called 'republican' . . . freedom" (Wood 2014, 50; and see also Grüne-Yanoff 2012, 638). The latter notion is familiar. "A person or group enjoys [republican] freedom to the extent that no other person or group has 'the capacity to interfere in their affairs on an arbitrary basis'" (Lovett 2014; Pettit 1997).

However, Pettit is clear that republican freedom does not mean avoiding certain influences over you. Rather, it designates a situation in which no one can have those influences: "to enjoy such non-domination, after all, is just to be in a position where no one *can* interfere arbitrarily in your affairs" (Pettit 1997, 107, emphasis added). A domineering position admittedly makes arbitrary influence easier, but it is not itself a form of influence (Pettit 1997). Since manipulation is a form of influence, Wood (and perhaps Grüne-Yanoff) seems to conflate the fact that some agents are in a position to manipulate with the action of manipulating. The action cannot be accused of "domination." Wood may try to correct his position into one of opposition to handing government the power to nudge. But that would not help explain why nudging (as opposed to giving the power to nudge) would be wrong.

Promoting a Worse Self

For Eric Cave, manipulative acts wrong the victim because they "bring out his worse rather than his better self . . . the victim acts—not against his will—but against his 'better judgment'" (Cave 2007, 134, quoting Joel Feinberg). Other philosophers suggest additional ways in which manipulation influences us to fall short of ideals for belief, desire, or emotion, to fail to track reasons, and otherwise to behave suboptimally and even to be defeated by our own suboptimal self (Gorin 2014, 97; Barnhill 2014, 72; Coons and Weber 2014, 15, 16).[10]

But who needs to adhere to a rational ideal every day in the cafeteria line? Even if "[m]anipulation . . . deliberately falls short of the persuasive ideal" (Barnhill 2014, 60), is that a big deal? In a logic class, falling short of a persuasive ideal is complete failure. But the point of getting lunch is different. So considerations about the non-ideal self are unlikely to substantiate a weighty moral reason against all genuine nudging.

Trust Violation

For Patricia Greenspan, the problem with manipulation, say, with Tom Sawyer's luring his chums to whitewash the fence, is that by involving deception and an unfair exchange it violates social trust (Greenspan 2003; and see also Buss 2005; Scanlon 1998, 298).

As mentioned already, not all manipulation involves deception (see also Greenspan 2003, 158–59). And in the paternalistic nudge setting, there is usually no "exchange" that might have been unfair. Greenspan clarifies: "The complaint [of unfairness] need not be that the manipulator is deceiving anyone, but rather that it is unfair for him to impose his own agenda, even supposing that it is a wiser or more worthy agenda or in aid of the common good" (2003, 158–59). However, in the case of nudges, no one has an "agenda" of, for example, eating unhealthfully—a plan of life or a deep commitment that might be unfairly suppressed. Nudges seek to help us overcome mere weaknesses. The only nudges Sunstein supports help make people's lives go better "as judged by their own preferences, not those of some bureaucrat" (Sunstein and Thaler 2008, 10; Sunstein 2014a).[11]

Abuse

Several authors warn that manipulative techniques can help ill-doers and harm-doers (Bovens 2008, 218; Hausman and Welch 2010, 135; White 2013; Wood 2014). Even Sunstein admits that nudges can be dangerous when they fall into commercial hands.

However, that does not show that using manipulative nudges is wrong. There are many tools that it is right to use although they could be abused (compare Greenspan 2003, 156). It is permissible to use knives to spread tahini, although others might use knives to stab innocents. Concern about potential abuse is a reason for tight oversight of manipulative nudges not against their use. Even if nefarious corporations and governments might use manipulation for nefarious purposes, manipulative nudging for the public's health usually remains ethically benign.

Benign Manipulation for Health: A Few Examples

On some accounts of Cafeteria's mechanism of action, this nudge is both manipulative and benign. Let me give additional examples of benign manipulation for health.

Instigating slight embarrassment in the interests of health is often manipulative, and benign. For example, smaller plates make people eat less, and some cafeterias offer smaller plates with a view to keeping diners healthier. Why don't diners return for seconds? Perhaps because they feel too embarrassed, even when any social sanctions would have been small (Chang and Marsh 2013; Kawachi 2014, 499). Tying unhealthy choice to slight embarrassment could be a benign nudge (Eyal 2014, 2015).

Good doctors are thoughtful about the patient's feelings and likely reactions. Their "difficult conversations" on bad prognoses, for example, seek to manage the outcome beneficially. This is a skill taught in "patient-doctor" courses, where it is said that what matters is not just disclosing information but communicating it and eliciting certain responses. Truth be told, that can involve a degree of manipulation. Words like "terminal" or even "cancer" are sometimes avoided or deferred in order not to extinguish the patient's hope or clog her attention before relaying important medical instructions. Econs would not benefit from clinicians with that training. This manipulation seems, however, benign or commendable on many occasions.

Some public health ads use emotional manipulation to make smoking less "cool" and attractive, or a stigmatized population more human, to viewers. It is true that some ads are not manipulative. They draw us to internalize truths only by revealing other truths, for instance, to see that stigmatized populations are also full-blown human beings by emphasizing their unique human traits. But some ads achieve welcome changes of heart through manipulation, and they also remain easy to justify. They may, for example, show a patient with a stigmatized condition as an amicable, hard-working individual and an admirable parent. Surely some patients with that condition are not very amicable or great parents. So such ads achieve their aim by creating an incorrect picture, even if what eventually ensues is a correct and a helpful picture. That is manipulation, albeit intuitively one of a benign sort.

Finally, TV and radio soap operas that broadcast fiction to promote safe sex or maternal and child health are gaining currency as means of health promotion (Solomon and DeJong 1989, 1988; Population Media Center 2015; Development Media International 2015). One way such fiction works is by role-modeling healthy behavior, and that is often manipulative. The fact that beautiful, rich protagonists act healthfully provides no good reason to act healthfully. Intuitively, however, effective soap operas for health remain ethically benign. So they exemplify benign manipulation for health.

In short, genuine nudges are manipulative, but can be ethically benign.

Notes

1. Occasionally they do describe nudging interventions as "manipulation" (Sunstein and Thaler 2008, 71; Sunstein 2014b, 145) or "manipulative" (Sunstein and Thaler 2008, 245), and recent writing seems to vacillate between concessions of peripheral or weak manipulation and its complete denial (see below).
2. Sunstein's statements on whether these nudges constitute manipulation are somewhat ambivalent, for example: "Some forms of framing could plausibly be counted as manipulative . . . some nudges can be counted as forms of manipulation . . . That is a strong point against them. Even when nudges target System 1, it might well strain the concept of manipulation to categorize them as such" (Sunstein, forthcoming, V.E.1, VII).
3. Rebonato (2008, 60) and Frances Kamm (orally) made similar points.
4. Even Anne Barnhill, according to whom manipulative tricks typically work against the interests of those they influence (2014), thinks that influences that actually/predictably promote our interests can remain manipulative (personal correspondence).
5. Besides, elsewhere in the same paper Sunstein denies that, all things considered, manipulation is always wrong (Sunstein, WIP).
6. Compare Greenspan (2003, 160). Hausman and Welch do write at one point that manipulative nudging is often permissible when it is more efficient than persuasion (Hausman and Welch 2010, 134). That might suggest merely weak opposition to nudging. Nonetheless, recall their strong language of disrespect.
7. "If [previous manipulations—including advertising and social norms—have influenced people to become smokers] perhaps we can say that public officials are permitted to meet fire with fire. But some people might insist that two wrongs do not make a right—and that if the government seeks to lead people to quit, it must treat them as adults, and appeal to their deliberative capacities" (Sunstein, WIP).
8. It is true that coercion likewise thwarts only a single enactment of that capacity. That is a reason not to strongly repudiate all coercion, at least not in the name of autonomy.
9. For example, "[p]eople are busy, and without a degree of paternalism, we would quickly be overloaded with the tasks of choice making, which would compromise our autonomy" (Sunstein 2014a, 21; see also Sunstein, forthcoming, V.B).
10. Barnhill does not hold all (nudging) manipulation to be *pro tanto* wrong, but analyzes features of manipulation that, in her view, make others say so.
11. Moti Gorin asked in conversation, What if the alleged wrongness of manipulative nudging consists in imposing an agenda on the nudgee, whether or not the nudgee has an agenda? Even if the nudgee should have rationally had the agenda of eating healthfully, say, still she sometimes lacks that agenda in actuality, and some libertarians oppose precisely the imposition of agendas.

References

Barnhill, Anne. 2014. "What Is Manipulation?" In *Manipulation: Theory and Practice*, edited by C. Coons and M. Weber. Oxford University Press. New York.

Baron, Marcia. 2014. "The Mens Rea and Moral Status of Manipulation." In *Manipulation: Theory and Practice*, edited by C. Coons and M. Weber. Oxford University Press. New York.

Berofsky, Bernard. 1983. "Autonomy." In *How Many Questions? Essays in Honor of Sidney Morgenbesser*, edited by L. S. Cauman, I. Levi, C. Parsons, and R. Schwartz. Hackett. Indianapolis.

Bovens, Luc. 2008. "The Ethics of Nudge." In *Preference Change: Approaches from Philosophy, Economics and Psychology*, edited by T. Grüne-Yanoff and S. O. Hansson. Springer. Berlin.

———. 2012. "Real Nudge." *European Journal of Risk Regulation* 1:43–46.

Buss, Sarah. 2005. "Valuing Autonomy and Respecting Persons: Manipulation, Seduction, and the Basis of Moral Constraints." *Ethics* 115(2):195–235.

Cave, Eric M. 2007. "What's Wrong with Motive Manipulation?" *Ethical Theory and Moral Practice* 10:129–44.

Chang, Julu, and Mary Marsh. 2013. *The Google Diet: Search Giant Overhauled Its Eating Options to "Nudge" Healthy Choices*. ABC News. January 25. Accessed January 27, 2015. http://abcnews.go.com/Health/google-diet-search-giant-overhauled-eating-options-nudge/story?id=18241908.

Christman, John. 1988. "Constructing the Inner Citadel: Recent Work on Autonomy." *Ethics* 99:109–24.

Coons, Christian, and Michael Weber. 2014. "Introduction: Investigating the Core Concept and Its Moral Status." In *Manipulation: Theory and Practice*, edited by C. Coons and M. Weber. Oxford University Press. New York.

Development Media International. 2015. Accessed January 27, 2015. http://developmentmedia.net/.

Donagan, Alan. 1977. "Informed Consent in Therapy and Experimentation." *Journal of Medicine and Philosophy* 2(4):307–29.

Eyal, Nir. 2015. "Nudge, Embarrassment, and Restriction—Replies to Voigt, Tieffenbach, and Saghai." *International Journal of Health Policy and Management* 4(1):53–54.

———. 2014. "Nudging by Shaming, Shaming by Nudging." *International Journal of Health Policy and Management* 3:1–4.

Faden, Ruth R., and Tom L. Beauchamp. 1986. *A History and Theory of Informed Consent*. Oxford University Press. New York.

Gorin, Moti. 2014. "Towards a Theory of Interpersonal Manipulation." In *Manipulation: Theory and Practice*, edited by C. Coons and M. Weber. Oxford University Press. New York.

Greenspan, Patricia. 2003. "The Problem with Manipulation." *American Philosophical Quarterly* 40(2):155–64.

Grüne-Yanoff, Till. 2012. "Old Wine in New Casks: Libertarian Paternalism Still Violates Liberal Principles." *Social Choice and Welfare* 38:635–45.

Hausman, Daniel M., and Brynn Welch. 2010. "To Nudge or Not to Nudge." *Journal of Political Philosophy* 18(1):123–36.

Hill, Thomas E., Jr. 1984. "Autonomy and Benevolent Lies." *Journal of Value Inquiry* 18:251–67.

Kawachi, Ichiro. 2014. "Applications of Behavioral Economics to Improve Health." In *Social Epidemiology*, edited by L. F. Berkman, I. Kawachi, and M. M. Glymour. Oxford University Press. New York.

Korsgaard, Christine. 1986. "The Right to Lie: Kant on Dealing with Evil." *Philosophy and Public Affairs* 15(4):325–49.

Lovett, Frank. 2014. "Republicanism." In *Stanford Encyclopedia of Philosophy*, edited by E. N. Zalta. Stanford University Press. Stanford, CA.

Mandava, A., and J. Millum. 2013. "Manipulation in the Enrollment of Research Participants." *The Hastings Center Report* 43(2):38–47.

Mitchell, Gregory. 2005. "Libertarian Paternalism Is an Oxymoron." *Northwestern University Law Review* 99:1245–77.

Pettit, Philip. 1997. *Republicanism: A Theory of Freedom and Government*. Oxford University Press. Oxford.

Population Media Center. 2015. Accessed January 27, 2015. https://www.populationmedia.org/.

Raz, Joseph. 1986. *The Morality of Freedom*. Clarendon. Oxford.

Rebonato, Riccardo. 2008. *Taking Liberties: A Critical Examination of Libertarian Paternalism*. Palgrave Macmillan. New York.

——— 2012. *Taking Liberties—A Critical Examination of Libertarian Paternalism*. Palgrave Macmillan. London.

Scanlon, T. M. 1998. *What We Owe to Each Other*. Harvard University Press. Cambridge, MA.

Scoccia, Danny. 2014. "Paternalism and Manipulation." Mimeo.

Shanker, Deena. 2014. *19 Supermarket Mind Games That Get You to Buy More Junk Food*. June 18. Accessed January 27, 2015. http://www.buzzfeed.com/deenashanker/ways-supermarkets -trick-you-into-buying-more-junk#.dxYYEwBx0.

Solomon, M. Z., and W. DeJong. 1988. "The Impact of a Clinic-Based Educational Videotape on Knowledge and Treatment Behavior of Men with Gonorrhea." *Sexually Transmitted Diseases* 15(3):127–32.

———. 1989. "Preventing AIDS and Other STDs through Condom Promotion: A Patient Education Intervention." *American Journal of Public Health* 79(4):453–58.

Sunstein, Cass R. 2014c. "Choosing Not to Choose." In *Behavioral Economics, Law, and Health Policy*. Harvard Law School. Cambridge, MA.

———. WIP. "Fifty Shades of Manipulation." February 16, 2015. Draft.

———. Forthcoming. "Nudging and Choice Architecture: Ethical Considerations." *Yale Journal on Regulation*.

———. 2014b. *Valuing Life: Humanizing the Regulatory State*. University of Chicago Press. Chicago.

———2014a. *Why Nudge? The Politics of Libertarian Paternalism*. Yale University Press. New Haven, CT.

Sunstein, Cass R., and Richard H. Thaler. 2008. *Nudge: Improving Decisions about Health, Wealth, and Happiness*. Yale University Press. New Haven, CT.

White, Mark D. 2013. *The Manipulation of Choice: Ethics and Libertarian Paternalism*. Palgrave MacMillan. New York.

Wilkinson, T. M. 2013. "Nudging and Manipulation." *Political Studies* 61:341–55.

Wood, Allen W. 2014. "Coercion, Manipulation, Exploitation." In *Manipulation: Theory and Practice*, edited by C. Coons and M. Weber. Oxford University Press. New York.

CHAPTER 7

The Political Morality of Nudges in Healthcare

Jonathan Gingerich

Nudges have sparked the interest of some moral philosophers, many of whom have thought that there is something ethically unsettling about nudges because of the sort of relationship between a government and its citizens that they entail or because of what nudges do to the deliberative capacities of people who are nudged. Daniel M. Hausman and Brynn Welch argue that nudges "may threaten the individual's control over her own choosing" and claim that to "the extent that they are attempts to undermine that individual's control over her own deliberation, as well as her ability to assess for herself her alternatives, they are *prima facie* as threatening to liberty, broadly understood, as is overt coercion" (2010, 123). Jeremy Waldron suggests that there is a "genuine worry" about Cass Sunstein's advocacy of nudges, and thinks that there is "an element of insult" in Sunstein's nudging (2014, §3). For these and other philosophers, nudges raise ethical concerns primarily or exclusively when used by governments to encourage their citizens to behave in particular ways and governments have at least a *pro tanto* reason to avoid nudging their citizens.

In this chapter, I reconstruct the moral philosophers' objections to nudges, explaining why we might think that nudges contain "an element of insult." I begin by considering and rejecting as overly simplistic interpretations of the moral philosophers' objection that focus on either how nudges diminish the number of choices that people make or how nudges aim to modify people's behavior without engaging with their rational capacities. The moral philosopher's objection can be more charitably understood as a worry about nudges insofar as they undermine democratic control of

PhD candidate, University of California, Los Angeles, Department of Philosophy. My thanks to Glenn Cohen, Daniela Dover, Rimon Elkotbeid, Tatiana Espinosa, Nir Eyal, Laura Gillespie, Pamela Hieronymi, Melissa Hughs, Brian Hutler, Christopher Robertson, Yashar Saghai, Seana Shiffrin, and the audience at the Petrie-Flom Center's 2014 Annual Conference.

default rules by making it more difficult for people to detect that the choice architecture in which they operate has been actively shaped by policymakers. I argue that this version of the objection to nudges is not really a worry about nudges, as a policy category, but a worry about compromising the integrity of individual decision-making in certain important contexts. Governments do not, then, have a *pro tanto* reason to refrain from nudging. Instead, governments ought to consider whether particular nudges prevent people from directly engaging with the reasons and values that bear on a decision that it is morally important for them to make for themselves. Finally, I discuss how governments might determine whether nudges in the field of healthcare are likely to interfere with the independence of such decisions.

Nudges and Respect for Choice

A central feature of moral philosophers' criticisms of nudges is a claim that, in some manner, nudges fail to respect nudgees as individual choosers, whether by failing to show appropriate regard for the choices that they make or by treating people as lacking the rational capacities that are central to the practice of choosing.[1] Waldron, for instance, claims that when I am nudged, "my choosing is being made a mere means to my ends by somebody else" (Waldron 2014, §4). Waldron "think[s] this is what the concern about dignity is all about" (Waldron 2014, §4). My choosing is treated as a mere means when a nudge fails to take seriously my capacities for deliberation as a part of me, and the fact that when I do something because I choose to do it, I invest my action with self-respect (Waldron 2014, §4). In this section, I explore why we might think that nudges fail to respect my choosing. I first consider two obvious interpretations of the moral philosophers' objection to nudges and reject both as overly simplistic. I then propose that the best understanding of the objection to nudges focuses on the possibility that nudges could undermine democratic control of choice architecture.

What the Moral Philosophers' Objection to Nudges Is Not

One very straightforward interpretation of the objection to nudges, which is advanced by some libertarian critics of nudging, holds that nudges disrespect me as a chooser because they reduce the number of options that I have to choose from, or the number of choices that I must make. But it is a truism that having more choices does not straightforwardly enhance my agency (Dworkin 1982, 60). In many contexts, having more choices limits both my welfare, by forcing me to make choices I would rather not make (like which health insurance plan to enroll in), and my autonomy, by forcing me to expend deliberative resources making choices that are not central to my agency (Sunstein, this volume). If I am nudged by my insurance to choose an optometrist from a relatively small network of optometrists, I might spend less time deliberating about which optometrist to use and more time deliberating about things that matter much more to me. So the complaint that nudges fail to respect nudgees as choosers cannot plausibly amount to the claim that nudges disrespect people as choosers just because they reduce the number of choices that they have.

We might instead think that this objection concerns the manner in which nudges interact with individuals' rational choice-making capacities. Nudges do not induce nudgees to behave in a manner that promotes their own or third-party welfare or deliberation through rational persuasion. Sometimes nudges consist of providing information, like graphic warnings on cigarette packages about the health effects of smoking. But nudges differ from argumentation in that, even when they consist of the providing information, they achieve their objectives through subrational processes. Arguably, graphic cigarette warnings "nudge" smokers to pay more attention to the long-term health effects of smoking not by providing an explanation of why they should focus their reasoning about cigarette purchases on long-term health consequences, but by relying on their reflexive response to the warning. Nudges may constitute a substitution of the nudger's judgment for my own, such that "my choosing is being made a mere means to my ends by somebody else" (Waldron 2014, §4) because they aim to elicit a specific behavior from me other than by rationally persuading me that I should behave in that way.

While this interpretation of the objection to nudges is more plausible than the first version that I considered, it remains unappealing. Our human rational agency is inevitably conditioned on and influenced by nonrational processes. Perhaps we should aspire to free our rational decisions from nonrational influences to the greatest extent possible, but it would be odd to think that the best way to do this is to reduce the effect of extraneous influences on every single choice we make. Further, it is not clear why we would want to avoid all nonrational interferences with deliberation that aim at a particular result. As the proponents of nudging frequently point out, even in the context of important decisions that should be made independently, some default rule is often necessary. Deciding whether to become an organ donor is a decision that many people think is an important one that individuals ought to make autonomously and with the use of their own rational, deliberative capacities. But what should happen with the organs of someone who has not made a decision about whether to be an organ donor or not? Given that having some default rule is inevitable, should the default be that people are organ donors or that they are not? And if, as humans, it is inevitable that nonrational processes impact individuals' rational decision-making so that many people stick with the default rule for organ donation, whatever it is, what rationale could there be for setting the default at not being a donor if being a donor is what most people would prefer if they did, in fact, give serious consideration to the question of whether to be an organ donor? It seems that even the fact that a nudge has the potential to make a particular outcome to a particular important decision more likely (other than by rational persuasion) is not, by itself, reason to be suspicious of nudges.[2]

Nudges and Democratic Control

Part of why nudges seem unlikely to interfere impermissibly with the independence of reasoning by individuals any more than rational persuasion or mandates is that nudges tend to succeed and fail at the level of populations. Consider an employer that changes the health insurance plan that its employees are enrolled in by default from plan A, a low-premium, high-deductible plan, to plan B, a moderate-premium, moderate-deductible plan, although it allows employees to choose easily which of the two plans to enroll in. The employer makes the change because such a plan is likely to be better, financially speaking, for most of its employees. Whether changing the default insurance plan succeeds or fails does not depend on whether employee X sticks with the default or elects to enroll in a different plan, and it also does not depend on whether employee X would be better off with plan A or plan B. There would be no good ground to object to the nudge if, in fact, most employees would like to enroll in plan B and only a small number of employees would like plan A, and if setting plan A as the default will result in more employees enrolling in plan A than plan B. The employer could know that most of its employees would prefer plan B—for instance, by surveying a random sampling of employees—it is impossible for the employer to know the health insurance preferences of all of its employees in advance. The default is going to be the insurance plan that some employees want but not what others want, and there must be some default. Setting plan B as the default looks like the best way to allocate the costs of decision-making to reduce costs as much as possible.

Focusing on how nudges function at the level of populations suggests that if nudges give rise to a moral concern, the concern has to do not with their impact on individual decision-making but on how they impact the choice architecture that a group of people relies on. Defaulting to plan A seems like a good rule to have if a plurality of employees would, if they thought about it, save at that rate. But consider a nudge to encourage employees to avoid financial shocks associated with unplanned healthcare expenditures by setting plan B as the default when, in fact, most employees would choose plan A if they really thought about it. This nudge looks much more like it fails to respect individual members of the population of employees as choosers. The objection to nudging could be formulated as follows:

> **N1:** Nudges disrespect nudgees as choosers when they make it more difficult for individual nudgees to choose according to the default choice that the collective of nudgees would prefer.

Here, "the default choice that the collective of nudgees would prefer" represents the appropriate aggregation of individual nudgees' choices. If a doctor routinely prescribes two versions of a drug, generic and branded, and 90% of patients want a generic and 10% want a brand-name drug, the majoritarian default choice would be the generic. According to this line of thought, nudges disrespect us as choosers when they treat our choices as something to be modified in pursuit of some further objective that we would not endorse, individually or in aggregate.

This objection needs further refinement because often there may be no fact of the matter as to what we would endorse, individually or in aggregate. The problem is not only that, given certain assumptions about how to aggregate individual preferences, it may be impossible to translate individual preferences into community-wide preferences, but also that individuals may not have an answer as to what their highest-order desires are (Korobkin 2009). An insurance plan may serve many patients who both want to want the best medicine available (and who think brand-name drugs are better than generics) and who want to want good healthcare at an affordable price (and who think this is provided by generics). It may be a rational failing of individuals to have unresolved conflicts between their preferences, but one can purchase pharmaceuticals without being fully rational. Even if they were prompted to reflect seriously about their higher-order preferences, many customers would not know what they prefer, or might simply pick among alternatives for no reason at all.

More abstractly, I might not have fully consistent desires about what choices I would like to make. For instance, I might like to make more choices than I possibly could make, given the limited amount of time and the limited deliberative resources that I have, and I might not have worked out rules about how to prioritize the various choices that I would like to make. Additionally, figuring out which choices are the most important for me to make is the work of a lifetime, not something that I could settle by setting aside a couple of hours or even a few days to think about it. Moreover, in many cases, there might not be any default choice that represents an aggregation of individual preferences about the default, even in principle. If this is the case, we might accept that N1 is only an objection to nudges in those cases where there is a clear majoritarian default choice. But thinking about the grounds of a principle that supports showing respect for majoritarian default choices can produce a revised objection. Nudges can fail to respect people as choosers when they promote some small set of individuals' default preferences at the cost of making it (at least marginally) more difficult for other people to get what they want. What matters is democratic control of nudges so that it is possible for us, together, to revise nudges if we want to do so. The objection to nudges might then be formulated as follows:

N2: Nudges disrespect nudgees as choosers when they make it more difficult for nudgees to democratically control the relevant choice architecture.

Nudging patients toward generics and away from brand-names would, then, be subject to criticism under N2 if a democratic majority of patients wanted branded drugs, or if most patients were not sure what they wanted to want but the nudge made it more difficult for them to exercise control over decisions about the default drugs in prescriptions. Of course, there are many different ways that a nudge could be under democratic control: a nudge might be implemented through a referendum, through a statute enacted by a legislature, or by an administrative agency overseen by an elected executive. There are many different forms that democratic oversight can take, but more significant to determining whether a nudge is subject to criticism under N2 is the aim of the nudge. N2 objects to nudges that have an anti-democratic aim in that they treat some people's preferences or commitments as more important than those of others in determining a default, just because of who they are.

We might still wonder why nudges, in particular, are a form of policymaking that we should worry about. Why think that there is a *pro tanto* reason to avoid nudging? Perhaps the thing to avoid is not nudges, but rather failures of democratic oversight of policymaking or counter-democratic aims of government officials.

For the moral philosophers' objection to nudges to work as an objection to nudges particularly, it should be able to explain why there is something more morally worrisome about nudges than about coercive policies. The focus on democratic control of choice architecture helps to explain how this might happen. As non-lying deception may be more difficult to detect than lies, it may be harder for nudgees to tell when nudging is going on than to tell when more coercive policies are in place.[3] If a hospital is designed so that its stairs and ramps are attractive and obvious, so that patients, visitors, and staff are more likely to walk than take an elevator or lift, it is hard for users of the hospital to immediately discern that the placement of stairs is the result of a policy that has an aim related to how they should get exercise. Even if they can tell, in the abstract, that the placement of the stairs represents a policy decision, the policy intervention is much less salient than would be a prohibition on using elevators by anyone who could take the stairs, or, for that matter, a requirement that elevator passengers fill out a waiver acknowledging the health risks of not walking enough before going up a few stories.

If the presence of nudges in our deliberative environments is more difficult to detect than the presence of more overtly coercive policies or than the presence of efforts at rational persuasion, we might think that nudges can undermine democratic control of choice architecture. Rather than thinking about the objectives that are being advanced by making stairs obvious and attractive and doing something to change the hospital's architectural decisions if they disagree with its objectives, hospital users are likely to go along with the nudge either because they do not notice that it is part of the choice architecture or, even if they notice it, because individually, they still have the freedom to take the elevator and so are not concerned to change the policy. The involvement of my choice in the outcome may make it less likely that I will object to the manner in which the choice was set up for me. After all, in the end I got what I wanted and at relatively little cost to me.

We might wonder whether nudges rely on this quality of non-transparency to function. In many cases, greater transparency might undermine nudges that are prima facie objectionable according to N2. If, collectively, the people enrolled in the insurance plan that nudges them to use generics do not want to use generics, the disclosure of the nudge might prompt a large number of insureds to actively choose brand-name drugs. There is a complication, however: the members of the insurance plan might prefer brand-name drugs but also have a higher-order desire not to have this preference. They might think that they themselves are irrational for wanting branded drugs when generics produce health outcomes that are just as good, and so, collectively, they might want not only a generic drug default but also want not to be prompted to think about the possibility of opting out by a disclosure. We might also think that nudges do not depend on being hidden to work because even when disclosure about a nudge is provided, nudgees are under pressure to see themselves as responsible for what they choose.

Suppose I work for an employer that offers health insurance through plan A (the low-premium, high-deductible plan) and plan B (the moderate-deductible, moderate-premium plan), and makes it extremely easy to select either plan, but offers plan A as the default. If I would rather have plan B but never fill out the simple form to enroll in plan B, whether out of procrastination, anxiety, laziness, or inattentiveness, and I end up with high out-of-pocket medical expenses that I would have avoided if I selected plan B, I might blame my employer for not making plan B the default, but I might also blame myself. Disclaiming responsibility would involve undermining my own rational agency and foregrounding my rational defects, a painful experience that I might seek to avoid.

We can now formulate a moral claim that is more specifically focused on nudges:

N3: Nudges disrespect nudgees as choosers when they make it more difficult for nudgees to democratically control the relevant choice architecture by making the ways in which choice architects have manipulated majoritarian default rules less obvious to nudgees.

This principle echoes Nir Eyal's suggestion that nudges are morally fine when they put nudgees on "automatic pilot" toward a particular course of action but make it easily possible for nudgees to abort automatic pilot. N3 suggests that nudges are morally objectionable when they make it difficult for us, collectively, to get off autopilot. To the extent that nudges make us feel alright about being governed from above, and make it less likely that we will organize democratically to change policies that do not suit us, we should be concerned about nudges.

Nudges and Healthcare

Some difficulties with the objection to nudging linger. Suppose that a city with many employees offers five health insurance plans, A, B, C, D, and E. The city changes the default insurance plan from A to B because public health experts tell the city that this will enhance the welfare of its employees in the long run. And suppose that this is a case where there is no default rule that the community of nudgees would or could democratically endorse—most employees do not know which plan they would choose if they thought about it, and even if they spent a lot of time deliberating about which plan to choose, most employees would end up just picking a plan more or less at random. Setting plan B as the default plan might reduce democratic control of the choice architecture relative to a decision to force employees to make a choice among the five plans as a condition of employment or relative to a penalty default rule, like making the default insurance plan the one that is obviously worse than the others. It seems strange to think that the city's nudge is morally problematic. It is strange to think that it is important to maintain a high level of democratic control over every single piece of choice architecture, at least as it remains, in principle, possible to exert democratic control.

If anything troublesome were happening in the case of the city's healthcare plans, it would be because the choice that the nudge is designed to shape is one that it is particularly important for individuals to make for themselves, by directly engaging with the values that bear on their decision. Seana Shiffrin suggests that "[i]t is valuable to have the opportunity to engage with a particular value, in some degree of isolation, to determine its significance to oneself and to respond appropriately to the reasons it presents" (Shiffrin 2004, 291). On this picture, choice architecture should not be designed in a manner that makes it difficult for people to engage directly with the reasons and values that bear on a decision that they face, when the area of decision is one where it is morally important for individuals to practice such direct engagement.

Consider a cancer patient who has to choose between two courses of treatment, one palliative and one involving aggressive chemotherapy, both of which are routinely provided to other patients with the same condition. It might be important that the patient's deliberations about which course of treatment to pursue without being pressured by considerations about whether her family will be bankrupted or severely financially strained by one or another of the treatment options, or about whether others will disapprove of or be inconvenienced by her decision.[4] We might think it important instead for the patient to be able to focus directly on values related to her own health and longevity, and some nudges might interfere with the patient's ability to do so. Indeed, in this situation, providing the patient with either course of treatment as a default option might signal to the patient that her healthcare providers would disapprove of her decision to pursue the other course of treatment.

Sometimes, when things are important to us, we are unlikely to be swayed by a default rule, especially one that provides an easy mechanism for opting out, because a decision that is important to us is precisely the sort of thing that we are likely to actively deliberate about. However, there are two reasons that we might remain concerned about the effect of nudges on decision-making. First, even in decisions that I regard as important, nudges might interfere with my direct engagement with values, even if they do not prevent deliberation. Setting the default rule for the aforementioned cancer patient as providing aggressive chemotherapy might not make it much less likely that the patient will actively deliberate about which course of treatment to pursue, but it might undermine her ability to engage in a focused deliberation about the values of health. She might take the setting of the default rule to indicate that it is appropriate for patients to want aggressive chemotherapy, or that her physicians endorse this treatment option.

Second, some decisions that are really important to me can also be emotionally fraught, especially in the context of healthcare. Deciding between aggressive chemotherapy and palliative treatment forces me to confront many different values that may be incompatible with one another. I might care about having a chance to prolong my life, about the environment in which I receive healthcare, about avoiding severe pain, and about maintaining cognitive function, and I may not be able to preserve access to all of these values that I care deeply about. This could be profoundly anxiety provoking, and might occasion avoidance. If a default is available, I might take the default as authoritative so that I need not endure the stress of directly engaging with the values that bear on a decision about my course of treatment. This does not end the inquiry about whether such a nudge is desirable because we might have further values that are served by making it easy for patients to avoid the anxiety provoked by making emotionally difficult decisions about medical treatment. But it is possible that, while collectively we recognize that when faced with such decisions we would be likely to avoid them by relying on defaults available to us, we might also collectively think it important that we overcome this avoidance and participate in the difficult but important direct engagement with values related to our health. If this is true of us, collectively, we might think it important to avoid nudging patients in either direction.

How do we know when we are in a context in which it is important for people to engage directly with values? These areas of decision will likely include "big personal decisions" that "address matters that comprise some of the primary bases of a meaningful or fulfilling life" (Tsai 2014, 78), but might also include "space to make even trivial choices purely on the basis of the small, specific reasons that trivial options provide" (Shiffrin 2004, 296). Returning to the example of the city's health insurance plan, the decision about which healthcare plan to enroll in might be such a decision, but whether it deserves this sort of protection will depend on questions about how important it is for individuals to make decisions about health insurance and on how important it is to maintain relatively direct democratic control of the choice architecture surrounding such decisions. This is a question that we must resolve by examining the values of healthcare, and determining whether decisions about insurance are the sort that merit insulation from other considerations than those that have to do with health, not by examining how nudges, in general, impact decision-making by nudgees.

Conclusion

The moral philosophers' objection to nudges claimed that nudges fail to adequately respect nudgees as choosers. I argued that it is implausible to interpret this objection to nudges as an objection to nudges reducing the number of options or choices that nudgees have, or an objection to nudges attempting to elicit a specific behavior other than through rational persuasion. A better interpretation of the objection to nudges is that nudges can make it more difficult for nudgees to democratically control the choice architecture in which they make decisions by remaining more hidden than other interventions, like mandates. But whether it is really objectionable to make choice architecture more hidden and more difficult to democratically control depends on how important the choices that the architecture shapes are to the people who make them. It is particularly in the context of choices where it is important for people to directly engage with a certain set of values that we might worry that nudges undermine democratic control of choice architecture, and this determination depends on substantive considerations about the situations in which people should have at least limited opportunities to engage with certain values directly. What is left of the moral philosophers' objection to nudges is not a claim that that there is a *pro tanto* reason to avoid nudging, but that as a psychological matter, because nudges may be more hidden than other policy interventions, we might wish to pay special attention to the possibility that nudges can undermine the independence of decisions in choice contexts that ought to be insulated.

Notes

1. I use the terms "nudger" to designate a person or institution who institutes a nudge and "nudgee" for a person who is the target of a nudge.
2. I leave open the possibility that in some contexts, such as decisions about organ donation or other posthumous uses of one's body might involve an asymmetry, such that a default rule of allowing posthumous use of a body is intrusive even if, on considered reflection, almost everyone would not have an objection to using their organs after their death. Thanks to Glenn Cohen for raising this point.
3. I owe this analogy to Seana Shiffrin.
4. This example closely tracks an example provided in Shiffrin 2004, 289.

References

Dworkin, Gerald. 1982. "Is More Choice Better Than Less?" *Midwest Studies in Philosophy* 7:47.

Hausman, Daniel M., and Brynn Welch. 2010. "Debate: To Nudge or Not to Nudge?" *Journal of Political Philosophy* 18:123.

Korobkin, Russell. 2009. "Libertarian Welfarism." *California Law Review* 97:1651.

Shiffrin, Seana Valentine. 2004. "Egalitarianism, Choice-Sensitivity, and Accommodation." In *Reason and Value: Themes from the Moral Philosophy of Joseph Raz*, edited by R. Jay Wallace et al. Clarendon. Oxford University Press. 270–302.

Tsai, George. 2014. "Rational Persuasion as Paternalism." *Philosophy and Public Affairs* 42:78.

Waldron, Jeremy. 2014. "It's All for Your Own Good." *The New York Review of Books*, October 9. Accessed February 25, 2016. http://www.nybooks.com/articles/2014/10/09/cass-sunstein -its-all-your-own-good/.

PART II **NUDGING AND PUBLIC HEALTH POLICY**

Introduction

Holly Fernandez Lynch

Public health has traditionally been an area in which government mandates, compulsion, and coercion have been accepted in the name of the greater good: the government can require vaccination, ban illicit drugs, require helmets and seatbelts, prohibit smoking in public places, and demand compliance with a wide variety of safety codes that may increase costs and burdens but protect health. In these contexts, we may be past the point of nudges and into the realm of straight paternalism. But when a nudge might work, should we ever proceed with a shove? And, on the flip side, if a nudge will not work, or will not work well enough, is that enough to justify the shove?

The chapters in this part focus on two important public health priorities: vaccination (particularly where herd immunity has not yet been achieved) and human nutrition (particularly in marginalized communities). As Jennifer Blumenthal-Barby and her coauthors explain in their chapter, reducing barriers to vaccination in India through the presence of reliable clinics and offering modest incentives rendered substantial improvement in vaccination rates—a nudge was relatively effective. On the other hand, Andrea Freeman describes a number of nudges related to food policy—nutrition labels, calorie counts, defaults, and design—that are simply not up to the challenge of effectively overcoming the wide variety of socioeconomic factors, market forces, and even evolutionary drives that contribute to poor food choices. In that context, she argues, nudges are just not enough.

There are a number of important conclusions that we may draw from these two examples. First, the fact that the nudge achieved a sixfold increase in vaccinations in the Indian village where it was implemented does not necessarily mean that it was justified. Ends do not always justify the means, as Blumenthal-Barby and her coauthors recognize, and we need to know more than just whether an intervention was effective in achieving a particular goal. For example, what if the nudge had manipulated parents into doing something that seriously violated their deeply held beliefs, or had some important unintended consequence? In order to evaluate whether the nudging was ethically appropriate, Blumenthal-Barby et al. argue that it must be assessed against standards of utility, justice, autonomy, legitimacy, transparency, and trust. In this case, they determine that the vaccine nudge satisfied the relevant criteria, but it is unclear that the analysis should end there.

This leads to the second point: simply because an ethically acceptable nudge is available does not necessarily mean that a more paternalist approach would be unacceptable. The Indian nudge was a dramatic success, but it still resulted in only a 38% full immunization rate for children, up from 6% in the control group. This is far below the approximately 90% coverage needed for herd immunity. A vaccine mandate, or enforceable penalty, may be the only way to achieve that goal, and could be justified given the risk of serious preventable disease. On the other hand, such an imposing requirement could have backfired if it led to reduced trust and evasion among parents who might have been otherwise willing to vaccinate their children with a slightly stronger or different nudge. That is an empirical question, but the point is simply that is not necessarily the case that you should or must begin at the lowest rung on the intervention ladder when the stakes are high.

Of course, mandates must also stand up to ethical scrutiny, and the ethical propriety of a mandate is a stand-alone inquiry. Simply because a nudge would not be sufficient to achieve the policy goal in question does not necessarily mean that a more paternalistic approach would be acceptable. Moving to the context of food and nutrition policy as discussed in Freeman's chapter, then, the solution to failed nudging is not necessarily individual restriction. Instead, it may be that the solution is more substantial regulation of commercial firms, as Freeman suggests, or even perhaps acknowledging that restrictions on liberty may be worse than the problem to be solved, such that no effective intervention would be ethically appropriate.

How might these principles be applied to a pressing public health issue in the United States today, namely, nonmedical (personal belief) exemptions from mandatory vaccination? These state-level policies have been cited as the source of recent outbreaks of preventable diseases that had been nearly eradicated in this country. Would it be possible or appropriate to nudge those seeking exemption toward compliance, for example, by making the bureaucratic hurdles required to obtain an exemption more substantial, such as requiring notarization of forms, hand-delivery, physician confirmation of information disclosure, explicit acknowledgment of risk, personal statements, and the like (Ropeik 2015)? This would likely have substantial salutary effect by logistically eliminating exemptions for those without deeply held objections to vaccination, as demonstrated by the fact that states in which it is more burdensome—but still possible—to obtain an exemption in fact have better vaccination rates than those states in which obtaining an exemption is easier, for example, checking a box and mailing a form (Vestal 2015; *The New York Times* 2015).

Beyond being effective, which is Freeman's primary mechanism by which to evaluate proposed nudges, this approach would also seem to meet the ethical test set forth by Blumenthal-Barby and her coauthors. Encouraging vaccination by making it more difficult to avoid would produce greater benefit than risk, meeting the utility requirement, and benefits and burdens would be fairly distributed, satisfying the justice requirement. There is no reason to question the legitimacy of the government's interests in this nudge, or reason for those with genuine objections to vaccine mandates to lose trust, as they would still be eligible for exemption. Thus, autonomy is preserved. Since this type of nudging is likely to be sufficiently effective in achieving the levels needed for herd immunity—and because some people do have such genuine objections that deserve legal protection—soft paternalism is preferable to the hard paternalist approach that would eliminate all nonmedical exemptions to vaccination outright.

Ultimately, public health contexts often require individual sacrifices of liberty for the protection of society. However, what the chapters in this part demonstrate is that policymakers have more than one tool in their toolbox to achieve such sacrifices, ranging from hope for true volunteerism to the encouragement of the nudge to the outright mandate in extreme cases. Each tool requires case-by-case analysis and justification, as explored in this part, as well as the one preceding it on the ethics of nudges in healthcare, and throughout this volume.

References

The New York Times. 2015. Editorial. "Vaccine Phobia in California." *The New York Times*, April 20. http://www.nytimes.com/2015/04/21/opinion/vaccine-phobia-in-california.html ?smid=pl-share.

Ropeik, David. 2015. "Vaccine Exemptions Should Be Harder to Get, But Don't Eliminate Them." *The LA Times*, February 9. http://www.latimes.com/opinion/op-ed/la-oe-0210 -ropeik-vaccine-exemption-ban-20150210-story.html.

Vestal, Christine. 2015. *In States with Looser Immunization Laws, Lower Rates. Pew Charitable Trusts, Stateline*. February 9. http://www.pewtrusts.org/en/research-and-analysis/blogs /stateline/2015/2/09/in-states-with-looser-immunization-laws-lower-rates.

CHAPTER 8

An Ethical Framework for Public Health Nudges
A Case Study of Incentives as Nudges for Vaccination in Rural India

Jennifer Blumenthal-Barby, Zainab Shipchandler,
and Julika Kaplan

Many people are concerned with issues in global health such as childhood immunization rates (United Nations 2013). Immunization is a highly cost-effective and beneficial preventative health measure; however, 1.5 million children under the age of 5 die from vaccine-preventable diseases annually (World Health Organization 2014). Some approaches to global health issues such as this have focused on mandates and coercion, but "softer" interventions, or "nudges," have garnered interest as they are generally regarded as more politically palatable. For example, in response to the low immunization rates in rural India, the Massachusetts Institute of Technology professors Abhijit Banerjee and Esther Duflo partnered with Seva Mandir, a nongovernmental organization in Rajasthan, India, between 2004 and 2007 to assess the impact of increased reliability of immunization services and small nonmonetary incentives on immunization rates in the tribal areas surrounding Udaipur. Using insights from behavioral economics, they randomized villages into three groups: a control group, a once monthly reliable immunization camp, and a once monthly reliable immunization camp with small incentives (women received raw lentils for every visit they made to the camps and a set of metal plates when their children completed the immunization course). These incentives can be described as "nudges" because they aim to predictably alter the behavior of the women participating in the immunization camps without forbidding choice (Thaler and Sunstein 2008, 6).[1] At the end of the 18-month program, rates of full immunization were 6% for children in the control group, 17% for children in the reliable camp group, and 38% for children in the incentives group. This amounted to a sixfold increase in vaccination rates in the incentives group, demonstrating that small incentives combined with improved reliability of services can have a significant impact on immunization rates (Banerjee et al. 2010).

Although this intervention had a positive impact on immunization rates, the use of incentives to encourage the uptake of preventive health services is ethically controversial (Kaplan 2013). Incentives are a form of influence that falls into the ambiguous ethical terrain between rational argument and coercion. Banerjee and Duflo faced criticism that their nudge intervention was immoral because it capitalized on the vulnerability of the poor through bribery; however, those who supported the intervention claimed that the researchers' study simply demonstrated the local people's need for a well-intentioned nudge (Banerjee et al. 2010). Our goal in this chapter is to determine whether the use of incentives in Banerjee and Duflo's study was morally permissible as a solution to the issue of low immunization rates in rural Udaipur and to provide recommendations for the ethically sound implementation of nonmonetary incentives or other nudges in similar settings. We develop an ethical framework for assessment by drawing on existing public health frameworks and frameworks for assessing nudges (including incentives) in healthcare and health policy. We then use this framework to analyze English translations of interviews that we conducted in April 2013 with twenty-nine mothers from five villages in rural Udaipur who participated in Seva Mandir's incentives intervention.[2]

Ethical Framework

Public health interventions require specific ethical consideration because they balance the risks and benefits faced by individuals with those faced by the population as a whole. We consider the contributions of Childress et al. (2002), the Nuffield Council (Hepple 2007), and Kass (2001) as representative of the primary concepts in public health ethics. Childress et al. (2002) emphasize general moral considerations such as utility, justice, respect for autonomous choice, and transparency and trust, while using "justificatory conditions" where utility might outweigh individual autonomy or justice: effectiveness, least infringement, and necessity of the given intervention to resolve conflicts are among the various moral considerations. The Nuffield Council introduces the intervention ladder, in which public health interventions that cause greater restrictions to individual choice are on a "higher rung" on the ladder and must be more strongly justified, and the stewardship model, which describes the legitimacy and roles of influencing parties (Hepple 2007).[3] Kass's public health ethics framework focuses on assessing effectiveness, knowledge of burdens and their minimization, and fair implementation (Antommaria 2013; Kass 2001).

The ethics of "nudging," or incentivizing, people to change their behaviors has developed its own literature, much of it focusing on questions of autonomy and manipulation. One of us has developed a framework for assessing the ethical permissibility of various nudge interventions (Blumenthal-Barby and Burroughs 2012). Assuming that a nudge aims to produce benefits, the framework involves two major domains: considerations regarding autonomy and considerations regarding the relationship between the influencing or incentivizing party and the recipients. Autonomy is preserved if the persons being influenced have and are aware of the presence of other options, and are also aware of and endorse (or were they made aware of, would endorse) being influenced by the particular mechanism in the particular decisional context. This is in contrast to persons viewing the influence as alienating, or moving them away from their core values.

An example of this contrast might be a nudge for someone who is simply afraid to accept a needed blood transfusion (likely autonomy preserving) versus a nudge for a Jehovah's Witness to accept a blood transfusion (likely autonomy threatening). Moreover, the intervention should be something that is reasonably expected and viewed as appropriate in the context of the relationship; should align with obligations that the nudger, or "incentivizer," has to the recipient parties; and should not result in damage to the relationship. Ashcroft (2011) has also developed a framework for thinking about the ethics of incentivizing—specifically, for assessing the impact of incentives on autonomy. On this framework, incentives should avoid overriding a person's considered values and should not cause subjects to ignore risks, benefits, and alternatives. They should also avoid functioning as fearful threats (for example, "incentivizing" someone with something that is rightfully hers or essential and withholding it if the person does not engage in said behavior) since threats are coercive by nature.

The ethical framework we developed to assess incentives as nudges for childhood vaccination in rural India integrates the public health ethics frameworks and ethical frameworks for assessing nudges described above (table 8.1).

Ethical Analysis

In this section of the chapter we use our ethical framework (summarized in table 8.1) to analyze the interviews that we conducted with twenty-nine mothers from five villages in rural Udaipur who participated in Seva Mandir's incentives intervention.

Utility

Assessing the utility of Banerjee and Duflo's intervention involves consideration of the benefits produced, the harms avoided or removed, and the balance of benefits over harms. Seva Mandir's incentive-based intervention produced a sixfold increase in complete vaccination rates in Udaipur, where immunization coverage rates for tuberculosis, polio, measles, diphtheria, pertussis, and tetanus were less than 2% in 2004 (Banerjee et al. 2010). This increase is far from the 90% coverage recommended by the World Health Organization for the basic immunization package and the amount needed to establish "herd immunity," the point at which enough of the population is immunized to protect the entire community; however, the intervention did lower child mortality rates significantly (Banerjee et al. 2010). Seva Mandir's intervention also provided a reliable source of healthcare in a region where public health facilities are characterized by high absenteeism: 45% of health workers are absent from their village-level health centers on any given workday (Banerjee et al. 2010). When asked what

Table 8.1. Integrated Ethical Framework for Assessing Public Health "Nudge" Interventions

Domain	Key Questions
Utility* (Childress et al. 2002; Kass 2001; Hepple 2007)	• What *benefits* are produced? • How are potential *harms* (physical, psychological, financial) avoided, prevented, and removed? • Is there an appropriate *balance* between benefits and harms and costs?
Justice (Distributive and Procedural) (Childress et al. 2002; Kass 2001)	• Are the benefits and the burdens *distributed fairly*? • Have *vulnerabilities* (health, poverty, literacy, age, geography) been given special consideration, such that no new vulnerabilities are created and existing ones are not exacerbated? • Is a vulnerable population *being used* for the benefit of the nudgers, or is a risk or burden being imposed on them that the nudgers would be unwilling to impose on themselves? • Has *public participation* by the affected parties been ensured?
Autonomy (Childress et al. 2002; Ashcroft 2011; Blumenthal-Barby 2012; Blumenthal-Barby and Burroughs 2012)	• Are *alternative* options present and not significantly blocked or burdened, and are the subjects *aware* of them (and the good and bad consequences of all options)? • Does the nudge intervention overbear the subjects' considered choices or values, thereby *thwarting* their autonomy? Or might it help them achieve their considered choices or values, thereby *enhancing* autonomy? • Does the nudge intervention cause the subjects to ignore risks, benefits, and alternatives, thereby undermining morally valid autonomous *consent*? • Are the subjects' *attitudes* (or would they be) positive or negative toward being nudged in the particular context? • Does the nudge intervention create a situation in which subjects act primarily out of *coercion* or threat (including fear of loss), thereby thwarting autonomy?
Legitimacy (Hepple 2007; Blumenthal-Barby 2012)	• Is the nudge intervention reasonably *expected* and viewed as appropriate in the context of the relationship? • Does the nudge intervention align with the *obligations* that the nudger has to the subjects?
Transparency and Trust (Childress et al. 2002)	• Is proper (material) information *disclosed* to subjects, and are transparency and truthfulness maintained? • Is trust built and maintained by honoring promises and commitments? • Are privacy and confidentiality protected?

* In public health contexts, utility may outweigh other domains such as autonomy if conditions of necessity, effectiveness, and least infringement are met (Childress et al. 2002).

motivated them to attend Seva Mandir's camp, one woman noted that "there is nobody there in the [government clinic], only one nurse," while another appreciated that Seva Mandir "is in our village and [provides] a facility." In addition, by providing an incentive, the intervention removed the harm of lost work time by fairly compensating the mothers for the work they missed during their visits to the camps; the value of the incentive (1 kilogram of lentils worth 40 rupees) was equivalent to three-quarters of a day's wage in the area (Banerjee et al. 2010). Finally, Seva Mandir's intervention provided vaccinations in a cost-effective way. The average cost of fully immunizing a child was cheaper for the sponsoring organization when incentives were used (1,102 rupees per child) than when they were not used (2,202 rupees per child) because the higher demand for immunization in camps with incentives spread the daily fixed cost of the camp over more children (Banerjee et al. 2010).

On the other hand, during our interviews, most of the women at Seva Mandir's vaccination camps were unable to state the risks and benefits of immunization, which represents a potential autonomy harm resulting from poor counseling. Furthermore, only twelve out of twenty-nine women correctly identified preventing disease as the purpose of immunization; others incorrectly reported that immunization either reduces the effects of or cures disease. In addition, several of the women at the camps falsely believed that immunization prevents fever when, in fact, immunization often causes fever as a side effect. There is also potential for decreased utility if women are uninformed about potential side effects, experience those side effects surprisingly, and then develop negative views about vaccination as a result. For example, the translator for the interviews noted that the women did not understand the counseling provided by the nurses, and "then the kids have fever and [the women] are afraid about that."

The benefits of immunization, including the potential to prevent death from disease, seem to outweigh the potential harms produced by Seva Mandir's intervention, such as the side effects of immunization (soreness, inflammation, and fever). However, it is important for public health and nudge interventions to minimize harms by counseling participants effectively. Ensuring that women understand the risks and benefits of immunization would not only increase the ethical permissibility of the intervention, but might also decrease the psychological harm from unexpected side effects and increase the number of children who return for full vaccination, maximizing the overall utility of the intervention.

Justice

Distributive justice involves distributing benefits and burdens fairly with special consideration of vulnerable populations. The population in this study exhibited several vulnerabilities: poverty, limited literacy, poor health, geographic isolation, and age (childhood). Udaipur is among the poorest districts in India, with more than 40% of households living below the poverty line at the time of the intervention (Banerjee, Deaton, and Duflo 2004). In this region, only 46% of adult males and 11% of adult females were literate at the time (Banerjee, Deaton, and Duflo 2004, 945). Health indicators in rural Udaipur are extremely poor, with high rates of malnourishment, anemia, and disease symptoms such as fever, fatigue, and headache (Banerjee, Deaton, and Duflo 2004, 946). Finally, the primary beneficiaries of this intervention were children, who are by nature vulnerable due to their dependent status (Lange, Rogers, and Dodds 2013). Based on a Rawlsian view of justice, which prioritizes the well-being of the most vulnerable, this population in particular deserves any public health interventions that would benefit them (Rawls 1971). On the other hand, however, their vulnerability also creates an obligation to consider the burdens of the intervention and whether these burdens might create or exacerbate non-welfare vulnerabilities; we examine this possibility in our discussion of autonomy.

Maximizing procedural justice involves ensuring public participation during the planning and implementation of a given intervention, especially by affected parties. Daniels's view is that one way to satisfy this condition is "accountability for reasonableness," in which the decision-making process is an open and transparent one, the rationale and anticipated outcomes of the program are made clear, and the stakeholders have a chance to voice their views and concerns (Daniels 2000; Daniels and Sabin 1997). While Daniels's views on procedural justice are focused on unresolved rationing problems, they can apply equally well here. In this case, Banerjee and Duflo's intervention began with a year-long survey in the villages served by Seva Mandir in which one thousand households and local health practitioners were interviewed to inquire about key health problems in the area. Next, Banerjee and Duflo convened a large conference with all stakeholders (Seva Mandir, local doctors, governmental officials, and village representatives) to discuss the concerns raised by the survey. The stakeholders identified low immunization rates as a priority issue during the conference, and Banerjee and Duflo implemented their experimental incentive-based intervention. Before beginning the experiment, Banerjee and Duflo held a community meeting in each village to explain the program and democratically obtain consent to proceed. Based on the conditions listed above, we believe this model fulfills the requirements of procedural justice.

Autonomy

First, we will consider whether Banerjee and Duflo's intervention overbore the participants' considered choice (for example, opposition to vaccination), which would alienate them from their values and preferences (Ashcroft 2011; London et al. 2012). Many of the tribal populations in rural Udaipur believe their children will catch the fatal "evil eye" if they are brought outside during their first year of life and therefore protect their children by putting black smudges on their faces or tying strings around their waists (Banerjee and Duflo 2011). Most of the children who were immunized at Seva Mandir's camps did have these visible protections from the "evil eye," suggesting that the people living in rural Udaipur might prefer to avoid vaccination, which requires them to bring their children outside. However, many of the participants we interviewed followed both traditional and allopathic treatment strategies and regarded these two systems as compatible and complementary: for example, they "go to the temple . . . [and] if it's not curing, they take [their children] to [the] hospital." We also found that women were failing to vaccinate their children not because they opposed immunization, but because they lacked access to vaccinations. When asked to explain why they sought immunization at Seva Mandir's camps, one interviewee said that "the government hospital [does] not inform [them] properly when to immunize," demonstrating their interest in accessing vaccination services. In addition, twenty-six of the twenty-nine women indicated that vaccination was important to them. Thus, there is no evidence that the nudge intervention alienated people from their established values and belief systems.

The second consideration is whether the nudge intervention created a situation in which the women accepted the incentive primarily out of fear of the loss of something essential (that is, if it took the form of a threat to them—either do this or do not receive food you need to live). This is a serious concern in Seva Mandir's nudge intervention because sixteen out of the twenty-nine women indicated that they sometimes or never had enough food. However, twenty-seven women claimed that the lentils did not heavily influence their decisions to attend the camps, with one woman stating, "it is fine if [we] do not get [the lentils]." In addition, lentils are locally available, so Seva Mandir is not incentivizing immunization with a one-time opportunity to get something the women could not easily get nearby.

The third consideration is whether the nudge intervention undermined the validity of the women's decisions to seek immunization by causing them to focus too narrowly on the incentive (Ashcroft 2011). Such myopic focus on the incentive could undermine the women's autonomy by causing them to ignore the risks and benefits of vaccination (London et al. 2012). There is empirical evidence that, for people living in poverty, an unconscious and "involuntary preoccupation with an unmet need" can occupy a significant amount of mental "bandwidth" and reduce cognitive performance (Mullainathan and Shafir 2013, 60). In this intervention, the women might have been reminded of their material poverty when considering whether to attend the incentivized camps, potentially resulting in a myopic focus on the incentive. In fact, some of the women referred to the lentils in their responses to questions that did not involve lentils directly, which might indicate that the incentive had a greater impact on their decisions than they realized or would admit. For example, when we asked the women for general suggestions to improve the immunization camps, one woman focused on the incentive more than expected, stating that although the lentils were of good quality, "there should be a proper place to keep [them]" and they should be brought directly to the camp.

A final consideration is whether the nudge incentive might have actually enhanced autonomy by helping participants implement behaviors they would endorse and employ were it not for other impeding factors (Ashcroft 2011). The value the women placed on their children's health was evidenced by the opinion they expressed during our interviews that vaccination is beneficial because it "keeps the sickness away" and the "child stays healthy." Although the mothers at Seva Mandir's immunization camps valued the healthcare services that were provided to them, as previously mentioned, it was difficult for them to access high-quality, affordable care. Seva Mandir's immunization program provided regular (monthly) access to vaccinations at a local facility, enhancing the autonomy of the mothers visiting the immunization camps by maximizing their ability to improve the health of their children. In addition to access and work barriers, people often experience "time inconsistency," which is the natural inclination to postpone small costs until a later point when they seem more urgent or necessary. In our interviews, twenty-eight out of twenty-nine women responded positively when asked whether they intended to bring their children back to finish the immunization course; however, in reality, only 52% of the children completed the immunization course after receiving at least one vaccination in the incentivized camps during Banerjee and Duflo's study (Banerjee et al. 2010). This discrepancy between intention and action suggests that the mothers in the study might have been inclined to postpone small costs such as walking to the immunization camps, waiting in line to have their children vaccinated, and managing the side effects of immunization (Banerjee and Duflo 2011). By offering incentives to help the mothers overcome time inconsistency, Seva Mandir's incentive-based immunization camps might have further enhanced the autonomy of the participants.

Legitimacy

According to the Nuffield Council, the state has a responsibility to provide conditions under which people can live healthy lives, protect citizens from harm caused by others, enhance the health of vulnerable groups such as children, and close the gap between the most and least healthy in society (Hepple 2007). In addition, one of us has argued that interventions should align with obligations that the nudger has to the recipients, should be expected and appropriate in the context of the relationship, and should not damage that relationship (Blumenthal-Barby 2012). Seva Mandir's immunization program was not funded or directed by the state, but it compensated for a deficiency in the public health services provided by the Indian government. This raises the question of whether Seva Mandir, as a nongovernmental organization, was justified in assuming the public health responsibilities of the state.

In this particular instance, Seva Mandir was maximizing the fulfillment of state objectives by extending immunization access to hard-to-reach, vulnerable populations; therefore, this intervention does not seem unexpected or inappropriate. In addition, there is no evidence that the intervention caused damage to the relationship between the "incentivizer" and the recipients. In fact, the incentive program might have even enhanced the relationship between the two parties. When we asked the women to describe their impressions of Seva Mandir as an organization, they made positive comments about Seva Mandir's impact on their communities and said they trusted the organization. For example, one of the women said, "[we] all know Seva Mandir," indicating that the organization's positive reputation is widespread. It also seems unlikely that Seva Mandir was perceived as overstepping its role in the community by incentivizing immunization. The local population did not verbalize objections to the incentive, which suggests that they did not view the intervention as inappropriate. Finally, trust is an essential component of a successful and ethical nudge intervention; therefore, a lack of understanding of local culture and traditions can negatively impact utility and autonomy when an outsider's priorities do not align with the priorities of the target population. In this study, positive relationships between parties stemmed from the familiarity of Seva Mandir with the local culture and customs.

Transparency and Trust

Transparency and trust involve protecting privacy and confidentiality, keeping promises and commitments, disclosing information, and building and maintaining trust between parties (Childress et al. 2002). Seva Mandir's intervention was transparent because vaccination was clearly mentioned as a prerequisite to the incentive by the traditional birth attendants (TBAs), who reminded potential participants when and where the camps would take place. Therefore, the women who came to the camps were easily able to recognize a causal relation between the vaccinations and the lentils. However, in order to achieve true transparency, Seva Mandir should have ensured that the participants were informed about the potential risks and benefits of vaccination. The risks of vaccination were not always specified to the women. This might have represented benevolent deception on the part of the nurses who administered the vaccinations in order to increase participation since the benefits of immunization often seem distant and abstract, while the risks of immunization are more salient. However, Seva Mandir was not, for example, concealing risks or nudging people toward vaccination to benefit the organization at the cost of the participants, which would have violated transparency and trust.

In addition to the incentive, we believe that trust of Seva Mandir had a significant impact on the women's decisions to attend the camps. Seva Mandir's long-standing relationship with the people of Udaipur allowed the organization to choose a culturally appropriate incentive. We believe that this trusting relationship between Seva Mandir and the people in rural Udaipur contributed to the success of the behavioral economics initiative; if an unknown organization had started an incentive-based program, it might have generated suspicion. The women also had trusting relationships with Seva Mandir employees such as the TBAs, who are selected by the community members themselves. One woman explained that "the TBA knows every woman, and if somebody has a child, she goes to the household and says, 'Today is a vaccination day, you must go.'" Although these exceptional levels of trust increased the women's motivation to attend the camps, they might have also reduced the participants' need to autonomously seek and understand information about the benefits and risks of immunization. In conclusion, we believe that the requirements of transparency and trust were fulfilled by Seva Mandir's intervention, but could have been enhanced through proper counseling to ensure that trust was maintained.

Conclusion

There is a prevailing assumption that public health interventions are beneficial as long as they improve the health of their target populations. However, through this case study, we have demonstrated that the design, implementation, and results of these interventions must be systematically subjected to ethical scrutiny, in addition to ensuring their benefit to public health. For example, in our ethical analysis of Seva Mandir's vaccination program, the high levels of trust between Seva Mandir and the participants might have compromised their autonomous decision to attend the incentivized immunization camps. Through our interviews, we found that the incentives were culturally appropriate, did not alienate the women from their established belief systems, and even enhanced their ability to access a valued health service. However, we also found that the incentive coupled with the vulnerability of the women due to their material poverty shifted their focus away from understanding the potential risks of vaccination. Our interviews led us to find that increases in vaccination rates did not necessarily equate to increased understanding of the risks and benefits of vaccination, which could have led to a more sustained impact in the region. In this case study, the benefits of incentivizing immunization vastly outweighed the potential harms to autonomous choice; however, other cases might require a more nuanced application of the utility section of our framework. Our hope is that this integrated ethical framework will help researchers and public health officials use behavioral economics interventions to improve public health in low-resource settings.[4]

Notes

1. We note that there is a vigorous definitional debate about nudges. For example, Thaler and Sunstein (2008, 6) refer to a nudge as "any aspect of choice architecture that alters people's behavior in a predictable way without forbidding an option or significantly changing their economic incentives," whereas Yashar Saghai refers to a nudge as an intentional altering of someone's behavior by triggering "shallow cognitive processes" without interfering with their freedom of choice (Saghai 2013, 5). So under some definitions incentives could be considered "nudges," and under others they might not be. We are unconcerned about the definitional debate in our chapter. Nothing in our ethical framework or analysis hangs on a particular definition. One of these authors has elsewhere argued that the most helpful way to think of these types of behavioral influencers as "non-argumentative but non-coercive influencers" (Blumenthal-Barby 2012, 349).
2. We are third-party researchers who are unaffiliated with either Seva Mandir or the Massachusetts Institute of Technology. We would like to thank Seva Mandir for giving us permission to conduct interviews with the women at their immunization camps.
3. Intervention ladder by Nuffield Council on Bioethics: do nothing or simply monitor the current situation; provide information; enable choice; guide choice through changing the default policy; guide choice through incentives; guide choice through disincentives; restrict choice; eliminate choice.

4. A limitation of our analysis is that we were only able to interview mothers in the incentive group who vaccinated their children, not mothers who did not participate and might have been opposed to vaccination or the incentive. Additional limitations were language and cultural barriers since we had to rely on a translator for our interviews, and the fact that our interviewer's (JK) presence could have influenced the subjects' responses.

References

Antommaria, Armand H. Matheny. 2013. "An Ethical Analysis of Mandatory Influenza Vaccination of Health Care Personnel: Implementing Fairly and Balancing Benefits and Burdens." *The American Journal of Bioethics* 13:30–37.

Ashcroft, Richard E. 2011. "Personal Financial Incentives in Health Promotion: Where Do They Fit in an Ethic of Autonomy?" *Health Expectations* 14:191–200.

Banerjee, A. V., E. Duflo, R. Glennerster, and D. Kothari. 2010. "Improving Immunisation Coverage in Rural India: Clustered Randomised Controlled Evaluation of Immunisation Campaigns with and without Incentives." *British Medical Journal* 340:c2220–c2220.

Banerjee, Abhijit, Angus Deaton, and Esther Duflo. 2004. "Health Care Delivery in Rural Rajasthan." *Economic and Political Weekly* 39:944–49.

Banerjee, Abhijit, and Esther Duflo. 2011. "Low-Hanging Fruit for Better (Global) Health?" In *Poor Economics: A Radical Rethinking of the Way to Fight Global Poverty*. Reprint ed. Public Affairs. New York. 41–70.

Blumenthal-Barby, J. S. 2012. "Between Reason and Coercion: Ethically Permissible Influence in the Context of Health Care and Health Policy." *Kennedy Institute of Ethics Journal* 22(4):345–66.

Blumenthal-Barby, J. S., and H. Burroughs. 2012. "Seeking Better Healthcare Outcomes: The Ethics of Using the 'Nudge.'" *The American Journal of Bioethics* 12:1–10.

Childress, James F., Ruth R. Faden, Ruth D. Gaare, Lawrence O. Gostin, Jeffrey Kahn, Richard J. Bonnie, Nancy E. Kass, Anna C. Mastroianni, Jonathan D. Moreno, and Phillip Nieburg. 2002. "Public Health Ethics: Mapping the Terrain." *Journal of Law and Medical Ethics* 30:170–78.

Daniels, N. 2000. "Accountability for Reasonableness." *British Medical Journal (Clinical Research Edition)*. 321:1300–1301.

Daniels, Norman, and James Sabin. 1997. "Limits to Health Care: Fair Procedures, Democratic Deliberation, and the Legitimacy Problem for Insurers." *Philosophy and Public Affairs* 26:303–50.

Hepple, Bob, ed. 2007. *Public Health: Ethical Issues*. Edited by Bob Hepple. Nuffield Council on Bioethics. London.

Kaplan, Julika. 2013. "An Ethical Analysis of Incentives as 'Nudges' toward Better Health Outcomes: A Case Study of Seva Mandir's Immunization Program in Rural Udaipur." *Independent Study Project (ISP) Collection* Paper 1537. http://digitalcollections.sit.edu/isp _collection/1537.

Kass, Nancy E. 2001. "An Ethics Framework for Public Health." *American Journal of Public Health* 91(11):1776–82.

Lange, Margaret Meek, Wendy Rogers, and Susan Dodds. 2013. "Vulnerability in Research Ethics: A Way Forward." *Bioethics* 27:333–40.

London, Alex John, David A. Borasky, Anant Bhan, and Ethics Working Group of the HIV Prevention Trials Network. 2012. "Improving Ethical Review of Research Involving Incentives for Health Promotion." *PLoS Medicine* 9:e1001193.

Mullainathan, Sendhil, and Eldar Shafir. 2013. "Freeing Up Intelligence." *Scientific American Mind* 25(1):58–63.

Rawls, John. 1971. *A Theory of Justice.* Rev. ed. Belknap Press of Harvard University Press. Cambridge, MA.

Saghai, Yashar. 2013. "Salvaging the Concept of Nudge." *Journal of Medical Ethics* 39:487–93.

Thaler, Richard, and Cass R. Sunstein. 2008. *Nudge: Improving Decisions about Health, Wealth, and Happiness.* Yale University Press. New Haven, CT.

United Nations. 2013. "Goal 4: Reduce Child Mortality Fact Sheet." Millennium Development Goals and Beyond 2015. http://www.un.org/millenniumgoals/pdf/Goal_4_fs.pdf.

World Health Organization. 2014. *Global Immunization Data: July 2014.* www.who.int /immunization/monitoring_surveillance/global_immunization_data.pdf.

CHAPTER 9

Behavioral Economics and Food Policy
The Limits of Nudging

Andrea Freeman

The U.S. Congress classified pizza as a vegetable for the purposes of satisfying fruit and vegetable quotas in public school lunches (Jalonick 2011) during a nationally recognized childhood obesity crisis. In the following year's spending bill, Congress prohibited the federal government from restricting the amount of salt in school lunches and created exceptions to whole grain requirements for pasta and tortillas (Pear 2014), despite extensive research linking high sodium and white flour to serious health and weight problems. These two legislative acts significantly impeded progress toward solving an urgent public health issue.

Faced with these types of limitations, the U.S. Department of Agriculture (USDA) has focused its efforts to reform unhealthy eating habits primarily on the Cornell Center for Behavioral Economics in Child Nutrition. The center's mandate is to conduct, sponsor, and disseminate research on food selection, with the objective of incorporating behavioral economics principles into the federal food programs, including the National School Lunch and School Breakfast Program, the Supplemental Nutrition Assistance Program, and the Food Stamp program. These programs primarily assist low-income individuals and disproportionately serve Blacks, Latinos, Indians, and other racially marginalized groups. The programs' success therefore has the potential either to perpetuate or to reduce existing socioeconomic and racial health disparities, which contribute significantly to broader inequality.

Behavioral economics represents only one tool among many available to the government to combat obesity and improve health outcomes. For example, the USDA uses high-impact marketing strategies, such as partnerships with fast food companies, to increase consumption of subsidized commodities, which include dairy, corn, wheat, meat, and soy (Shanker 2015; Butler 2014; Fields 2004). These tactics depart significantly from the principles of choice architecture, which is a form of libertarian paternalism that focuses on the environments in which people make choices. Dividing food policy into three categories—hard paternalism, aggressive soft paternalism, and gentle soft paternalism—highlights the differences in the government's approaches that depend on its objective. This categorization suggests that financial concerns, such as subsidies and industry goodwill, compel the use of strategies proven to influence consumer behavior. Health concerns, in contrast, tend to generate less impactful policies.

The Cornell Center's studies indicate that nudging, a form of institutional design that seeks to alter behavior predictably without foreclosing options or dramatically changing costs, has the potential to influence food selection. These studies do not, however, demonstrate a significant link between nudging techniques and improved health outcomes. Further, even when experiments show that behavioral economics can positively alter food selection, the USDA has not widely implemented changes to school lunchrooms or other federal food programs accordingly. Nonetheless, the USDA continues to invest in behavioral economics research and favor gentle soft paternalism to boost health through nutrition.

This chapter begins by exploring the three different forms of paternalism available in the food policy arsenal, emphasizing the behavioral economics principles and studies of the Cornell Center. It then discusses the potential of nudging strategies to reduce obesity and improve health outcomes within a number of constraints. It interrogates the disproportionate harm these constraints inflict on socially marginalized communities and concludes by proposing a shift in food policy to a harder paternalistic framework.

Paternalism in Food Policy

The government employs a broad range of tactics to meet its nutritional, health, and subsidized commodity sales goals. Most of them represent some form of paternalism, the desire to influence or alter people's behavior in their own self-interest. Other strategies reflect a mandate to create or sustain a market for subsidized commodities or to satisfy the demands of the food industry. Some paternalistic measures seek to alter the method of arriving at a choice ("means paternalism"), and others strive to affect the choice itself ("ends paternalism") (Sunstein 2013, 1855–56). Paternalistic methods can be either "hard" or "soft" (Sunstein 2013, 1858–61). With hard paternalistic measures, the government makes the choice for the consumer, or creates significant penalties, usually economic, for making a different choice. Soft paternalism is libertarian; it preserves personal choice. Paternalistic strategies generally lie on a spectrum between these extremes.

This chapter divides soft paternalism into two further categories: aggressive and gentle. Aggressive soft paternalism motivates primarily through economic incentives, and includes marketing techniques such as creating and marketing new food products. Gentle soft paternalism seeks to alter behavior through information provision and other cognitive strategies, including nutrition labeling, public school lunchroom design, and food payment method innovations. Both forms of soft paternalism strive for asymmetry, aiming to have little or no impact on fully rational individuals while creating opportunities for large gains for individuals who experience bounded rationality (Simon 2000). The negative effects of time, information, and cognitive processes on optimal decision-making create bounded rationality. Food decisions are particularly susceptible to bounded rationality because of the powerful motivations behind them, including hunger, sensory stimulation, and the desire for immediate gratification.

Gentle Soft Paternalism

Gentle soft paternalism in food policy consists primarily of nutrition labeling requirements, imposed through the Nutrition Labeling and Education Act (NLEA) and Patient Protection and Affordable Care Act (PPACA), and research into choice architecture, through funding of the Cornell Center. The Cornell Center investigates the effects on student food selection of a variety of nudging techniques, including payment systems, pre-ordering, priming through the availability of "trigger foods" (foods that influence selection by their presence, even though they are not themselves selected), convenience, branding, and descriptive food naming (Cornell Center for Behavioral Economics in Child Nutrition Programs 2014). This research relies on a number of behavioral economics observations that may affect food selection.

The foundational behavioral economics principles of the Cornell Center's project are as follows: (1) lack of self-control, resulting from a desire for immediate gratification or simple hunger, is an obstacle to healthy food selection; (2) people tend to select default options because they value what they already possess more highly than items they have not yet acquired; (3) people engage in mental accounting that inclines them to use up an amount designated for a certain type of purchase before delving into another "account"; (4) people prefer items with fixed costs over ones with variable costs; (5) food decisions more often depend on emotional factors, such as stress and comfort, than on rational cognitive processing; and (6) environmental factors, including noise, lighting, and distractions, influence food choice (Just, Mancino, and Wansink 2007). Other psychological conditions that affect food selection are reactance, an aversion to choices that others appear to force on us (Watanabe 2011), and self-attribution, the satisfaction associated with making our own decisions in our own best interests (Just and Wansink 2009).

Based on these underlying principles and insights, the Cornell Center's researchers design nudges intended to help students and other food program participants overcome their cognitive biases. One of these nudges is the preselection of food. Preselection counters struggles with self-control and impulsivity and allows students to make intellectual, instead of emotional, food choices (Gupta 2014; Hanks, Just, and Wansink 2013). Another nudge is the creation of a default option of fruit instead of fries in school lunchrooms (Just and Wansink 2009). For food stamp recipients, the center proposes designating some stamps exchangeable only for healthy foods, to take advantage of the mental accounting process (Just, Mancino, and Wansink 2007). In lunchrooms, permitting payment by prepaid debit cards for nutritious foods while allowing only cash payments for less healthy items promotes healthier choices (Wansink, Just, and Payne 2010). Displaying healthy foods prominently and accessibly appeals to positive emotional impulses (Just and Wansink 2009). Smaller tables combined with brighter lights can render the quality and amount of food consumed more salient, leading to a desire to choose better (Stroebel and De Castro 2004).

The Cornell Center also tests the effects of eliminating some unhealthy choices altogether. One study removed chocolate milk from eleven school cafeterias in Oregon (Hanks, Just, and Wansink 2014). As a result, students in those schools drank 10% less milk overall and wasted 29% percent more milk. Their consumption of both sugar and calories decreased. Nonetheless, the study concludes that chocolate milk should remain in school cafeterias. It further recommends shifting the position of white milk to the front of the cafeteria and ensuring that one-third to one-half of the milk on display is white.

In another study, researchers sent an email containing a nutritional report card to the parents of twenty-seven students from kindergarten to twelfth grade in an upstate New York school (Wansink, Just, and Patterson 2012). The report informed parents how many fruits, vegetables, starches, milk, snacks, and à la carte items their children selected from the cafeteria every day for six weeks. The study compares the food choices of students whose parents received emails with a control group. Children whose parents received the report cards took 8% more servings of fruits and vegetables while chocolate chip cookie purchases by this group fell by 56% percent. The study concludes that nudging parents to influence their children's choices is easy, inexpensive, and effective.

Other studies demonstrate that convenience and branding affect food selection. For example, selling apple slices instead of whole apples increases apple sales (Wansink et al. 2013). Children select more apples when a character icon appears with the apple (Wansink, Just, and Payne 2012). Also, adults may be more willing to try new foods that have appealing descriptive names, such as "Satin Chocolate Pudding" instead of "Chocolate Pudding" and "Grandma's Zucchini Cookies" instead of "Zucchini Cookies" (Wansink, van Ittersum, and Painter 2005). The Cornell Center views information as one of the key elements of food selection. This perspective accords with nutritional information's primacy in food policy. Under the PPACA, chain restaurants with more than twenty outlets must post calorie counts (21 U.S.C. §343(q)(5)(H)). The definition of "restaurant" includes vending machines, movie theaters, and grocery stores (Federal Register 79, no. 230 2014). These requirements bring food providers closer in line with food manufacturers, which must display a label titled "Nutrition Facts" listing calories, sugars, fat, saturated fat, vitamins A and C, calcium, iron, fiber, and carbohydrates on their products. Manufacturers may also voluntarily post other nutritional content.

Choice architecture and nutrition labeling are gentle soft paternalistic tactics because they impose minimal, if any, costs on consumers, institutions, and corporations, while unequivocally preserving the individual's ability to make his or her own food choices.

Aggressive Soft Paternalism

Aggressive soft paternalism also maintains personal choice but creates strong incentives for individuals to make specific food selections through the regulation of taxes and advertising. Additionally, it seeks to influence consumers through marketing strategies employed to sell subsidized commodities, which involve substantial expenditures of taxpayer dollars. Aggressive soft paternalism has either a direct or indirect economic impact on consumers and businesses, as opposed to simply an emotional or behavioral one. These methods therefore tend to be more effective than the intellectual and cognitive appeals of gentle soft paternalism. The marketing of subsidized commodities, however, is not clearly paternalistic because it advances the government's objective of promoting certain agricultural industries instead of the individual's self-interest in good health. Nonetheless, to the extent that individuals' interests are aligned with their government's goals, these tactics are paternalistic because policies that advance the common good also benefit the individual, even if indirectly.

Several scholars advocate for the imposition of "junk food taxes" on either consumers or manufacturers to make healthy food relatively more affordable in comparison and to correct for the artificially low cost of fast food resulting from agricultural subsidies. Although other countries, most notably Mexico, successfully use taxes to control harmful food consumption, the United States generally resists this type of measure (O'Connor 2016). In 2014, however, the City of Berkeley became the first municipality to impose a soda tax (Goetz 2014). Studies of this tax will indicate its potential efficacy in reducing soda consumption. Research to date demonstrates that significant price increases deter some Americans from unhealthy eating, but minor alterations in price do not affect consumer behavior (Golan, Mancino, and Unnevehr 2009). Manufacturers, however, may be more responsive than consumers to small changes in costs through taxation because of their scale of production.

Restrictions on food advertising, another form of aggressive soft paternalism, generate strong opposition from food companies, which argue that First Amendment commercial speech principles guarantee freedom in advertising. Thus, although countries such as England, Ireland, South Korea, Spain, and France restrict food advertising directed at children (World Cancer Research Fund International 2014), Congress has failed to pass similar bills modeled on World Health Organization guidelines and American Academy of Pediatrics recommendations. So far, organizations representing food corporations and advertising agencies that oppose these bills have lobbied successfully for self-regulation instead of government intervention. An exception to this trend is the proposed rule restricting the advertisement of specific products in school lunchrooms (Federal Register 79, no. 38 2014, 10693). These restrictions, however, would guide rather than foreclose companies' advertising, by allowing, for example, ads for Diet but not regular Coca-Cola.

The USDA's attempts to promote dairy consumption through marketing represent another form of aggressive soft paternalism. To reduce the surplus of high-fat milk resulting from the federal Dietary Guidelines' advice to consume low-fat dairy products, the USDA used a dairy farmers' check-off program to establish a marketing branch, DMI (U.S. Department of Agriculture 2010). DMI created the wildly successful, twenty-year "Got Milk?" advertising campaign featuring celebrities with milk moustaches. It also entered into covert partnerships with fast food companies to devise new products with increased amounts of cheese, such as Dominos' seven-cheese American Legends pizza line (Moss 2010). DMI additionally worked with supermarket chains to set up sampling displays of cheese products across the country.

Aggressive soft paternalistic strategies generally succeed at altering consumer behavior. That is why the industry strongly opposes their implementation when threatened with reduced sales, and the government seeks to hide its use of these tactics when they run against consumer interest.

Hard Paternalism

Bans and restrictions represent the hardest form of paternalism in food policy. Congress, state legislatures, and municipal bodies have overlapping authority to prohibit or limit food ingredients, based on their harmfulness to health or other reasons, such as import rules. Congress, however, is generally reluctant to regulate harmful foods. For example, in 2013, the U.S. Food and Drug Administration (FDA) proposed removing trans fats from its "generally recognized as safe" category. This proposal came more than fifteen years after medical research revealed that trans fats cause 7,000 deaths and 20,000 heart attacks in the United States every year (U.S. Food and Drug Administration 2013). Instead of responding to these discoveries with a ban, as other countries did, the FDA took the less aggressive path of imposing labeling requirements on products containing trans fats over a five-year span (U.S. Food and Drug Administration 2013).

The last time the FDA declared a food additive unsafe was in 1969, when it banned the artificial sweetener cyclamate due to its links to birth defects, bladder cancer, and liver damage (Pierson, Hsu, and Morin 2013). There are many food ingredients banned in other countries, however, that remain legal and in common usage in the United States, despite their links to serious health issues such as brain cancer, nerve cell deterioration, organ damage, infertility, and birth defects. These ingredients include petroleum-based artificial dyes, olestra, brominated vegetable oil, potassium bromate, azodicarbonamide, butylated hydroxyanisole (BHA), butylated hydroxytoluene (BHT), the synthetic growth hormones rBGH and rBST, and arsenic (Calton and

Calton 2013). They are present in a range of popular foods, from M&Ms to milk to macaroni and cheese.

State and local governments, on the other hand, have experimented with harsher restrictions. Twenty-one states ban the sale of unpasteurized milk (Hendrick and Far-quhar 2012.). California and New York City banned trans fats from restaurants (Public Health Law Center 2009). New York Mayor Michael Bloomberg attempted to ban the sale of large sugar-sweetened beverages, but a judge overturned the ban (New York Statewide Coalition of Hispanic Chambers of Commerce v. New York City Department of Health and Mental Hygiene 2014). Mississippi, conversely, has a law prohibiting food bans by the state (M.S. S.B. 2687 2013). These laws represent hard paternalism because they remove choice from the consumer, except for Mississippi's statute, which takes a strong anti-regulatory stance.

Instead of banning foods outright, the government can place restrictions on them, by location, amount, or consumer. For example, the FDA imposed some limits on the amounts of fat, calories, sugar, and sodium in products sold in school vending machines and cafeterias, such as sodas and sports drinks, beginning in 2015 (Federal Register 78, no. 125 2014, 39068). These requirements follow on the heels of states, including California, Massachusetts, and New York, that restrict the amount of fat and sugar in products that school lunchrooms sell to students (CA S.B. 12 2005; Rock 2005). A San Francisco law conditioned the inclusion of toys in McDonalds' Happy Meals, marketed to children, on the meals' meeting certain nutritional standards (Park 2011). These restrictions constitute hard paternalism because they limit consumers' control over their food choices.

Government subsidies also function as a type of hard paternalism because financial support for certain foods creates high supply levels. Subsidization lowers costs for farmers and producers, which allows them to harvest and produce more. Wider availability of the food item combined with lower production costs leads to lower prices, which induce consumers to purchase more. The dairy, corn, soy, and wheat industries receive substantial support from the USDA, leading to their presence in a large number of products available in grocery stores, restaurants, and federal food programs. (Coppess and Paulson 2014; Collins 2014; Kick 2014). The USDA also distributes formula, containing either dairy or soy, free through its nutrition program for Women, Infants, and Children (Freeman 2013, 2015a).

In some instances, subsidies create a surplus that can drive other food policies and practices geared toward selling the surplus to consumers (Freeman 2015c). For example, the subsidies that the USDA provides to corn growers go primarily to large agricultural operations. These large-scale farms use growing techniques that render the corn they produce unpalatable for direct consumption. The farmers must therefore sell this corn to other industries, primarily sweetened beverage manufacturers, which use high-fructose corn syrup in soft, energy, and sports drinks. This interdependency gives the USDA a high stake in the sales of these beverages, which may account for the government's reluctance to ban them from schools.

Limits on the Effectiveness of Gentle Soft Paternalistic Food Policy

Food policy grounded in gentle soft paternalism, specifically nudging and nutrition labeling, faces major obstacles to the effective reform of eating habits and the broader goal of improving health outcomes (Freeman 2015b). The Cornell Center identifies price, income, and information as the three major elements of food selection (Just, Mancino, and Wansink 2007). Convenience and taste are also significant. Research shows, however, that preferences for unhealthy food are "sticky," meaning resistant to change through behavioral and cognitive manipulation, for a number of reasons. One is that food companies devote large amounts of resources to finding the ideal combination of sugar, salt, and fat that will make food addictive (Moss 2013). The pleasure and comfort induced by the resulting products may have particular appeal to individuals who struggle financially or suffer from health issues. Food companies also study how to increase consumption once hunger is satiated, focusing on emotional rather than nutritional needs (Lambert et al. 1991; McCormick 2001). Behavioral economics techniques employed by food marketers, in addition to social conditions and industry capture of government policy, also reduce the potential to improve food selection and health through cognitive-based methods.

Information about the nutritional content of food, delivered on menu boards and product labels, may affect food selection but does not appear to improve health outcomes. One study reports that, although adults and teenagers notice calorie counts in restaurants, they do not alter their choices because of them (Harnack et al. 2008). Behavioral economics provides two possible explanations for this. First, information acquisition simply may not have the power to increase self-control. Individuals tend toward impulsivity in food selection, and environmental factors at the point of purchase, such as colors, smells, and positioning of products, often exert greater influence than rational thinking about diet and health. Second, people have a limited capacity to process new information—they simply do not have room for it in their heads at the moment that they confront it.

Another study shows that posted calories can lead to healthier choices, but that consumers reward themselves for making better selections by adding on an unhealthy item, such as fries or a dessert, making the overall meal less healthy (Wisdom, Downs, and Loewenstein 2010). Studies of nutrition labels on packaged products similarly reveal no decrease in intake of calories, saturated fats, or sodium (Variyam 2008). Instead, research indicates that nutrition information is most valuable to consumers who are already healthy, leading to no overall societal benefit (Variyam 2005; Wisdom, Downs, and Loewenstein 2010). This outcome is inapposite to the goals of asymmetric paternalism (Camerer et al. 2003), because the information affects only those who appear to be operating with full rationality while having no impact at all on those experiencing bounded rationality.

Labeling might, however, have a greater effect on consumer behavior if its messages were clearer. The former head of the FDA, David Kessler, proposed a radical change to product labeling that would list the three top ingredients, the number of calories per serving, and the amount of additional ingredients on a clearly visible label on the front of each product (Kessler 2014). This design might increase consumers' comprehension of the nutrition label and lead to healthier choices. Also, using plain language about the actual effects on the body of consuming the product appears to alter behavior. For example, six corner stores in predominantly Black Baltimore neighborhoods posted large, brightly colored signs on refrigerators that contained sweetened beverages stating how long it would take to walk off the calories in the drink (Bleich et al. 2014). There was a corresponding decrease in the number of calories purchased and the amount of adolescent shoppers selecting sugary beverages dropped from 98% to 89%. Similarly, a study conducted at Massachusetts General Hospital used labels coded with red, yellow, and green (colors associated with traffic lights) to indicate items that were healthy, less healthy, or contained little or no nutritional value (McGreevey 2012). This intervention increased sales of healthy foods and decreased purchases of unhealthy ones.

Despite these promising results, there are significant structural constraints on the ability of any type of information to improve health. The relationship between price and income, identified as crucial to food selection by the Cornell Center, represents more than a desire to maximize the amount of calories available for purchase on a fixed budget. Price and income are two factors among many socioeconomic conditions that determine food choice, including wealth (assets beyond income), debt, neighborhood, access to transportation, number of jobs held, and familial responsibilities, including childcare. The potential for behavioral economics to alter food selection becomes irrelevant when the sole purveyor of grocery items in a neighborhood does not offer any products with healthful ingredients. Similarly, if fast food is the only type of restaurant within walking distance, working families who rely on public transportation and have limited time to cook will eat it. In these and other ways, a person's socioeconomic status and race, both correlated to and distinct from class, determine food choice.

Social and economic constraints render the nutritional content of government-provided food of paramount importance. Food assistance is essential for the 50 million Americans living under the poverty line (Boyer 2014), the 31 million children eating school lunches (Hellmich 2013), and the more than 9 million women and children receiving Special Nutritional Assistance for Women and Children (U.S. Department of Agriculture 2014). Children in school lunch programs consume more than half of their daily calories at school (Story, Kaphingst, and French 2006). Although market forces shape the eating environment outside schools, particularly in low-income and rural areas, the government has the power to act independently of the market and provide nutritious food in the sites where it exercises control.

Instead, unfortunately, the market presently operates inside, in addition to outside, schools. Fast food companies provide essential financial support to underfunded schools and receive access to classrooms and cafeterias in return (Freeman 2007). The food industry also maintains a close relationship with the government through well-resourced lobbying efforts, generous political campaign contributions, and a "revolving door" between prominent government and industry positions. Food companies' resulting influence manifests itself in many areas of food policy, including the development of standards for school lunches and the recommendations provided by the federal Dietary Guidelines (Nestle 2007).

Food Oppression: Disproportionate Racial and Socioeconomic Effects of USDA Policy

The harms arising from industry control over food policy are universal, but they have a disproportionate negative impact on certain communities. For example, selling subsidized commodities to consumers primarily through fast food, prepackaged processed foods, and sweetened beverages disproportionately harms low-income, urban communities of color. Individuals living in these settings have diets high in fast food and "junk" foods due to structural factors that include lack of access to healthy foods in their neighborhoods (Freeman 2007). These groups also rely heavily on food assistance programs such as school lunches and food banks (Feeding America 2010). Health data reveal racial disparities in food-related illnesses and deaths, with Blacks, Latinos, Native Hawaiians, and other racialized groups suffering from significantly higher incidences of many serious food-related conditions such as cancer, heart disease, diabetes, and high blood pressure (Hurt et al. 2010; Center for Medicare Advocacy 2014; Agency for Health Care Research and Quality 2011). The disproportionate, harmful impact on socially and politically marginalized individuals of food policy is a form of food oppression.

Food oppression is institutional, systemic, food-related action or policy that physically debilitates a socially subordinated group (Freeman 2013). Food oppression theory attributes racial and socioeconomic health disparities to policies and practices that appear neutral yet disproportionately harm vulnerable individuals. Popular narratives about personal responsibility exacerbate these disparities by obscuring the structural factors that truly determine food choice and negating the government's responsibility to ensure its citizens' good health. Racial stereotypes that, for example, characterize Blacks and Latinos as lazy, weak-willed, and unintelligent (Puhl and Heuer 2012), embodied in tropes such as the "welfare queen" and the "illegal immigrant," further the misperception that health corresponds to individual attributes.

The food policy focus on behavioral economics embraces the paradigm of health as a reflection of personal choice. Behavioral economics research's role in food policy is to use government resources to discover how to alter individual decision-making in one's own interest. Approaching food policy from this perspective veils the structural factors that create and enforce the parameters of food choice, causing them to disappear from view as health determinants. Racial stereotyping reinforces the ideas that structural reform would be both irrelevant and futile, making strategies such as behavioral economics appear more appropriate. Therefore, although behavioral economics has some potential to improve health by influencing individual choice, it will not be effective unless it is only one of many policy tools used to expand the choices of less privileged individuals. Expending resources on behavioral economics without enacting laws and regulations designed to improve the health of individuals who depend on federal food programs therefore represents a form of food oppression.

Conclusion

"[W]hen social welfare calls for a stronger response [than nudging], we should give it serious consideration" (Sunstein 2013, 1835). Poor diet and exercise overtook smoking as the leading cause of premature deaths in the United States in 2014 (National Center for Chronic Disease Prevention and Health Promotion 2015). The high number of illnesses and deaths associated with poor nutrition, particularly in comparison to similarly situated nations (Tandon et al. 2000, 18), along with dramatic racial health disparities point to the need for direct interventions in the form of hard paternalistic measures. The USDA should alter agricultural subsidies to reflect desired consumption choices, emphasizing fruits and vegetables over milk, corn, soy, meat, and wheat. To achieve this, the USDA should not be tasked with the conflicting roles of promoting both healthy eating and agricultural industries. It should be free from the influence of the food and beverage industries through campaign contributions, lobbying efforts, and revolving door positions.

The USDA should also transform school lunches by taking choice architecture to its logical conclusion and offering only healthy food choices. Faced with this reality, hungry students will eat. Generally, the USDA should shift its resources away from behavioral economics, information provision, and education, and toward systemic changes in the food system that would promote the production and distribution of healthy food to individuals serviced by nutrition assistance programs. As a first step, the USDA should recognize the limits of nudging, and prioritize consumer over industry health.

References

Agency for Healthcare Research and Quality. 2011. "Disparities in Health Care Quality among Racial and Ethnic Minority Groups: Selected Findings from the AHRQ 2010 NHQR and NHDR." http://www.ahrq.gov/qual/nhqrdr10/nhqrdrminority10.htm.

Bleich, Sara N., Julia A. Wolfson, Seanna Vine, and Y. Claire Wang. 2014. "Diet-Beverage Consumption and Caloric Intake among US Adults, Overall and by Body Weight." *American Journal of Public Health* 104:3. http://ajph.aphapublications.org/doi/pdf/10.2105/AJPH.2013.301556.

Boyer, Dave. 2014. "That's Rich: Poverty Level under Obama Breaks 50 Year Level." *Washington Times*, January 7. http://www.washingtontimes.com/news/2014/jan/7/obamas-rhetoric-on-fighting-poverty-doesnt-match-h/?page=all.

Butler, Kiera. 2014. "How the US Government Helps McDonald's Sell Junk Food." *Mother Jones*, June 23. http://www.motherjones.com/environment/2014/06/usda-dairy-checkoff-mcdonalds-taco-bell.

Calton, Mira, and Jayson Calton. 2013. *Rich Food Poor Food: The Ultimate Grocery Purchasing System*. Primal Blueprint Publishing. Malibu.

Camerer, Colin, Samuel Issacharoff, George Loewenstein, Ted O'Donoghue, and Matthew Rabin. 2003. "Regulation for Conservatives: Behavioral Economics and the Case for 'Asymmetric Paternalism.'" *University of Pennsylvania Law Review* 151: 1211–54.

The Center for Media and Democracy. 2013. "National Corn Growers Association." Source-Watch. September 9. http://www.sourcewatch.org/index.php/National_Corn_Growers_Association.

Center for Medicare Advocacy, Inc. 2014. "Racial and Ethnic Healthcare Disparities." http://www.medicareadvocacy.org/medicare-info/health-care-disparities/.

Collins, Laura. 2014. "The 2014 Farm Bill Subsidy Reforms Don't Go Far Enough." American Action Forum. http://americanactionforum.org/research/the-2014-farm-bill-subsidy-reforms-dont-go-far-enough.

Coppess, Jonathan, and Nick Paulson. 2014. "Agriculture Risk Coverage and Price Loss Coverage in the 2014 Farm Bill." FarmdocDAILY. February 20. http://farmdocdaily.illinois.edu/2014/02/arc-and-plc-in-2014-farm-bill.html.

Cornell Center for Behavioral Economics in Child Nutrition Programs. 2014. "Grants & Research." http://ben.dyson.cornell.edu/grants-and-research.html.

Feeding America. 2010. "When the Pantry Is Bare: Emergency Food Assistance and Hispanic Children." http://www.feedingamerica.org/hunger-in-america/our-research/latino-hunger-research/latino-hunger-exec-summ.pdf.

Fields, Scott. 2004. "The Fat of the Land: Do Agricultural Subsidies Foster Poor Health?" *Environmental Health Perspectives* 112, no. 14:A820–A823. http://www.ncbi.nlm.nih.gov/pmc/articles/PMC1247588/.

"Food Labeling; Nutrition Labeling of Standard Menu Items in Restaurants and Similar Retail Food Establishments." 2014. *Federal Register*. December 1. https://www.federalregister.gov/articles/2014/12/01/2014-27833/food-labeling-nutrition-labeling-of-standard-menu-items-in-restaurants-and-similar-retail-food#h-14.

Freeman, Andrea. 2007. "Fast Food: Oppression through Poor Nutrition." *California Law Review* 95:2221.

———. 2015a. "'First Food' Justice: Racial Disparities in Infant Feeding as Food Oppression." *Fordham Law Review* 83:3053, 3068.

———. 2015b. "Transparency for Food Consumers: Nutrition Labeling and Food Oppression." *American Journal of Law and Medicine* 41:315–30.

———. 2013. "The Unbearable Whiteness of Milk: Food Oppression and the USDA." *University of California at Irvine Law Review* 4:1251, 1253.

———. 2015c. "The 2014 Farm Bill: Farm Subsidies and Food Oppression." *Seattle University Law Review* 38:1271, 1280.

Goetz, Gretchen. 2014. "Berkeley Puts First Soda Tax on the Books." *Food Safety News.* November 6. http://www.foodsafetynews.com/2014/11/berkeley-puts-first-soda-tax-on-the -books/#.VKMsIyvF8c0.

Golan, Elise, Lisa Mancino, and Laurian Unnevehr. 2009. "Food Policy: Check the List of Ingredients." U.S. Department of Agriculture Economic Research Service. June 1. http://www.ers.usda.gov/amber-waves/2009-june/food-policy-check-the-list-of-ingredients .aspx#.VL7KHi7F9XA.

Gupta, Sonam. 2014. "The Effects of Pre-Selection and Behavioral Nudges on Food Item Selection by Middle School Children, Association of Public Policy Analysis and Manage- ment." Association for Public Policy Analysis and Management. November 7. http://appam .confex.com/appam/2014/webprogram/Paper11016.html.

Hanks, Andrew, David Just, and Brian Wansink. 2014. "Chocolate Milk Consequences: A Pilot Study Evaluating the Consequences of Banning Chocolate Milk in School Cafeterias." *PLOS One.* April 16. http://www.plosone.org/article/info%3Adoi%2F10.1371%2Fjournal.pone .0091022.

———. 2013. "Pre-Ordering School Lunch Encourages Better Food Choices by Children." *JAMA Pediatrics* 167:7. http://papers.ssrn.com/sol3/papers.cfm?abstract_id=2473781.

Harnack, Lisa J., Simone A. French, J. Michael Oakes, Mary T. Story, Robert W. Jeffrey, and Sarah A. Rydell. 2008. "Effects of Calorie Labeling and Value Size Pricing on Fast Food Meal Choices: Results from an Experimental Trial." *International Journal of Behavioral Nutrition and Physical Activity* 5:63. http://www.ncbi.nlm.nih.gov/pmc/articles /PMC2621234/.

Hellmich, Nanci. 2013. "More Kids Skip School Lunch, But Breakfasts Are Up." *USA Today*, August 21. News sec. 3A. http://www.usatoday.com/story/news/nation/2013/08/20/school -breakfast-up-lunch-down/2673275/.

Hendrick, Scott, and Doug Farquhar. 2012. "Summary of Raw Milk Statutes and Administra- tive Codes." National Conference of State Legislatures. http://www.ncsl.org/documents /agri/NCSL_Raw_Milk_Memo.pdf.

Hurt, Ryan T., Christopher Kulisek, Laura A. Buchanan, and Stephen A. McClave. 2010. "The Obesity Epidemic: Challenges, Health Initiatives, and Implications for Gastroenterolo- gists." *Gastroenterology & Hepatology* 6(12):780–92. http://www.ncbi.nlm.nih.gov/pmc /articles/PMC3033553/pdf/GH-06-780.pdf.

Jalonick, Mary Clare. 2011. "Pizza Is a Vegetable? Congress Says Yes." *NBC News.* Novem- ber 15. http://www.nbcnews.com/id/45306416/ns/health-diet_and_nutrition/t/pizza -vegetable-congress-says-yes/#.VKM8zCvF8c0.

Just, David R., Lisa Mancino, and Brian Wansink. 2007. "Could Behavioral Economics Help Improve Diet Quality for Nutrition Assistance Participants?" *U.S. Department of Agriculture Economic Research Report No. 43.* http://www.ers.usda.gov/media/196728/err43_1_.pdf.

Just, David, and Brian Wansink. 2009. "Smarter Lunchrooms: Using Behavioral Economics to Improve Meal Selection." *Choices* 24:3. http://www.choicesmagazine.org/magazine/article .php?article=87.

Kessler, David. 2014. "Toward More Comprehensive Food Labeling." *New England Journal of Medicine* 371:193. http://www.nejm.org/doi/full/10.1056/NEJMp1402971.

Kick, Chris. 2014. "The 2014 Farm Bill Brings Dairy Policy Change." *Farm and Dairy*, January 30. http://www.farmanddairy.com/news/new-farm-bill-brings-dairy-policy-changes /174331.html.

Lambert, Kelly Gurley, Tara Neal, Jill Noyes, Conway Parker, and Pamela Worrel. 1991. "Food-Related Stimuli Increase Desire to Eat in Satiated and Hungry Human Subjects." *Current Psychology* 10(4):297. http://link.springer.com/article/10 .1007%2FBF02686902#page-1.

"Local School Wellness Policy Implementation under the Healthy, Hunger-Free Kids Act of 2010." 2013. *Federal Register* 78, no. 125, June 28. http://www.gpo.gov/fdsys/pkg/FR-2013 -06-28/pdf/2013-15249.pdf.

"Local School Wellness Policy Implementation under the Healthy, Hunger-Free Kids Act of 2010." 2014. *Federal Register* 79, no. 38, February 26. http://www.fns.usda.gov/sites/default /files/Local_School_Wellness_Proposed_Rule_022614.pdf.

McCormick. 2001. "Americans Crave Meats and Sweets." Press release. http://www .theuandigroup.com/pdfs/mccormick.pdf.

McGreevy, Sue. 2012. "Enlightened Eating." *Harvard Gazette*, January 19. http://news.harvard .edu/gazette/story/2012/01/enlightened-eating/.

Moss, Michael. 2013. *Salt Sugar Fat: How the Food Giants Hooked Us*. Random House. New York.

———. 2010. "While Warning about Fat, U.S. Pushes Cheese Sales." *The New York Times*, November 7, sec. A1. http://www.nytimes.com/2010/11/07/us/07fat.html?pagewanted=all.

National Alliance for Nutrition and Activity. 2010. "National Health Priorities: Reducing Obesity, Heart Disease, Cancer, Diabetes, and Other Diet- and Inactivity-Related Diseases, Costs, and Disabilities." http://cspinet.org/new/pdf/cdc_briefing_book_fy10.pdf.

National Center for Chronic Disease Prevention and Health Promotion. 2015. "Smoking and Tobacco Use." Centers for Disease Control and Prevention. http://www.cdc.gov/tobacco /data_statistics/fact_sheets/fast_facts/.

Nestle, Marion. 2007. *Food Politics: How the Food Industry Influences Nutrition and Health, Revised and Expanded Edition*. University of California Press. Oakland.

New York Statewide Coalition of Hispanic Chambers of Commerce v. New York City Department of Health and Mental Hygiene, 23 N.Y.3d 681 (2014).

O'Connor, Anahad. 2016. "Mexican Soda Tax Followed by Drop in Sugary Drink Sales." *The New York Times*, January 6. http://well.blogs.nytimes.com/2016/01/06/mexican-soda-tax -followed-by-drop-in-sugary-drink-sales/?_r=0

Park, Madison. 2011. "Happy Meal Toys No Longer Free in San Francisco." *CNN*. December 1. http://www.cnn.com/2011/11/30/health/california-mcdonalds-happy-meals/.

Pear, Robert. 2014. "In Final Spending Bill, Salty Food and Belching Cows Are Winners." *The New York Times*, December 14, sec. A1. http://www.nytimes.com/2014/12/15/us/politics/in -final-spending-bill-salty-food-and-belching-cows-are-winners.html?_r=0.

Pierson, David, Tiffany Hsu, and Monte Morin. 2013. "FDA Action Would Effectively Ban Trans Fats." *Los Angeles Times*, November 7. http://articles.latimes.com/2013/nov/07 /business/la-fi-fda-trans-fat-20131108.

Public Health Law Center. 2009. "Transfat Bans: Policy Options for Eliminating the Use of Artificial Trans Fats in Restaurants." William Mitchell College of Law. http:// publichealthlawcenter.org/sites/default/files/resources/phlc-policy-trans-fat.pdf.

Puhl, Rebecca, and Chelsea Heuer. 2012. "The Stigma of Obesity: A Review and Update." *Obesity* 17(5):941. http://onlinelibrary.wiley.com/doi/10.1038/oby.2008.636/full.

Rock, Carol. 2005. "Sampling Healthier Foods: It May Be Hard Sell to Feed Kids Well." *LA Daily News*, September 23. http://www.thefreelibrary.com/SAMPLING+HEALTHIER +FOODS+IT+MAY+BE+HARD+SELL+TO+FEED+KIDS+WELL.-a0136578439.

Shanker, Deena. 2015. "Milking It: How the US Government Helped McDonald's Climb Out of its Sales Rut." *Quartz*, October 29. http://qz.com/533505/how-the-us-government-helped -mcdonalds-climb-out-of-its-sales-rut/.

Simon, Herbert A. 2000. "Bounded Rationality in Social Science: Today and Tomorrow." *Mind & Society* 1:25–29. http://link.springer.com/article/10.1007/BF02512227#page-1.

Story, Mary, Karen Kaphingst, and Simone French. 2006. "The Role of Schools in Obesity Prevention." *Childhood Obesity* 16:111.

Stroebel, Nanette, and John De Castro. 2004. "Effect of Ambience on Food Intake and Food Choice." *Nutrition* 20:821–38.

Sunstein, Cass. 2013. "The Storrs Lectures: Behavioral Economics and Paternalism." *Yale Law Journal* 122:1826–85.

Tandon, Ajay, Christopher J. L. Murray, Jeremy A. Lauer, and David B. Evans. 2000. "Measuring Overall Health System Performance for 191 Countries." World Health Organization GPE Discussion Paper No. 30. http://www.who.int/healthinfo/paper30.pdf.

U.S. Department of Agriculture. 2010. "Report to Congress on the National Dairy Promotion and Research Program and the National Fluid Milk Processor Promotion Program 2008 Program Activities." 28:4.

———. 2014. "WIC—The Special Supplemental Nutrition Program for Women, Infants and Children: Nutrition Program Facts." http://www.fns.usda.gov/sites/default/files/WIC-Fact -Sheet.pdf.

U.S. Food and Drug Administration. 2013. "FDA Targets Trans Fat in Processed Foods." *Consumer Updates*. November 7. http://www.fda.gov/ForConsumers/ConsumerUpdates /ucm372915.htm.

———. 1994. "Nutritional Labeling and Education Act (NLEA) Requirements (8/94-2/95)." http://www.fda.gov/iceci/inspections/inspectionguides/ucm074948.htm.

Variyam, Jayachandran N. 2008. "Do Nutrition Labels Improve Dietary Outcomes?" *Health Economics* 17:695–708.

———. 2005. "Nutrition Labeling in the Food-Away-From-Home Sector, an Economic Assessment." U.S. Department of Agriculture, Economic Research Service, Economic Research Report 4. http://webarchives.cdlib.org/sw1tx36512/http://www.ers.usda.gov /publications/err4/err4.pdf.

Wansink, Brian, David Just, Andrew Hanks, and Laura E. Smith. 2013. "Finger Fruits: Pre-Sliced Fruit in Schools Increases Sales, Selection, and Intake." *American Journal of Preventative Medicine* 44(5):477. http://papers.ssrn.com/sol3/papers.cfm?abstract_id =2473208.

Wansink, Brian, David Just, and Rich Patterson. 2012. "Nudging Healthier Choices through Nutritional Report Cards." *Journal of Nutrition Education and Behavior Poster Abstracts* 44(4S):S78. http://ben.cornell.edu/pdfs/abstracts2012/nudges.pdf.

Wansink, Brian, David Just, and Collin Payne. 2012. "Can Branding Improve School Lunches?" *Archives of Pediatric and Adolescent Medicine* 166(10):967. http://papers.ssrn.com/sol3/papers .cfm?abstract_id=2079828.

———. 2010. "Payment Systems That Nudge Healthier School Lunch Choices." *Journal of the Federation of American Societies for Experimental Biology* 24 (Meeting Abstract Supplement) 322.1. http://www.fasebj.org/cgi/content/meeting_abstract/24/1_MeetingAbstracts /322.1.

Watanabe, Teresa. 2011. "L.A. Schools' Healthful Lunches Panned by LAUSD District Students." *Los Angeles Times*, December 17. http://articles.latimes.com/2011/dec/17/local/la-me-food-lausd-20111218.

Wisdom, Jessica, Julie S. Downs, and George Loewenstein. 2010. "Promoting Healthy Choices: Information versus Convenience." *American Economic Journal: Applied Economics* 2(2):164–78.

Woldow, Dana. 2012. "USDA's My Plate Should Step Up to Marketing Plate." *Civil Eats.* January 20. http://civileats.com/2012/01/20/usda's-myplate-should-step-up-to-marketing-plate/.

World Cancer Research Fund International. 2014. "Restrict Food Advertising and Other Forms of Commercial Promotion." June 11. http://www.wcrf.org/int/policy/nourishing-framework/restrict-food-marketing.

PART III **BEHAVIORAL ECONOMICS
AND HEALTHCARE COSTS**

Introduction

Matthew J. B. Lawrence

The chapters in this part use behavioral economics to shed light on, and propose partial solutions to, diverse aspects of the healthcare spending problem: Christopher T. Robertson and David V. Yokum look at policymakers' decisions about how much cost sharing to impose on insurance beneficiaries; Ameet Sarpatwari and colleagues discuss doctors' decisions about whether to prescribe branded or generic drugs; and Jim Hawkins investigates regulators' decisions about how closely to watch consumer credit arrangements in the self-pay medical market. These represent just a few of the many fronts on which we could attack the spending problem. Among other options, we might cause Americans to live healthier lives and so reduce the need for healthcare; we might provide more preventive care and thereby avoid costlier emergency care; we might encourage the invention of cheaper treatments and so reduce the actual cost of care; or we might give people less, or less costly, healthcare than they currently receive.

While we can (and the chapters in this part do) fight the battle against healthcare spending on multiple fronts, we ultimately have only one weapon at our disposal: behavior. The fundamental mechanism through which man-made laws, norms, or institutions alter real-world outcomes is by changing the behavior of individuals upstream from those outcomes.

The trouble is that it can be hard to know how (or how much) new laws, norms, or institutions will actually change behavior (and so outcomes), and so whether any particular reform will create more savings than costs. We are not behavioral marksmen. Intellectual property rules intended to spur the invention of cheaper treatments can instead promote inventions that add much cost and little value. Disclosure rules intended to encourage better (because better informed) decision-making may fail to do so (Ben-Shahar and Schneider 2011).

Indeed, the Affordable Care Act's (ACA) mandate that people purchase health insurance—backed up by the threat of tax penalties and the enticement of tax subsidies—has been deemed a success in states where one in three people subject to it complied (Dan 2014). One in three! That low standard reflects not any failing in the ACA, but rather our appreciation of just how hard it can be to prompt a particular change in the way people behave.

The authors of the chapters in this part are well aware of this challenge. While they all draw on behavioral economic theory to take on the problem of healthcare spending, I think all would also agree that, ultimately, the only way to know for sure how a particular law or institution will change behavior is to try it in practice. Indeed, they all say as much. Robertson and Yokum recognize that they cannot measure the actual magnitude of the "decisional burden" associated with giving patients healthcare spending choices that they identify. Hawkins calls for more research into the "case for intervening in the relationships between patients, doctors, and third-party medical creditors" because "translating studies conducted in one context into other contexts can lead to inaccuracy." And Sarpatwari et al. rely exclusively on context-specific support in evaluating the efficacy of interventions intended to cause physicians to prescribe (or pharmacists to provide) generic drugs.

Furthermore, the authors all appear to agree that the medical context is distinctive in ways that make reflexive application of behavioral economics especially problematic. Sick patients and busy, highly experienced (and stressed) doctors may not behave in the same way as the college students whose decision-making forms the basis for most behavioral economic theory. Robertson and Yokum emphasize that medical decisions are "profoundly difficult" because they are made in the face of scientific uncertainty and also because they implicate "existential questions about whether and how to live." Hawkins points out that, in addition to the distinctiveness of healthcare decisions, patients often lack the information about medical products and services that they usually have as to other products. And Sarpatwari and colleagues show that doctors can also be distinctive, pointing out, for example, that doctors are creatures of habit and learn better through interaction than didactic lectures.

This "knowledge problem" has been offered as a critique of behavioral economics. What good is a theoretical account of behavior, the story goes, if it recognizes that the particularities of context could always be outcome-determinative?

While recognizing the limitations of behavioral economics, the chapters in this part beg to differ. They demonstrate again and again that behavioral economic theory can help us regulate better—here, help us address the problem of healthcare spending—in three ways, despite the challenge posed by the knowledge problem.

First, a theoretical account tells us where to look; it suggests how we should focus our inquiry. Hawkins's analysis provides a nice illustration of this suggestive power. He first identifies potential problems with consumer credit in self-pay medical markets—optimism, a halo effect, and an automation effect—by applying behavioral economic theory. But he goes further, building on the theory to focus on and problematize particular aspects of consumer credit contracts in financing IVF in the real world.

Robertson and Yokum also demonstrate the value-added of behavioral economics' suggestive power. They show how behavioral economics predicts a significant unrecognized cost to cost sharing—"decisional burden" on the beneficiary—that could impact the desirability *vel non* of this means of reducing healthcare spending. Yes, additional context-specific research may show that this burden is tiny in some cases (or massive in others), but without behavioral economic insights any such burden might have gone completely unnoticed.

Second, a theoretical account gives us a common language that allows us to determine how closely contexts are related in the first place. This is how Hawkins is able to zero in on research into consumer credit markets for financing cell phones and the like to inform his analysis of how people pay for IVF. And it is how Sarpatwari et al. are able to generalize from actual studies of physician behavior to develop our understanding of how physicians learn and, so, how to educate them about generic drugs.

Third, theory gives us something better than mere guesswork to act upon in situations where we have no choice but to act. Hawkins puts it well: sometimes we "cannot wait for perfect knowledge." The problem of medical spending is just such a situation. The faster we get context-specific research the better, but policymaking cannot wait for certainty, which may itself be an unattainable goal. As such, solutions to the problem of healthcare spending based on behavioral economic theory—bedeviled by the knowledge problem though they might be—are better than solutions based on nothing at all.

References

Ben Shahar, Omri, and Carl Schneider. 2011. "The Failure of Mandated Disclosure." *University of Pennsylvania Law Review* 259:647.

Dan, Carrie. 2014. "In Polling Obamacare, a Label Makes a Big Difference." NBC News. May 12. http://www.nbcnews.com/politics/first-read/polling-obamacare-label-makes-big -difference-n102861.

CHAPTER 10

Cost Sharing as Choice Architecture

Christopher T. Robertson and David V. Yokum

Even while the Affordable Care Act (ACA) is insuring greater numbers of Americans, there is a contrary trend for the health insurance coverage to become thinner and thinner. Health insurance plans increasingly feature larger deductibles, co-pays, co-insurance, and reference prices, which are all forms of "cost sharing, " as they shift payment responsibility from insurer to patient (Kaiser Family Foundation 2014). Compared to being fully insured, an exposure to cost sharing creates a disincentive for patients to consume wasteful healthcare. However, cost sharing also causes several well-known normative problems, three of which we review herein, but argue that they can be fixed through more precision in the design of cost-sharing mechanisms. A fourth problem relates to the subject of this volume. What we refer to as the "decisional burden" is potentially endemic to any cost-sharing mechanism. It is a subjective disutility experienced by patients when navigating a difficult, and potentially unwanted, choice among a complex set of options. This burden may undermine the quality of decisions rendered, and worsen the satisfaction with any outcome.

In what follows, we explain how cost sharing can be understood as a form of choice architecture, then review and distinguish three other normative objections to this particular mechanism of reducing wasteful healthcare spending. We then identify two alternatives to cost sharing, which are useful as analytical benchmarks for comparison. We next review selections from the behavioral economics and judgment and decision-making literatures to illustrate three ways in which cost sharing may be problematic: choice overload, cognitive scarcity, and facilitation of regret. We conclude

The opinions expressed in this paper are those of the authors in their individual capacities. For a longer discussion of these and related themes, see Christopher T. Robertson and David V. Yokum, "The Burden of Deciding for Yourself: The Disutility Caused by Out-of-Pocket Healthcare Spending," *Indiana Health Law Review* 11 (2014): 609.

that the decisional burden is a real disadvantage of using patient cost sharing as a mechanism for rationing healthcare. Nonetheless, in a world of epistemic uncertainty and heterogeneity of values, it may be understandable for consumers to prefer cost sharing—if carefully designed and implemented—as the least-bad rationing mechanism among the alternatives.

Cost Sharing as Choice Architecture

Over the past several decades, cost sharing—deductibles, co-payments, co-insurance, reference pricing, and other forms—has become a primary tool to reduce the cost of health insurance (Kaiser Family Foundation 2014). Cost sharing has both a distributional function (as to how much the insurer versus the patient pays at the point of consumption) and a behavioral function (as to whether the patient chooses to consume versus decline certain healthcare) (Robertson 2013, 2014a). The behavioral function is a form of distributed rationing since it asks the patient to determine whether the healthcare in question is worth the cost to the patient. If cost sharing can reduce consumption of healthcare, or shift patients toward less expensive forms of healthcare, it may reduce the cost of insurance premiums ex ante. It may also counteract some of the pro-consumption biases that currently exist in the healthcare system, and even make the economy more efficient as individuals trade for other healthcare options and other forms of non-healthcare consumption that deliver higher value (Robertson 2013, 2014a).

Because cost sharing creates an incentive for individual consumers to make socially desirable choices (to reduce wasteful healthcare consumption), while nonetheless preserving the freedom of individuals to choose otherwise, it can be considered a tool of "choice architecture." More narrowly, Thaler and Sunstein (2008, 6) define a nudge as "any aspect of the choice architecture that alters people's behavior in a predictable way without forbidding any options or significantly changing their economic incentives." On this definition, cost sharing may be a form of choice architecture, but may not be a nudge, because it overtly manipulates incentives (Sellinger and White 2012). Although scholars have begun to consider the ethics of choice architecture in healthcare (for example, Blumenthal-Barby and Burroughs 2012), and this volume is a major contribution to that literature, cost sharing has not yet been extensively evaluated in this light.

To be sure, the increasing use of cost sharing has been controversial, for all sorts of other reasons. An initial practical problem is the lack of price transparency in the American healthcare market (Reinhardt 2006; Ubel, Abernathy, and Zafar 2013), which prevents patients from performing the cost-benefit analysis that cost sharing presumes. States are legislating, federal officials are investigating, and entrepreneurs are starting new enterprises, all seeking to improve this situation.

From a normative perspective, there are three standard objections to cost sharing. An initial concern is that cost sharing may be so large in comparison to the patient's wealth that it actually forecloses healthcare consumption options for patients, and thereby undermines the core functions of insurance, namely, guaranteeing access to care and protection from financial risk (Schoen et al. 2008; Bloche 2007). Under-insurance can lead to other problems, including bankruptcies and foreclosures (Bashshur, Smith, and Stiles 1993; Himmelstein et al. 2009; Gross and Notowidigdo 2011; Robertson, Egelhof, and Hoke 2008). In other work, we have suggested and begun to test ways in which this serious problem can be addressed through careful design of cost-sharing policies (Robertson 2013, 2014a; Robertson et al. 2014).

A second concern is that, in addition to discouraging consumption of low-value healthcare (as intended), cost sharing may cause patients to decline high-value health-care too. This problem has been documented empirically (Swartz 2010; Remler and Greene 2009). From a theoretical perspective, cost sharing often exposes patients to only a small portion of the costs of healthcare (18% is a typical co-insurance rate), so patients must make radical errors toward nonconsumption to overcome what is other-wise a strong subsidy for consumption. Such an outcome is possible with hyperbolic discounting. Even if a real problem in the aggregate, policymakers often lack the epis-temic and normative basis to overrule such a patient's decisions to decline care (Rob-ertson 2014b; Elhauge 1994). Nonetheless, this problem can also be addressed through careful insurance design in which cost sharing is reduced or eliminated for high-value healthcare (Chernew et al. 2007).

A third normative concern is that cost sharing is unfair to those who are unluckily sick (Hoffman 2010; Bloche 2007). This concern raises several interesting normative questions, including how responsibility for sickness should be allocated more funda-mentally (Wikler 1987). Nonetheless, one of us (CR) has argued elsewhere that much of this objection can also be resolved through careful insurance design (Robertson 2014a).

Decisional Burden and the Alternatives to Cost Sharing

A fourth concern is our focus here. How does cost sharing affect the patient's decision-making process, the outcomes of those decisions, and the patient's satisfac-tion with those outcomes? In one of the few papers to consider this dimension, even in passing, Bruce Vladeck has written: "Consumers . . . don't wish to be forced to make rational trade-offs when they are confronted with medical care consump-tion decisions. [M]edical care is about living and dying, something considered by many to be of a rather different character from the purchase of tomatoes" (Vladeck 1981, 211).

In this sense, a cost-sharing burden makes the patient's healthcare decisions—which are already profoundly difficult, as they are made in the grips of scientific uncertainty with existential questions about whether and how to live—even more difficult. As we show below, this difficulty can lead to stress, lack of certainty, cogni-tive load, and other disutility, which we call collectively "decisional burden."

To understand whether, how, and to what extent cost sharing actually creates decisional burden disutility, it is useful to identify the counterfactual world that would obtain without cost sharing. In principle, there are two different ways that the decisional burden could be eliminated: (1) outsource the rationing function, which will likely reduce the choice set of treatments available to the patient at the point of consumption; or (2) increase the costs of insurance premiums (or tax outlays) ex ante, which has the effect of sinking certain costs. Consider each.

The first alternative to cost sharing is to outsource the rationing function to someone else—whether it is the physician, the insurer, a government regulator, or some third party—to receive the pricing information and then decide whether the treatment's benefits to the patient are worth its cost to the insurer (Elhauge 1996; Robertson 2014b). One way of doing so is for a rationer to use its own cost-benefit assessments, and then create a subset of all possible treatment options that survive the rationing test, as does the National Institute for Clinical Effectiveness (NICE) in the United Kingdom (Loewenstein 2012). This solution has the immediate consequence of reducing the patient's autonomy and access to healthcare since there will be instances in which the outsourced rationer excludes treatments from the choice set (that is, declines care) that the patient himself would have preferred to consume.

The second alternative is to forgo the price signal rationing function altogether. As Vladeck has suggested, "[a]s a society, we may be prepared to pay a substantial economic premium to insulate people from having to make such decisions" (Vladeck 1981, 212). The health insurance premiums would be inflated in two ways: first, more healthcare would be consumed; and second, the producers and providers of that healthcare would significantly increase their prices charged since they would not be competing along the dimension of price. Depending on how these higher costs are distributed, it might make health insurance unaffordable ex ante, or even if affordable, would force tradeoffs between other spending priorities (for example, housing or nutrition) against the marginally higher health insurance premiums. In this sense, a patient who buys insurance sans-rationer pays ex ante for healthcare that she would not choose to consume ex post, if she had to bear those costs at the point of consumption. This is a waste, which is a prima facie harm to the consumer.

Behavioral Science on the Decisional Burden

Given the unattractive features of these alternatives, cost sharing may appear attractive as a rationing mechanism. However, research from the behavioral sciences sheds light on the decisional burden potentially associated with cost-sharing mechanisms. The burden might be experienced in at least two forms: first, the quality of the decision itself might be worsened; and, second, even if choice quality is not worsened, the decision-maker may feel less satisfied.

We approach these issues from several angles. We begin by considering how features of the choice set affect decision-making. Specifically, additional choices can, somewhat paradoxically, actually worsen decision quality and satisfaction. We then turn to consider characteristics of the decision-maker himself. Our case study is cognitive capacity and, in particular, how consideration of stressful financial constraints can itself deteriorate cognitive performance. Finally we examine how outsourcing a decision avoids the potential for regret, especially of a self-blame variety.

Choice Overload

Compared to cost sharing, the alternative to outsourcing the rationing function has the ultimate effect of reducing the number of options available to the patient at the point of consumption (because the rationer screens out options according to its own cost-benefit analysis). This reduction is, prima facie, undesirable. Yet a variety of experimental and field studies have revealed a "paradox of choice," wherein the availability of more choice options actually decreases decision quality and satisfaction (Schwartz 2009). Thus, cost sharing may preserve choices only at our peril.

Iyengar and Lepper, in now famous work, provided several controlled experimental examples of the phenomenon (2000). In one study, they found that customers at an upscale grocery store were more likely to sample jams from a choice set of twenty-four flavored jam possibilities, but—paradoxically—they were actually more likely to purchase a jam when confronted with a limited set of six flavored jams only. A second study found that undergraduate students were more likely to complete an extra credit essay, and that the essays were of higher quality, if the instructor afforded only six rather than thirty topic possibilities. Subjects in a third study selected from a choice set of either six or thirty chocolates. Those in the limited choice set condition were more satisfied with the taste of their chosen chocolate and experienced less regret than their counterparts confronted with the larger array of chocolates. Based on these results, the authors postulated a "choice overload hypothesis," namely, that "although the provision of extensive choices may sometimes still be seen as initially desirable, it may also prove unexpectedly demotivating in the end" (996).

Subsequent empirical work has confirmed the problem of choice overload in more naturalistic settings. Proctor & Gamble experienced a 10% increase in overall sales after it reduced the number of versions of Head and Shoulders shampoo from 26 to 15 (Osnos 1997). Sethi-Iyengar, Huberman, and Jiang examined enrollment rates in the 401(k) retirement benefit plans of approximately 800,000 employees in 650 plans across 70 industries, as a function of the number of plan options offered (which ranged from 2 to 59) (2004). Carefully controlled regression analyses revealed that, all else equal, the addition of every 10 funds was associated with a 1.5% to 2.0% reduction in enrollment. Participation was highest when only 2 options were offered (75%), but lowest when 59 funds were available (60%). Enrollment rates in Medicare Advantage have also been found to first rise, but then decline, as the number of choices proliferates (McWilliams et al. 2011; but see Bundorf and Szrek 2010, failing to find a similar dynamic in Medicare Part D).

Why might a proliferation of options decrease choice quality and satisfaction? Several explanations have been proposed, which are not mutually exclusive (Scheibehenne, Greifeneder, and Todd 2010). The first is that as the number of options increases, it becomes more time consuming (and ultimately cognitively impossible) to exhaustively compare all the option attributes. A person must instead rely on simple heuristics, such as a satisficing rule (Gigerenzer and Gaissmaier 2011). Although efficient, such heuristics can lead to systematic biases and, thus, relatively suboptimal choice quality. Moreover, choosers may suffer anxiety because they realize the complexity of the choice has made it impossible to choose optimally (Iyengar, Wells, and Schwartz 2006). An increased choice set might introduce multiple attractive options, and deciding becomes more difficult (Fasolo, McClelland, and Todd 2007). Finally, counterfactual thinking and regret are more likely because a larger choice set is more likely to have an attractive second-best, non-chosen alternative.

From this perspective, outsourcing the rationing decision—and thus limiting choice—can actually provide benefits, namely, avoiding the disutility associated with choice overload. Indeed, the choice overload problem is potentially even greater in the domain of health (relative to consumer choices about jams and chocolates) since decision difficulty is typically compounded by the need to understand scientifically complex treatments, often with substantial uncertainty as to likely outcomes. Thus, whereas it might take thirty jams to overload a consumer choice about basic food preferences, even a handful of medical treatment options might quickly exert a similar overload.

It is worth emphasizing that the disutility emerges in two ways, namely, decision quality and decision satisfaction. Regarding quality, a patient overwhelmed with the choice might turn to a simplifying heuristic, such as just reflexively declining care or blindly deferring to his physician, who may suffer from biases of her own, including conflicting interests (Beaver, Bogg, and Luker 1999; Robertson, Rose, and Kesselheim 2012). This can result in a different—and potentially worse—decision than if a fuller consideration were given.

Although there is no direct evidence about patient decision-making on this point, a study of physicians by Redelmeier and Shafir reveals the underlying psychological phenomenon (1995). Physician-subjects were asked to consider an elderly patient with osteoarthritis, who will soon visit an orthopedic surgeon for possible hip replacement, but in the meantime had to stop taking several attempted non-steroidal, anti-inflammatory medications due to inefficacy or adverse effects. The decision was whether to prescribe a new medication or forgo it until the orthopedic consult. Half of subjects were told the remaining options were ibuprofen and piroxicam, while the other half were told only ibuprofen had yet to be tried. In line with a choice overload effect, 72% of subjects prescribed a drug when only ibuprofen was available, but they were less likely to prescribe a drug when both ibuprofen and piroxicam were available. As the authors interpreted the finding, "[a]pparently, the uncertainty in deciding between two similar medications led some physicians to avoid this decision altogether and recommend not starting any new medication" (304).

Cognitive Scarcity

The second alternative to cost sharing holds constant the number of choices available to the patient, but eliminates the price criterion for evaluation. Within cost sharing, this criterion can create disutility, even aside from choice overload, because of the way that it enhances the complexity of the patient's decision.

Human rationality is "bounded," as Herbert Simon explains, as people have limited abilities to "work out the consequences of their actions, to conjure up possible courses of action, to cope with uncertainty (including uncertainty deriving from the possible responses of other actors), and to adjudicate among their many competing wants" (Simon 2000, 25). People cope with the barrage of complexity by adopting cognitive heuristics or otherwise reducing their full consideration of the decision problem (Kahneman 2013; Gilovich, Griffin, and Kahneman 2002). Because only a subset of information is considered, systematic biases can emerge.

Our cognitive capacity is not, however, a static feature. The same complex decision can become more difficult, and more prone to bias, as the decision-maker becomes distracted, fatigued, overwhelmed with stress, and so forth (Mullainathan and Shafir 2013). This is particularly relevant in the medical decision-making context, where life and limb often hang in the balance, and the decisions are made in suboptimal circumstances.

More specifically, the very consideration of financial constraints can induce suboptimal decision-making. Research by Mani et al. (2013) is revealing on this point. In one experiment, shoppers at a New Jersey mall made a series of hypothetical, financial-based decisions about needing to fix their cars. Subjects were assigned to one of two conditions: a "hard" condition, wherein high costs were implicated (for example, the car would take $1,500 to fix), or an "easy" condition involving lower costs (for example, the car would take only $150 to fix). Subjects then completed two tests of cognitive function, and reported demographic information, including wealth. "Poor" and "rich" subjects performed equally well on the cognitive tests following easy decisions. After hard decisions, in contrast, the poor subjects performed substantially worse. As the authors interpreted it, "[p]reoccupation with pressing budgetary concerns leaves fewer cognitive resources available to guide choice and action" (976). Three additional experiments replicated Mani's finding, as well as ruled out alternative explanations, such as math anxiety, a lack of real-world financial incentive, or that the cognitive tests themselves induced undue cognitive load. It also confirmed the effect size was substantial, akin to a full night of sleep deprivation, the effect of chronic alcoholism, or a 13 point decrease in IQ. In other words, consideration of stressful financial constraints can seriously undermine cognitive performance. The authors warn that "policy-makers should beware of imposing cognitive taxes on the poor just as they avoid monetary taxes on the poor" (980).

A different thread of research has focused, not on financially induced mental constraints, but more generally on the effects of depleted mental resources. Fatigue, for instance, can seriously undermine the ability to think critically, even about important life decisions. One field study of Israeli judges found that the proportion of parole grants was tightly coupled with number of hours since the judge last took a break (Danziger, Levav, and Avnaim-Pesso 2011). As the time lengthened—and thus the judge became more fatigued—it became significantly less likely that the parole request would be granted. As soon as a break occurred, the proportion of parole grants returned to the same rate seen at the beginning of the morning. Without purporting to say which set of decisions was more accurate or appropriate, this research evinces the relationship between decision outcomes and depleted mental resources.

These threads of research are suggestive for understanding the cognitive effects of cost-sharing burdens in healthcare. (Although, given the limited research on cognitive scarcity in healthcare specifically, it remains to be seen just how well results generalize to this domain.) Consideration of financial costs has the potential to undermine a fuller consideration of the nonfinancial choice features, such as likelihood of outcomes and quality of life.

This is not to suggest that mental effort should not be spent on considering the financial constraints. Rather the question is who: whether the patient, or someone else, should be making this exertion. Cost sharing may not be the most efficient allocation of effort. Patients sense this difficulty: survey research has shown that U.S. health consumers are equivocal about the idea of discussing costs with physicians in the clinical encounter (Sommers et al. 2013).

Facilitation of Regret

Cost sharing may also cause subjective disutility if it creates opportunities for regret. Richard Thaler has argued that, similarly to tourists preferring a resort that includes food and drink in the cost, health insurance buyers "choose not to choose." With a fulsome insurance plan, consumers sink the costs of healthcare, so that at the point of consumption, they need not make choices about money in ways that they may later potentially regret (Thaler 1980; see also the foreword to this volume, by Cass Sunstein). This regret dynamic is not peculiar to out-of-pocket spending, but arises whenever there is a difficult decision, and one solution is to outsource the choice to someone else. Thaler explains that, when there are two different surgical procedures from which to choose, "[c]learly in this situation a rational consumer would want the physician to make the choice and furthermore, he would not want to know that a choice existed!" (1980, 53). That way, patients who suffer a bad outcome need not experience any regret for the choice made.

Connolly and Reb, through a series of careful laboratory experiments, have delineated several different types of regret (Connolly and Reb 2012). Noting that regret is a transitive verb—one typically regrets something—there is a distinction based on the target of regret. With *outcome regret* the target is the outcome of the decision, whereas with *process regret* the target is the decision-making process itself. Consider a patient who forgoes implantation of a surgical stent and then, months later, suffers a heart attack. The patient might experience regret: that the heart attack occurred (outcome regret); that he did not more carefully consider the pros and cons of implanting the stent (process regret); or both. The key difference is that process regret, unlike outcome regret, is "centrally concerned with mechanisms of self-criticism and justification" (Connolly and Reb 2005, S31). More particularly, when a poor decision outcome occurs, "individuals tend to ask themselves whether the decision, or the process that led up to it, was justified[; i]f it was partially or entirely unjustified, we feel regret, the intensity of which is increased by the seriousness of the outcome" (S31).

When a cost-sharing scheme is replaced by an other-rationing scheme, a patient can be shielded from process regret. The decision is outsourced to someone else. If a treatment is declined, a patient might regret any ensuing bad outcome, but she will not be in a position of feeling the pang of self-blame that is process regret. If the other-rationer also prevents the patient from becoming aware of other options, she may also thereby avoid outcome regret. Cost sharing thus increases these psychic costs.

Conclusion

We identified two counterfactuals for thinking about the causal effects of cost sharing along this dimension, and reviewed three potential mechanisms of disutility: choice overload, depletion of cognitive capacity, and facilitation of regret. We conclude that the decisional burden of cost sharing is a real problem.

Nonetheless, the behavioral science results are descriptive, not prescriptive. And we are unable to compare the size of this disutility with the diminishment of choices that comes with outsourcing the rationing function or the runaway costs that come with simply forgoing the rationing function altogether. This difficulty may explain why different political communities and different insurance plans in the market reach different conclusions about these ultimate questions.

Advocates of cost sharing must pay closer attention to these disadvantages of this particular mechanism for rationing healthcare. Indeed, perhaps sustained attention will yield ways to improve the mechanisms of cost sharing, so as to reap its advantages while minimizing some of these psychic costs.

Regardless, in a world of epistemic uncertainty and heterogeneity of values, it is not irrational for consumers to prefer cost sharing—if carefully designed and implemented—as the least-bad rationing mechanism among the alternatives, which either reduce access to healthcare or sink costs for unwanted healthcare. Thus, insurance designers and policymakers may likewise have reasons to favor cost sharing, notwithstanding these burdens that it imposes.

References

Bashshur, Rashid, Dean G. Smith, and Renee A. Stiles. 1993. "Defining Underinsurance: A Conceptual Framework for Policy and Empirical Analysis." *Medical Care Review* 50:199.

Beaver, K. J., B. Bogg, and K. A. Luker. 1999. "Decision-Making Role Preferences and Information Needs: A Comparison of Colorectal Cancer and Breast Cancer." *Health Expectations* 2:266.

Bloche, M. Gregg. 2007. "Consumer-Directed Health Care and the Disadvantaged." *Health Affairs* 26:1315, 1318.

Blumenthal-Barby Jennifer, and Hadley Burroughs. 2012. "Seeking Better Health Care Outcomes: The Ethics of Using the Nudge." *The American Journal of Bioethics* 12(2):41284.

Bundorf, M. K., and H. Szrek. 2010. "Choice Set Size and Decision Making: The Case of Medicare Part D Prescription Drug Plans." *Medical Decision Making* 30(5):582–93.

Connolly, Terry, and Jochen Reb. 2005. "Regret in Cancer-Related Decisions." *Health Psychology* 24:S29–S41.

———. 2012. "Regret Aversion in Reason-Based Choice." *Theory and Decision* 73:35–51.

Chernew, Michael, et al. 2007. "Value-Based Insurance Design." *Health Affairs* 26:w195, w195–w196.

Danziger, Shai, Jonathan Levav, and Liora Avnaim-Pesso. 2011. "Extraneous Factors in Judicial Decisions." *Proceedings of the National Academy of Sciences* 108:6889–92.

Elhauge, Einer. 1996. "The Limited Regulatory Potential of Medical Technology Assessment." *Virginia Law Review* 82:1525.

———. 1994. "Allocating Health Care Morally." *California Law Review* 82:1457, 1480.

Fasolo, Barbara, Gary H. McClelland, and Peter M. Todd. 2007. "Escaping the Tyranny of Choice: When Fewer Attributes Make Choice Easier." *Mark Theory* 7:13–26.

Gigerenzer, Gerd, and Wolfgang Gaissmaier. 2011. "Heuristic Decision Making." *Annual Review of Psychology* 62:451–82.

Gilovich, Thomas, Dale Griffin, and Daniel Kahneman, eds. 2002. *Heuristics and Biases: The Psychology of Intuitive Judgment.* Cambridge University Press. Cambridge.

Gross, T., and M. J. Notowidigdo. 2011. "Health Insurance and the Consumer Bankruptcy Decision: Evidence from Expansions of Medicaid." *Journal of Public Economics* 95:767.

Himmelstein, David U., et al. 2009. "Medical Bankruptcy in the United States, 2007: Results of a National Study." *American Journal of Medicine* 122:741, 744–45.

Hoffman, Allison K. 2010. "Three Models of Health Insurance: The Conceptual Pluralism of the Patient Protection and Affordable Care Act." *University of Pennsylvania Law Review* 159:1873, 1922–32.

Iyengar, Sheena S., and Mark R. Lepper. 2000. "When Choice Is Demotivating: Can One Desire Too Much of a Good Thing?" *Journal of Personality and Social Psychology* 79:995–1006.

Iyengar, Sheena S., Rachael E. Wells, and Barry Schwartz. 2006. "Doing Better But Feeling Worse: Looking for the 'Best' Job Undermines Satisfaction." *Psychological Science* 17:143–50.

Kahneman, Daniel. 2002. *Thinking, Fast and Slow*. Farrar, Straus & Giroux. New York.

Kaiser Family Foundation. 2012. "2012 Annual Survey." *Kaiser Family Foundation Employer Health Benefits* 4. http://kff.org/private-insurance/report/employer-health-benefits-2012 -annual-survey/.

Loewenstein, George, et al. 2012. "Can Behavioral Economics Make Us Healthier?" *British Medical Journal* 344:1, 2.

Mani, Anandi, et al. 2013. "Poverty Impedes Cognitive Function." *Science* 341:976–80.

McWilliams, J. M., C. C. Afendulis, T. G. McGuire, and B. E. Landon. 2011. "Complex Medicare Advantage Choices May Overwhelm Seniors—Especially Those with Impaired Decision Making." *Health Affairs* 30(9):1786–94.

Mullainathan, Sendhil, and Eldar Shafir. 2013. *Scarcity: Why Having Too Little Means So Much*. Macmillan. New York.

Osnos, E. 1997. "Too Many Choices? Firms Cut Back on New Products." *Philadelphia Inquirer*, 27:D1, D7.

Redelmeier, Donald A., and Eldar Shafir. 1995. "Medical Decision Making in Situations That Offer Multiple Alternatives." *Journal of the American Medical Association* 273:302–5.

Reinhardt, Uwe E. 2006. "The Pricing of US Hospital Services: Chaos behind a Veil of Secrecy." *Health Affairs* 25:57.

Remler, Dahlia K., and Jessica Greene. 2009. "Cost Sharing : A Blunt Instrument." *Annual Review of Public Health* 30:293.

Robertson, Christopher T. 2014b. "A Presumption against Expensive Healthcare Consumption." *Tulsa Law Review* 49:627.

———. 2014a. "Scaling Cost Sharing to Wages." *Yale Journal of Health Policy, Law, and Ethics* 14:239.

———. 2013. "The Split Benefit: The Painless Way to Put Skin Back in the Healthcare Game." *Cornell Law Review* 98:921.

Robertson, Christopher T., Richard Egelhof, and Michael Hoke. 2008. "Get Sick, Get Out: The Medical Causes of Home Foreclosures." *Health Matrix: Journal of Law-Medicine* 18:65.

Robertson, Christopher T., Susannah Rose, and Aaron S. Kesselheim. 2012. "Effect of Financial Relationships on the Behaviors of Health Care Professionals: A Review of the Evidence." *Journal of Law, Medicine, and Ethics* 40:452, 458.

Robertson, Christopher T., David Yokum, Nimish Sheth, and Keith Joiner. 2014. "A Random- ized Experiment of the Split Benefit Health Insurance Reform to Reduce High-Cost, Low-Value Consumption." *Innovation and Entrepreneurship in Health* 1:5.

Scheibehenne, Benjamin, Rainer Greifeneder, and Peter M. Todd. 2010. "Can There Ever Be Too Many Options? A Meta-Analytic Review of Choice Overload." *Journal of Consumer Research* 37:409–25.

Schoen, Cathy, et al. 2008. "How Many Are Underinsured? Trends among U.S. Adults, 2003 and 2007." *Health Affairs Web Exclusive*. June 10.

Schwartz, Barry. 2004. *The Paradox of Choice: Why More Is Less*. Harper Perennial. New York.

Sellinger, Evan, and Kyle Pawys White. 2012. "What Counts as a Nudge?" *The American Journal of Bioethics* 12:11.

Sethi-Iyengar, Sheena, Gur Huberman, and Wei Jiang. 2004. "How Much Choice Is Too Much? Contributions to 401(k) Retirement Plans." In *Pension Design and Structuring: New Lessons from Behavioral Finance*, edited by Olivia S. Mitchell and Stephen P. Utkus. Oxford University Press. New York. 83–95.

Simon, Herbert A. 2000. "Bounded Rationality in Social Science: Today and Tomorrow." *Mind & Society* 1:25.

Sommers, Roseanna, et al. 2013. "Focus Groups Highlight That Many Patients Object to Clinicians' Focusing on Costs." *Health Affairs* 32:338.

Swartz, Kathryn. 2010. "Cost Sharing : Effects on Spending and Outcomes." *Robert Wood Johnson Foundation Research Synthesis Report* 20:1.

Thaler, Richard. 1980. "Toward a Positive Theory of Consumer Choice." *Journal of Economic Behavior & Organization* 1:39.

Thaler, Richard, and Cass Sunstein. 2008. *Nudge: Improving Decisions about Health, Wealth, and Happiness.* Yale University Press. New Haven, CT.

Ubel, Peter A., Amy P. Abernathy, and S. Yousuf Zafar. 2013. "Full Disclosure—Out-of-Pocket Costs as Side Effects." *New England Journal of Medicine* 369:1484.

Vladeck, Bruce. 1981. "The Market v. Regulation: The Case for Regulation." *Milbank Quarterly* 59:209, 210–11.

Wikler, Dan. 1987. "Who Should be Blamed for Being Sick?" *Health Education Quarterly* 14:11.

CHAPTER 11

Using Behavioral Economics to Promote Physicians' Prescribing of Generic Drugs and Follow-On Biologics
What Are the Issues?

Ameet Sarpatwari, Niteesh K. Choudhry, Jerry Avorn,
and Aaron S. Kesselheim

Spending on prescription medications—both small-molecule drugs and biological products—totaled $271 billion in 2013 and continues to rise (Centers for Medicare and Medicaid 2014). Brand-name products have served as the primary driver of this growth, increasing 13% in price in 2013 alone (Schondelmeyer and Purvis 2014).

In stark contrast, generic drug prices have fallen on average in recent years (Thomas 2012). Generic drugs are copies of small-molecule brand-name drugs usually made by distinct manufacturers. They contain the same active ingredients and have been approved as interchangeable with their corresponding brand-name drugs by the U.S. Food and Drug Administration (FDA). Because they do not require the same long process of basic science development and expensive array of clinical trials, generic drugs are substantially cheaper than brand-name drugs if sold in a competitive marketplace. Use of generic drugs has reduced healthcare costs by more than $1 trillion in the past decade (Martin 2013).

Despite the meaningful savings that generic drugs have provided, however, they remain underused in many clinical scenarios. One reason is that many physicians remain skeptical of generic drug safety and effectiveness. Physicians' opinions are shaped, of course, by the educational resources used to learn about drugs. Brand-name manufacturers spend $30 to $60 billion per year on marketing their products to U.S. physicians (Gagnon and Lexchin 2008). By contrast, generic manufacturers typically do not engage in promotion.

Another potential source of healthcare savings in the near future may arise from the availability of follow-on biologic drugs. Such complex molecules, generally derived

This work is derived from an article previously published in *PLoS Medicine*: Ameet, Sarpatwari, Niteesh K. Choudhry, Jerry Avorn, and Aaron S. Kesselheim, "Paying Physicians to Prescribe Generic Drugs and Follow-On Biologics in the United States," *PLoS Medicine* 12 (2015): e1001802.

from living cells, are predicted to account for 20% of all prescription drug costs worldwide by 2017 (IMS Institute for Healthcare Informatics 2013). In 2009, Congress authorized the FDA to approve "biosimilar" versions of biologic drugs that could be approved without the manufacturer needing to conduct the same costly clinical trials as the originator. Eighteen such products are available in the European Union and cost on average 20% to -25% less than their innovator counterparts (Grabowski, Guha, and Salgado 2014).

Many U.S. policymakers and payers support greater use of generic drugs and anticipate the FDA's first approval of a follow-on biologic. Physician-centered tactics intended to encourage generic drug prescribing range from traditional information-supplying efforts to more recent payments to prescribers who demonstrate high generic prescribing rates. Both types of interventions are likely to become more prevalent as urgency grows to offset rising healthcare spending. In this chapter, we explore clinical, legal, and ethical issues regarding these programs.

Approval and Use of Generic Drugs and Follow-On Biologics

The Hatch-Waxman Act of 1984 established a new regulatory process for efficient approval of generic drugs called the Abbreviated New Drug Application (ANDA) pathway, prompting a dramatic surge in generic drug use. By 2012, 84% of all prescriptions were filled with generic drugs (Thomas 2012), up from 15% before 1984. These products reach patients through two primary mechanisms: bioequivalent substitution and therapeutic substitution. Substitution of follow-on biologics will mirror these general categories. Before we evaluate the role that behavioral economics interventions can play in these marketplaces, we first review the relevant features of generic and follow-on biologic drugs.

Generic Drug Testing

A generic manufacturer's ANDA is approvable if the manufacturer can prove to the FDA that its product is "bioequivalent" to the corresponding brand-name drug. Meeting this standard requires the generic manufacturer to perform pharmacokinetic and pharmacodynamic studies of its product, which are traditionally conducted in animal models and in a limited number of healthy human volunteers over short periods of time. If these studies show that the generic manufacturer's version of the drug delivers the same active ingredient into the body in the same concentration and with the same timing as the brand-name version, additional comparative clinical trials in large numbers of patients are not necessary.

A critique of the ANDA approval process is that it is not rigorous enough to account for generic versions of so-called narrow therapeutic index (NTI) drugs, drugs for which a small change in dose "produces clinically significant and undesirable alterations" (Levy 1998, 501). Concerns about the safety of generic NTI drugs, however, have not been confirmed in any systematic trials. Some authors of this chapter led two studies that systematically reviewed data from head-to-head randomized-controlled trials (RCTs) of brand-name and generic NTI drug pairs. The first, an investigation of cardiovascular drugs, found that the sole RCT of the antiarrhythmic procainamide (Pronestyl) failed to detect a significant difference in ventricular premature beats while all five RCTs of the anticoagulant warfarin (Coumadin) reported non-significant differences in coagulation times (Kesselheim et al. 2008). The second, a meta-analysis of seven RCTs, uncovered no significant change in the rate of uncontrolled seizures in patients receiving brand-name versus bioequivalent generic antiepileptics (Kesselheim et al. 2010). Thus, the ANDA approval process generally leads to safe and effective generic drugs, and there are no evidence-based clinical reasons not to use them for the vast majority of patients in the vast majority of conditions.

Bioequivalent versus Therapeutic Substitution of Generic Drugs

While physicians often directly prescribe generic drugs, most generic drug use arises from two types of substitution. In bioequivalent substitution, a prescription for a brand-name drug is replaced with a chemically equivalent generic that supplies the same quantity of active ingredient to the target site. In therapeutic substitution, a brand-name drug is replaced with a non-bioequivalent generic drug that has a similar mechanism of action.

Bioequivalent Substitution

Bioequivalent substitution is extremely common and often occurs automatically through drug product selection laws in every state that either mandates or authorizes pharmacists to substitute a less-expensive generic for a brand-name medication. One reason why drug product selection laws are so important is the unique relationship of the patient, prescriber, and payer in the pharmaceutical marketplace. For brand-name prescription drugs intended for outpatient settings, the physician writes the prescription for the medication; the pharmacist dispenses and sells the medication; and the patient (or her insurer) pays for the medication. Separation of the prescription-writing act from the prescription-paying act has long been understood to lead to disconnects between medication use and payment that persist to the present day (Allan, Lexchin, and Wiebe 2007). Drug product selection laws permit these price disconnects to be bridged by the pharmacist.

Bioequivalent substitution of generic drugs can nevertheless be circumvented by patients and physicians with varying ease depending on the choice architecture adopted by a state. Some states, for example, explicitly require pharmacists to obtain patient consent to substitute a prescription for a brand-name drug with a bioequivalent generic product while others do not. Likewise, some states make it relatively easy for physicians to require pharmacists to "dispense as written" prescriptions, permitting prescription pads with a pre-printed instruction rather than mandating a handwritten order. In a 2011 study, physicians and patients directed pharmacists to dispense as written nearly 5% of 5.6 million prescriptions (Shrank et al. 2011a).

Therapeutic Substitution

Therapeutic substitution involves substitution of non-bioequivalent products. Therapeutic substitution is possible because most classes of drugs contain multiple chemically related but distinct drugs that share a common mechanism of action. For example, eight different cholesterol-lowering statins have been approved by the FDA that achieve their clinical effect by inhibiting the HMG CoA reductase enzyme in the cholesterol biosynthesis pathway.

On a practical level, therapeutic substitution requires more active involvement of prescribers, pharmacists, and patients than bioequivalent substitution. State drug product selection laws do not permit therapeutic substitution at the pharmacy level without a new prescription from the physician. However, therapeutic substitution offers additional possibilities to reduce spending because many new brand-name drugs do not offer significant benefits over and above existing generics within the same drug class. An evaluation of the Medicare Part D insurance program by the nonprofit news organization ProPublica found that improving the prescribing of just 913 physicians to reflect common therapeutic substitution practices would have saved taxpayers $300 million in 2011 (Ornstein, Weber, and LaFleur 2013).

Continued Underutilization of Generic Drugs

Despite the widespread availability of high-quality generic drugs and the potential for bioequivalent and therapeutic substitution, generic drug use remains suboptimal. Gellad et al. estimated that Medicare could save $1.4 billion annually simply by matching the generic drug prescribing rates of the Veterans Affairs Health System for four common medications used to treat diabetes (Gellad et al. 2013). As noted, some state laws contribute to this underuse by implementing a choice architecture that undercuts bioequivalent substitution. One study found that drug product selection laws requiring patient consent prior to generic substitution experienced 25% lower rates of substitution than states that did not require patient consent (Shrank et al. 2010). Other states have imposed heightened barriers for pharmacists to substitute prescriptions for brand-name NTI drugs.

Social factors also contribute to generic drug underuse. Although 56% of 1,054 commercially insured patients reported that Americans should use more generic drugs in a 2007 study, only 38% stated that they prefer generics (Shrank et al. 2009). Skepticism about generic drugs is not limited to patients. In one 2011 survey, one-fourth of practicing physicians reported harboring concerns over generic drug safety and effectiveness (Shrank et al. 2011b).

Follow-On Biologic Substitution

The ANDA process served as a model for the abbreviated approval pathway for follow-on biologics established under the Biologics Price Competition and Innovations Act (BPCIA) of 2009. To qualify for the pathway, a follow-on biologic must have the same mechanism of action, route of administration, and dosage form as the innovator product and not be meaningfully different with regard to safety, purity, or potency. When follow-on biologics are approved by the FDA, a select few will be deemed interchangeable, while most will simply be approved as members of the same drug class to treat the same conditions.

The scientific standards put forth by the FDA about follow-on biologics largely mirror those adopted by the European Union, where such drugs have a longer track record. Yet concerns about follow-on biologics remain, including difficulties with establishing the similarity of complex molecules made by different manufacturers and the possibility that even small variations in follow-on biologic products may induce immune responses or lead to variable effects on patients (Liang and Mackey 2011). As a result, some professional societies, patient groups, and innovator manufacturers have urged state legislatures to enact carve-outs to their drug product selection laws that would make it harder for pharmacists to substitute innovator biologics with follow-on products, even those deemed interchangeable by the FDA (Macdonald and Stanton 2014).

Physician-Centered Tools to Promote Generic Drug Use

In the face of underuse of generic drugs in both bioequivalent and therapeutic substitution contexts, physician-centered efforts to promote evidence-based use of generic drugs have taken multiple forms with varying evidentiary support. These strategies, which harness developments in behavioral economics, can be applied to increase uptake of follow-on biologics once such products are available in U.S. markets.

Information-Supplying Programs

Information-supplying programs are among the most conspicuous of the behavioral strategies aimed at changing generic prescribing practices. Such programs seek to combat the massive asymmetry in drug-specific information reaching physicians and to address general cost-effectiveness data deficits. Formulary support, for example, provides physicians with information from national guidelines and patients' co-payment costs to facilitate a choice of medication that is safe, effective, and affordable. In 2008, Fischer et al. published an evaluation of the largest rollout of a community-based e-prescribing system with formulary decision support in the country. In a pre-post investigation spanning 18 months, the investigators found a 3.3% absolute increase in generic drug prescribing by physicians given a color-coded breakdown (green, blue, and red) of preferred formulary (that is, generic), non-preferred formulary, and non-formulary medications, translating to an estimated savings of $845,000 in prescription drug costs per 100,000 people (Fischer et al. 2008).

Academic detailing capitalizes on behavioral insights exploited by brand-name drug manufacturers, which demonstrate greater physician responsiveness to individually tailored information on optimal prescription drug use through in-person, interactive sessions with trained educators rather than didactic lectures. As opposed to brand-name drug sales representatives, however, academic detailers seek to present physicians with neutral evidence-based educational materials developed by university-based experts. Academic detailing has been shown to have a positive influence on physician prescribing practices. In a meta-analysis of twenty-eight studies, the Cochrane Collaboration reported a 5.6% median risk difference in compliance with desired practices between physician recipients of academic detailing and controls, leading to the conclusion that such programs "have effects on prescribing that are relatively consistent and small, but potentially important" (O'Brien et al. 2008, 2).

Recently, researchers have begun studying the incorporation of so-called nudges—subtle interventions that "change people's behavior in a predictable way without forbidding any options or significantly changing their economic incentives" (Thaler and Sunstein 2009, 6)—into information-supplying programs. Stenner and colleagues, for example, observed a statistically significant increase in the proportion of generic medication prescriptions issued by users of an e-prescribing system that returned searches for a medication with a list programmed to place generic drugs first and in larger, bolder font. This difference persisted two years after the intervention and was consistent across specialties (Stenner, Chen, and Johnson 2010). Similarly, Patel et al. found a statistically significant increase in generic prescribing of three drug classes—statins, proton-pump inhibitors, and beta-blockers—combined following the adoption of an e-prescribing system query default that returned only generic drugs (Patel et al. 2014). Such nudges can correct for inherent cognitive biases like choice overload—the likelihood that physicians will maintain the status quo when presented with many rather than few alternatives—in addition to countering habits and false perceptions concerning generic drugs.

Financial Incentives

Financial incentives have also emerged as a tool to promote physician prescribing of generic drugs. In 2007, Blue Care Network in Michigan ran a 90-day program that offered physicians $100 for every patient who switched from a brand-name to a generic cholesterol-lowering medication. While the program cost $2 million, it saved $6 million, including $1 million in out-of-pocket patient costs, in just 5 months (Fuhrmans 2008). In New York, two insurance companies crafted broader programs that were not limited to a particular drug class. Excellus BlueCross provided an elevated office visit reimbursement rate for physician groups that increased their generic drug fill rates by 5% or more, reducing out-of-pocket expenditures by 10% to 12%

(Fuhrmans 2008), while Independent Health paid physicians who prescribed 70% or more generic drugs monthly bonuses (Solomont 2008). None of the companies discussed the impact of their programs on health outcomes, and no scientific studies of such payments have yet been performed.

News of insurance schemes to financially reward prescribing of generic drugs prompted widespread criticism that the insurers were placing profits over patients. In response to public outcry, politicians in several states introduced legislation prohibiting or regulating such initiatives (Fender 2008). However, the efforts proved largely unsuccessful.

Since the controversy over the direct payments for using generic drugs, insurers have been more subtle about applying financial incentives to stimulate use of generic drugs. A 2010 national survey found that it is commonplace for insurers to make generic drug prescribing one factor among many in annual "pay-for-performance" bonuses (Med-Vantage 2011). In California, for example, seven insurers use a common physician performance measure that includes generic drug prescribing for several common conditions like hypertension and depression (Yegian and Yanagihara 2013).

Legal Considerations

In the debate over the public health implications of paying physicians to switch from brand-name to generic drugs, one point was largely neglected—the risk that such programs might expose physicians and parties paying them to liability under the anti-kickback provision of the Social Security Act, commonly known as the anti-kickback statute (AKS). Originally enacted in 1972, the AKS prohibits parties from offering or soliciting payment to induce the purchase of items paid for by a federal healthcare program. AKS violations constitute felonies punishable by up to $25,000 and/or five years' imprisonment (21 U.S.C. §1320a-7b). Violators also face civil penalties of $50,000 per breach, treble damages, and exclusion from participation in federal healthcare programs (21 U.S.C. §1320a-7a). The latter penalty has been termed a corporate death sentence because the federal health insurance programs Medicare and Medicaid account for a substantial fraction of healthcare reimbursement.

Passage of the Patient Protection and Affordable Care Act (PPACA) in 2010 resulted in two key alterations to the AKS. First, it created an indirect private right of action. Whereas the federal government previously exercised sole discretion to file AKS claims, PPACA made AKS violations *de jure* violations of the False Claims Act (21 U.S.C. §1320a-7b). The False Claims Act authorizes *qui tam* actions, or whistleblower lawsuits, which enable individuals with private knowledge to make claims on behalf of the federal government and to share between 15% and 30% of any judgment.

Second, PPACA lowered the scienter requirements for AKS violations. The AKS is explicitly limited to knowing and willful inducements, which courts have struggled to define. In *Hanlester Network v. Shalala*, the Court of Appeals for the Ninth Circuit held that violators must have both knowledge of the AKS and the specific intent to violate it (1995, 1400). Other courts have reached different conclusions. In *United States v. Jain*, for example, the Court of Appeals for the Eighth Circuit required that violators only have knowledge that the conduct "was wrongful rather than proof that . . . it violated a known legal duty" (1996, 441). The circuit split complicated AKS enforcement efforts and ultimately prompted congressional clarification in PPACA, which clarified that violations required neither knowledge of the AKS nor the specific intent to disobey it (21 U.S.C. §1320a-7b).

To our knowledge, no cases have been brought under the AKS involving physicians prescribing under insurance schemes that offer payments for use of generic drugs. Liability in such instances is nonetheless possible. Since Medicare Part D and Medicaid provide payment for prescription medications, physicians who accept financial rewards for prescribing generic drugs or follow-on biologics could be seen as accepting kickbacks to refer their patients "for the furnishing of any item . . . for which payment may be made in whole or in part under a Federal healthcare program" (21 U.S.C. §1320a-7b).

The identity of the inducer, however, is critical in a potential violation. The AKS exempts "any amount paid by an employer to an employee . . . for employment in the provision of covered items or services" (21 U.S.C. §1320a-7b). Hospitals and managed care organizations that employ physicians can therefore safely incorporate generic drug or follow-on biologic prescribing as a measure in their pay-for-performance schemes.

The AKS additionally does not prohibit physicians from accepting generic drug or follow-on biologic bonuses from private health plans. In 2013, the secretary of Health and Human Services opined that qualified health plans offered through PPACA's exchanges are not federal healthcare programs and, thus, fall outside the scope of the AKS (Radick 2013). Despite the nonlegally binding nature of the secretary's statement, the executive branch has signaled its intent not to pursue AKS claims involving qualified health plans. Given the increasing popularity of pay-for-performance programs and the rising costs and use of brand-name drugs, it is likely that many qualified health plans will explore offering physicians financial incentives to promote greater generic drug and follow-on biologic use.

The Ethics of Promoting Generic Drug and Follow-On Biologic Use

The fact that physicians can safely accept financial incentives for prescribing generic drugs and follow-on biologics from private health plans, qualified health plans, and employers without violating the AKS does not necessarily imply that they should. Inducements to encourage brand-name drug prescribing—including gifts and meals offered by brand-name drug company marketing representatives—have been frequently criticized. Studies have shown that such programs result in commencing treatment-naïve patients on medication therapy that was not indicated (and could therefore place the patient at risk of side effects without a reasonable possibility of benefit) or lead to unnecessary and expensive prescribing (Blumenthal 2004).

While the threats of over-prescribing, prescription drug adverse events, and high patient costs make interventions targeting the use of brand-name drugs ethically problematic, they generally do not apply to physician-centered programs that encourage generic drug prescribing. First, generic drug promotional programs are characterized by different motivations than those underlying brand-name drug inducements. Parties that financially benefit from greater relative generic drug use—employers and insurers—lack vested interests in overprescribing.

Generic drug use is also less dangerous overall than brand-name drug use. As generic drugs have been in wide use for an extended period of time, their benefit-to-risk ratios and features such as complications in specific subpopulations tend to be more well known to the prescribing physician. In a review of all brand-name drugs introduced between 1975 and 1999, Lasser et al. found that half of all safety withdrawals and additions of black box warnings took place within two and seven years of approval, respectively (Lasser et al. 2002). The average time between the launch of a brand-name drug and the arrival of its first generic competitor is more than twelve years (Grabowski, Long, and Mortimer 2014).

Finally, generic drug use has less cost-associated toxicity. The chief benefit of generic substitution is the replacement of expensive brand-name drugs with cheaper, effective, and safe products. The resulting reduction in out-of-pocket costs increases patient health outcomes via improved medication adherence. Medication non-adherence is a common and increasingly recognized problem affecting more than one in four U.S. patients with hypertension, hyperlipidemia, and diabetes (Fischer et al. 2010). One key contributor to non-adherence is the high cost of brand-name drugs; one-third of Americans reported not filling a prescription or taking a reduced dose as a result of the drug's high out-of-pocket costs (Rector and Venus 2004). By contrast, generic drugs' lower prices promote adherence to essential medications. A study of six classes of chronic medications between 2001 and 2003, for example, found 12.6% greater adherence among patients who commenced treatment with a generic rather than a brand-name drug (Shrank et al. 2006).

We believe that these differences support offering physicians financial incentives to promote generic drug use over brand-name drug use. The distortive impact that financial incentives could have in clouding clinical decision-making with the prospect of profit, however, suggests that policymakers should be circumspect about the situations in which they are used. Financial incentives are generally not appropriate for therapeutic or noninterchangeable follow-on biologic substitution (table 11.1). Generic drugs proposed as part of therapeutic substitution have different active ingredients, and noninterchangeable follow-on biologics need not demonstrate clinical equivalence to the innovator product. Therapeutic substitution and noninterchangeable follow-on biologic substitution therefore expose patients to marginally greater risk than bioequiv-

Table 11.1. Evaluation of Physician-Centered Strategies to Promote Generic Drug
and Follow-On Biologic Prescribing

Type of Program	Traditional Strategies	Direct Financial Incentives
Example	Formulary support and academic detailing	$100 bonus for every prescription switched
Appropriateness as applied to		
Small-molecule drugs		
Bioequivalent substitution	Recommended	Recommended
Bioequivalent substitution of narrow therapeutic index drugs	Recommended	Not recommended*
Therapeutic substitution	Recommended	Not recommended
Biologics		
Interchangeable follow-on biologic substitution	Recommended	Not recommended*
Noninterchangeable follow-on biologic substitution	Recommended	Not recommended

* Pending further evidence.

alent and interchangeable follow-on biologic substitution. Financial incentives should likewise not be offered to physicians for initiating treatment-naïve patients on generic drugs or follow-on biologics, as payments could prompt unnecessary treatment or preclude clinically preferable treatment with a non-bioequivalent brand-name drug.

Instead, physician payments should be limited to bioequivalent substitution of non-NTI drugs. Further comparative effectiveness research studies are currently being organized to evaluate generic NTI drugs, including recent funding calls for bioequivalence studies of the antidepressant bupropion and the antihypertensive metoprolol (Edney 2014). Similarly, while some follow-on biologics have been safely used in the European Union for several years, their evidence base continues to evolve. Given this knowledge, it would not be prudent to extend financial incentives to bioequivalent substitution of NTI drugs or to interchangeable follow-on biologic substitution until there is more widely accepted assurance of safety and effectiveness in the U.S. market.

To encourage treatment initiation on generic drugs or follow-on biologics, therapeutic or noninterchangeable follow-on biologic substitution, or bioequivalent NTI or interchangeable follow-on biologic substitution, policymakers can instead rely on underused nonfinancial behavioral strategies. Formulary support, academic detailing, and e-prescribing nudges can improve decision-making and help physicians overcome the habit of thinking about and referring to drugs by their brand names as well as the false perception that generic drugs are less effective than brand-name drugs without changing the cost-benefit calculus of drug selections. In a 2011 survey, however, just 34% of office-based physicians reported even having a basic electronic health record system through which effective formulary support or e-prescribing nudges can be implemented (Hsiao et al. 2012), and only a handful of state governments sponsor academic detailing initiatives. Incentives should be considered to encourage insurers to develop formulary applications that can work with common electronic health record systems, which are already being promoted by the federal government to implement meaningful use standards. More research is also needed to test a wider spectrum of nudges like default generation of e-prescriptions for interchangeable generic drugs or follow-on biologics when available and publication of physicians' generic drug and follow-on biologic prescribing rates.

Even the incorporation of so-called nudges within traditional physician-centered strategies poses less risk of undue influence than bonuses. Implementation of an e-prescribing system that returns physician-initiated searches for a medication with lists programmed to place generic drugs first in larger and bolder font (Stenner, Chen, and Johnson 2010), for example, can correct for inherent cognitive biases like choice overload—the likelihood that physicians will maintain the status quo when presented with many rather than few alternatives—in addition to countering habits and false perceptions without changing the cost-benefit calculus of drug selections. More research is needed to develop and test a wider spectrum of nudges that can be applied at the point of prescribing.

Conclusion

Several strategies have emerged to optimize generic drug prescribing that can be applied to follow-on biologics when available. They include information-supplying programs and physician bonuses. These programs are largely legal and ethical. While the AKS prohibits Medicare Part D insurance providers and Medicaid managed care organizations from offering physicians financial incentives to prescribe generic drugs, it does not prevent private health plans, qualified health plans, and employers from doing the same. These incentives should be encouraged for bioequivalent substitution of non-NTI drugs and may be justified for bioequivalent substitution of NTI drugs and interchangeable follow-on biologic substitution following the emergence of further support. Current knowledge about the differences in the benefits and risks of non-bioequivalent drugs, however, militate against using financial incentives for therapeutic or noninterchangeable follow-on biologic substitution. Such substitution should be promoted by information-supplying programs alone, which pose less of a threat to override clinical decision-making.

References

Allan, G. Michael, Joel Lexchin, and Natasha Wiebe. 2007. "Physician Awareness of Drug Cost: A Systematic Review." *PLoS Medicine* 4:1491.

Blumenthal, D. 2004. "Doctors and Drug Companies." *New England Journal of Medicine* 351:1887–88.

Centers for Medicare and Medicaid. 2014. "NHE Factsheet." http://www.cms.gov/Research
-Statistics-Data-and-Systems/Statistics-Trends-and-Reports/NationalHealthExpendData
/NHE-Fact-Sheet.html.

Edney, Anna. 2014. "Generic-Drug Testing Goes Widespread in U.S. FDA Effort." Bloomberg.
February 22. http://www.bloomberg.com/news/2014-02-21/first-u-s-testing-of-generic
-drugs-is-unveiled-by-fda.html.

Fender, Jessica. 2008. "Bill Bans Incentives to Prescribe Generics." *Denver Post*, April 29.
http://www.denverpost.com/ci_9090030.

Fischer, Michael A., Christine Vogeli, Margaret Stedman, Timothy Ferris, M. Alan Brookhart,
and Joel S. Weissman. 2008. "Effect of Electronic Prescribing with Formulary Decision
Support on Medication Use and Costs." *Archives of Internal Medicine* 168:2437–38.

Fischer, Michael A., Margaret R. Stedman, Joyce Lii, Christine Vogeli, William H. Shrank,
M. Alan Brookhard, and Joel S. Weissman. 2010. "Primary Medication Non-Adherence:
Analysis of 195,930 Electronic Prescriptions." *Journal of General Internal Medicine*
25:288.

Fuhrmans, Vanessa. 2008. "Doctors Paid to Prescribe Generic Pills." *Wall Street Journal*,
January 24. http://online.wsj.com/news/articles/SB120114138064112219.

Gagnon, Marc-André, and Joel Lexchin. 2008. "The Cost of Pushing Pills: A New Estimate of
Pharmaceutical Promotion Expenditures in the United States." *PLoS Medicine* 5:31.

Gellad, Walid F., Julie M. Donohue, Xinhua Shao, Maria K. Mor, Carolyn T. Thorpe, Jeremy
Smith, Chester B. Good, Michael J. Fine, and Nancy E. Morden. 2013. "Brand-Name
Prescription Drug Use among Veterans Affairs and Medicare Part D Patients with
Diabetes." *Annals of Internal Medicine* 159:108.

Grabowksi, Henry, Rahul Guha, and Maria Salgado. 2014. "Biosimilar Competition: Lessons
from Europe." *Nature Reviews Drug Discovery* 13:100.

Grabowski, Henry, Genia Long, and Richard Mortimer. 2014. "Recent Trends in Brand-Name
and Generic Drug Competition." *Journal of Medical Economics* 17:207.

Hanlester Network v. Shalala, 51 F.3d 1390, 1400 (9th Cir. 1995).

Hsiao, Chun-Ju, Sandra L. Decker, Esther Hing, and Jane E. Sisk. 2012. "Most Physicians Were
Eligible for Federal Incentives in 2011, But Few Had EHR Systems That Met Meaningful-
Use Criteria." *Health Affairs* 31:1.

IMS Institute for Healthcare Informatics. 2013. "The Global Use of Medicines: Outlook
through 2017." http://www.imshealth.com/deployedfiles/imshealth/Global/Content
/Corporate/ IMS%20Health%20Institute/Reports/Global_Use_of_Meds_Outlook_2017
/IIHI_Global_Use_of_Meds_Report_2013.pdf9.

Kesselheim, Aaron S., Alexander S. Misono, Joy L. Lee, Margaret R. Stedman, M. Alan
Brookhart, Niteesh K. Choudhry, and William H. Shrank. 2008. "Clinical Equivalence of
Generic and Brand-Name Drugs Used in Cardiovascular Disease: A Systematic Review and
Meta-Analysis." *Journal of the American Medical Association* 300:2524.

Kesselheim, Aaron S., Margaret R. Stedman, Ellen J. Bubrick, Joshua J. Gagne, Alexander S.
Misono, Joy L. Lee, M. Alan Brookhart, Jerry Avorn, and William H. Shrank. 2010.
"Seizure Outcomes Following the Use of Generic versus Brand-Name Antiepileptic Drugs:
A Systematic Review and Meta-Analysis." *Drugs* 70:618.

Lasser, Karen E., Paul D. Allen, Steffie J. Woolhandler, David U. Himmelstein, Sidney M.
Wolfe, and David H. Bor. 2002. "Timing of New Black Box Warnings and Withdrawals for
Prescription Medications." *Journal of the American Medical Association* 287:2216.

Levy, Gerhard. 1998. "What Are Narrow Therapeutic Index Drugs?" *Clinical Pharmacology & Therapeutics* 63:501.

Liang, Brian A., and Timothy Mackey. 2011. "Emerging Patient Safety Issues under Health Care Reform: Follow-On Biologics and Immunogenicity." *Therapeutics and Clinical Risk Management* 7:490–91.

Macdonald, Gareth, and Dan Stanton. 2014. "Biosimilars, Bio-Differences: Breakdown of US State Substitution Laws." *BioPharma-Reporter*. April 18. http://www.biopharma-reporter .com/Markets-Regulations/Biosimilars-bio-differences-Breakdown-of-US-State-substitution -laws.

Martin, Timothy W. 2013. "Drugstores Press for Pricing Data." *Wall Street Journal*, March 27. http://online.wsj.com/articles/SB10001424127887323466204578382990730159644.

Med-Vantage. 2011. "2010 National P4P Survey." http://www.imshealth.com/deployedfiles /ims/ Global/Content/Solutions/Healthcare%20Analytics%20and%20Services/Payer%20 Solutions/Survey_Exec_Sum.pdf.

O'Brien, Mary Anne, A. D. Oxman, D. A. Davis, R. B. Haynes, N. Freemantle, and E. L. Harvey. 2008. "Educational Outreach Visits: Effects on Professional Practice and Health Care Outcomes." *Cochrane Database Systematic Review* 4:2.

Ornstein, Charles, Tracy Weber, and Jennifer LaFleur. 2013. "Medicare's Failure to Track Doctors Wastes Billions on Name-Brand Drugs." ProPublica. November 18. http://www .propublica.org/article/medicare-wastes-billions-on-name-brand-drugs.

Patel, Miteesh S., Susan Day, Dylan S. Small, John T. Howell, Gillian L. Lautenbach, Eliot H. Nierman, and Kevin G. Volpp. 2014. "Using Default Options within the Electronic Health Record to Increase the Prescribing of Generic-Equivalent Medications." *Annals of Internal Medicine* 161:S44.

Radick, Robert. 2013. "The Anti-Kickback Statute and the Affordable Care Act: A Law Enforcement Tool Suddenly Goes Missing." *Forbes*. November 13. http://www.forbes .com/ sites/insider/2013/11/13/the-anti-kickback-statute-and-the-affordable-care-act-a-law -enforcement-tool-suddenly-goes-missing/.

Rector, Thomas S., and Patricia J. Venus. 2004. "Do Drug Benefits Help Medicare Beneficia- ries Afford Prescribed Drugs?" *Health Affairs* 23:215.

Schondelmeyer, Stephen W., and Leigh Purvis. 2014. "Rx Price Watch Report." AARP. http://www.aarp.org/content/ dam/aarp/ppi/2014-11/rx-price-watch-report-AARP-ppi- health.pdf.

Shrank, William H., Niteesh K. Choudhry, Jessica Agnew-Blais, Alex D. Federman, Joshua N. Liberman, and Jun Liu. 2010. "State Generic Substitution Laws Can Lower Drug Outlays under Medicaid." *Health Affairs* 29:1384.

Shrank, William H., E. R. Cox, Michael A. Fischer, J. Mehta, and Niteesh K. Choudhry. 2009. "Patients' Perceptions of Generic Medications." *Health Affairs* 31:549.

Shrank, William H., Tuyen Hoang, Susan L. Ettner, Peter A. Glassman, Kavita Nair, Dee DeLapp, June Dirstine, Jerry Avorn, and Steven M. Asch. 2006. "The Implications of Choice: Prescribing Generic or Preferred Pharmaceuticals Improves Medication Adherence for Chronic Conditions." *Archives of Internal Medicine* 166:335.

Shrank, William H., Joshua N. Liberman, Michael A. Fischer, Jerry Avorn, Elaine Kilabuk, and Andrew Chang. 2011a. "The Consequences of Requesting 'Dispense as Written.'" *American Journal of Medicine* 124:311.

Shrank, William H., Joshua N. Liberman, Michael A. Fischer, Charmaine Girdish, Troyen A. Brennan, and Niteesh K. Choudhry. 2011b. "Physician Perceptions about Generic Drugs." *Annals of Pharmacotherapy* 45:33–34.

Solomont, E. B. 2008. "Insurers Pay Doctors to Push Generic Drugs." *The New York Sun*, July 16. http://www.nysun.com/business/insurers-pay-doctors-to-push-generic-drugs/81992/.

Stenner, Shane P., Qingxia Chen, and Kevin B. Johnson. 2010. "Impact of Generic Substitution Decision Support on Electronic Prescribing Behavior." *Journal of the American Medical Informatics Association* 17:681.

Thaler, Richard H., and Cass R. Sunstein. 2009. *Nudge: Improving Decisions about Health, Wealth, and Happiness*. Penguin Books. New York. 6.

Thomas, Katie. 2012. "Brand-Name Drug Prices Rise Sharply, Report Says." *The New York Times*, November 29. http://www.nytimes.com/2012/11/29/business/cost-of-brand-name-prescription-medicines-soaring.html.

United States v. Jain, 93 F.3d 436, 441 (8th Cir. 1996).

Yegian, Jill, and Dolores Yanagihara. 2013. "Value Based Pay for Performance in California." Integrated Healthcare Association. http://www.iha.org/pdfs_documents/p4p_california/Value-Based-Pay-for-Performance-Issue-Brief-September-2013.pdf.

CHAPTER 12

Toward Behaviorally Informed Policies for Consumer Credit Decisions in Self-Pay Medical Markets

Jim Hawkins

For patients considering healthcare that is not covered by insurance, such as fertility care, plastic surgery, or dental care, medical credit cards offer a way to finance these services. Although they are a relatively recent innovation in medical credit (Willis 2008), these medical creditors are a significant commercial force. For instance, in 2013, CareCredit, LLC, a major medical credit card provider, had 4 million cardholders as customers and 175,000 doctors' offices as partners (Zibel 2013). In its dental practice group alone, CareCredit has provided credit to 20 million patients (CareCredit, LCC 2014b).

In this chapter, I argue that consumers using third-party medical credit likely suffer from behavioral biases that cause them to make irrational decisions and that policymakers should attempt to correct these errors. I recognize the weaknesses in the current case for intervening in this market; policymakers need new research to assess the case for regulation. Despite these weaknesses, however, I suggest ways that the relationships between doctors and third-party lenders likely cause patients to make suboptimal decisions.

Because government officials have scrutinized CareCredit's lending activities in the past year, this chapter discusses CareCredit as its primary example of a medical credit provider. Specifically, I examine CareCredit's contract with physicians who offer Care-Credit to their customers and its recent settlements with the New York attorney general and the Consumer Financial Protection Bureau (CFPB).

Little academic literature addresses medical credit cards (Jacoby 2009). In a law review article in 2010, I discussed a study I did of fertility clinic websites and their presentations of credit products (Hawkins 2010). That article also pointed out that little law governs the relationship between creditors and doctors. While the Truth in Lending Act requires creditors to disclose pricing information to borrowers, nothing requires doctors to make any disclosures about their financial relationships with lenders (Hawkins 2010). Thus, this chapter also hopes to contribute to that general discussion.

Introduction to Medical Credit Providers

For physicians in markets where patients self-pay, third-party financing is important because many patients lack the money to pay for services. Healthcare consultants urge doctors to have patients use third-party credit providers instead of the doctors' extending credit themselves by performing services and then seeking repayment afterward (Jacoby and Holman 2010). Third-party credit providers are attractive to physicians because the creditor brings in additional business by providing patients with the money they need for the care. At the same time, the third-party creditor bears the risk of nonpayment. If patients cannot pay their bills, the creditor, not the doctor, suffers. As icing on the cake, physicians are not legally liable for arranging credit for patients (Jacoby and Holman 2010). As a result, many physicians partner with medical credit providers. I did a study in 2008–9 of fertility clinic websites, and I found that 48.5% of clinics' websites mention credit. Of course, many offices may mention credit to patients in person, but my study measured only websites. Of those websites mentioning credit, 62.1% of those websites mentioned a limited number of credit options. They did not simply suggest that patients turn to loans or credit cards to finance the care. Instead, they would state that they partnered with one or two specific creditors. Clinics seem to see relationships with creditors as a selling point—52.4% market themselves based on the credit or market the credit itself (Hawkins 2010).

CareCredit's marketing and the agreement between physicians and CareCredit illustrate the benefits doctors obtain by partnering with third-party lenders. CareCredit's website describes how partnering with CareCredit will "increase production by enabling more patients the ability to accept, and immediately begin, recommended care without having to decline, delay or compromise treatment because of insurance benefits" (CareCredit, LCC 2014d). The marketing to physicians also emphasizes that doctors do not bear any responsibility for nonpayment: "Receive payment in two business days, with no responsibility if the patient delays payment or defaults" (CareCredit, LLC 2014c). An agreement between doctors and Springstone Financial, LLC, another popular third-party lender, is even more clear: "The Springstone Program is a non-recourse program for the Doctor, meaning that Springstone will not seek repayment from the Doctor if the patient fails to repay the loan" (Springstone Financial, LCC 2014b).

The agreement between CareCredit and physicians does impose some risk of nonpayment on doctors by giving CareCredit the right to refuse to pay the physician in some circumstances such as fraud. But in general, CareCredit's rights against the doctor for patient nonpayment are limited to CareCredit's taking the right to the payments that patients owe to the physician as collateral (CareCredit, LCC 2014a).

Finally, CareCredit agrees to indemnify the doctor for damages relating to the consumer credit agreement's failure to comply with the law, so CareCredit takes on the risk of legal problems from the loan (CareCredit, LCC 2014a). CareCredit attempts to minimize such problems by instructing physicians to not violate any law in a way that would make CareCredit liable, such as ensuring the truthfulness of disclosures about the credit plan (CareCredit, LCC 2014a).

For patients, third-party creditors offer promise and peril. For some patients who need money for medical procedures, third-party creditors offer a way to buy services now and pay later. Also, because the creditor partners with the doctor, the search costs for credit are lower. Patients might feel uncomfortable explaining their infertility to a loan officer at a bank when the officer asks about the reason the patient needs the money, for instance, making searching for credit outside a doctor's office costly (Meyer 2005).

On the other hand, taking on debt for medical procedures can lead to financial distress, as demonstrated empirically for medical debt in general. Medical debt is associated with bankruptcy filings (Himmelstein et al. 2009). This debt is not merely a product of the cost of services—the cost of servicing medical debt adds to expenses (Sugden 2012). Even for those patients who do not seek refuge in bankruptcy, medical debt is a leading cause of collection activity, and medical debt harms consumers' credit reports (Rukavina 2014).

Behavioral Anomalies in Medical Credit Markets

Patients who obtain credit from third-party lenders that partner with their doctors likely depart from the rational actor model of decision-making. First, medical consumers likely exhibit the same biases from which other credit card users suffer. A rich literature demonstrates that credit card users are excessively optimistic (Bar-Gill 2004). For instance, they believe they can pay off a card's balance before the teaser rate ends, and they underestimate the likelihood that they will borrow at post-introductory rates (Bar-Gill and Bubb 2012). Also, consumers are myopic, focusing on present benefits and not readily assessing risks and future costs (Kilborn 2005). Surveys demonstrate that credit card customers focus more on short-term benefits such as teaser rates, rewards, rebates, and the lack of an annual fee (Slowik 2012). In summary, myopia and optimism are the "two underlying biases [that] jointly contribute to [a cardholder's] underestimation of many future costs" (Bar-Gill and Bubb 2012, 976).

CareCredit's agreements reflect over-optimism because around 85% of borrowers agree to CareCredit's deferred-financing plan as opposed to a plan in which the borrower pays interest for the duration of the loan, for instance, at 14.90% APR, but does not risk a large jump in the interest rate (Consumer Financial Protection Bureau 2013; CareCredit, LLC 2014e). Under the deferred-financing plan, patients pay nothing if the debt is fully repaid by the end of the promotional period, but they pay 26.99% interest for the entire borrowing period if they do not completely repay the debt by the end (CareCredit, LLC 2014e). This structure is a classic form of framing that causes patients to focus on the fixed, short-term costs instead of the long-term, contingent costs (Bar-Gill 2012). Many patients entering these deferred-payment transactions likely think the credit will be free for them, but 25% of patients in these plans fail to repay during the promotional period ("Patients Using Health Credit Cards?" 2013). Those patients substantially underestimate the cost of the credit and of the entire medical transaction because they do not consider the 26.99% finance charge. This failure to apprehend the true cost of the credit creates a behavioral market failure because consumers think the product costs less than what they actually end up paying, causing them to misjudge the cost relative to the value of the product (Bar-Gill 2012).

In addition to teaser rates, a salesperson for a medical credit provider explained to me that she provided training for doctors' offices that appears to capitalize on consumers' tendencies to neglect the overall cost of credit by focusing on just the individual payment amounts (Sunstein 2006). For instance, "instead of telling patients that [in vitro fertilization] will cost a large fixed sum, Capital One trained clinic staff to present the payment in a monthly payment amount that appeared more manageable" (Hawkins 2010, 859).

But beyond general poor decision-making, an important area that behavioral economists have overlooked in the context of medical credit is the relationships between the patient, the doctor as the arranger of credit, and the credit provider. I argue that these relationships have two potential effects: a halo effect in which borrowers view creditors more positively because of the doctor's involvement and an automation effect in which the salience of the lending decision is diminished.

First, partnerships between lenders and doctors might create a halo effect, causing the patient to evaluate the credit differently because patients trust doctors (Downs and Lyons 1991; Lieberman 2002). While there is not currently direct evidence of such a halo effect, studies have shown that patients want their doctors to make treatment decisions for them (Korobkin 2014). It is not a large conceptual leap to think this trust may also apply to the doctor's preferred credit provider. The confirmation bias—that is, people's tendency to "seek out evidence that confirms their prior beliefs" (Leslie 2010, 314)—may work against any resistance a patient has to using credit or using the doctor's preferred credit provider if the patient is unwilling to question the doctor's recommendations. Studies have shown, for instance, that patients "interpret data showing poor outcomes of treatments as unavoidable events beyond the physician's control" (Frank 2007, 205–6). Thus, the trust patients place in their physicians may cause them to view the associated credit provider more positively than they otherwise would because of the halo effect. If patients view third-party creditors as related to the doctor, they might either be confused about the relationship between the two or be at least affected by it.

The CareCredit agreement recognizes the confusion that patients might have over which party is providing credit. The agreement requires physicians to hold in trust any payments to CareCredit that the doctor inadvertently accepts from patients, and it grants CareCredit a limited power of attorney to cash payments for CareCredit mistakenly made out to the doctor (CareCredit, LLC 2014a). While the agreement also prohibits the doctor from representing the financing as an "in-house" payment plan, some practices disregard this prohibition (Hawkins 2010). The agreement actually facilitates the confusion because the physician grants CareCredit "a nonexclusive license to use [the doctor's] name, trademarks, logos or other marks in connection with the administration and operation of the Program" (CareCredit, LCC 2014a). Springstone Financial, LLC's agreement is the same (Springstone Financial, LLC 2014b).

In addition to the halo effect, having a partnership between doctors and credit providers likely decreases the salience of the borrowing to the patient, creating an automation effect. If a patient does not have to leave the doctor's office, talk to any outside personnel, or wait more than a few seconds for a response (CareCredit, LCC 2014c), the transaction becomes relatively painless and almost automatic. Sixty-five percent of CareCredit cardholders signed up in their doctor's office ("Patients Using Health Credit Cards?" 2013), and the Capital One salesperson I spoke to had the impression that everyone who needed credit and qualified for the doctor's preferred credit provider chose that provider (Hawkins 2010). The speed at which someone can spend matters, and Springstone Financial, LLC, as one example, emphasizes in its marketing the speed at which patients obtain loans (Springstone Financial, LLC, 2014b). Again, while there is not currently direct empirical support for this effect, in other contexts, research has demonstrated its existence. For instance, after states automated toll booth payments on highways, research found that the reduced salience caused toll rates to be 20% to 40% higher than in nonautomatic systems (Finkelstein 2007). The ease of obtaining credit may cause people to take out loans they would otherwise avoid, or it may dissuade people from searching for better deals.

The salience of the lending decision is also diminished by the stressful situation many self-pay patients find themselves in at the moment they make the decision to borrow money in the doctor's office. For some patients, the decision to borrow will be made at the same time as other critical decisions, like whether to have dental work done or whether to undergo fertility treatments. These circumstances will involve stress and distractions that tax cognitive resources, suggesting that biases and suggestions will have more influence. As Barr and colleagues explain:

> The amount of information people can and do attend to is limited. Moreover, cognitive load has been shown to affect performance in everyday tasks. To the extent that consumers find themselves in challenging situations that are unfamiliar, tense, or distracting, all of which consume cognitive resources, less focused attention will be available to process the information that is relevant to the decision at hand. (Barr, Mullainathan, and Shafir 2012, 442)

Thus, third-party credit offered in a doctor's office likely poses greater risks than credit decisions generally.

These effects of the relationship between doctors and third-party creditors have the potential to cause real harm (Hawkins 2010). Patients may get worse deals because they are led by their physician instead of by detached, rational analysis. Worse, patients may take on debt that could lead to collection activity, financial distress, or bankruptcy.

Lawmaking under Uncertainty

The problem with the preceding analysis is that it imports findings about consumer credit behavior from contexts outside that of third-party medical credit providers, leaving uncertainty about whether consumers of medical credit act in the same way as other credit card users. For optimal policymaking, we need empirical research on behavior within specific markets. Otherwise, translating studies conducted in one context into other contexts can lead to inaccuracy (Bar-Gill 2012). While common within literature on healthcare and consumer credit, importing studies from one context into another one is problematic. For one thing, it often involves using results from experiments with students in laboratories on people making decisions with real consequences (Beales 2008).

Consider the seemingly unassailable proof that people are overly optimistic (Kahneman 2011). Generalized proof of this phenomenon has led academics to call on the CFPB to step into payday loan markets because they have translated studies about optimism in other contexts into that market (Bar-Gill and Warren 2008). The problem, however, is that payday loan consumers do not appear to exhibit significant over-optimism (Mann 2014; Fritzdixon, Hawkins, and Skiba 2014). For instance, Fritzdixon and colleagues surveyed consumers of title lending, a close cousin to payday lending that involves month-long loans. They asked how long people thought it would take to completely pay off their loans. The standard literature about optimism bias suggests that people would predict a very short repayment term because they are overly optimistic. Fritzdixon and colleagues found, however, that 50% of borrowers predicted taking four or more months to completely repay the debt (Fritzdixon, Hawkins, and Skiba 2014). Payday and title lending consumers, like all consumers, likely suffer from other cognitive defects, but the point is that we need market-specific data to ensure that regulation is solving the right behavioral market failures.

Credit decisions in the context of healthcare are different from normal credit decisions on a number of levels. Healthcare is much more complicated than other purchases. In addition, healthcare consumers often lack information about the costs of services and about the quality of individual health service providers. Also, healthcare decisions often involve insurance, which complicates how much the patient will actually pay and poses a risk of moral hazard.

In order to assess the degree to which consumers of medical credit are predictably irrational, new research needs to be done. Regarding the over-optimism bias's influence on patients picking deferred interest plans, it would be helpful to policymakers to understand the extent to which people borrowing from medical creditors believe they will repay their debt within the promotional period. Researchers could survey borrowers at the time they open their credit card accounts, asking whether the borrower believes she will repay the debt within the required timeframe. Then, those survey responses could either be compared against the general population of medical credit borrowers in deferred interest plans or against the actual outcome for the borrower who took the survey. Ronald Mann's work on payday lending follows a similar strategy to access borrowers' optimisms in that market (Mann 2014).

To assess the effects of the doctor's serving as the arranger of the credit relationship between the patient and the third-party medical credit provider, research could compare the outcomes for patients using credit provided by independent creditors and creditors partnering with medical practices. Data could come from bankruptcy filings or credit reporting bureaus. Alternatively, a survey-based approach could help policymakers understand the extent to which medical borrowers considered options beyond those presented by their physicians. Finally, following Oren Bar-Gill's approach, researchers could explore whether a rational choice framework explains the characteristics of these contracts, and if not, explore a behavioral explanation (Bar-Gill 2012).

Yet, despite the uncertainty that a new context provides, policymakers still should consider intervening in this market. First, switching to a behaviorally informed approach to medical credit has risks and costs, but so does staying with rational choice theory that merely uses product attribute-style disclosures. We know that approach is oversimplified (Vandenbergh, Carrico, and Bressman 2011). Legislating cannot wait for perfect knowledge (Orszag 2008).

Moreover, despite the differences between medical credit and credit in general, self-pay markets are particularly apt places to apply behavioral economics principles because the costs are more transparent to consumers, unlike other healthcare contexts where prices are deliberately concealed (Schneider and Hall 2009; Reinhardt 2001) or difficult to predict because of uncertainty about the patient's responsibility (Bohnsack and Hawig 2013). Also, unlike other contexts where patients make decisions and "lack of information on success rates and other costs and benefits makes that decision extremely difficult to make well" (Monahan 2006, 820), self-pay consumers in fertility markets, for instance, can often see success rates on the provider's website (Hawkins 2013). Finally, moral hazard problems plague healthcare markets that are not self-pay because of the influence of health insurance, but these problems are not present in the self-pay environment because consumers internalize the full cost of treatment (Korobkin 2014). Thus, despite the fact that specific empirical research has not proven that borrowers in this context are acting suboptimally, there is still a strong case for behaviorally informed regulation.

Policy Responses

In other consumer credit contexts, behavioral economics has shaped policy, yielding beneficial results. Unfortunately, recent regulatory enforcement actions by the CFPB and New York attorney general against medical credit providers have reached settlements that do not generally recognize the cognitive limits of patients. This section discusses the success of behaviorally informed credit laws in other consumer credit environments as well as the limited usefulness of the recent regulatory settlements in the healthcare context.

One popular example of behavioral economics' influence on credit regulation is Texas's payday and auto title lending laws. Before 2012, Texas placed few restrictions on payday and auto title lenders because these businesses operated under a loophole in the state's usury laws (Hawkins 2012). An empirical study by Marianne Bertrand and Adair Morse of disclosures about how borrowers actually acted when repaying their payday loans, what Bar-Gill calls pattern-of-use disclosures, motivated Texas to change its laws (Bertrand and Morse 2011; Hutchings and Nance 2012). Texas now requires that payday and auto title lenders disclose to customers "information regarding the typical pattern of repayment of deferred presentment transactions and motor vehicle title loans" (Tex. Fin. Code Ann. §393.223(a)). Providing this information combats over-optimism or other behavioral biases because it corrects borrowers' faulty predictions about how they will use the product. Bertrand and Morse found that the pattern-of-use disclosures reduced "the take-up of future payday loans by 11% in the subsequent 4 months"(Bertrand and Morse 2011, 1865).

In contrast to this and other successful legal changes outside of medical credit, recent settlements between CareCredit and the New York attorney general and the CFPB appear less likely to protect consumers of medical credit. In 2013, the attorney general of New York settled a controversy with CareCredit, and the settlement agreement included consumer protection measures, including a cooling-off period and disclosures to make consumers aware of the high interest rate at the end of the teaser rate period ("Patients Using Health Credit Cards?" 2013). Later in 2013, the CFPB settled with CareCredit, also requiring a disclosure-based consumer protection measure. CareCredit agreed to contact new consumers within seventy-two hours of taking out a credit card loan with a promotional interest rate and explain "that interest at the rate of 26.99 percent (or the applicable interest rate at the time) will be incurred from the date of purchase and charged if the original balance is not paid by the end of the promotional period" (CFPB/GE Consent Order 2013).

From a behavioral economics standpoint, other than the cooling-off period, the rules generated by these two settlements only disclose attributes of the CareCredit product, not the ways that consumers will actually use these products (Bar-Gill 2012). Disclosing the fact that a teaser rate will end will not affect people suffering from the optimism bias because such people will not think that information applies to them

(Bar-Gill 2012). If people are overly optimistic about whether they will pay off the debt during the promotional period, they will underestimate the likelihood that they will incur the interest at the higher rate (Jolls, Sunstein, and Thaler 1998).

Instead of disclosures about the medical credit product's attributes, governments should push medical creditors to disclose information about the consumer's probable future use of the credit. For instance, following Bertrand and Morse's and Texas's lead, policymakers could require medical creditors to disclose average use information about deferred-cost arrangements. The disclosure could feature a graphic depiction of the number of borrowers who fail to pay during the promotional period.

Another problem with these settlement rules is that the entity implementing them—CareCredit—has a significant incentive to evade the rules. Firms' opposition to a behaviorally informed law affects the law's efficacy (Willis 2013; Barr, Mullainathan, and Shafir 2012). To again take an example from the context of fringe lending, auto title lenders have been extremely successful in evading even strict laws. To evade usury caps on interest rate charges, auto title lenders have offered open-ended credit plans secured by vehicles in Kansas, they have operated as Credit Service Organizations instead of as lenders in Texas, and they have offered only loans for more than $2,500 in California (Hawkins 2012). Because medical credit providers benefit substantially from consumers' underestimating the likelihood that they will pay a higher interest rate for their loans, it is likely that these credit providers will find creative legal solutions to ensure that over-optimism endures.

As an alternative to the New York attorney general's and the CFPB's approaches, policymakers should work with doctors who partner with lenders to implement reforms. The main benefits that third-party lenders bring to medical practices—more customers, no risk of nonpayment, and no legal liability—persist for doctors even if the government requires doctors to make pattern-of-use disclosures to combat over-optimism. These pattern-of-use disclosures are designed to lead borrowers to pick traditional payment plans, not deferred-financing plans, but they are not designed to cause borrowers not to take out loans at all. Thus, because doctors are much less likely to try to evade or thwart legal intervention, governments should focus on the medical practices partnered with the creditor.

A final problem with the New York attorney general's and CFPB's approach is that their enforcement actions do not address the halo and automatic effects that the relationships between lenders and doctors likely create. In the past, I argued that the government should require disclosures about doctors' financial relationships with third-party lenders and should require doctors to offer multiple credit sources to combat problems associated with the doctor-creditor relationship (Hawkins 2010). If patients were made aware of other options and were aware of the financial incentives doctors have in offering specific types of credit, they would likely be more wary of just automatically going with the doctors' lenders. At the very least, requiring multiple choices would force borrowers to engage in the decision-making process.

Conclusion

While the case for intervening in the relationships between patients, doctors, and third-party medical creditors requires more research, policymakers should consider implementing behaviorally informed laws and regulations to mitigate suboptimal decision-making. Consumers considering whether to take out a loan from a medical creditor recommended by a doctor's office likely make the decision too quickly, trusting the doctor and focusing on the medical (and not the financial) situation. Policymakers should aim reforms at the medical practices themselves instead of at lenders in order to avoid having the creditor—who likely opposes reforms—implement them.

References

Bar-Gill, Oren. 2004. "Seduction by Plastic." *Northwestern University Law Review* 98:1373–1434.

———. 2012. *Seduction by Contract: Law, Economics, and Psychology in Consumer Markets.* Oxford University Press. New York.

Bar-Gill, Oren, and Ryan Bubb. 2012. "Credit Card Pricing: The Card Act and Beyond." *Cornell Law Review* 97:967–1017.

Bar-Gill, Oren, and Elizabeth Warren. 2008. "Making Credit Safer." *University of Pennsylvania Law Review* 157:1–101.

Barr, Michael S., Sendhil Mullainathan, and Eldar Shafir. 2012. "Behaviorally Informed Regulation." In *The Behavioral Foundations of Public Policy*, edited by Eldar Shafir. Princeton University Press. Princeton, NJ.

Beales, J. Howard. 2008. "Competition Protection and Behavioral Economics: To BE or Not to BE?" *Competition Policy International* 4:149–67.

Bertrand, Marianne, and Adair Morse. 2011. "Information Disclosure, Cognitive Bias, and Payday Borrowing." *Journal of Finance* 66:1865–93.

Bohnsack, Jim, and Scott Hawig. 2013. "Choosing the Right Strategy for Point-of-Service Collections." *Healthcare Registration* 22:1–12.

CareCredit, LLC. 2014a. "Card Acceptance Agreement for Participating Professionals." http://www.carecredit.com/agreement/CareCreditPPA_REV04-2013.pdf.

———. 2014b. "Help More Patients Get Care with Convenient Financing Options." http://www.carecredit.com/practices/dental/.

———. 2014c. "How CareCredit Works." http://www.carecredit.com/practices/dental/cc-works.html/.

———. 2014d. "Increased Production." http://www.carecredit.com/practices/dental/inc-production.html.

———. 2014e. "Terms & Conditions for CareCredit Payment Plans." http://www.carecredit.com/payment_calculator/terms.html.

CFPB/GE Consent Order. 2013. http://files.consumerfinance.gov/f/201312_cfpb_consent-order_ge-carecredit.pdf.

Consumer Financial Protection Bureau. 2013. "CFPB Orders GE CareCredit to Refund $34.1 Million for Deceptive Health-Care Credit Card Enrollment." http://www.consumerfinance

.gov/newsroom/cfpb-orders-ge-carecredit-to-refund-34-1-million-for-deceptive-health-care -credit-card-enrollment/.

Downs, A. Chris, and Phillip M. Lyons. 1991. "Natural Observations of the Links between Attractiveness and Initial Legal Judgments." *Personality & Social Psychology Bulletin* 17:541–47.

Finkelstein, Amy. 2007. "E-ZTax: Tax Salience and Tax Rates." *National Bureau of Economic Research* Working Paper No. 12924.

Frank, Richard G. 2007. "Behavioral Economics and Health Economics." In *Behavioral Economics and Its Applications*, edited by Peter Diamond and Hannu Vartianen. Princeton University Press. Princeton, NJ. 205–6.

Fritzdixon, Kathryn, Jim Hawkins, and Paige Marta Skiba. 2014. "Dude, Where's My Car Title?: The Law, Behavior, and Economics of Title Lending Markets." *University of Illinois Law Review* 2014:1013–58.

Hawkins, Jim. 2012. "Credit on Wheels: The Law and Business of Auto-Title Lending." *Washington & Lee Law Review* 69:535–606.

———. 2010. "Doctors as Bankers: Evidence from Fertility Markets." *Tulane Law Review* 84:841–98.

———. 2013. "Selling ART: An Empirical Assessment of Advertising on Fertility Clinics' Websites." *Indiana Law Journal* 88:1147–79.

Himmelstein, David U., Deborah Thorne, Elizabeth Warren, and Steffie Woolhandler. 2009. "Medical Bankruptcy in the United States, 2007: Results of a National Study." *American Journal of Medicine* 122:741–47.

Hutchings, Sealy, and Matthew J. Nance. 2012. "Credit Access Business: The Regulation of Payday and Title Loans in Texas." *Consumer Finance Law Quarterly Report* 66:76–93.

Jacoby, Melissa B. 2009. "The Debt Financing of Parenthood." *Law & Contemporary Problems* 72:147–75.

Jacoby, Melissa B., and Mirya R. Holman. 2010. "Managing Medical Bills on the Brink of Bankruptcy." *Yale Journal of Health Policy, Law, and Ethics* 10:239–97.

Jolls, Christine, Cass R. Sunstein, and Richard Thaler. 1998. "A Behavioral Approach to Law and Economics." *Stanford Law Review* 50:1471–1550.

Kahneman, Daniel. 2011. *Thinking, Fast and Slow.* Farrar, Straus and Giroux. New York. 260.

Kilborn, Jason J. 2005. "Behavioral Economics, Overindebtedness and Comparative Consumer Bankruptcy: Searching for Causes and Evaluating Solutions." *Emory Bankruptcy Developments Journal* 22:13–45.

Korobkin, Russell. 2014. "Comparative Effectiveness Research as Choice Architecture: The Behavioral Law and Economics Solution to the Health Care Cost Crisis." *Michigan Law Review* 112:523–74.

Leslie, Christopher R. 2010. "Rationality Analysis in Antitrust." *University of Pennsylvania Law Review* 158:261–353.

Lieberman, Joel D. 2002. "Head over the Heart or Heart over the Head? Cognitive Experiential Self-Theory and Extralegal Heuristics in Juror Decision Making." *Journal of Applied Social Psychology* 32:2526–53.

Mann, Ronald J. 2014. "Assessing the Optimism of Payday Loan Borrowers." *Supreme Court Economic Review* 22:105–32.

Meyer, Mark C. 2005. *Lifestyle Lending Offers Innovation and Growth for Credit Unions.* Filene Research Institute. 8.

Monahan, Amy B. 2006. "The Promise and Peril of Ownership Society Health Care Policy." *Tulane Law Review* 80:777–848.

Orszag, Peter. 2008. "Health Care and Behavioral Economics." http://www.cbo.gov/sites /default/files/cbofiles/ftpdocs/93xx/doc9317/05-29-nasi_speech.pdf.

"Patients Using Health Credit Cards?" 2013. *Health Care Collector* 27:9.

Reinhardt, Uwe E. 2001. "Can Efficiency in Health Care Be Left to the Market?" *Journal of Health Politics, Policy and Law* 26:967–92.

Rukavina, Mark. 2014. "Medical Debt and Its Relevance When Assessing Creditworthiness." *Suffolk University Law Review* 46:967–82.

Schneider, Carl E., and Mark A. Hall. 2009. "The Patient Life: Can Consumers Direct Health Care?" *American Journal of Law and Medicine* 35:7–65.

Slowik, Jonathan. 2012. "Credit Card Act II: Expanding Credit Card Reform by Targeting Behavioral Biases." *UCLA Law Review* 59:1292–1341.

Springstone Financial, LLC. 2014a. "Patient Welcome." https://secure.springstoneplan.com /patients/.

———. 2014b. Program Terms and Conditions.

Sugden, Ryan. 2012. "Sick and (Still) Broke: Why the Affordable Care Act Won't End Medical Bankruptcy." *Washington University Journal of Law & Policy* 38:441–74.

Sunstein, Cass R. 2006. "Boundedly Rational Borrowing." *University of Chicago Law Review* 73:249–70.

Sunstein, Cass R., and Richard H. Thaler. 2008. *Nudge: Improving Decisions about Health, Wealth, and Happiness*. Yale University Press. New Haven, CT.

Vandenbergh, Michael P., Amanda R. Carrico, and Lisa Schultz Bressman. 2011. "Regulation in the Behavioral Era." *Minnesota Law Review* 95:715–81.

Willis, Lauren E. 2008. "Against Financial-Literacy Education." *Iowa Law Review* 94:197–285.

———. 2013. "When Nudges Fail: Slippery Defaults." *University of Chicago Law Review* 80:1155–1229.

Zibel, Alan. 2013. "GE Capital to Refund up to $34 Million Over CareCredit Medical Credit Cards." *Wall Street Journal*, December 10.

PART IV **CROWDING OUT**

Introduction

Neel Shah

No one has more at stake in making healthcare a good value than those who purchase it in bulk—namely, employers who are trying to keep premiums low and insurers who are trying to hold on to as much of those premiums as possible. That is why employers and insurers are putting considerable effort into "nudging" their employees or healthcare providers to make healthier decisions. In the plurality of cases where we know what these healthier decisions are (exercise for people who are obese), rewarding someone for a healthy behavior with cold, hard cash seems like an effective way to reinforce the behavior. Moreover, if a reward (or penalty) promotes a healthy behavior while also preventing more expensive healthcare down the road, everybody seems to win.

The trouble is that sometimes these incentives do not appear to promote healthy behavior for very long, or even at all. In some cases, counterintuitive as it may seem, a monetary reward for a healthy behavior may even cause people to double down on less healthy behaviors. As a result, for employers, insurers, and everyone else with a stake in improving healthcare value, the effects of incentives on behaviors can be challenging to predict.

Underlying this puzzle is a key insight from cognitive psychology: the way all of us value health behaviors is often distorted by the current status of our health. For example, if we are very healthy, we may undervalue healthcare services. (Try naming your favorite routine screening test—pap smears? Colonoscopies perhaps?) Similarly, if we are very unhealthy or sick, we may overvalue care. (What wouldn't you want done if your life were unexpectedly in danger?) The reasons why we do or do not make certain decisions about our health are complex and often disconnected from the actuarial value of the decision that an insurance company might calculate.

Enter the idea of motivational "crowding out." As Kristen Underhill points out in chapter 13, our motivations fall into two categories: extrinsic motivation, in which the reward is "separable" from the desired result of the action (for example, getting cold, hard cash for losing weight), and intrinsic motivation, which includes everything else (like personal satisfaction). The traditional view of incentive design is that extrinsic motivations created by rewards or penalties sum additively with preexisting intrinsic motivations. What we are now learning from a growing base of empirical data is that in many cases, extrinsic motivations may attenuate or even entirely displace intrinsic ones.

Both the theory and the empirical demonstration of motivational crowding out in the health domain are at nascent stages. Underhill advances the theory of motivational crowding out by presenting a framework for understanding an array of mechanisms by which motivational crowding out may take place. She parses and defines five key cognitive processes of crowding out, which she calls "signaling effects," "overjustification," "impaired self-determination," "endogenous preference formation," and "learned helplessness." Despite this apparent complexity, there are two fundamental assumptions: (1) extrinsic incentives are necessary only because of an asymmetry in the way the principal and agent value a certain behavior, and (2) what links the cognitive processes of crowding out is that there are often also asymmetries in the way the principal and the agent value the incentive itself.

Crowding out from "signaling" (a familiar concept to economists) results when the type and size of the incentive reveals information to the agent that indicates that the principal values the behavior less than he does. Crowding out from "impaired self-determination" occurs when the incentive adulterates the agent's own intrinsic motivations (such as altruism) in specific cases where intrinsic motivation alone should be sufficient. Underhill demonstrates the utility of parsing these heterogeneous cognitive processes by placing them in the context of common, real-world examples, ranging from organ donation to corporate wellness. She acknowledges that there is some evidence that crowding out effects may be overcome by making rewards or penalties large enough, but argues that case-specific understanding of these processes may allow principals to design incentives that are not only effective, but also more efficient and less expensive.

In chapter 14, Aditi Sen and colleagues add an additional dimension of complexity by providing new empirical evidence that theories on motivational crowding out may not be generalizable to all health behaviors. One of the key concerns in applying financial incentives to personal health in particular is the high degree of preexisting intrinsic motivation compared to other domains. Using data from two randomized controlled trials of workplace weight loss programs, Sen et al. investigate the impact of various extrinsic incentive designs (individual versus group rewards, and graduated employer reward matching) on the scores of a pre-validated psychometric test that measures intrinsic motivation. Because all participants have relatively high intrinsic motivation to lose weight at baseline, loss of intrinsic motivation (as theoretically predicted), should be straightforward to detect.

This is not what they find. Sen et al. test for motivational crowding out by looking for differences in intrinsic motivation between the incentive groups and a control group at different points in time. For both incentive designs, no significant difference in intrinsic motivation was detected. This observation persists even across different baseline weights, financial statuses, and starting motivation levels.

Sen et al. further illustrate the pragmatic challenges of collecting this type of data. Experimental trials are expensive. As a result, sample size is small, a problem that is compounded by missing data from participants who dropped out (approximately one-third of the participants in each arm). Sen et al. therefore perform a sensitivity analysis to test the possibility that those who dropped out may have had less intrinsic motivation to lose weight to begin with. While this requires some leaps of faith, again, they fail to detect motivational crowding out.

Taken together, these chapters make clear that theoretical heterogeneity and empirical inconsistency pose significant challenges to the study of motivational crowding out in healthcare. Nonetheless, Underhill and Sen et al. help point the way toward important next steps of inquiry in complementary ways. If motivational crowding out is more challenging to detect empirically in some settings than others, it is helpful to understand how different cognitive processes may account for this. Similarly, as we parse the relative influence of different processes, it will be important to empirically validate them in context.

CHAPTER 13

Extrinsic Incentives, Intrinsic Motivation, and Motivational Crowding Out in Health Law and Policy

Kristen Underhill

Commentary on carrots and sticks abounds; indeed, all law may be viewed as a system of rewards and penalties. Conventional economic theory would suggest that offering incentives for good behavior is likely to yield more of it, while penalties are likely to deter bad behavior. But behavioral economics scholarship prompts a second look at how incentives and incentive-based policies may have counterintuitive effects. A subset of this work concerns motivational crowding out: a process by which imposing an extrinsic reward or penalty may reduce individuals' "intrinsic" motivation for good behavior (Frey and Jegen 2001; Gneezy, Meier, and Rey-Biel 2011). Controversial scholarship in this area has raised concerns that echo throughout law, philosophy, and economics. These concerns include not only instrumental worries about efficiency and behavioral impacts of incentives, but also deeper concerns about whether incentives impair autonomy (Grant 2012) or prompt the deterioration of individual or collective morality over time (Bowles 2008; Grant 2012; Sandel 2012; Schwartz and Sharpe 2010). This chapter sets aside moral concerns to focus on instrumental impacts; that is, whether motivational crowding out can render an incentive inefficient or detrimental for behavior.

The concept of motivational crowding out initially derived from research conducted in psychology and economics in the 1970s, beginning in contexts such as blood donation (Titmuss 1970; Arrow 1972) and educational achievement (Deci 1972; Lepper, Green, and Nisbett 1973), and expanding to encompass a broad range of incentives aimed at maximizing health, productivity, and educational accomplishments (Cerasoli, Nicklin, and Ford 2014; Gneezy, Meier, and Rey-Biel 2011). Health policy has been at the forefront of discussions on crowding out, in part due to Richard Titmuss's initial text on incentives for blood donation, but also due to the growing popularity of incentives to motivate behaviors such as smoking cessation, medication adherence, exercise, organ donation, and high-quality patient care. To date, however, concerns about motivational crowding out in health policy have been "muddled" (Schlesinger 2012), lacking a clear understanding of the processes by which crowding out occurs.

A closer look at the crowding-out literature reveals an important reason for confusion: the impact of incentives on motivation is inescapably complex, and there are multiple mechanisms by which incentives can interfere with intrinsic motives. Where motivational crowding out occurs, changing the incentive structure may help to disrupt these effects. But importantly, remedies for crowding-out effects must be tailored to the specific mechanisms at work in a given context. Remedies that mitigate crowding out due to one causal process (for example, increasing the size of the incentive, using prizes instead of penalties) may backfire if another process is actually in play. Careful empirical study is therefore needed to identify the cognitive mechanisms that give rise to motivational crowding out in each context, and to test mechanism-specific ways to limit potential harms due to crowding-out effects. Of course, even where crowding-out effects persist, incentives may nevertheless have a net beneficial effect on behavior, or they may be preferable to other policy options. The goal of the current analysis, however, is to suggest that incentives can be optimized by considering design features that limit crowding out.

This chapter proceeds in several steps. I first provide a conceptual overview of motivational crowding out in response to incentives, which draws on empirical research from economics, psychology, and law. I then illustrate heterogeneity in the causes of motivational crowding out by discussing three examples of incentives proposed or implemented in health law: incentives for organ donation, pay-for-performance programs for individual physicians, and wellness programs implemented by insurers or workplaces. I conclude by noting the importance of responding to specific crowding-out processes when designing incentive-based policies, suggesting how solutions for crowding-out problems can flow from the mechanisms driving these effects.

Motivational Crowding Out

Distinguishing between "intrinsic" and "extrinsic" motivations is essential for understanding motivational crowding out. Although the boundaries between these two categories may blur (Feldman 2011), "extrinsic," or "instrumental," motivation generally denotes a desire for a result that is "separable" from the action itself, such as obtaining a financial benefit or avoiding a penalty (Benkler 2004, 279; Ryan and Deci 2000, 55). In contrast, "intrinsic" motivations generally include all other motives, such as enjoyment, morality, reciprocity, and civic duty (Feldman and Perez 2012; Ryan and Deci 2000).

When a principal offers an incentive for a task, whether the incentive is a positive reward or a negative penalty, the goal is to shape agents' choices by adding to their extrinsic motivation (Grant 2012). To use Titmuss's classic example, a principal may offer to pay agents to donate blood on the assumption that the reward will increase overall motivation to donate (Titmuss 1970). Early studies tended to assume that rewards would unequivocally increase agents' motivation, leading to improved performance and increased effort (Rummel and Feinberg 1998). This conventional view has been described as the "separability assumption" (Bowles 2008, 1606) or the idea that extrinsic and intrinsic motivations are "additive" (Sandel 2012, 122; Walton 2012, 436). But more recent studies in psychology and economics began to question this premise. For example, evaluations revisiting Titmuss's premise have demonstrated that payment for blood donations may reduce donations, particularly among women and older donors (Glynn et al. 2003; Mellstrom and Johannesson 2008). Meta-analyses have now shown that incentives can sometimes reduce overall motivation, intrinsic motivation, and desirable behavior in many contexts, such as volunteering, tax payment, educational achievement, physical activity, recycling, and whistleblowing (Cerasoli, Nicklin, and Ford 2014; Deci, Koestner, and Ryan 1999; Feldman and Lobel 2010; Feldman and Perez 2012; Rummel and Feinberg 1998).

On the strength of these findings, incentives are now understood to have two effects: a "relative price" effect by which they increase incentivized behavior, and a less predictable effect by which they can diminish or amplify intrinsic motivations (Frey and Jegen 2001, 593). "Motivational crowding out" is the most common term for a reduction of intrinsic motivation, while the lesser-known phenomenon "motivational crowding in" occurs when an incentive increases intrinsic motivations (Frey and Jegen 2001, 593). Importantly, crowding out need not reverse the expected impact of an incentive. Instead, the direction of an incentive's effect on behavior will depend on whether the crowding-out effect or the relative price effect dominates (Frey and Jegen 2001). Where the crowding-out effect is stronger, the incentive will provoke a net reduction in desired behavior, thwarting the incentive scheme. But crowding out may be offset by a larger relative price effect; even if intrinsic motivation drops, overall behavior may improve if the relative price effect is dominant (Frey and Jegen 2001).

Processes Giving Rise to Crowding Out

A review of the literature on motivational crowding out suggests that there are at least four broad types of cognitive mechanisms that drive effects. I provide brief descriptions here. Each of these four categories represents a way in which an incentive can cause an absolute loss of intrinsic motivation, such that intrinsic motivation is lower than it would have been in the absence of the incentive.

Signaling Effects

The broadest category is signaling effects, based on the premise that the presence, size, and type of an incentive conveys information to agents. Agents faced with an incentive for performance may adjust their beliefs about (1) the burden or importance of a task (Bénabou and Tirole 2006); (2) the principal's perception of the agent (Frey and Jegen 2001); (3) the principal's own values, including whether it is morally acceptable to offer payment for the given task (Bénabou and Tirole 2006; Falk and Kosfeld 2006); (4) social norms surrounding the task itself (Bowles and Hwang 2008; Kahan 2003); and (5) whether the decision to undertake the task should be framed as an exchange (signaling the need for selfishness) or as a moral choice (Bowles 2008; Gneezy 2003). When agents update their beliefs about the task itself, the principal's perceptions or values, the social norms surrounding a task, or the appropriate mode for reasoning about a task, these new beliefs may undermine their preexisting motivations. For example, offering a large incentive for organ donation may signal to agents that (1) being a donor is burdensome or personally costly; (2) the principal believes agents to be too selfish to donate without an incentive; (3) the principal has bad moral values, as evidenced by the willingness to pay for organs; (4) the prevailing social norms are so unsupportive of donation that an incentive is needed to counteract popular sentiment; or (5) the decision to donate organs should be governed by market norms rather than other values. According to crowding-out theory, each of these beliefs may reduce individuals' willingness to donate.

Incentives can also signal information about the agent to observers, leading agents to fear "image-spoiling" when incentives change the social meaning of an act from a marker of good character to a suggestion of profit-seeking (Bénabou and Tirole 2006). For example, an agent's unrewarded decisions to donate organs may display her altruism, leading to reputational benefits. If others know that she received an incentive to donate, however, they may decide that she did so for selfish greed or financial need, thereby minimizing the reputational rewards of her choice. For an agent concerned about the reputational effects of her choices, this shift may be enough to deter donation altogether.

Signaling mechanisms also affect agents' interpretation of their own behavior, leading to what might be called "self-image-spoiling" when agents attribute their actions to reward-seeking rather than good character (Deci, Koestner, and Ryan 1999). This can influence not only willingness to engage in an initial task (for example, an agent may be less willing to donate blood for payment because paid donations do not give him the "warm glow" of an altruistic activity (Imas 2014), but also willingness to engage in repeated tasks if incentives are removed. For example, if someone has been paid for an initial blood donation, he may subsequently attribute his actions to the payment, rather than believing that he donated blood for altruistic reasons. If payments become unavailable in the future, the agent may no longer believe himself to be sufficiently altruistic to donate.

Overjustification and Impaired Self-Determination

A second set of crowding-out processes are collectively known as "overjustification" and "impaired self-determination" (Bénabou and Tirole 2003; Bregn 2013; Frey and Jegen 2001). These theories begin with the premise that agents derive benefits from behaving in intrinsically motivated ways, and one benefit is the perception of control over their behavior. When a principal offers an incentive for a task that an agent is already motivated to do, the agent may perceive his own motivations to be rendered unnecessary (the combination of intrinsic and extrinsic motives "overjustifies" the task). Because the principal is manipulating the agent's extrinsic motivation by supplying an incentive, the agent further perceives that he has given up some control over his behavior. This is often described as a displacement of the "locus of control," or "locus of causality," from the agent to the principal, which causes the agent to lose some of the benefits of perceived self-determination. Without these benefits, the agent is less intrinsically motivated to complete the task, even if his new extrinsic motivation compensates for this loss through the relative price effect. The agent need not accept the incentive; he could reject the reward (and therefore the principal's attempt to shape his behavior) by refraining from the task. But the presence of an incentive inevitably makes the agent's choices "reactive" (Bénabou and Tirole 2003, 504), whereby either task completion or noncompletion may reflect his reaction to the incentive plan rather than his intrinsic motivations. (Whether incentives actually impair autonomy is a moral concern, but for instrumental purposes, the relevant dynamic is the agent's perception of lost autonomy.) In the organ donation example, incentivized agents may perceive that their donation choice reflects not only their intrinsic motives, but also the principal's influence on their choices, diminishing the extent to which the decision is purely self-determined. This can reduce the motivation to donate, as it no longer confers the satisfaction of a self-determined choice.

Endogenous Preference Formation

A third explanation is endogenous preference formation, by which incentives can produce long-term changes in actual preferences for extrinsic compared to intrinsic rewards. Preference adaptation has been explained either by "cultural transmission" of new preferences over time or by the imitation of successful (rewarded) individuals (Bar-Gill and Fershtman 2005, 842; Bowles 2008). In brief, this would occur if the presence of incentives for organ donation and other activities produced a long-term change in social preferences, reducing preferences for (unrewarded) altruistic activities, and increasing preferences for activities that are rewarded. Several studies have demonstrated short-term variants of preference adaptations in response to incentives, including incentives for contributing to public goods (Bar-Gill and Fershtman 2005), incentives for accepting undesirable public works projects in one's community (Frey and Oberholzer-Gee 1997), and negative incentives (penalties) for breach of contract (Bohnet, Frey, and Huck 2001) and tortfeasance (Deffains and Fluet 2012).

"Learned Helplessness"

Finally, one research team has demonstrated in several studies that where incentives lack a clear link to performance quality (for example, awards for participation but not performance), they may create "learned helplessness" (Eisenberger and Cameron 1996). That is, agents may associate low-effort activity with reward or conclude that they cannot influence the size of rewards through good performance. This lack of control causes a general loss of motivation, including motivation for the incentivized task. Learned helplessness theory, however, may be relevant only for tasks requiring creativity or high effort (Eisenberger and Cameron 1996), and other crowding-out researchers have expressed concern that the link between "uncontrollable positive outcomes" and loss of motivation lacks empirical support (Deci, Koestner, and Ryan 1999).

Mechanisms of Crowding Out and Incentive-Based Health Policies

As the prior section demonstrated briefly, crowding-out effects are heterogeneous. These effects may complicate the impacts of incentive-based policies in health policy, to which I now turn. This section considers three uses (or, rather, two uses and one explicit non-use) of financial incentives in health policy, indicating the specific mechanisms hypothesized to drive crowding-out effects.

Incentives for Organ Donation

Despite the continued shortage of donor organs available for transplant, the 1984 National Organ Transplant Act firmly criminalized the transfer of organs for "valuable consideration," with exemptions only for blood, sperm, and eggs (42 U.S.C. §274e). In a recent test of this law, plaintiffs in the Ninth Circuit case *Flynn v. Holder* sought to interpret these exemptions to include bone marrow cells donated through peripheral blood stem cell apheresis, a process largely indistinguishable from blood donation. This would permit a nonprofit corporation to implement a program paying individuals $3,000 for donations. The court agreed that compensating agents who donated bone marrow by apheresis was indeed lawful, but upheld a ban on compensation for donations by aspiration, a more invasive procedure. In doing so, the Ninth Circuit recognized concerns about crowding out as a valid basis for legislation, noting congressional testimony that warned of the "collapse" of the voluntary organ donation system if compensation were allowed (*Flynn v. Holder* 2012, 859–62). A subsequent notice of proposed rulemaking released by the U.S. Department of Health and Human Services reclassified blood stem cell apheresis as a non-compensable donation, justified by Congress's intent to "encourage altruistic donations" (78 Fed. Reg. 60,810, 60,812 (Oct. 2, 2013)).

Using financial incentives to encourage organ donation may activate several mechanisms of crowding out. Although scholars and regulators have recognized the relevance of crowding out, these concerns are generally based on extrapolation from other fields, such as blood donation. The extent of potential crowding out as applied to organ donation is therefore controversial and has not been empirically documented

(Epstein 2008; Mahoney 2009); future research should consider several mechanisms. One is image-spoiling, by which receipt of payment for donation may interrupt agents' ability to signal their altruism to observers or themselves; without this reputational benefit, donation is no longer worthwhile for image-motivated agents. Other signaling mechanisms may also be relevant, including whether incentives convey unsupportive social norms (that is, payment is needed because so few people are willing to donate), task danger or burden (that is, payment is needed because donating organs is dangerous or costly), bad values on the part of the principal (that is, for those who oppose the commodification of human organs, offering payment for organs is immoral and may prompt a refusal to deal with the principal), or the need for self-interested reasoning when deciding to donate or not.

Payment-for-Performance in Healthcare

Pay-for-performance, or "P4P," refers to the practice of paying healthcare providers based on performance metrics, which has been highly controversial as applied to payment for individual clinicians (Eijkenaar et al. 2013; Magrath and Nichter 2012). A principal concern has been that incentive-based payments will crowd out providers' intrinsic motivations to provide high-quality care due to the providers' loss of perceived control, which may be exacerbated by divergence between providers' and payers' perceptions of quality care (Eijkenaar et al. 2013). As before, however, despite much discussion, empirical studies have yet to investigate different mechanisms of crowding-out effects in this context. A 2008 review of the evidence on P4P documented only two studies considering physician motivation or satisfaction, of which one found no harmful effects on motivation, and the other found an increase in physicians' perception of work-related pressure after payment was linked to annual objectives (Christianson, Leatherman, and Sutherland 2008).

Several potential mechanisms may yield crowding out as a response to P4P—namely, impaired self-determination; signaling the payer's view that the providers cannot be trusted to provide high-quality care absent an incentive; signaling that it is appropriate for providers to make care decisions that consider self-gain; and when payers' and providers' metrics for "quality" differ, signaling that the payer has inappropriate values. Other scholars have raised concerns that resonate in framing effects and endogenous preference adaptation (Schwartz and Sharpe 2010), with several empirical studies showing that providers may focus on incentivized care while neglecting other tasks (Eijkenaar et al. 2013).

Wellness Programs

Aided by the Affordable Care Act (Osilla et al. 2012), employers and health insurers have increasingly instituted wellness programs—incentive programs managed by health insurers and employers to encourage individual policyholders or employees to achieve health goals or participate in healthy behaviors (for example, attending clinical visits, visiting gyms). These programs enable insurers or employers to vary health insurance premiums for program participants by up to 30% to 50% depending on participation or achievement of health status indicators (Osilla et al. 2012). Such programs are expanding to other health insurance contexts. For example, the state of Iowa plans to institute a "Healthy Behavior Incentive Protocol" as part of the Medicaid program. Under a §1115 Medicaid demonstration waiver, nonexempt Medicaid participants in Iowa will be charged premiums unless they participate in required "healthy behaviors," including a health risk assessment and annual exam (Centers for Medicare and Medicaid Services 2014). Although participants cannot lose their Medicaid coverage due to nonpayment (making the payments more of a penalty than a "premium" as traditionally understood), the state will have authority to collect overdue payments.

Economic evidence on wellness programs is generally favorable or mixed for both cost savings and health outcomes (Baicker, Cutler, and Song 2010; Osilla et al. 2012), but commentators have raised concerns on the grounds of crowding out (Madison, Volpp, and Helpern 2011). Again, these tend to be speculative at present, without prior research investigating specific mechanisms. Potential processes of interest may include self-image spoiling (if agents attribute their healthy activities to incentives rather than intrinsic motivations); impaired self-determination; signaling principal hostility or bad values (for example, a lack of respect for privacy in health decisions); signaling that health decisions should be made through market-based reasoning; or prompting changed preferences for extrinsic compared to intrinsic rewards for healthy behaviors. Each of these mechanisms would raise questions on instrumental grounds—namely, whether crowding-out effects are sufficiently strong as to make the incentive programs harmful or inefficient.

Incentive Architecture: Tailoring Crowding-Out Remedies to Causal Mechanisms

The three examples above show the heterogeneity of cognitive processes that may drive crowding out, either in a single context or across different incentive programs. Although some have suggested that it is possible to remedy all reductions in effort caused by crowding out by making incentives very large (Frey and Jegen 2001; Hollander-Blumoff 2011), this may be unnecessarily expensive. A more nuanced set of solutions responding to specific causal mechanisms may mitigate crowding out more efficiently by responding to the precise mechanisms at work.

Take, for example, crowding out due to impaired self-determination, a possibility in the P4P context. One option for reducing crowding out due to perceived loss of autonomy and displacement of control is to involve agents in the design of the incentive structure, using participatory processes to define program metrics. Several scholars have noted that P4P programs have been more acceptable to providers when they involved the clinicians directly in choosing and defining performance targets (Eijkenaar et al. 2013; Magrath and Nichter 2012). Agents with meaningful participation in the incentive development process may also be less likely to perceive the incentive scheme as a signal that they are personally untrustworthy, that they are insufficiently dedicated to their performance, or that the institution setting the incentives has inappropriate or hostile values (Frey 1997). At least one empirical study has demonstrated that incentives designed as bonuses are less likely than penalties to provoke reduced self-determination and the perception of principal hostility (Fehr and Gachter 2002). But although using positive incentives and involving agents in incentive design may alleviate crowding out attributed to loss of self-determination or signaling principal hostility, it may do little to contain crowding out due to other mechanisms, such as image-spoiling or endogenous preference adaptation.

Where crowding out occurs due to image-spoiling or self-image-spoiling, using a mandate rather than a positive reward may help to avoid crowding out by affirming value systems (Bowles and Hwang 2008). Of course, mandates and defaults may not always be normatively attractive; a mandate to donate organs after death, for example, may attract widespread opposition in the United States, where in 2012 only 60% of drivers had granted permission for donation (U.S. Department of Health and Human Services 2013). Where mandates or defaults are unavailable, image-spoiling and self-image-spoiling may also be responsive to changing incentives to in-kind rewards rather than cash payments, offering a menu of incentives (Bénabou and Tirole 2006), or permitting agents to publicly donate their incentive to others (Mellstrom and Johannesson 2008; Beretti, Figuières, and Grolleau 2013). Some of these tweaks may also be useful for limiting signals about whether the principal has inappropriate market-driven values, or about whether self-interested behavior is the appropriate mode of reasoning in a given context.

Endogenous preference adaptation may be the crowding-out mechanism most resistant to remedy. Oren Bar-Gill and Chaim Fershtman have suggested that where there are reputational reasons for good behavior, actively taxing good behavior can increase the reputational payoff of good acts, limiting a shift away from reputation concerns and toward extrinsic motivations (Bar-Gill and Fershtman 2005). For example, charging people fines to become organ donors can amplify the signal they send to others about their altruism, making donation more attractive for its reputational benefits. Ian Ayres has collected several examples of effective anti-incentives that harness similar dynamics (Ayres 2011).

Conclusion

Despite its prominence in scholarship on the use of incentives in health law, the concept of motivational crowding out has been ambiguous, with few commentators considering the full range of empirically supported mechanisms by which extrinsic incentives may interact with intrinsic and reputational motivations. In this chapter, I have aimed to define the phenomenon more precisely, to show some of the heterogeneity in crowding out as a response to incentives in health policy, and to gesture toward the ways in which incentive architecture remedies for crowding out should match the specific cognitive mechanisms at work.

References

Arrow, Kenneth J. 1972. "Gifts and Exchanges." *Philosophy and Public Affairs* 1:343–62.

Ayres, Ian. 2011. *Carrots and Sticks: Unlock the Power of Incentives to Get Things Done.* Bantam. New York. 1–240.

Baicker, Katherine, David Cutler, and Zirui Song. 2010. "Workplace Wellness Programs Can Generate Savings." *Health Affairs* 29:1–8.

Bar-Gill, Oren, and Chaim Fershtman. 2005. "Public Policy with Endogenous Preferences." *Journal of Public Economic Theory* 7:841–57.

Bénabou, Roland, and Jean Tirole. 2003. "Intrinsic and Extrinsic Motivation." *Review of Economic Studies* 70:489–520.

———. 2006. "Incentives and Prosocial Behavior." *The American Economic Review* 96: 1652–78.

Benkler, Yochai. 2004. "Sharing Nicely: On Shareable Goods and the Emergence of Sharing as a Modality of Economic Production." *Yale Law Journal* 114:273–358.

Beretti, Antoine, Charles Figuières, and Gilles Grolleau. 2013. "Using Money to Motivate Both 'Saints' and 'Sinners': A Field Experiment on Motivational Crowding Out." *Kyklos* 66:63–77.

Bohnet, Iris, Bruno S. Frey, and Steffen Huck. 2001. "More Order with Less Law: On Contract Enforcement, Trust, and Crowding." *American Political Science Review* 95:131–44.

Bowles, Samuel. 2008. "Policies Designed for Self-Interested Citizens May Undermine 'The Moral Sentiments': Evidence from Economic Experiments." *Science* 20:1605–9.

Bowles, Samuel, and Sung-Ha Hwang. 2008. "Social Preferences and Public Economics: Mechanism Design when Social Preferences Depend on Incentives." *Journal of Public Economics* 92:1811–20.

Bregn, Kirsten. 2013. "Detrimental Effects of Performance-Related Pay in the Public Sector? On the Need for a Broader Theoretical Perspective." *Public Organization Review* 13:21–35.

Centers for Medicare and Medicaid Services. 2014. "Iowa Marketplace Choice Plan: Special Terms and Conditions." Iowa Department of Human Services. https://dhs.iowa.gov/sites /default/files/Marketplace%20Choice%20STCs.pdf.

Cerasoli, Christopher P., Jessica M. Nicklin, and Michael T. Ford. 2014. "Intrinsic Motivation and Extrinsic Incentives Jointly Predict Performance: A 40-Year Meta-Analysis." *Psychological Bulletin* 140:980–1008.

Christianson, Jon B., Sheila Leatherman, and Kim Sutherland. 2008. "Lessons from Evaluations of Purchaser Pay-for-Performance Programs." *Medical Care Research and Review* 65:5S–35S.

Deci, Edward L. 1972. "The Effects of Contingent and Noncontingent Rewards and Controls on Intrinsic Motivation." *Organizational Behavior and Human Performance* 8:217–29.

Deci, Edward L., Richard Koestner, and Richard M. Ryan. 1999. "A Meta-Analytic Review of Experiments Examining the Effects of Extrinsic Rewards on Intrinsic Motivation." *Psychological Bulletin* 125:627–68.

Deffains, Bruno, and Claude Fluet. 2012. "Legal Liability When Individuals Have Moral Concerns." *Journal of Law, Economics, and Organization* 29:930–55.

Eijkenaar, Frank, Martin Emmert, Manfred Scheppach, and Oliver Schöffski. 2013. "Effects of Pay for Performance in Health Care: A Systematic Review of Systematic Reviews." *Health Policy* 2:115–30.

Eisenberger, Robert, and Judy Cameron. 1996. "Detrimental Effects of Reward: Reality or Myth?" *American Psychologist* 51:1153–66.

Epstein, Richard A. 2008. "The Human and Economic Dimensions of Altruism: The Case of Organ Transplantation." *Journal of Legal Studies* 37:459–501.

Falk, Armin, and Michael Kosfeld. 2006. "The Hidden Costs of Control." *The American Economic Review* 96:1611–30.

Fehr, Ernst, and Simon Gachter. 2002. "Do Incentive Contracts Crowd Out Voluntary Cooperation?" Institute for Empirical Research in Economics—University of Zurich. IEW-Working Papers. 034. http://ideas.repec.org/p/zur/iewwpx/034.html.

Feldman, Yuval. 2011. "The Complexity of Disentangling Intrinsic and Extrinsic Compliance Motivations: Theoretical and Empirical Insights from the Behavioral Analysis of Law." *Washington University Journal of Law and Policy* 35:11–51.

Feldman, Yuval, and Orly Lobel. 2010. "The Incentives Matrix: The Comparative Effectiveness of Rewards, Liabilities, Duties, and Protections for Reporting Illegality." *Texas Law Review* 88:1151–1211.

Feldman, Yuval, and Oren Perez. 2012. "Motivating Environmental Action in a Pluralistic Regulatory Environment: An Experimental Study of Framing, Crowding Out, and Institutional Effects in the Context of Recycling Policies." *Law and Society Review* 46:405–41.

Flynn v. Holder, 634 F.3d 852 (9th Cir. 2012).

Frey, Bruno S. 1997. "A Constitution for Knaves Crowds Out Civic Virtues." *The Economic Journal* 443:1043–53.

Frey, Bruno S., and Reto Jegen. 2001. "Motivation Crowding Theory: A Survey of Empirical Evidence." *Journal of Economic Surveys* 15:589–611.

Frey, Bruno S., and Felix Oberholzer-Gee. 1997. "The Cost of Price Incentives: An Empirical Analysis of Motivation Crowding Out." *The American Economic Review* 87:746–55.

Glynn, Simone A., Alan E. Williams, Catharie C. Nass, James Bethel, Debra Kessler, Edward P. Scott, Joy Fridey, Steven H. Kleinman, George B. Schreiber, and Retrovirus Epidemiology Donor Study. 2003. "Attitudes toward Blood Donation Incentives in the United States: Implications for Donor Recruitment." *Transfusion* 43:7–16.

Gneezy, Uri. 2003. "The W Effect of Incentives." University of Chicago Working Paper. https://ideas.repec.org/e/pgn18.html. 1–40.

Gneezy, Uri, Stephan Meier, and Pedro Rey-Biel. 2011. "When and Why Incentives (Don't) Work to Modify Behavior." *Journal of Economic Perspectives* 25:191–210.

Grant, Ruth W. 2012. *Strings Attached: Untangling the Ethics of Incentives*. Princeton University Press. Princeton, NJ. 1–224.

Hollander-Blumoff, Rebecca. 2011. "Intrinsic and Extrinsic Compliance Motivations: Comment on Feldman." *Washington University Journal of Law and Policy* 35:53–67.

Imas, Alex. 2014. "Working for 'Warm Glow': On the Benefits and Limits of Prosocial Incentives." *Journal of Public Economics* 114:14–18.

Kahan, Dan M. 2003. "The Logic of Reciprocity: Trust, Collective Action, and Law." *Michigan Law Review* 102:71–103.

Lepper, Mark R., David Greene, and Richard E. Nisbett. 1973. "Undermining Children's Intrinsic Interest with Extrinsic Reward: A Test of the 'Overjustification' Hypothesis." *Journal of Personality and Social Psychology* 28:129–37.

Madison, Kristin M., Kevin G. Volpp, and Scott D. Halpern. 2011. "The Law, Policy, and Ethics of Employers' Use of Financial Incentives to Improve Health." *The Journal of Law, Medicine and Ethics* 39:450–68.

Magrath, Priscilla, and Mark Nichter. 2012. "Paying for Performance and the Social Relations of Health Care Provision: An Anthropological Perspective." *Social Science and Medicine* 75:1778–85.

Mahoney, Julia D. 2009. "Altruism, Markets, and Organ Procurement." *Law and Contemporary Problems* 72:23–35.

Mellstrom, Carl, and Magnus Johannesson. 2008. "Crowding Out in Blood Donation: Was Titmuss Right?" *Journal of the European Economic Association* 6:845–63.

Osilla, Karen Chan, Kristin Van Busum, Christopher Schnyer, Jody Wozar Larkin, Christine Eibner, and Soeren Mattke. 2012. "Systematic Review of the Impact of Worksite Wellness Programs." *American Journal of Managed Care* 18:e68–e81.

Rummel, Amy, and Richard Feinberg. 1988. "Cognitive Evaluation Theory: A Meta-Analytic Review of the Literature." *Social Behavior and Personality* 16:147–64.

Ryan, Richard M., and Edward L. Deci. 2000. "Intrinsic and Extrinsic Motivations: Classic Definitions and New Directions." *Contemporary Educational Psychology* 25:54–67.

Sandel, Michael J. 2012. *What Money Can't Buy: The Moral Limits of Markets.* Farrar, Straus and Giroux. New York. 1–256.

Schlesinger, Mark. 2012. "Crowding Out: Multiple Manifestations, Muddled Meanings." *Journal of Health Politics, Policy and Law* 37:851–64.

Schwartz, Barry, and Kenneth Sharpe. 2010. *Practical Wisdom: The Right Way to Do the Right Thing.* Riverhead Books. New York. 1–324.

Titmuss, Richard M. 1970. *The Gift Relationship: From Human Blood to Social Policy.* Allen and Unwin. London. 1–339.

U.S. Department of Health and Human Services. 2013. *2012 National Survey of Organ Donation Attitudes and Behaviors.* Washington, DC. 1–118.

Walton, Nina. 2012. "Crowding Theory and Executive Compensation." *Theoretical Inquiries in Law* 13:429–56.

CHAPTER 14

Do Financial Incentives Reduce Intrinsic Motivation for Weight Loss?

Evidence from Two Tests of Crowding Out

Aditi P. Sen, David Huffman, George Loewenstein, David A. Asch,
Jeffrey T. Kullgren, and Kevin G. Volpp

While financial incentives for good performance have not traditionally been used in domains such as personal health, policymakers are increasingly interested in approaches that introduce such incentives. In healthcare, incentives have been used successfully in a number of field experiments testing programs to promote weight loss, smoking cessation, drug abstinence, and medication adherence (Volpp et al. 2008a; Volpp et al. 2009; Silverman et al. 1996; Silverman et al. 1999; Donatelle et al. 2004; Heil et al. 2008; Higgins et al. 1993; Higgins et al. 1994; Higgins et al. 2000; Volpp et al. 2008b). These demonstrations have potentially important policy implications, building a case for using financial incentives to shift individuals toward making better health-related choices, with benefits for both the individuals involved and society at large.

The idea of using financial incentives for health is not, however, without potential concerns. One of these is the possibility, suggested by a long line of research in psychology (Deci, Koestner, and Ryan 1999; Deci and Ryan 1985; see also Gneezy, Meier, and Rey-Biel 2011), that such financial incentives might crowd out intrinsic motivation. To the extent that introducing incentives crowds out some form of pre-existing intrinsic motivation, this might lead to a decline in effort once incentives are removed to a lower level than if incentives had never been introduced. For example, if an incentive is of relatively low value, it may suggest to an individual that the task at hand is of little value; in turn, this new signal could crowd out any intrinsic motivation the individual may have for the task (see Gneezy, Meier, and Rey-Biel 2011 for a fuller discussion). In turn, if the long-run decrease in effort more than offsets the short-term gains, an intervention featuring temporary incentives could on net be counterproductive. Even if incentives are permanent, their net effects may be negative if the crowding-out effect is larger than the incentive effect. These issues highlight the importance of a more precise understanding of the relationship among incentive design (for example, size, length of time in place), motivation, and performance.

While the issue of incentives and intrinsic motivation in health has been identified as an important topic for research (for example, Shaw 2007; Halpern, Madison, and Volpp 2009; Marteau, Ashcroft, and Oliver 2009), there is little empirical evidence on the direct effects of financial incentives on motivation in the context of health behavior. Existing research on crowding out may not be generalizable to the context of personal health behaviors for several reasons. Most of the evidence in psychology on the crowding-out hypothesis comes from laboratory studies involving tasks such as puzzle solving or drawing pictures, with subject pools consisting of college students and young children (for a review, see Deci, Koestner, and Ryan 1999). It is unclear whether such results generalize to the domain of health and to adults who are likely to have strong prior intrinsic motivation to overcome health problems. That is, the strength or robustness of intrinsic motivation in the domain of personal health might be different than in domains where it has typically been explored to this point (for more discussion of motivation in health setting versus previous evidence from psychology, see Promberger and Marteau 2013).

There is so far little in the way of "smoking gun" evidence of crowding out in field studies on incentives and health; behavior often exhibits a trend back toward baseline levels after incentives are removed (John et al. 2011; Sutherland, Christianson, and Leatherman 2008), but this likely reflects lack of sustainability of interventions post-intervention and is not by itself evidence of crowding out. None of the incentive studies we are aware of demonstrate that behavior falls below baseline post-intervention, which would indicate crowding out (for an overview, see Promberger and Marteau 2013). At least two studies have even found evidence that incentives may "crowd in" motivation. For example, Charness and Gneezy (2009) found that college students who were paid to attend the gym continued to have higher attendance rates than those in the control arm even after incentives were removed, potentially due to habit formation, and Volpp et al. (2009) found that participants who previously received incentives for smoking cessation maintained higher quit rates than control arm participants fifteen months post-incentives.

Our study provides new evidence on whether or not financial incentives affect intrinsic motivation, focusing on the case of weight loss. Our approach involves measuring intrinsic motivation in the field using a survey tool developed by psychologists to measure crowding out as described above (Ryan and Connell 1989). There are some advantages of such an approach; while crowding out might take a relatively long time to manifest in terms of behavior and thus empirical evidence based on an outcome such as weight might be missed in the limited time window of a follow-up period, the impact on motivation itself should happen more quickly. A decrease in motivation should in principle manifest already during the intervention itself, as well as being apparent during the period immediately post-intervention. A survey-based approach is thus a useful complement to previous studies that only observed behavior (which is also observed here). We know of only one previous study that has measured the effect of incentives on motivation levels in a health-related setting; Ledgerwood and Petry (2006) use a different survey tool to measure motivation in the context of a substance use program and find no difference in motivation levels among those who had previously received incentives to change substance use and a control group three months after the incentives were removed, suggesting that financial incentives did not crowd out intrinsic motivation.

The ideal data for studying the impact of incentives on direct measures of intrinsic motivation for weight loss would involve experiments conducted in the field with multiple measures of motivation for each participant over time, across different types of incentive interventions and different populations. We conducted two such field experiments, with different populations and different types of incentives, and we measured intrinsic motivation at baseline and then two subsequent times for each person: at the end of the active phase of the intervention and three months post-intervention. Our field experiments took place within the context of workplace wellness programs, which also makes the results relevant for assessing potential impacts of incentives for health-related behaviors adopted by employers.

Our main finding is that incentives have no systematic impact on intrinsic motivation for weight loss. This is generally true across different types of incentives, and across both of the different field experiments and study populations. Participants reported high levels of intrinsic motivation initially, and there was essentially no change during the six-month intervention period or the three-month follow-up period. These results are reproduced for sub-populations of interest, such as those differing in terms of initial levels of motivation and initial weight, as well as those who earned relatively more versus less money through financial incentives.

Thus, there is neither behavioral nor direct evidence of crowding out in this setting. That is, participants who received incentives had equal or lower weights compared both to control participants and to their own baseline weights at the end of the follow-up period and they also maintained their baseline levels of intrinsic motivation. From a policy perspective, our results suggest that incentives are unlikely to cause crowding out (in this setting) and that, therefore, they have the potential to promote behavior change in both the short and the long terms. We cannot, however, conclude that the value of incentives in this setting is net-positive since this would require determining the (monetary) value of weight loss outcomes in the program (benefits) so that this value could be compared to the value of the incentives (costs).

Experimental Design

We used data from two randomized controlled trials of workplace weight loss programs to evaluate the relationship among motivation, incentives, and weight loss. Both studies offered substantial financial rewards for meeting weight loss goals to overweight individuals over six months, followed by a three-month no-incentive follow-up period. The studies tested different incentive designs for weight loss, as described below.

Study 1 tested the effectiveness of individual versus group rewards for weight loss (versus control) (Kullgren et al. 2013a). Participants in the individual rewards arm were told that they could receive $100 per month for being at or below their monthly target weight while those in the group rewards arm were put into an (anonymous) group with four other participants and told that at the end of each month, $500 would be split among those members of the group who had met their weight loss goal (that is, if two participants out of five achieved their goal, each would receive $250; if all five met their goal, each would receive $100).

Study 2 tested the effectiveness of deposit contract incentive designs with various levels of employer matching (no match, 1:1 match, 2:1 match) (Kullgren et al. 2013b). In the basic deposit contract arm (no match), participants were given the chance to deposit between $1 and $3 per day (up to $84) into an individual account (deposits were not mandatory). The money was then refunded at the end of the month for every day in that month that an individual weighed in and was at or below his target weight for that day. In the 1:1 match group, participants were again given the chance to deposit between $1 and $3 per day (up to $84) into an individual account, and whatever they deposited was matched 1:1 by their employer as an additional incentive. The final arm used a 2:1 match for participants' deposit contracts. As reported in Kullgren et al., 2013a and 2013b, neither study showed behavioral evidence of crowding out based on measured weight (that is, participants in intervention arms had equal or lower weights compared both to control participants and to their own baseline weights). In this chapter, we analyze data collected during each study on the interaction of financial incentives and intrinsic motivation for weight loss to consider the question of crowding out.

In both studies, we measured intrinsic and extrinsic motivation at baseline, at the end of the incentives period (six months), and at the end of the follow-up period (nine months). This allowed us to gather consistent measures of motivation across two studies that offered different incentive schemes for achieving the same weight loss goal (losing one pound per week for twenty-four weeks) and to see how these measures of motivation changed over time for participants in the incentive arms versus control and whether they differed across incentive schemes.

We used the Treatment Self-Regulation Questionnaire (TSRQ) to measure intrinsic motivation for weight loss on a scale of 1–7. The TSRQ was developed in the psychology literature as a means of eliciting individuals' reasons for engaging in certain behaviors, and was initially used to assess intrinsic and extrinsic motivation for participating in academic and pro-social activities among children (Ryan and Connell 1989). It has since been validated across a number of settings and health behaviors (Levesque et al. 2007) and was used in relation to a variety of health-related behaviors (Williams et al. 1996; Williams et al. 1998; Williams, Freedman, and Deci 1998; Williams et al. 2002). Previous studies have typically not considered changes in intrinsic motivation over time (that is, before and after a behavior change program), or how motivation changes due to other components of the program such as incentives. We test for differential changes in these motivation scores over time by study arm. In the presence of crowding out, we would expect to see a relatively greater decrease in intrinsic motivation in financial incentive arms than in the control arms.

Empirical Results: The Effect of Incentives on Intrinsic Motivation for Weight Loss
Empirical Strategy and Statistical Tests

We use non-parametric statistical tests (Wilcoxon rank-sum/Wilcoxon-Mann-Whitney tests for independent samples and Wilcoxon signed-rank tests for paired samples) to test changes in intrinsic motivation over time due to small sample size concerns and the non-normality of our intrinsic motivation measure (heavily skewed to the right). Where appropriate, we use conservative bonferroni adjustment for multiple comparisons to conserve the overall type I error rate (for example, to compare any of the incentive arms to the control group in a study).

We focus on three key tests. First, we test the change in intrinsic motivation over time *within each control and incentive condition* in each study (significant changes of this type are shown in figs. 14.1 and 14.2) (test 1). Second, we test the difference in the *change* in intrinsic motivation over time *between incentive arms and control arms*; to do this, we construct zero to six, six to nine, and zero to nine month differences and test these differences across arms using Wilcoxon rank-sum tests and correcting for multiple comparisons as appropriate (for example, correcting for two simultaneous tests to test the 0–6 month change in any incentive arm versus control in study 1 where there were two incentive arms) (test 2). Third, we test the difference in the change in intrinsic motivation over time *among incentive arms* within each study, using a similar procedure as described above (test 3). Test 2 is the key test of crowding out of intrinsic motivation by financial incentives as it assesses differential changes in intrinsic motivation over time in incentive versus control arms.

Baseline Intrinsic Motivation among Voluntary Participants

Before presenting evidence on crowding out, we first verify that randomization was successful in generating similar baseline levels of intrinsic motivation across incentive and control conditions. Table 14.1 reports average baseline values for the intrinsic motivation component of the TSRQ measure. There is only one difference across arms that is significant at the 5% level, between incentive arm 3 and the control group in study 2. Otherwise baseline intrinsic motivation scores are not significantly different across the arms in each study.

The baseline measures are also informative in that they show that initial levels of intrinsic motivation were high: motivation scores can range from 1 to 7, and mean

Table 14.1. *Mean Intrinsic Motivation by Arm at Baseline*

ARM	Mean Score (standard deviation) [incentive type]	
	Study 1	Study 2
Control	5.995 (1.356)	6.789 (0.388)
Incentive arm 1	6.487 (0.607) [Individual rewards]	6.618 (0.543) [No match]
Incentive arm 2	6.449 (0.741) [Group rewards]	6.538 (0.567) [1:1 match]
Incentive arm 3	N/A	6.405 (0.663) [2:1 match]

Note: The difference in baseline intrinsic motivation between control and incentive arm 3 is significant at the 5% level (*p*-value 0.0257); however, once adjusted for multiple comparisons it is no longer significant.

baseline scores in both studies were uniformly at or above 6. These high levels indicate that the weight loss patients in our study considered themselves highly intrinsically motivated to lose weight, shedding some light on the strength of intrinsic motivation for this and similar health behaviors. There is also a technical implication of the high initial values, which is that floor effects pose no difficulty for our key research question; given that initial scores are high, there is plenty of "room" for financial incentives to reduce intrinsic motivation through crowding out should this effect be present.

Evidence of Crowding Out

To see whether external incentives are associated with crowding out of intrinsic motivation for weight loss, we show changes in intrinsic motivation over time, by arm (fig. 14.1). Crowding out of intrinsic motivation by incentives would be illustrated by a decline over time in motivation in the incentive arms that is greater than any downward trend in motivation for the control groups. The results in figure 14.1 show little evidence of crowding out. In study 1, there is no statistically significant decline over time within any of the control or incentive conditions for any time horizon (for example, between baseline and six months). In study 2, there are significant declines in intrinsic motivation in the no match arm and the control arm between zero and nine months; however, given that there are no differential declines in incentive arms

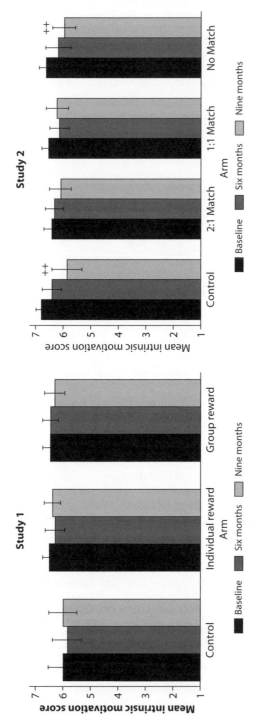

FIGURE 14.1 Average intrinsic motivation scores by arm. *Error bars show two standard errors. ** indicates a change from zero to six months that is significant at the 5% level. ++ indicates a change from zero to nine months that is significant at the 5% level.*

versus control, this suggests that there is no evidence of crowding out due to incentives (test 1).

We test specifically for crowding out by testing for differential changes in intrinsic motivation over time between incentive arms and control (test 2). There are no statistically significant differences either in the change in intrinsic motivation over time, comparing any of the incentive arms to the respective control group, or comparing any of the incentive arms to other incentive arms in each study. The overall conclusion, replicated across both studies, is that financial incentives do not appear to lead to a drop in intrinsic motivation for weight loss; this finding appears to be robust to various types of financial incentives (that is, cash rewards and deposit contracts).[1]

We also have measures of some sources of extrinsic motivation, and thus can investigate whether the incentives affect these types of extrinsic motivation. For example, if participating in a weight loss initiative with financial incentives in a workplace setting makes participants feel pressure from those implementing the program (in particular, their employers), this could affect extrinsic motivation levels. (Alternatively, if incentives simply offer a financial nudge but do not exert any type of social or other pressure, extrinsic motivation would likely not be significantly affected.) Figure 14.2 shows average extrinsic motivation by arm over time for each study. There are no significant changes within or across arms over time in either of these two measures.

We find no crowding-out effects in the aggregate study populations; however, there is the potential for heterogeneity in crowding-out effects across participants.[2] We test whether participants experience crowding out differentially based on their baseline weight or how much money they earned via incentives since we might expect that those who earned more in incentives would be more likely to experience any crowding out or to experience relatively more crowding out if financial incentives crowd out intrinsic motivation. We find no evidence of differential changes in intrinsic motivation over time between those with relatively higher versus lower baseline weight categories in either study. When we consider financial earnings, we consider those who earned more than the median amount of money during the intervention period versus those who lost less than the median amount in study 1 and those who lost versus gained money during the intervention period (conditional on making a deposit) in study 2.[3] Again, we find no evidence of significant changes in intrinsic motivation within earning category over time or across categories over time. Though we are limited by small sample sizes, these results provide further suggestive evidence in support of our main finding of no crowding out of intrinsic motivation by financial incentives.

Sensitivity Analyses of Missing Data

In the results reported thus far, our sample included only those participants with non-missing intrinsic motivation scores at baseline, 6, and 9 months, resulting in sample sizes of 76 and 80 in study 1 and 2, respectively. About one-third of participants in

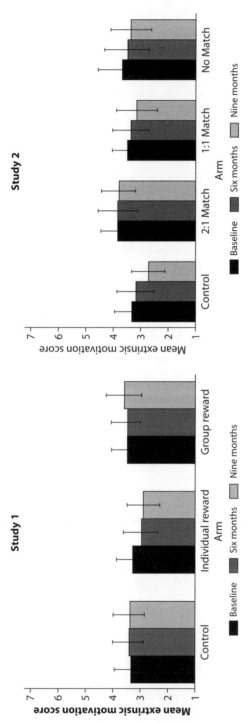

FIGURE 14.2 Average extrinsic motivation scores by arm. *Error bars show 2 standard errors.*

each arm has missing data and is therefore dropped. The missing rate across incentive and non-incentive arms is similar in both studies. The characteristics of these omitted participants suggest that there are no systematic differences in baseline intrinsic motivation between participants who completed and participants who did not complete subsequent questionnaires. The populations also do not differ with regard to baseline weight or self-reported health status, or self-reported income level, education, and race.

There is evidence, however, that participants with missing data were less likely to have a weight recorded at 6 months and 9 months, though it is important to view these numbers in the context of missing weight data, which is relatively low at approximately 17% averaged across both studies at 6 months and 12% at 9 months. The fact that those with missing data were less likely to have a recorded weight suggests that they might have been more likely to drop out of the study. It is impossible to know the direction of causality between missing motivation data and missing weight measurements in this case; if dropping out is an indicator of reduced intrinsic motivation, however, we may miss this decline in our survey measures and this may bias our results. We conducted two sensitivity analyses to examine the implications of missing data and, in particular, the potential that participants with missing weight data might have also had reduced intrinsic motivation.[4] The results of these sensitivity analyses strengthen our conclusion that financial incentives do not appear to crowd out intrinsic motivation for weight loss in our setting.

Discussion

We have presented evidence that providing monetary incentives for achieving weight loss goals does not crowd out intrinsic motivation for weight loss. We directly measured intrinsic motivation over time in two randomized controlled trials of financial incentives for weight loss and find that individuals who enrolled in voluntary workplace weight loss programs were highly motivated at baseline and that incentives did not crowd out this intrinsic motivation whether they were designed as deposit contracts or cash rewards. In addition, we find no difference in effect across subpopulations of particular interest, including those who won more or less money through incentives.[5]

This lack of crowding out is consistent with behavioral evidence of the long-run effects of incentives seen in the field. To our knowledge there is no behavioral evidence that indicates crowding out from field studies on health behavior; that is, no study has actually observed a decline in performance below baseline after removal of incentives, which would be a direct sign of crowding out. We complement this behavioral evidence with direct evidence that financial incentives do not reduce intrinsic motivation in the case of weight loss.

Further, there are a number of incentive studies that even find some prolonged beneficial effects, consistent with "crowding in," or habit formation (Charness and

Gneezy 2009; Acland and Levy 2010; Volpp et al. 2009). It remains unclear what features of incentives prevent crowding out and promote crowding in. For example, incentive magnitude and duration are likely to be important in encouraging long-run behavior change. If incentives are not in place long enough for recipients to achieve progress and realize some benefit from the behavior (for example, weight loss), or if incentives are too small to be salient, then they are unlikely to result in habit formation. Future work on the relationship between incentive design and habit formation will be extremely valuable.

Incentives have been used successfully to promote health behaviors, particularly in the short run. Many studies, however, have found that incentive effects do not persist over the long run and that performance declines following the removal of incentives. In order to understand what might be driving these performance drops—and, therefore, how we might be able to prevent them—it will be important to understand the mechanisms by which incentives shape behavior. It will also be valuable to understand how these mechanisms vary across behaviors; for example, effective incentives for "good" behaviors (for example, going to the gym) may be different from those to stop engaging in "bad" behaviors (for example, smoking). Incentive studies in education have demonstrated further that the effect of incentives can be increased through careful targeting of recipients (Gneezy, Meier, and Rey-Biel 2011). Thus, there remains much to learn about how incentives can promote long-run behavior change and be designed in a cost-effective manner.

The results of this chapter are relevant to the debate on whether financial incentives can be an effective component of policy interventions designed to foster better individual health outcomes and improved public health. Our findings indicate that incentives need not reduce intrinsic motivation, at least in the context of health, and that we ought to be cautious in generalizing crowding out results from pro-social behaviors or activities such as puzzles to personal health behaviors among adults. It is important to recognize that our study is limited to two types of incentives (group versus individual, deposit contracts) for a particular health behavior. In future work, it will be important to assess whether crowding out occurs in other settings. Indeed, our findings highlight the value of future research on decision-making under incentives, outside of the lab and across different types of incentives and populations, to improve understanding of when crowding out may happen and when it tends not to happen.

Notes

1. One potential concern is that censoring could prevent us from observing crowding out even if it occurs. A nontrivial fraction of our participant population rates themselves at the maximum value of 7 on the TSRQ scale at baseline. Thus, we may be concerned that the true intrinsic motivation level for some of these individuals lies above 7, but our scale is

unable to capture this. To test this, we check whether there is any evidence of crowding out among the sub-sample of individuals who state an initial motivation level that is below the maximum, and thus are not subject to censoring; between 55% and 59% of the sample in each study has baseline intrinsic motivation below 7. We find that the changes in intrinsic motivation over time in this sub-population are small in magnitude and far from significant. Thus, there is also little evidence of crowding out among the restricted sample for which censoring problems do not apply, and we conclude that the lack of crowding out cannot be explained simply by censoring.

2. For example, Charness and Gneezy (2009) find that their results are driven by the sub-group of individuals who were new gym-goers versus those who had been members before the study.

3. In study 2, we divide incentive arm participants into those who earned positive versus negative amounts overall because take-up of deposit contracts was very low; only twenty-two participants out of eighty made deposits and either earned or lost money.

4. First, we compared changes in motivation over time between those who were missing any motivation measure (for example, missing the nine-month motivation measure but not the six-month measure) and those who had complete data. If missing data was an indicator of reduced motivation and drop-out, we would expect that participants missing some data experienced greater declines in intrinsic motivation over time than those with complete data. We find no significant differences in the change in intrinsic motivation among those with some missing data relative to those with complete data. Second, we redo the analyses presented above, assuming that those with missing motivation data have a decline in intrinsic motivation that is equal to the mean change in the 10% of the sample with the biggest motivation decrease (rather than dropping these participants from our sample). This is a strong assumption since approximately one-third of our data were dropped due to missing motivation and using this method we assign this third a relatively large decrease in intrinsic motivation over time. Even with this strong assumption, however, there is still no evidence of the differential decreases in intrinsic motivation over time in incentive versus control arms that would indicate crowding out.

5. A potential concern is that we do not have wide baseline heterogeneity in motivation scores, suggesting that the survey tool we use to measure motivation, the TSRQ, may have some limitations in settings such as ours (in particular, among a population that volunteers to participate in a behavior change program). While the uniformly high baseline levels of intrinsic motivation leave "room to fall," and thus make it more likely that we could detect crowding out should it exist, the lack of heterogeneity in these measures makes it difficult to establish any links between intrinsic (or extrinsic) motivation and actual behavior (for example, baseline intrinsic motivation associated with higher weight loss in a weight loss program as seen in Williams et al., 1996). We measure motivation using the TSRQ because it has been widely used in the field of psychology to study intrinsic motivation and, in particular, crowding out of intrinsic motivation by financial incentives. Future work should experiment with new and different types of scales to capture behavior and motivation among this type of population, as well as in populations whose baseline motivation is likely to be lower, and across a variety of healthcare settings and incentive designs.

References

Acland, Dan, and Matthew Levy. 2010. "Habit Formation and Naiveté in Gym Attendance: Evidence from a Field Experiment." Unpublished paper.

Barkema, Harry G. 1995. "Do Job Executives Work Harder When They Are Monitored?" *Kyklos* 48:19–42.

Benabou, Roland, and Jean Tirole. 2003. "Intrinsic and Extrinsic Motivation." *Review of Economic Studies* 70(3):489–520.

Charness, Gary, and Uri Gneezy. 2009. "Incentives to Exercise." *Econometrica* 77(3):909–31.

Deci, Edward L., Richard Koestner, and Richard M. Ryan. 1999. "A Meta-Analytic Review of Experiments Examining the Effects of Extrinsic Rewards on Intrinsic Motivation." *Psychological Bulletin* 125(6):627–68.

Deci, Edward L., and Richard M. Ryan. 1985. *Intrinsic Motivation and Self-Determination in Human Behavior.* Plenum. New York.

Donatelle, Rebecca J., Deanne Hudson, Susan Dobie, Amy Goodall, Monica Hunsberger, and Kelly Oswald. 2004. "Incentives in Smoking Cessation: Status of the Field and Implications for Research and Practice with Pregnant Smokers." *Nicotine & Tobacco Research* 6(2):S163–S179.

Gneezy, Uri, Stephan Meier, and Pedro Rey-Biel. 2011. "When and Why Incentives (Don't) Work to Modify Behavior." *Journal of Economic Perspectives* 25(4):1–21.

Halpern, Scott D., Kristin M. Madison, and Kevin G. Volpp. 2009. "Patients as Mercenaries?: The Ethics of Using Financial Incentives in the War on Unhealthy Behaviors." *Circulation Cardiovascular Quality and Outcomes* 2:514–16.

Heil, Sarah H., Stephen T. Higgins, Ira M. Bernstein, Laura J. Solomon, Randall E. Rogers, Colleen S. Thomas, Gary J. Badger, and Mary Ellen Lynch. 2008. "Effects of Voucher-Based Incentives on Abstinence from Cigarette Smoking and Fetal Growth among Pregnant Women." *Addiction* 103(6):1009–18.

Higgins, Stephen T., Gary J. Badger, and Alan J. Budney. 2000. "Initial Abstinence and Success in Achieving Longer-Term Cocaine Abstinence." *Experimental and Clinical Psychopharmacology* 8(3):377–86.

Higgins, Stephen T., Alan J. Budney, Warren K. Bickel, Florian Foerg, R. Donham, and Gary J. Badger. 1994. "Incentives Improve Outcome in Outpatient Behavioral Treatment of Cocaine Dependence." *Archives of General Psychiatry* 51(7):568–76.

Higgins, Stephen T., Alan J. Budney, Warren K. Bickel, John R. Hughes, Florian Foerg, and Gary Badger. 1993. "Achieving Cocaine Abstinence with a Behavioral Approach." *American Journal of Psychiatry* 150(5):763–69.

John, Leslie, George Loewenstein, Andrea Troxel, Laurie Norton, Jennifer Fassbender, and Kevin Volpp. 2011. "Financial Incentives for Extended Weight Loss: A Randomized, Controlled Trial." *Journal of General Internal Medicine* 26(6):621–26.

Just, David, and Joseph Price. 2013. "Using Incentives to Encourage Healthy Eating in Children." *Journal of Human Resources* 48(4):855–72.

Kullgren, Jeffrey T., Andrea B. Troxel, George Loewenstein, David A. Asch, Laurie A. Norton, Lisa Wesby, Yuanyuan Tao, Jingsan Zhu, and Kevin G. Volpp. 2013a. "Individual- versus Group-Based Financial Incentives for Weight Loss: A Randomized, Controlled Trial." *Annals of Internal Medicine* 158(7):505–14.

Kullgren Jeffrey T., Andrea B. Troxel, George Loewenstein, David A. Asch, Laurie A. Norton, D. Gatto, Yuanyuan Tao, Jingsan Zhu, H. Schofield, J. A. Shea, David A. Asch, T. Pellathy, J. Driggers, and Kevin G. Volpp. 2013b. "A Mixed-Methods Randomized Controlled Trial of Employer Matching of Deposit Contracts to Promote Weight Loss." Academy of Health Annual Research Meeting. Oral presentation.

Ledgerwood, David M., and Nancy M. Petry. 2006. "Does Contingency Management Affect Motivation to Change Substance Use?" *Drug and Alcohol Dependence* 83(1): 65–72.

Levesque, Chantal S., Geoffrey C. Williams, Diane Elliot, Michael A. Pickering, Bradley Bodenhamer, and Phillip J. Finley. 2007. "Validating the Theoretical Structure of the Treatment Self-Regulation Questionnaire (TSRQ) across Three Different Health Behaviors." *Health Education Research* 21:691–702.

Marteau, Theresa M., Richard E. Aschcroft, and Adam Oliver. 2009. "Using Financial Incentives to Achieve Health Behaviour." *British Medical Journal* 338:983–85.

Promberger, Marianne, and Theresa M. Marteau. 2013. "When Do Financial Incentives Reduce Intrinsic Motivation? Comparing Behaviors Studied in Psychological and Economic Literatures." *Health Psychology* 32(9):950–57.

Royer, Heather, Mark Stehr, and Justin Sydnor. 2012. "Incentives, Commitments and Habit Formation in Exercise: Evidence from a Field Experiment with Workers at a Fortune-500 Company." NBER (National Bureau of Economic Research) Working Paper No. 18580.

Ryan, Richard M., and James P. Connell. 1989. "Perceived Locus of Causality and Internalization: Examining Reasons for Acting in Two Domains." *Journal of Personality and Social Psychology* 57(5):749–61.

Shaw, Joanne. 2007. "Is It Acceptable for People to Be Paid to Adhere to Medication? No." *British Medical Journal* 335(7613):233.

Silverman, Kenneth, Mary Ann Chutuape Stephens, George E. Bigelow, and Maxine L. Stitzer. 1999. "Voucher-Based Reinforcement of Cocaine Abstinence in Treatment-Resistant Methadone Patients: Effects of Reinforcement Magnitude." *Psychopharmacology* 146(2):128–38.

Silverman, Kenneth, Conrad J. Wong, Stephen T. Higgins, Robert K. Brooner, Ivan D. Montoya, Carlo Contoreggi, Annie Umbricht-Schneiter, Charles R. Schuster, and Kenzie L. Preston. 1996. "Increasing Opiate Abstinence through Voucher-Based Reinforcement Therapy." *Drug and Alcohol Dependence* 41(2):157–65.

Sutherland, Kim, Jon B. Christianson, and Sheila Leatherman. 2008. "Impact of Targeted Financial Incentives on Personal Health Behavior: A Review of the Literature." *Medical Care Research and Review* 65(6):36S–78S.

Volpp, Kevin G., Leslie K. John, Andrea B. Troxel, Laurie Norton, Jennifer Fassbender, and George Loewenstein. 2008a. "Financial Incentive-Based Approaches for Weight Loss: A Randomized Trial." *Journal of the American Medical Association* 300:2631–37.

Volpp, Kevin G., George Loewenstein, Andrea B. Troxel, Jalpa Doshi, Maureen Price, Mitchell Laskin, and Stephen E. Kimmel. 2008b. "A Test of Financial Incentives to Improve Warfarin Adherence." *BMC Health Services Research* 8:272.

Volpp, Kevin G., Andrea B. Troxel, Mark V. Pauly, Henry A. Glick, Andrea Puig, David A. Asch, Robert Galvin, Jingsan Zhu, Fei Wan, Jill DeGuzman, Elizabeth Corbett, Janet Weiner, and Janey Audrain-McGovern. 2009. "A Randomized Controlled Trial of Financial Incentives for Smoking Cessation." *New England Journal of Medicine* 360:699–709.

Williams, Geoffrey C., Zachary R. Freedman, and Edward L. Deci. 1998. "Supporting Autonomy to Motivate Patients with Diabetes for Glucose Control." *Diabetes Care* 2:1644–51.

Williams, Geoffrey C., Marylene Gagné, Richard M. Ryan, and Edward L. Deci. 2002. "Facilitating Autonomous Motivation for Smoking Cessation." *Health Psychology* 21(1):40–50.

Williams, Geoffrey C., Virginia M. Grow, Zachary R. Freedman, Richard M. Ryan, and Edward L. Deci. 1996. "Motivational Predictors of Weight Loss and Weight-Loss Maintenance." *Journal of Personality and Social Psychology* 70(1):115–26.

Williams, Geoffrey C., Gail C. Rodin, Richard M. Ryan, Wendy S. Grolnick, and Edward L. Deci. 1998. "Autonomous Regulation and Long-Term Medication Adherence in Adult Outpatients." *Health Psychology* 17(3):269–76.

PART V **BEHAVIORAL ECONOMICS AND THE
DOCTOR-PATIENT RELATIONSHIP**

Introduction

Aaron S. Kesselheim

The doctor-patient relationship is the key cog in the nearly $4 trillion U.S. healthcare system. When someone signs up for health insurance, selecting a primary care provider is among the first requirements. Physicians serve as patients' conduits to receiving all forms of medical care, including diagnostic services, therapeutic drugs, and medical devices, and access to hospitals, rehabilitation centers, and other healthcare institutions.

The centrality of the doctor-patient relationship is also reflected in the strong feelings attached to potential perturbations to that relationship. One of the key themes in the debates leading up to the 2010 Affordable Care Act (ACA), which extended the prospect of healthcare insurance to nearly all U.S. citizens for the first time, was whether patients would be able to keep their own physicians. Some previous health reform proposals never gained traction in part because people were not confident that their relationships with their physicians would remain intact. Similarly, patients worry about the possibility that outside interests may infringe on their dealings with their physicians. For example, one recent survey showed that more than two-thirds of patients were concerned that pharmaceutical companies have too much influence over their physicians' prescribing practices.

The functional and psychological importance of the doctor-patient relationship in the U.S. healthcare system makes the application of behavioral economics theory to it a sensitive issue. Behavioral economics allows clinicians to better understand how patients actually make decisions, knowledge that can also then be used to affect how those decisions are made. But as Alexander M. Capron and Donna Spruijt-Metz explain in this part, in recent decades the medical establishment has moved (not altogether easily) from a traditional paternalistic attitude toward patients into a more collaborative framing of the doctor-patient relationship that emphasizes fully informed consent and shared decision-making. To seek to inject a more subtle type of paternalism in the form of behavioral economics tools that can powerfully and even unconsciously shape patients' health choices threatens to undermine the doctor-patient relationship, unless done carefully and guided by the highest-quality evidence.

The chapters in this part focus on different tools of behavioral economics and how they interact with the doctor-patient relationship. In her chapter, Jennifer L. Zamzow examines the use of decision aids in helping physicians empower patients to make optimal choices about future emotional states. Capron and Spruijt-Metz address the applicability of preference data gathered—perhaps unknowingly—from patients through their mobile health applications. Ester Moher and Khaled El Emam describe two randomized studies of variations to the informed consent document and how these affect patients' subsequent health disclosures.

These authors bring three different perspectives to the alignment of behavioral economics and the doctor-patient relationship. Zamzow comes close to calling it an ethical obligation for physicians to use behavioral economics tools in effectively helping patients through difficult health-related crises (at least in the context of affective forecasting). Capron and Spruijt-Metz are skeptical of overreaching but ultimately conclude that data gathered from mobile health and other similar tools and used for behavioral economics goals can be a positive development, when designed with patients' input. Moher and El Emam empirically assess the process of using informed consent with behavioral economics cues, finding paradoxical outcomes that diverge from what physicians, and even patients, may want.

Thus, behavioral economics can lead to both substantial promise and important perils for the doctor-patient relationship. How do we implement these principles in a way that supports positive outcomes and avoids the potential risks? Not surprisingly, the leading answer is more research. Zamzow describes the need for research to show how to develop the right sort of decision aids and to know when in the process to deploy them. Capron and Spruijt-Metz describe how data from mobile health technologies can supplement traditionally gathered data to improve patient decision-making, but also call for research to ensure that the correct inferences are being drawn from the data. Moher and El Emam's hypothetical experimental studies, if confirmed with real patients making actual decisions, suggest that a substantial amount of additional research is needed to better understand patients' goals related to the use of their data for research and how they interact with the informed consent process.

To this point, most research focusing on the intersection of behavioral economics and the doctor-patient relationship has involved understanding and moderating addictive behaviors like smoking and alcohol overuse, improving health-related goals like exercise and weight loss, and attempting to promote medication adherence. Thus, the intersection of behavioral economics and the doctor-patient relationship has largely been in the aid of augmenting goals that most doctors and patients share. The chapters in this part consider the application of behavioral economics beyond this controversy-free zone to other facets of the doctor-patient relationship, including aiding patients' emotional state in coping with illness (Zamzow), expanding to even seemingly trivial behaviors that might be registered by mHealth devices (Capron and Spruijt-Metz), and covering the informed consent process (Moher and El Emam). Other less consensus-driven areas representing the future of behavioral economics and the doctor-patient relationship that are either hinted at or explicitly discussed in other parts of this book include choices between different equally valid therapeutic options or cost containment.

Testing these applications of behavioral economics in relation to the doctor-patient relationship will take a sustained commitment of resources and close involvement from doctors, patients, and other affected parties. It is hard to imagine foundation sources or individual payers, which have funded much of the behavioral economics research thus far, being able to sufficiently integrate such a confluence of stakeholders. It may therefore make sense for the government to take a more prominent role. Current National Institutes of Health funding of behavioral economics is spread across the different centers and is only a partial focus of the Office of Behavioral and Social Sciences Research. In 2013 President Barack Obama created a Behavioral Insights Team in the Office of Science and Technology Policy to translate research insights from behavioral economics into improvements in federal programs and policies. The next step is to create a broader centralized resource that can help fund and organize this work—a National Center for Behavioral Economics—redeploying resources from the agency's existing programs in a manner similar to the 2011 creation of the National Center for Advancing Translational Sciences. Such an investment is warranted because as the chapters in this part (and the rest of the book) show, the benefits of behavioral economics are substantial in helping promote positive health outcomes from the doctor-patient relationship and reducing waste and inefficiency in healthcare delivery.

CHAPTER 15

Affective Forecasting in Medical Decision-Making
What Do Physicians Owe Their Patients?

Jennifer L. Zamzow

Imagine a patient who was involved in an accident that crushed his spine and left him paralyzed. The patient now requests that all life-sustaining treatment be withdrawn because he does not want to live as a paraplegic. Many would argue that so long as the patient is competent, we need to respect his decision. But what if the patient requests that life-sustaining treatment be withdrawn because he mistakenly believes that life as a paraplegic would be worse than death for him? Though it is not uncommon for patients who become paralyzed to initially see this condition as a fate worse than death, many of these patients adapt over time. Studies have found that while individuals with disabilities report being less happy, on average, than individuals without disabilities, their mean life-satisfaction scores indicate that many individuals with disabilities are still generally satisfied with life (Brickman, Coates, and Janoff-Bulman 1978; Oswald and Powdthavee 2008). While we do not want to force life-sustaining treatment on those who really would rather die than live in their conditions, we also do not want patients to go without life-sustaining treatment due to mistaken beliefs about what life will be like for them in their conditions.

If patients want to choose treatment options that will lead to the best subjective quality of life, it is essential that their beliefs about how they will feel under various conditions are accurate. Consequently, *affective forecasting*—predicting how an outcome will impact one's experiential quality of life—is an essential step in choosing between medical treatments with different potential outcomes. This raises an impor-

I am grateful to Alex London, David Danks, and Rosa Terlazzo for helpful comments on this paper. I would also like to thank audiences at the Harvard Behavioral Economics, Law, and Health Policy Conference, the Georgetown Emotions and Emotionality Workshop, the 4th Annual Conference on Values in Medicine, Science, and Technology, and the 7th Annual Rocky Mountain Ethics Congress.

tant question for medical ethics: do physicians have an obligation to help their patients make more accurate affective forecasts?

Why Physicians Have an Obligation to Help Their Patients Make More Accurate Affective Forecasts

Most will probably agree that affective forecasting is important for good medical decision-making, but some may question whether this should give physicians any special obligations. It might seem that judgments about how the patient will feel about different outcomes are the patient's responsibility because, while the physician is supposed to be an expert on the medical information, the patient is supposed to be the expert on her own beliefs, desires, values, and experiences. Hence, though the physician has a responsibility to inform the patient of the chance of becoming paralyzed from surgery, for instance, the physician would not have a responsibility to inform the patient of how she might feel about being paralyzed.

The problem is that even if patients do have privileged access to their own beliefs, desires, values, and experiences, this is not sufficient for making good affective forecasts. The consistent finding in the empirical work on affective forecasting is that people are not always accurate predictors of their own future feelings (Brickman, Coates, and Janoff-Bulman 1978; Christensen-Szalanski 1984; Halpern and Arnold 2008; Hoerger et al. 2009; Sieff, Dawes, and Loewenstein 1999; Wilson and Gilbert 2003). In general, people are inclined to overestimate the effect that events will have on their emotional reactions and well-being, a phenomenon known as the *impact bias* (Wilson and Gilbert 2003). People often predict they will be happier about future positive events and more upset about future negative events than they actually end up feeling. There are a number of psychological mechanisms that can lead to affective forecasting errors, three of which have received a great deal attention in medical decision-making. First, people have a tendency to focus narrowly on what will change as the result of the focal event and fail to anticipate the extent to which other events will influence their thoughts and emotions. Second, people have a tendency to underestimate the effect of powerful psychological defenses that serve to ameliorate the impact of negative events on their overall well-being. Third, people tend to underestimate how quickly they will adapt to change. Each of these phenomena can lead people to overestimate the impact that a particular event will have on their future feelings (Gilbert et al. 1998).

If people are such poor predictors of their own future feelings, this suggests that merely having privileged access to one's own experiences, beliefs, desires, and values is not sufficient for making accurate predictions about how one will feel in the future. Patients are not without hope, however, for researchers have found a number of ways to help reduce impact bias. Having individuals consider their available coping mechanisms and how they have adapted to situations in the past, for example, can reduce immune neglect and help individuals better predict adaptation (Halpern and Arnold

2008; Peters et al. 2014; Ubel, Loewenstein, and Jepson 2005; T. D. Wilson et al. 2000). This suggests that patients could benefit from assistance with their affective forecasting when making medical decisions. Still, we need more than the fact that patients could benefit from help with their affective forecasting to show that physicians have an obligation to help them with this.

Physicians clearly have some duties to help their patients make prudent medical decisions. Unlike auto mechanics, bankers, or sales representatives, physicians have a professional duty of beneficence, which gives them an obligation to try to help their patients engage in good deliberation and make good decisions. However, physicians do not have a duty to assist their patients with everything related to their medical decisions. Patients likely need help with many tasks related to their medical decisions—planning their finances, getting their affairs in order, and the like—and we do not think physicians have a responsibility to assist their patients with all of these tasks. I argue that making predictions about how one will feel under various conditions is different, however. Assisting patients with their affective forecasting should be among the professional duties of physicians because whereas physicians are not in a good position qua physicians to help their patients with their finances and other matters, they are in a good position qua physicians to assist their patients with their affective forecasting given their special knowledge, perspective, and potential resources.[1] Their experience with other patients in similar situations gives them a better sense for what it is like for patients in such conditions, their third-person perspective may lead them to better appreciate different aspects of the decision, and it is more efficient to provide physicians with decision aids and other resources to assist their patients than to have patients try to acquire such information on their own.

Why Physicians Are in a Good Position to Assist Their Patients with Their Affective Forecasting
Physicians Have Special Knowledge

When thinking about how we will feel about different future outcomes, we often consult our own past experience. But what if a patient has to make a prediction about how she will feel under conditions that are unlike anything she has previously experienced? It is easy to predict that you would not enjoy being incontinent or having severe anxiety even if you have never experienced these before, but in order to compare different treatment options, patients often need to make more specific predictions. They need to predict how positive or negative particular conditions are likely to be, how long they might experience them, and so on, and these can be difficult predictions to make if the patient is not familiar with the condition.

One thing that can help patients make better predictions in unfamiliar situations is to know how other patients tend to experience these conditions. Knowing something about what it is like for other people in similar situations can be a good starting point for understanding what it might be like for you (Gilbert 2009). Since physicians interact with other patients with similar conditions, they will generally have a better idea of how other patients tend to experience such conditions than a new patient will. Of course, we should not expect physicians to be able to perfectly predict how their patients will feel about given outcomes. For one thing, physicians' judgments of their patients' quality of life do not always match patients' judgments (Boyd et al. 1990; Sonn et al. 2013; K. A. Wilson et al. 2000). For instance, in one study eliciting people's utility judgments for colostomies, Boyd et al. (1990) found that patients with colostomies assigned higher utilities to colostomies than physicians specializing in treating the disease. However, the physicians' utility ratings were still closer to actual colostomy patients' than were the ratings of patients who did not have colostomies. So unless the patient has dealt with the condition or knows someone who has dealt with it, the physician likely has better insight as to what the quality of life tends to be for patients with that condition than a patient who has not yet adapted to the full effects of her condition, which puts physicians in a good position to assist their patients with their affective forecasting.

Physicians Have a Different Perspective

A second way in which physicians are in a good position to help their patients make better affective forecasts is that they can offer a different perspective or point of view on the situation. Research has shown that people have difficulty predicting what they will want and how they will behave in a different affective state than they are currently in (Loewenstein 2005). This is especially worrisome for patients facing tough medical decisions because changes in their medical conditions are likely to lead to changes in their affect, which can make it difficult to predict their future preferences and behavior.

The problem with trying to make important decisions in a temporarily "hot" state is not that emotions are always bad for decision-making; a certain amount of emotional engagement is necessary for good decision-making. The problem arises when temporary emotions overwhelm us, making it difficult to appreciate how things might be different in the future. Similarly, it can be difficult to appreciate how things might be different in the future if the future will involve strong emotions that we are not currently experiencing.

The point is not that physicians necessarily have a better perspective than patients but merely that they have a different perspective, and this will make different factors salient to the physician than to the patient. If these factors are relevant to how the patient is likely to feel in the future, then drawing the patient's attention to these factors can provide her additional insight. To the extent that physicians can help patients appreciate factors that may not have been salient to them otherwise, physicians should be able to help patients make better predictions and better decisions than they would make without getting input from a different point of view.

It Is More Efficient for Physicians to Have Access to Training and Resources

Instead of requiring each patient to go out on her own and find information about the factors that are likely to influence her affective forecasts and the factors that are likely to influence her actual experiences, it would be much more efficient for the medical profession to provide resources and decision aids to physicians who can then use them to help guide patients through the process of thinking about what it might be like for them to experience different medical conditions. Having a guide for physicians can make it not only less burdensome for physicians to help their patients, but decision aids can also be more effective than physicians' unaided judgments at minimizing errors and biases on the part of physicians (Bornstein and Emler 2001). For instance, decision aids can draw physicians' attention to factors that physicians tend to underestimate, such as the effect of chronic pain or clinical depression on one's subjective experience (Wolff et al. 2012). This will not completely eliminate bias on the part of physicians, but it will likely still be better than having patients try to make predictions about how they might feel under various conditions on their own if patients do not know what factors they should consider, how they should process these factors, or what information to seek out in order to make more accurate affective forecasts. Decision aids can also help minimize the opportunities for physicians to manipulate patients' decisions by taking advantage of framing effects or other cognitive biases.[2]

Implications for Medical Practice
Which Physicians Have a Duty to Assist the Patient with Her Affective Forecasting?

If the above argument is correct and physicians do, in fact, have an obligation to assist their patients with their affective forecasting, what will such an obligation look like in practice? One of the first questions we need to ask is which physicians have this obligation. When patients are faced with difficult medical decisions, they often have many different medical professionals working with them. Who among these medical professionals has a duty to help the patient with her affective forecasting? In general, the physicians in the best position to help patients develop a more realistic understanding of how different conditions might impact their experiential quality of life will be those who have knowledge of how other patients tend to respond to similar conditions and who have knowledge of the particular patient and an established relationship of trust. Who is in the best position to provide information to the patient is not the only relevant question, however. On a shared decision-making model, patients and physicians work together to reach healthcare choices. Consequently, the question of which physicians have a duty to assist the patient with her affective forecasting will also depend on the role of the physician in the shared decision-making process with the patient. Those who will play a primary role in the shared decision-making process and who will be involved with the patient at the ultimate point of decision-making will have the strongest obligation to participate in the affective forecasting intervention. It is important for these physicians to be aware of the patient's beliefs about how she will feel under different conditions so they can have a better understanding of the patient's treatment preferences.[3]

When Should Physicians Intervene?

Now that we have identified who should be involved in the affective forecasting intervention, we can ask when in the decision-making process they should intervene. It might seem that the most efficient way to help patients would be to wait for them to request help or to wait for them to show clear signs of needing help. However, I think this approach underestimates how difficult it is both for the physician and for the patient to recognize a need for assistance with affective forecasting. Affective forecasting errors are ubiquitous, yet people tend to be unaware of how inaccurate they can be at predicting their own future feelings, so patients might not recognize their need for help with their affective forecasting. It is also difficult for physicians to recognize when a particular patient is in danger of making affective forecasting errors. One problem with affective forecasting is that it can be difficult to determine whether a particular individual making a particular affective forecast is making an error. For one thing, we do not know whether a prediction is correct until after the fact. In some cases, we might not even be able to tell after the fact whether the patient made a good or bad affective forecast. Just because one's prediction turns out to be wrong does not mean it was a bad prediction. There could have been some significant change in the patient's circumstances that affected her experience but the patient had no way of knowing about it in advance. Furthermore, our knowledge of affective forecast errors is based on base rates. For instance, we can know that, in general, people tend to not be as depressed after losing a loved one as they predict, but it is harder to determine whether a particular individual in a particular situation will be as depressed as she thinks she will be. Since we cannot know all of the factors that will influence a patient's affective forecast or her actual experience of an event, it can be difficult to tell whether a particular patient's affective forecast is reasonable. Hence, if physicians only offer assistance when they believe their patient is exhibiting clear signs of a forecasting error, they might miss out on helping a number of patients who are in danger of making poor affective forecasts without even realizing it.

Instead of trying to recognize individual cases in which intervention is necessary, we should focus on determining the kinds of cases in which intervention will be most beneficial and intervene proactively in these situations. Physicians should intervene proactively in at least two kinds of cases: (1) cases where the stakes are high (for example, where different treatment options will lead to very different outcomes and where the outcomes will significantly affect one's experiential quality of life); and (2) cases where patients typically have a poor understanding of what it is like to have a certain condition or undergo a certain treatment (for example, colostomies, paraple-gia, etc.).[4] This will allow physicians to focus their time and resources on the cases where the patient's affective forecasting is likely to matter most without requiring either the patient or the physician to first recognize that there is a problem with this particular patient's affective forecasts that needs to be addressed. Of course, some patients may need help that goes beyond what an individual physician can provide. While physicians might be in a good position to help their patients with their affective forecasting, they might not be able to personally assist patients with special underlying needs that hinder their ability to make accurate affective forecasts. For instance, if a patient is severely depressed or anxious or is having great difficulty processing her emotions or thinking about what life might be like for her under different conditions, the physician may need to refer the patient to a psychiatrist, support group, or other resources.

Implications for Medical Training and Resources

If there is a duty for physicians to assist their patients with their affective forecast-ing and if the best way to do so is through the use of decision aids, this will clearly have implications for the medical profession regarding medical resources and train-ing. The medical profession needs to provide physicians with easily interpretable and accessible research on patient outcomes, quality of life judgments, and so on.[5] They also need to provide physicians with decision aids that can help guide them through the process of presenting the relevant information to patients and prompting reflec-tion in a way that will help minimize bias.

Since patients' choices can be significantly influenced by the way in which infor-mation is presented, decision aids must be designed carefully. More empirical research needs to be done to determine the best ways to proactively assist patients with their affective forecasts, but we can begin to make progress by raising some of the ques-tions and issues that should be considered when developing affective forecasting in-terventions. One important factor to consider when giving patients information about what it is like for other patients who have faced similar medical conditions is who to include in the sample. Should we give patients information about the experiences and subjective quality of life of the average patient in their condition or of patients like them? In cases where we have reliable data available on individual or group differences in patient outcomes that might be relevant to a particular patient, this information should generally be conveyed to her; patients should know if they are in a group that is significantly more or less vulnerable to particular conditions or outcomes. However, although more specific information can often be more useful, it is sometimes difficult to determine whether a patient's membership in a particular group will be important. Even when we have reliable data on individual or group differences, whether this will be relevant for a particular patient might depend on idiosyncratic factors such as how strongly the patient identifies with the group or demographic in question. For example, some patients' religious values might significantly affect how they experience a given condition while other patients' religious values might not.

Another factor that needs to be considered is the extent to which abstract and concrete information should be incorporated. If physicians provide patients with abstract information about how patients (or patients like them) who have a particular condition tend to report their experiences and quality of life on various measures, this might give patients a better idea of what the average patient believes about her condition and about the range of experiences, but it might also be too abstract for the patient to get a real phenomenological sense of what it is like for the patients to experience the condition. Patients may have difficulty understanding the statistics or what they should take away from them, or they may not be sufficiently moved by them because they are not emotionally salient. Patients could also be presented with more concrete information about what it is like for a patient with a certain condition by having them actually meet patients with a given condition or by presenting the patient with narratives or other depictions of what life is like from actual patients. The worry with presenting patients with more detailed information from a small sample is that it is more difficult to convey the likelihood of actually experiencing the particular outcomes they are presented with, which could leave patients with a less accurate overall picture of what to expect in their case. Even if both positive and negative patient outcomes are presented, if these outcomes are not presented in proportion to actual patient outcomes, this could lead patients to be more or less optimistic than they should be. There are also tradeoffs in terms of how much information to provide; sometimes presenting patients with too much information causes them to experience information overload and make worse decisions (Ubel 2002). In order to know how we should present information to patients, we need to have a better sense for how these and other factors influence patients' judgments. Once we know how patients' judgments might be influenced, we then need to consider what tradeoffs we should make to most effectively help patients and physicians.

It is also important that the decision aids are constructed so as to promote a dynamic interaction between the patient and the physician. This will give the physician a better opportunity to ensure that the patient understands the relevant information and is able to integrate it with her own values, traits, coping mechanisms, social support, and so on. Playing an active role in the conversation will also give the physician a better sense for the patient's beliefs, values, and preferences, which will put the physician in a better position to help the patient make treatment choices that accord with her values.

Conclusion

In order for patients to make good medical decisions, it is important that they are able to make accurate predictions about how various conditions will impact their experiential quality of life. Though it may seem that making predictions about how the patient will feel in the future is something that only the patient should be responsible for, I have argued that assisting patients with their affective forecasting should be among the professional duties of physicians.

Physicians have a professional duty of beneficence, which gives them an obligation to try to help their patients engage in effective deliberation and make good decisions when they are in a good position qua physicians to help, and physicians are in a good position qua physicians to assist their patients with their affective forecasting given their unique knowledge, perspective, skills, and potential resources. Their experience with other patients in similar situations gives them a better sense for what it is like for patients in such conditions, their third-person perspective may lead them to better appreciate different aspects of the decision, and it is more efficient to provide physicians with decision aids and other resources to assist their patients than to have patients try to acquire such information on their own.

I do not wish to suggest that physicians are in a better position than patients to determine what is in the patient's "best interest." The physician's role is not to just tell the patient how she is likely to feel or what is in the patient's best interest, but rather to guide the patient through the process of determining this for herself. The physician can work with the patient to help the patient determine what is in her best interest by helping her overcome some of the obstacles to affective forecasting. The advantage of such an approach is that patients can benefit from physicians' unique perspective and access to information and resources without necessarily being steered into making a particular decision. If the patient can develop more accurate predictions about what life might be like for her under different conditions, then she will be in a better position to make her own treatment choices rather than simply having to rely on the treatment recommendation of the physician. In this way, physicians can help patients make medical decisions that better align with their values without constraining their choice set.

Notes

1. While I think assisting patients with their affective forecasting should be among the professional obligations of physicians, I do not think it should be a legal obligation.
2. We will not be able to entirely eliminate the possibility that physicians could use affective forecasting interventions as an opportunity to manipulate patient preferences. We should do what we can to minimize such temptations, but we ultimately have to have trust in physicians to honor their fiduciary obligations to promote their patients' interests.
3. The obligation to assist the patient with her affective forecasting should fall on whomever is playing the primary role in shared decision-making. In some cases this may be nurses or other medical professionals.
4. For instance, the general public tends to overestimate the negative impact of having a colostomy and being on dialysis but tends to significantly underestimate the negative impact of mental illness and chronic pain (Wolff et al. 2012). Any time there are significant differences between quality of life judgments of individuals who have the condition versus

those who do not, physicians should intervene to try to make sure a patient who has not yet experienced the full effects of a particular condition has an accurate picture of what it might be like for her.

5. Similar pushes have been made in patient-centered outcomes research and comparative-effectiveness research for obtaining data on health outcomes and clinical effectiveness of treatments to help medical professionals and patients weigh alternatives and make better choices (see, for example, *Patient-Centered Outcomes Research Institute*).

References

Bornstein, Brian H., and A. Christine Emler. 2001. "Rationality in Medical Decision Making: A Review of the Literature on Doctors' Decision-Making Biases." *Journal of Evaluation in Clinical Practice* 7:97–107.

Boyd, Norman F., Heather J. Sutherland, Karen Z. Heasman, David L. Tritchler, and Bernard J. Cummings. 1990. "Whose Utilities for Decision Analysis?" *Medical Decision Making* 10:58–67.

Brickman, Philip, Dan Coates, and Ronnie Janoff-Bulman. 1978. "Lottery Winners and Accident Victims: Is Happiness Relative?" *Journal of Personality and Social Psychology* 36:917–27.

Christensen-Szalanski, Jay J. J. 1984. "Discount Functions and the Measurement of Patients' Values: Women's Decisions During Childbirth." *Medical Decision Making* 4:47–58.

Gilbert, Daniel. 2009. *Stumbling on Happiness*. Random House. New York.

Gilbert, Daniel T., Elizabeth C. Pinel, Timothy D. Wilson, Stephen J. Blumberg, and Thalia P. Wheatley. 1998. "Immune Neglect: A Source of Durability Bias in Affective Forecasting." *Journal of Personality and Social Psychology* 75:617–38.

Halpern, Jodi, and Robert M. Arnold. 2008. "Affective Forecasting: An Unrecognized Challenge in Making Serious Health Decisions." *Journal of General Internal Medicine* 23:1708–12.

Hoerger, Michael, Stuart W. Quirk, Richard E. Lucas, and Thomas H. Carr. 2009. "Immune Neglect in Affective Forecasting." *Journal of Research in Personality* 43:91–94.

Loewenstein, George. 2005. "Hot-Cold Empathy Gaps and Medical Decision Making." *Health Psychology* 24:S49–S56.

Oswald, Andrew J., and Nattavudh Powdthavee. 2008. "Does Happiness Adapt? A Longitudinal Study of Disability with Implications for Economists and Judges." *Journal of Public Economics* 92:1061–77.

Patient-Centered Outcomes Research Institute. Accessed December 12, 2014. http://www.pcori.org.

Peters, Stacey A., Simon M. Laham, Nicholas Pachter, and Ingrid M. Winship. 2014. "The Future in Clinical Genetics: Affective Forecasting Biases in Patient and Clinician Decision Making." *Clinical Genetics* 85:312–17.

Sieff, Elaine M., Robyn M. Dawes, and George Loewenstein. 1999. "Anticipated versus Actual Reaction to HIV Test Results." *American Journal of Psychology* 112:297–311.

Sonn, Geoffrey A., Natalia Sadetsky, Joseph C. Presti, and Mark S. Litwin. 2013. "Differing Perceptions of Quality of Life in Patients with Prostate Cancer and Their Doctors." *The Journal of Urology* 189:S59–S65.

Ubel, Peter A. 2002. "Is Information Always a Good Thing? Helping Patients Make 'Good' Decisions." *Medical Care* 40:V39–V44.

Ubel, Peter A., George Loewenstein, and Christopher Jepson. 2005. "Disability and Sunshine: Can Hedonic Predictions Be Improved by Drawing Attention to Focusing Illusions or Emotional Adaptation?" *Journal of Experimental Psychology: Applied* 11:111–23.

Wilson, Kerry A., Anthony J. Dowling, Mohamed Abdolell, and Ian F. Tannock. 2000. "Perception of Quality of Life by Patients, Partners and Treating Physicians." *Quality of Life Research* 9:1041–52.

Wilson, Timothy D., and Daniel T. Gilbert. 2003. "Affective Forecasting." *Advances in Experimental Social Psychology* 35:345–411.

Wilson, Timothy D., Thalia Wheatley, Jonathan M. Meyers, Daniel T. Gilbert, and Danny Axsom. 2000. "Focalism: A Source of Durability Bias in Affective Forecasting." *Journal of Personality and Social Psychology* 78:821–36.

Wolff, Jonathan, Sarah Edwards, Sarah Richmond, Shepley Orr, and Geraint Rees. 2012. "Evaluating Interventions in Health: A Reconciliatory Approach." *Bioethics* 26:455–63.

CHAPTER **16**

Behavioral Economics in the Physician-Patient Relationship
A Possible Role for Mobile Devices and Small Data

Alexander M. Capron and Donna Spruijt-Metz

Behavioral economics seems to be everywhere these days, used by people who want us to do all sorts of things, for our own good or theirs. Drawing on the results of experiments about human cognition and behavior and on a tidal wave of data regarding what people do and how they interact, behavioral economists are telling marketers how to rearrange items on grocery store shelves and restaurateurs the food on their buffets, employers how to tweak the presentation of retirement savings options, and lenders how to entice students with a dizzying array of college loan choices (Cadena and Keys 2013). Whether people are being nudged toward a choice that will make them better off or being led down the primrose path, their decisions are shaped by the way their environment is constructed and their options are framed and even by the manipulation of their ability to process relevant facts. When businesses use this knowledge to exploit well-known biases and weaknesses in human reasoning and behavior to get people to misperceive their own interests without being aware that they are, they may be criticized for unfair or deceptive practices (Thaler and Sunstein 2009, 134–46). Conversely, when the aims are benign, one is among the "choice architects" who exercise "libertarian paternalism" to make it more likely that people—not "mandated" but "choosing freely"—will pick the behaviors that "make their lives longer, healthier, and better" (Thaler and Sunstein 2009, 5).

Should physicians' intentional use of the precepts and techniques of behavioral economics to nudge patients toward better health be regarded as unproblematic because physicians are subject to an ethical duty to act beneficently? At first blush, the answer is "no." Bioethicists have spent the past five decades—with substantial support from the law—trying to get physicians to engage their patients in a mutually respectful

We thank Amy Hulbert, University of Southern California Gould School of Law class of 2016, for invaluable assistance in research.

dialogue about the available therapeutic options, with the aim of helping each patient to arrive at an active, informed decision about which option best fits the patient's goals and preferences (Capron 1974; Faden and Beauchamp 1986). That is a far cry from the libertarian paternalism of Thaler and Sunstein, which is, after all, still paternalism, the scourge from which bioethics has aimed to free the physician-patient relationship. Medical paternalism may rest on the ethical injunction that physicians must place their patients' interests foremost, especially ahead of the physicians' own interests, but this commitment has traditionally been embodied in the Hippocratic pledge to "follow that system of regimen which, *according to my ability and judgment, I consider for the benefit of my patient*, and abstain from whatever is deleterious and mischievous" (emphasis added).

Behavioral economists could reassure physicians taking this traditional approach to the practice of medicine that they need not apologize for doing so since a core premise of the field is that most of our decisions originate in something other than a clear understanding of our own aims and their rational pursuit, even when we are most convinced of the rationality of our decision-making (Cohen 2013). In this view, caring physicians are not merely permitted but actually obligated to determine patients' best interests because deferring to patients' "autonomous choices" seems unwise since people often lack clear, stable preferences; have incomplete information; and are prevented by a variety of cognitive dysfunctions from accurately perceiving their true interests and objectives (Ménard 2010, 231; Sunstein and Thaler 2003, 1162). Likewise, "reasoning failure" interferes with patients making the decisions that will achieve those objectives (Aggarwal, Davies, and Sullivan 2014; Sunstein 2003, 767).

It would thus appear that behavioral economics is on the side of the traditional Hippocratic physician who not only decides which course of action is right for each patient based on the physician's objectivity and superior knowledge but also cleverly steers patients toward that right course of action. We believe, however, that behavioral economics can be used for exactly the opposite purpose, that is, as a tool for physicians who want to build therapeutic relationships with patients based on the principles of biomedical ethics, especially respect for persons. Further, the conscientious and creative application of mobile devices and wireless technologies (mHealth) and the "small data" they generate should enhance the capacity of behaviorally informed and ethically oriented physicians to learn what patients want out of treatment, to guide them through the minefield of decision-making about their medical conditions, and to help them act in ways that are aligned with those decisions and that are most likely to achieve the goals they have chosen.

The Challenges Behavioral Economics Poses for Physicians

Besides these contrasting uses of behavioral economics in justifying—and assisting—beneficent paternalism in medicine, on the one hand, or mutual decision-making informed by mHealth, on the other, the field also poses some interesting challenges for physicians' practice of their profession. Its findings and insights loom especially large, however, for physicians practicing in a more traditional, paternalistic fashion.

First, the very sorts of biases, cognitive limitations, and decision-making defects that provide the rationale for physicians behaving paternalistically toward patients also afflict physicians. Like the rest of us, physicians make snap judgments that are wrong; their rapport with, or conscious or unconscious aversion to, individual patients can alter their diagnoses or the care they provide; and their perceptions of their current patients are often distorted by the availability heuristic, which leads people to rely on salient memory rather than statistically valid information (Sunstein 2003, 756–63). "[P]hysicians may mistake symptoms of one disease for those of another disease they've seen more often. Or they may fall prey to 'confirmation bias,' which leads them to rapidly assemble information into an accurate diagnosis—or misconstrue the evidence before them" (Crichton 2007).

Second, physicians' efforts to do what is individually best for each patient are undermined by the natural tendency to presume that their own values and goals—or the values and goals that they have found in prior patients—are also those of the current patient. Countering that tendency would necessitate that they get to know each patient well, an objective that is not supported by the structure or financing of healthcare, which emphasizes acute over chronic care and pays physicians much more for interventions than conversations, nor aided by the typical physician's communication skills. "[A]lthough the medical profession has long recognized that doctors communicate poorly with patients, physicians receive little training to improve that interaction. Historically, medical education has regarded communication skills with an indifference that approaches contempt. It's unscientific, it's hand-holding, it's bedside manner. Yet it's clearly important" (Crichton 2007).

Further, physicians' attempts to get around the challenge of trying to infer their patients' preferences by looking at what these patients have chosen in the past may be stymied since those choices may themselves have been engineered by the existing "choice architecture." Except when they are extreme outliers on a particular matter, most people accept whichever option has been positioned as the preferred one, partly because of the positive power of behavioral manipulation and partly to avoid the burden of having to evaluate the range of options available (Saghai 2013a, 499; Schwartz 2003). The tidal wave of data that are being generated by the rapidly growing "Internet of things"—the 13 billion phones, chips, sensors, implants, and other Internet-connected devices that existed as of 2013, which are expected to balloon to 50 billion by 2020 (Pew Research Center 2014; Tucker 2014)—and gathered into huge databanks provide a wealth of information about how to produce the best outcomes for patients (as judged by their physicians) and which options were most preferred by patients. Choice architects in health plans and insurance companies use this sort of "big data" to construct the array of preferred options. Thus, any conclusions a physician might draw from a particular patient's past "choices" may not accurately represent the patient's true preferences (assuming that such preferences have survived his experience of selecting a series of default options in previous medical encounters). Finally, in nudging patients toward outcomes that physicians regard as healthier, physicians may, unfortunately, create uncertainty and fear, lead to stigma and unjust discrimination, infringe privacy, and lack an evidence base and thereby risk failing to promote good health or actually cause harm (ten Have et al. 2011, 671).

Some of these challenges will be mitigated as behavioral economists better understand the connections between behaviors and health outcomes and how particular nudges change behavior. In this process, they will rely not only on laboratory experiments but also on "big data" about the choices people make and the actions they take. By accessing such data on a different scale, physicians may be able to use behavioral economics more ethically as well as more effectively.

The Sources and Uses of "Small Data"—and Some Problems

One way to view "big data" about a population is as a collection of all the "small data" about the habits, activities (including purchases and travel), current status and location, general and specific preferences, and so forth of identifiable individuals in that population. Increasingly, people—and their physicians—can gain access to the "digital traces" of their lives that are stored as sets of small data (Estrin 2014). Such data could be used both in enriching clinicians' understanding of people's actual choices and behaviors and in allowing real-time monitoring of, or even intervention in, health-related choices and behaviors.

The relevant digital material comes from at least three sources. The first consists of "personal devices and Internet services specifically designed for self-tracking (Fitbit, Patients like me, quantifiedself.com, and so forth)," and the second is the "much richer corpus of data that we generate every day, just by virtue of our normal activities" in the presence of a host of common mobile technologies like GPS-enabled smartphones, tablets, and laptops that "leave a continuously updated 'trail of data breadcrumbs' behind us" (Estrin 2014, 32). The resulting traces do not relate narrowly to matters of health but could still be helpful to someone trying to understand our lives, including our health status and behaviors. The third source is a rapidly growing group "of new mobile health information and sensing technologies (mHealth)" that can (or in the near future will) not only "support continuous health monitoring" but also "encourage healthy behaviors to prevent or reduce health problems, support chronic disease self-management, enhance provider knowledge, reduce the number of healthcare visits, and provide personalized, localized, and on-demand interventions in ways previously unimaginable" (Kumar at al. 2013, 228–29).

These sources—general self-surveillance, digital traces of daily life, and mHealth— can complement the data about individuals that reside in electronic health records (EHRs), though they are distinct from EHRs, which "capture data reported by clinicians, not patients; and data about clinical treatment, not day-to-day activities" (Estrin

2014, 32). The promise of mHealth is that it will allow biological and behavioral monitoring and interventions "that are personalized and delivered in real time," that cost-effectively "enhance the possibility of scaling surveillance," and that can "capitalize on small, but frequent, intervention doses at a timing that is more optimal for the user" (Spruijt-Metz, Nilsen, and Pavel 2015, 120).

But for this promise to be fulfilled, technical and legal problems need to be addressed. First, mHealth assessments of patients' conditions depend not only on precise and frequent data from sensors and mobile devices but also on engineers, psychologists, and medical experts working together to generate algorithms that can combine those data with other information (such as self-reports and physicians' findings) and produce usable information that allows reliable inferences to be drawn about a patient's "physiologic, psychological, emotional, and environmental state" (Estrin 2014, 32). Second, notwithstanding the considerable enthusiasm for mHealth, rigorous research on the technologies' efficacy is needed to avoid premature adoption that could lead to avoidable injuries or unjustified expenditures. The assessments produced by all mHealth systems must be subjected to meticulous reliability and validity testing, which commercial developers may not be able or willing to provide, given the speed with which new technical capabilities are being developed, and which academics may be ill-equipped and poorly funded to undertake (Riley et al. 2013).

Third, the status of the data will have to be clarified: are they like personal (albeit automatically generated) diaries or "protected health information" to whose collection and dissemination the Health Insurance Portability and Accountability Act (HIPAA) might apply? Fourth, popular acceptance of mHealth may be held back by privacy concerns arising from data generated by self-surveillance programs and ubiquitous mobile devices being stored "casually, perhaps promiscuously, somewhere in 'the cloud'" (Kang et al. 2012, 809). Alternatives to such dumping (such as "vaults" and "guardians") have been suggested, but care will be needed to avoid the lack of interoperability that has hampered the utility of EHRs.

A further legal issue involves ownership of, and access to, the data. Since the companies that control the devices or programs through which the data are collected, such as mobile phone service providers or the websites where data are recorded, such as Facebook, are interested in monetizing people's data (for example, by parsing it for behavioral targeting and advertising), the default terms in their contracts—which most people, in a classic illustration of behavioral economics, click through without reading (Kang et al. 2012, 824)—allow the companies to collect, process, and sell the data, in some cases even to the individual whose device (such as a Fitbit bracelet) generates the data. If the success of mHealth depends on people owning, or at least having ready and inexpensive access to, their own data—what activists call "data liberation"—then the companies collecting the data, such as mobile carriers, need to see a business advantage to making it available. Estrin is hopeful that the companies will do so since, "if the standard interfaces to personal digital tracks spark a cottage industry of app makers who process small data and put it to work for subscribers," then "they could increase the value of the consumers' engagement with the underlying digital services," just as mobile apps have greatly increased the value of smartphones for consumers (Estrin 2014, 34).

Relationships and Data in "Personalized Paternalism"
Conversations and "Small Data": The Foundation for Identifying Goals and Influences

If they are to eschew libertarian paternalism in favor of a more patient-centered approach, physicians need to understand the goals, values, or specific objectives that would, if fulfilled, constitute both beneficent action and respect for each patient. "Small data" about the patient, competently analyzed and accessible on an ongoing basis, will help some by showing what patients like to do (work, travel, garden, hike, read books, attend concerts, etc.) and even when and with whom (spouses, children, grandchildren, friends, co-workers, strangers, etc.). Such data can also provide clues about how patients' well-being and activities are affected by changes in health or by different medical interventions, and about how various features of the environment also affect patients' behavior, choices, and health status. They are more detailed and more reliable than what patients or family members typically report to physicians during office visits since they are free of the errors of memory and selective reporting that color normal narratives. The fabric woven from these digital strands can be precious for the same reason that physicians can learn so much from home visits where patients can be observed in their natural habitat; at its best, the digitally derived information is akin to a continuous home visit by an omniscient observer. Thus, they provide valuable supplements to, albeit not replacements for, self-reports.

Indeed, if physicians are to truly understand their patients' preferences, habits, and triggers for action, they need candid and insightful conversations with them, a prescription provided thirty years ago by Jay Katz in *The Silent World of Doctor and Patient* (1984) based on having delved deeply into the historical, organizational, and psychological factors that steer physicians to act paternalistically. Katz probed how emotions such as faith, hope, and fear influence the decision-making of physicians as well as patients. He paid particular attention to physicians' most difficult challenge, namely, acknowledging uncertainty (their own and the field's) in their encounters with patients. Only when a physician has built a mutually respectful relationship with a patient can the physician openly reveal her uncertainties in arriving at diagnoses and prognoses and in providing care; these uncertainties confront the physician in evaluating the patient's situation and need to be understood by the patient if the latter is to appreciate the situation and its implications for achieving the hoped-for outcomes.

The point of engaging the patient in an ongoing dialogue is to learn each patient's wishes and fears rather than relying on the physician's imaginative suppositions regarding such matters. Being forthcoming about the true nature of the situation is a means of helping the patient to be honest and thoughtful in the process. Katz closed his book by asking whether patients can be trusted to participate more fully in the decisions that affect their well-being, to which he replied: "I believe patients can be trusted. If anyone were to contest that belief, I would ask: Can physicians be trusted to make decisions for patients? This book has argued that both must be trusted, but that they can only be trusted if they first learn to trust each other" (Katz 1984, 229).

Physicians striving to achieve such a trusting relationship must be prepared to ground their conclusions about what is best for each patient on conversations that are as complete, candid, and ongoing as they can make them, while avoiding those heuristics that rely on generalizations about patients based on their age, gender, ethnicity, and type of disease. By combining conversation with small data, physicians have a real possibility of understanding what patients want and how the environment affects patients' actions and decisions.

When Is It All Right to Nudge Patients?

Once a physician and a patient have identified the latter's values and preferences about treatments and outcomes, they will want to increase the likelihood that the patient will achieve the identified objectives. If physicians tell patients how they use default options, decision frames, incentives and disincentives, and other behavioral tools to shape patients' perceptions and hence to steer their decisions and actions, do they risk losing the power of those stratagems while at the same time inviting criticism that they are manipulating their patients and not relying on voluntary, informed decision-making?

One could say that so long as the set of choices a patient can make is not altered or the patient's freedom of choice substantially diminished, the use of nudges would not be paternalistic because the physician has merely increased the likelihood, not determined, that a particular choice will be made (Saghai 2013a, 2013b). More importantly, revealing one's reliance on behavioral stratagems is not necessarily at odds with still being able to use them. For example, with the agreement of a patient who wants to stop a behavior such as smoking or over-eating, a physician could set up a disincentive scheme in which regular assessments of the patient's behavior lead to the imposition of financial penalties for nonperformance. Properly designed, even modest financial nudges can have an outsized effect on patients' behavior without depriving them of autonomous choice, assuming they remain free to stop the program whenever they wish.

A more complex example would be a patient who, facing a potentially frightening diagnosis, expresses reluctance to make choices among treatment options or perhaps even to be informed of the results of a diagnostic test. It is possible to regard such a person as having removed himself from the realm of autonomy and informed consent, but besides trying to help the patient regain his capacity to participate actively in decisions about his care, a physician need not adopt either of the two common approaches for this situation, that is, regarding the patient as incapacitated and thus shifting decision-making to a surrogate, or allowing the patient to slip into a "whatever you say, Doc" mode. Instead, the physician could say something like the following:

> There are three possible treatments (A, B, and C), all of which are used to treat cases like yours. If you don't want to choose among them, I will take that to mean that you want option A. I happen to believe that A offers the best chance of producing the outcome you prefer, but you may come to believe that it is leading to a result you don't want or is creating side effects you don't like. You will always have the possibility to switch to B or C, or, having done so, to go back to A. Starting with A is not my decision; it is yours because we both know that A is the treatment we will use now if you don't express a choice to start with some other.

Thus, a default choice would be used but not for the usual reason (that is, in response to inertia and the status quo bias) but rather to reinforce the patient's connection with the treatment selected. In accepting this approach, the patient is not simply saying "yeah, whatever," but something closer to "this decision is so momentous that I don't want to bear the burden of making it. My family is very worried, and if I make a choice that doesn't turn out well, I'll feel responsible for their disappointment, on top of everything else." Part of the physician's therapeutic role entails relieving the patient's immediate distress, such as by temporarily lifting some of the burden of decision-making from the patient's shoulders, but without substituting someone else—the physician or a surrogate—as the decision-maker. Instead, the situation has been structured in light of the reality that some course of action must be undertaken (which could include "just observe, but do not intervene"), and the default (plainly announced and, hence, a "choice" that the patient can change at any time) is the course of action most likely to provide the benefits the patient wants. This reflects Katz's sophisticated view of consent that rejects deceit or coercion as paternalistic but fully accepts—indeed, insists on—the role that unconscious processes and unexamined assumptions play in the mutual decision-making carried out by physician and patient. Moreover, creating such a strategy as a means of preserving a form of choice for patients who feel unable to choose should remind physicians of the need to examine problems in their own decision-making processes, which are subject to the availability heuristic, confirmation bias, and other weaknesses.

By using small data to assess the patient's condition, behavioral strategies can be broken down into small units and personalized to the patient. Sometimes, the data—particularly when derived from the "digital traces" left by our ordinary mobile devices—would merely trigger an intervention: for example, a nurse calling a daughter or a neighbor to check on an elderly patient whose level of activity, as reflected in positional data sent by her smart phone, has declined over several days. Such an action is not paternalistic because it reflects the expectations worked out by the clinician and patient, which led the latter to have her personal digital "life data" supplied (in an analyzed fashion) to her physician for exactly such use.[1] More ambitious forms of monitoring, custom-designed for a particular patient's situation, though perhaps relying on fairly simple and inexpensive sensors, are likely to develop rapidly in the coming years, not the least because our aging demographic will fuel demand for such modalities. Sophisticated algorithms will allow clinicians to detect conditions and evaluate the effectiveness of health interventions earlier than otherwise possible—such as revealing changes in mental or physical health from a slow or sudden decrease in "gait velocity" as detected by in-home monitors (Austin et al. 2011).

Computational models can also use real-time data to estimate "an individual's readiness to change, motivations, and barriers" and, more ambitiously, "to inform a dynamic user model of an individual" that draws not only on purely observational data (by relying on such novelties as Bluetooth-enabled medication dispensers) but also the results of having the individual undertake particular tasks, such as playing "adaptive cognitive computer games, specifically designed to monitor metrics of working memory, executive function, divided attention, and verbal fluency" (Rivera and Jimison 2013, 43). Besides providing reports of the sort that might come from a visitor in the patient's home, the analysis of data from a monitoring system can "be used to tailor just-in-time, adaptive messages for encouragement and feedback to better enable a person's ability to change" (Rivera and Jimison 2013, 43). Indeed, it is this potential to personalize and temporalize nudges to a particular person in a particular time and place that is probably the most exciting aspect of applying small data to healthcare.

"Personalized Paternalism": Ethical and Effective Clinical Nudging

Many of the interventions that will occur—such as using a television, a computer, or a phone to convey simple reminders ("It's time to take your afternoon pills"), or having a health coach talk with the individual through a two-way camera/display on a tablet—would simply be more frequent forms of the advice that physicians and nurses have traditionally conveyed in person. But other interventions could involve more pointed use of behavioral economics. For example, since people tend to discount future (negative) consequences as against present pleasure, the positional signal in a recovering drug addict's cell-phone could trigger a message if he gets off the bus at the park where he used to go to buy drugs (Johnson et al. 2011), reminding him of the times he has been arrested and sent to jail and mentioning that his health coach will be dropping by his apartment that evening and will be very unhappy that he was hanging out in the drug park.

The point of these examples is simply to indicate that, with the agreement and cooperation of patients, small data that are specific to the behaviors, attitudes, and objectives of each individual can be used to personalize behavioral nudges through just-in-time messages based on the characteristics and circumstances of each person, conveyed at the moment when the person most needs the nudge and will be most receptive to it. By relying on conversation, mutual respect, and shared decision-making between patient and healthcare professional and on the creative use of the burgeoning field of mHealth, which involves the collection and analysis of small data, clinicians' nudges could be not only more effective but also more ethical.

Notes

1. The main concern would be to ensure that the data reports are being managed by someone—surely not solely the physician—with a reasonable level of oversight. One would not want a situation in which a monitored patient collapsed at home but was not found until it was too late to remedy the cause and/or consequences of her collapse because data transmitted from her home generated a report that indicated a serious problem, which went unnoticed for hours or even days.

References

Aggarwal, Ajay, Joanna Davies, and Richard Sullivan. 2014. "'Nudge' in the Clinical Consultation—an Acceptable Form of Medical Paternalism?" *BMC Medical Ethics* 15(1):31.

Austin, Daniel, Tamara L. Hayes, Jeffrey Kaye, Nora Mattek, and Misha Pavel. 2011. "Unobtrusive Monitoring of the Longitudinal Evolution of In-Home Gait Velocity Data with Application to Elder Care." *Conference Proceedings of the IEEE Engineering in Medicine and Biology Society*:6495–98.

Cadena, B. C., and B. J. Keys. 2013. "Can Self-Control Explain Avoiding Free Money? Evidence from Interest-Free Student Loans." *Review of Economics and Statistics* 95(4):1117–29.

Capron, Alexander M. 1974. "Informed Consent in Catastrophic Disease Research and Treatment." *University of Pennsylvania Law Review* 123(2):340–438.

Cohen, Shlomo. 2013. "Nudging and Informed Consent." *The American Journal of Bioethics* 13(6):3–11.

Crichton, Michael. 2007. "Where Does It Hurt?" *The New York Times*, April 1. http://www .nytimes.com/2007/04/01/books/review/Crichton.t.html?n =Top%2FFeatures%2FBooks%2FBook%20Reviews&_r=0 (reviewing Groopman, Jerome. 2007. *How Doctors Think*. Houghton Mifflin. New York).

Estrin, Deborah. 2014. "Viewpoint: Small Data, Where n=me." *Communications of the ACM* 57(4):32–34.

Faden, Ruth R., and Tom L. Beauchamp. 1986. *A History and Theory of Informed Consent*. Oxford University Press. New York.

Johnson, Kimberly, Andrew Isham, Dhavan V. Shah and David H. Gustafson. 2011. "Potential Roles for New Communication Technologies in Treatment of Addiction." *Current Psychiatry Reports* 13(5):390–97.

Kang, Jerry, et al. 2012. "Self-Surveillance Privacy." *Iowa Law Review* 97(3):809–47.

Katz, Jay. 1984. *The Silent World of Doctor and Patient*. The Free Press. New York.

Kumar, Santosh, et al. 2013. "Mobile Health Technology Evaluation: The mHealth Evidence Workshop." *American Journal of Preventive Medicine* 45(2):228–36.

Ménard, Jean-Frédérick. 2010. "A 'Nudge' for Public Health Ethics: Libertarian Paternalism as a Framework for Ethical Analysis of Public Health Interventions?" *Public Health Ethics* 3:229–38.

Pew Research Center. 2014. "The Internet of Things Will Thrive by 2025." http://www.pewinternet.org/2014/05/14/internet-of-things/.

Riley W. T., R. E. Glasgow, L. Etheredge, and A. P. Abernethy. 2013. "Rapid, Responsive, Relevant (R3) Research: A Call for a Rapid Learning Health Research Enterprise." *Clinical and Translation Medicine* 2(1):10.

Rivera, Daniel E., and Holly B. Jimison. 2013. "Systems Modeling of Behavioral Change." *IEEE Pulse* 4(6):41–47.

Saghai, Yashar. 2013a. "The Concept of Nudge and Its Moral Significance: A Reply to Ashcroft, Bovens, Dworkin, Welch and Wertheimer." *Journal of Medical Ethics* 39:499–501.

———. 2013b. "Salvaging the Concept of Nudge." *Journal of Medical Ethics* 39:487–93.

Schwartz, Barry. 2003. *The Paradox of Choice: Why More Is Less.* HarperCollins. New York.

Spruijt-Metz, D., W. Nilsen, and M. Pavel. 2015. "mHealth for Behavior Change and Monitoring." In *mHealth: Multidisciplinary Verticals,* edited by Sasan Adibi. CRC Press. Boca Raton, FL.

Sunstein, Cass R. 2003. "Hazardous Heuristics." *The University of Chicago Law Review* 70:751–80.

Sunstein, Cass R., and R. H. Thaler. 2003. "Libertarian Paternalism Is Not an Oxymoron." *The University of Chicago Law Review* 70:1159–1202.

ten Have, Marieke, et al. 2011. "Ethics and Prevention of Overweight and Obesity: An Inventory." *Obesity Review* 12(9):669–79.

Thaler, Richard H., and Cass R. Sunstein. 2009. *Nudge: Improving Decisions about Health, Wealth, and Happiness.* Penguin. New York.

Tucker, Patrick. 2014. *The Naked Future: What Happens in a World That Anticipates Your Every Move?* Penguin. New York.

CHAPTER 17

The Perilous Promise of Privacy
Ironic Influences on Disclosure of Health Information

Ester Moher and Khaled El Emam

As a patient, you may care both about the procedures you receive and how health-related information you disclose is collected, stored, and used. For example, in the case of newborn screening, a small blood sample is taken from infants at birth to test for a variety of rare but potentially devastating diseases. Screening is often conducted on a "presumed consent" basis; consent for secondary uses is usually not obtained at all (Laberge, Kharaboyan, and Avard 2004; Wildeman and Downie 2001; Kosseim and Jospe 2011). Several cases in both Canada and the United States have raised consent issues in these situations: just because a parent does not object to the initial screening (for example, for disease state) does not mean they would also not object to use of the sample for research (that is, secondary use). In some cases, data collected under presumed consent has been ordered to be destroyed, at great cost to researchers. For example, in British Columbia, Canada, in 2010 parents launched a class action lawsuit alleging a breach of privacy, when they learned that their infants' blood samples were being retained for secondary research purposes without consent (Kosseim and Jospe 2011). Similar cases in Minnesota and Texas (Minnesota Department of Health 2012; Doerr 2010) have resulted in the destruction of blood spots after seventy days.

These cases suggest that patients have strong concerns over secondary access to their health information. Experts now suggest a more extensive, lengthy consent process in which secondary uses of data are explicitly highlighted (Willison et al. 2003), and where assurances of anonymity or privacy (that is, that personally identifying information is not linked with responses) and confidentiality (any protective behavior taken by the researcher, for example, storing data on a secure server) are explicit (Carney et al. 2000). Health professionals are encouraged to include written privacy policies containing anonymity and confidentiality assurances when informing patients about the risks and benefits associated with disclosing health information (U.S. Department of Health and Human Services 2006; Government of Ontario 2004). For example, in the United States, the Health Insurance Portability and Accountability Act (HIPAA) of 1996 notes that the following elements are required in order to present a complete privacy policy to a participant:

- what personal information (PI) is
- how PI will be collected and used
- who has access to PI
- how PI is protected
- how you can gain access to your own PI
- who to contact in case of a suspected breach

Similarly, most research ethics boards require that participants be given an affirmation that data will be held privately, as well as a general description of security measures taken to protect against data breach (Public Works and Government Services Canada 2005).

These policies implicitly suggest that individuals are rational with regard to privacy in two ways. First, these policies suggest that more knowledge of anonymity and confidentiality practices will encourage feelings of safety. Second, these policies suggest that if participants are given more information about anonymity and confidentiality practices, they will make better-informed, preference-consistent disclosure decisions. However, these recommendations for transparency have not been empirically validated, suggesting a potential intention-action divide. Indeed, ensuring anonymity and confidentiality may have unintended negative consequences on the quality of data collected, such as reduced response rates and dishonest or misleading reporting by respondents (Acquisti, John, and Loewenstein 2009; El Emam et al. 2014; Moher 2013).

Ironic Effects of Anonymity and Confidentiality

Individuals do state a preference for full assurances of anonymity and confidentiality (Nair et al. 2004). Some evidence suggests that their intuitions are correct: when anonymity is assured, individuals indeed report increased incidence of sensitive behaviors, suggesting more comfort disclosing anonymously (Berman, McCombs, and Boruch 1977; Durant, Carey, and Schroder 2002; Fidler and Kleinknecht 1977; Goodstadt and Gruson 1975; Muhlenfeld 2005; Singer 1978; Tracy and Fox 1981; Warner 1965). Some literature further suggests that confidentiality assurances also increase response rates (Singer, Von Thurn, and Miller 1995; Esposito, Agard, and Rosnow 1984; Ford et al. 1997). Thus, informing individuals that their responses will remain anonymous or confidential might promote greater, and more accurate, disclosure.

However, other studies have demonstrated that individuals, when responding anonymously, are less accurate reporters of their own behavior (Esposito, Agard, and Rosnow 1984; Lelkes et al. 2012; Acquisti et al. 2008). For example, Mazar and colleagues (2008; see also Zhong, Bohns, and Gino 2010) demonstrate that when reporting is anonymous, individuals are particularly vulnerable to misreporting their own behavior. Further, presenting confidentiality assurances can counterintuitively encourage individuals to withhold information (Acquisti, John, and Loewenstein 2009; Durant, Carey, and Schroder 2002; Frey 1986; Reamer 1979; Singer, Hippler, and Schwarz 1992; Singer 1993; Willison et al. 2009; Haer and Meidert 2014), particularly when information being withheld is sensitive in nature (John, Acquisti, and Loewenstein 2011). However, when confidentiality practices are not mentioned, suggesting that no protections are in place, individuals are more inclined to give that same information. Individuals may thus see confidentiality as a warning instead of as a description of safety, which may induce skepticism (Lewandowsky et al. 2012; Woods and McNamara 1980). As a consequence, individuals may "clam up" and fail to take advantage of a safe avenue for information sharing.

This contradiction in the literature suggests that the presence of an assurance likely interacts with contextual factors to either encourage or inhibit disclosure. The former group of studies, largely conducted in-person or with paper-and-pencil surveys, suggests that providing assurances (perhaps in tandem with a personal communication to a researcher) can promote a sense of security. The latter group, largely conducted in online settings, suggests that assurances could backfire. We thus formulate the following hypotheses:

H1: Assurances of anonymity and confidentiality will discourage disclosure in an online survey setting.
H2: Disclosure rates will correlate negatively with how much subjective attention is paid to assurances of anonymity and confidentiality: those who report paying more attention to assurances should be least likely to disclose.

Given these hypotheses, we suggest that assurances of anonymity and confidentiality can be overwhelming. Perhaps we can redesign assurances from a behavioral economics approach to reduce discrepancy between intent of assurance and outcomes.

Summary of Studies

In the studies reported in this chapter, we examined the role of anonymity and confidentiality assurances on disclosure rates. We used the privacy statement in a standard research consent form to manipulate presence or absence of anonymity and confidentiality assurances. In study 1, we examined responses with some artificial conditions; in study 2, we extended findings to consider possible moderators of the effect. For all reported studies, ethics approval was obtained from the Children's Hospital of Eastern Ontario's Research Institute Research Ethics Board.

Study 1: Effects of Assurances on Disclosure Rates

In our first study, we sought to examine whether including assurances of anonymity and confidentiality reduced willingness to disclose sensitive health information in respondents (H1). We recruited 501[1] participants from Crowdflower.[2]

Methods

Participants read a consent letter before completing a short survey on personal health. Three factors were varied (and highlighted with italics) in each consent form:

Anonymity: When we guaranteed anonymity, participants were explicitly told that their responses could not be linked to any personally identifying information (for example, their name). When anonymity was not guaranteed, there was no mention of this statement.

Confidentiality: When we guaranteed confidentiality, participants were explicitly told that the responses they provided would be stored on a secure server, and that information could only be accessed by the researcher. When confidentiality was not guaranteed, there was no mention of this statement.

Sector: Participants were told that the study was being conducted either by a publicly funded, university-affiliated research group (our lab) or by a (fictitious) privately funded research firm ("Smyth Marketed Health"). We hypothesized that individuals may be more willing to disclose to a public versus a private research group.

Upon completion of the study, participants were appropriately debriefed.

Measurement and Analysis

We experimentally manipulated anonymity, confidentiality, and research sector in a $2 \times 2 \times 2$ factorial design. Participants in all conditions were asked to disclose demographics, followed by health information. Health information was elicited by asking participants to report on whether they had experienced any of seventeen health incidents. For example, participants were asked whether they had ever had a heart attack (low sensitivity), as well as whether they had ever had a sexually-transmitted infection (high sensitivity).[3] Responses were coded as a personal admission ("I have been diagnosed"), family admission (immediate or distant family member diagnosed), denial (no known diagnosis), or nonresponse ("Prefer not to say") (Joinson and Paine 2007).

We measured disclosure rates in two ways. First, we examined social "distance" of health behaviors. We assigned higher scores to more socially "near" responses (for example, "I have had a heart attack"), and lower scores to more socially "distal" responses (for example, "A distant family member has had a heart attack"). We reasoned that when participants feel that their privacy is threatened, they will be less likely to admit to having personally engaged in an unsavory health behavior, and may instead make a partial confession by admitting to the health behavior in the broader bracket of extended family, for example. This partial or distal admission may offer some amount of ego-protection to the individual, as a disclosure has occurred, but poor self-image associated with admission is minimized (Peer, Acquisti, and Shalvi 2014). We standardized and summed responses from all items, creating a Health Behaviors Index, and used this index to represent near versus distal responses. As a second measure of disclosure, we examined the number of "Prefer not to say" selections (opt-outs) across the study. Due to the nature of our study, we were unable to verify whether participants were telling the truth. However, given the random assignment of participants, we assume that approximate incidence rates across conditions should be roughly equal. As such, any deviations in incidence rate are likely to be the result of our manipulations, rather than differences in real incidence rates.

Results

Demographics

There were no main effects of gender, $p > 0.30$, but there were marginally significant effects of age, $F(1, 432) = 3.62$, $p = 0.06$, and significant effects of income, $F(1, 397) = 9.03$, $p < 0.01$, and employment status, $F(1, 419) = 6.39$, $p < 0.01$, on condition.[4] All were included in all further analyses as covariates.

Main Study

As a first measure of disclosure, we examined how socially "proximal" participants reported health behaviors to be. We observed a significant Anonymity x Confidentiality x Sector interaction, $F(1, 387) = 4.26$, $MSE = 245.16$, $p < 0.05$, $\eta^2 = 0.01$, such that when disclosing to a public institution anonymously, participants were less likely to admit to sensitive health behaviors when they were assured of confidentiality (see fig. 17.1; H1). No other significant effects were observed, $Fs < 2$, $ps > 0.20$.

As a second measure of disclosure, we examined the number of "Prefer not to say" response selections. There was a marginally significant Anonymity x Confidentiality interaction, $F(1, 387) = 2.89$, $MSE = 14.62$, $p = 0.09$, $\eta^2 = 0.01$, such that when anonymity was assured, presence of a confidentiality assurance reduced disclosure (as in John, Acquisti, and Loewenstein 2011; H1). Again, no other main effects or interactions were observed, $Fs < 1.5$, $ps > 0.20$.

Here, we observe that when participants were asked to disclose to a public institution (left side of graph), presence of an assurance of confidentiality significantly reduces disclosure when anonymity has already been guaranteed (bars 3 and 4 from

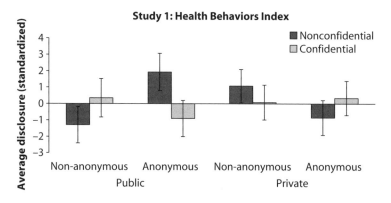

FIGURE 17.1 Health behaviors, standardized, across conditions, study 1

left). No differences were observed when participants were asked to disclose to a private institution (right side of graph).

Discussion

This study suggests that when anonymity is assured, confidentiality assurances discourage individuals from disclosing sensitive health information and encourage choosing nonresponse options (H1). No other main effects or comparisons were observed, suggesting that these effects are not due to simply presenting (or omitting) assurances, but rely on the interplay between assurances and context, such as to whom information is being disclosed.

Of particular interest, we observed these effects when messages of anonymity and confidentiality were embedded within a consent form, which is mandatory (or at least considered best practices) for health-related data acquisition. Previous studies have demonstrated that privacy cues, when triggered by contextual variables, can differentially influence disclosure decisions in a negative way (John, Acquisti, and Loewenstein 2011). Study 1 suggests that this effect can be observed when security messages are embedded in consent materials, rather than in the questions themselves.

Study 2: Subjective Attention to Consent Forms

One account for findings in study 1 is that by highlighting anonymity and confidentiality assurances with italicized font, we encouraged participants to pay more attention to the assurances relative to other parts of the form. Perhaps more attention to anonymity and confidentiality assurances may have encouraged greater counterintuitive focus on security breaches (H2). As such, we were interested in whether the effects observed in study 1 would be moderated by subjective attention to the consent form.

Methods

Again, we recruited participants (N=286) through Crowdflower. Materials and methods were similar to those in study 1. We experimentally manipulated whether the consent form contained assurances. Additionally, following completion of health information disclosures, participants were asked how much attention they had paid to the consent form. They were able to respond with one of four options: memory for the consent form was vivid; they remembered glossing through the form; they did not read the consent form; or they did not remember the form at all. We coded responses in a hierarchical order, such that greater scores were associated with less subjective attention to the consent form. As such, the present study was a 2 (Assurance: assured of anonymity and confidentiality versus unassured) x 4 (Consent form attention: vivid, glossed through, not read, not noticed) factorial design.

Results

Demographics

There were no significant main effects or interactions on gender, all $ps > 0.30$. However, there was a significant main effect of age on assurance, $F(1, 280)=8.12$, $MSE=0.43$, $p < 0.01$, such that participants reported being older in the assured condition. Age is thus included in all further analyses as a covariate.

Main Study

We subjected disclosure scores to a 2 (Assurance) x 4 (Consent form attention) analysis of variance (ANOVA). There was a significant Assurance x Consent form attention interaction, $F(3, 273)=2.65$, $MSE=0.21$, $p < 0.05$, $\eta^2=0.03$, such that greater disclosure was associated with less subjective attention to the consent form, but only when the consent form included assurances. This interaction was qualified by a main effect of Assurance, $F(1, 273)=6.95$, $MSE=0.21$, $p < 0.01$, $\eta^2=0.02$, such that participants disclosed more information after reading a consent form containing assurances than without (fig. 17.2). Further, the interaction was also qualified by a main effect of Consent form attention on disclosure, $F(3, 273)=4.01$, $MSE=0.21$, $p < 0.01$, $\eta^2=0.04$, such that participants disclosed more when attention to the consent form was lower (H2).

To further examine the Assurance × Consent form attention interaction, we next examined the robustness of Consent form attention across conditions by examining assured and unassured groups separately with univariate ANOVAs. We observed a significant main effect of Consent form attention on assured disclosures, $F(3, 126)=3.82$, $MSE=0.25$, $p < 0.05$, $\eta^2=0.09$, such that disclosures increased as Consent form attention decreased. However, a main effect was not observed when participants were unassured, $F < 1.5$, $p > 0.20$.

Here, we observe that as memory for the consent form is reduced (x-axis, moving from left to right), willingness to disclose increases for those participants who were

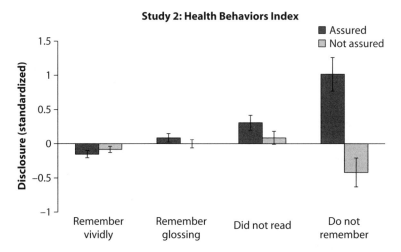

FIGURE 17.2 Health behaviors, standardized, across conditions, study 2

assured (dark bars), but does not increase for those participants who were not assured (light bars).

To further understand this effect, we examined the correlation between subjective attention to the consent form and disclosure of health information. Overall, we observed a significant negative correlation between disclosure and attention, $r(286)=0.18$, $p < 0.01$, suggesting that greater subjective attention to the consent form was associated with less disclosure. Further, when we examined this correlation separately for participants who received assurances relative to those who saw no assurance, we found a robust negative correlation for the former group, $r(129)=0.28$, $p < 0.01$, and no significant relationship for the latter group, $r(157)=0.08$, $p=0.33$. Together, these findings further suggest that disclosure is negatively associated with presence of assurances, particularly when greater attention is paid to them.

Finally, as in study 1, we examined non-response in a 2 × 4 ANOVA. There was a significant main effect of assurance on disclosure, $F(1, 273)=3.76$, $MSE=0.43$, $p=0.05$, $\eta^2=0.01$, such that participants selected nonresponse options more frequently when they were assured versus unassured. Thus, presence of assurances decreased the number of questions that participants responded to.

Discussion

Results of study 2 further demonstrate that assurances may negatively influence disclosure of sensitive health information. When participants paid more attention to the consent form, they disclosed less. When the consent form included an assurance of anonymity or confidentiality, this effect was robust, suggesting that more attention drawn to privacy statements in particular could trigger reduced disclosure.

General Discussion

These two studies suggest that when anonymity and confidentiality are assured, individuals may be less likely to disclose health information, particularly when assurances are explicit (Durant, Carey, and Schroder 2002; Frey 1986; John, Acquisti, and Loewenstein 2011; Lelkes et al. 2012; Haer and Meidert 2014). In study 1, we varied anonymity, confidentiality, and sector information and highlighted this information in the consent form. When anonymity was assured, presence of a confidentiality assurance more than doubled the number of nonresponse options selected (H1); similarly, omitting a confidentiality assurance more than doubled the likelihood of admitting to unsavory health behaviors.[5]

It seems that messages of anonymity and confidentiality counterintuitively encourage individuals to view such assurances as warnings, rather than as messages of safety. That is, individuals instead consider why these assurances are present—to protect against breaches—and incorrectly intuit that the risk of disclosure has increased (John, Acquisti, and Loewenstein 2011; Lewandowsky et al. 2012; Woods and McNamara 1980).

In study 2, we measured subjective attention to the consent form, and observed that assurances encouraged disclosure, but only when participants reported paying less attention to the consent form (H2). These findings shed light on a mixed literature we noted earlier, suggesting that inconsistencies might not reflect changes in preferences, but may instead reflect the role of a moderator—attention to consent forms.

Together, these studies suggest that despite the good intentions of researchers and health practitioners, quality and quantity of data collected may be influenced negatively by disclosing protective measures such as anonymity and confidentiality practices. Further, these findings suggest that researchers who do observe an increased disclosure after implementing more comprehensive consent forms might actually be observing a reduced reading rate among participants. Previous literature has demonstrated that longer, less readable consent forms common in clinical settings (Curtis et al. 1996; McDonald et al. 2009; Hopper, TenHave, and Hartzel 1995) are more likely to be skimmed for information or skipped over entirely (Dresden and Levitt 2001). As such, more comprehensive consent forms are unlikely to jointly increase disclosure and improve understanding of consent processes. More likely, researchers and clinicians may be getting one at the cost of the other.

However, minimizing privacy information to participants poses an additional ethical issue: without being fully informed, an individual cannot provide *informed* consent. One practical solution could be to improve the readability of the language contained in the consent form. For example, some research suggests that when consent forms are simplified, individuals are inclined to disclose more when provided with assurances (Moher and El Emam, in prep). This work suggests that complexity of the assurance could unnecessarily concern a participant. Alternatively, one could design consent forms, and associated assurances, using expandable sections that allow basic information to be gathered by all participants, with the option of more in-depth reading for those who are interested.

Clinical and Practical Applications

The present studies suggest that patients do not make privacy decisions rationally: they are less inclined to disclose information when they are explicitly made aware of protection measures. Further, this effect is strongest when participants report paying attention to those notices. This work suggests that well-intentioned legal codes developed to protect participants (for example, Personal Information Protection and Electronic Documents Act, HIPAA) might unwittingly be discouraging participation, perhaps by overwhelming participants with complex information. Though providing no privacy information refutes the principles of informed consent, clearly providing assurances that are long and complex is also harmful. A middle ground must be sought, though an obvious psychological, ethical, and legal question exists with respect to how much information should be provided.

Limitations and Future Research

Future research should focus on examining these effects with a real clinical sample. In the present work, participants were reporting health behaviors that were of relatively no consequence. Patients, however, might be prescribed different treatments depending on their responses, and as such, consequences of nondisclosure are greater. Thus, it is possible that the relatively low risk associated with disclosure in this study facilitated effect sizes. Alternatively, because most patients have relatively little knowledge of medicine, it is possible that unless they are made explicitly aware of potential health interactions (that is, that an undisclosed medication they already take could interact negatively with a new one being prescribed), they may continue to manage their images in ways that unintentionally compromise care.

In addition, future work should examine how to best inform individuals when anonymity and confidentiality practices are in place (Willison et al, 2007). It is clear that an explicit, lengthy consent form outlining procedures may discourage participation; however, this is often the gold standard for legal and ethical purposes.

Notes

1. We excluded sixty-five of these participants who did not complete the study as instructed.
2. Crowdflower is an online crowdsourcing tool, used for recruiting for online surveys. Participants from Canada and the United States were compensated with a nominal fee ($0.25) for participation.
3. For brevity, sensitivity results have not been reported. They can be obtained by request from the authors of this chapter.

4. These effects demonstrate that across conditions, there were some deviations in age, income, and employment status. As such, we control for each of these variables in all analyses.
5. We replicated findings of study 1 in a second study where we eliminated any highlighting of anonymity and confidentiality assurances in the consent form. We observed that confidentiality assurances again reduced disclosure.

References

Acquisti, Alessandro, Stefanos Gritzalis, Costas Lambrinoudakis, and Sabrina De Capitani di Vimercanti, eds. 2008. *Digital Privacy: Theory, Technologies, and Practices.* Auerbach Publications. Boca Raton, FL.

Acquisti, Alessandro, Leslie K. John, and George Loewenstein. 2009. "What Is Privacy Worth?" Arizona Biltmore Resort & Spa. Phoenix.

Berman, John, Harriet McCombs, and Robert Boruch. 1977. "Notes on the Contamination Method: Two Small Experiments in Assuring Confidentiality of Responses." *Sociological Methods and Research* 6(1):45–62.

Carney, Patricia A., Berta M. Geller, Howard Moffett, Molly Ganger, Matson Sewell, William E. Barlow, Nancy Stalnaker, et al. 2000. "Current Medicolegal and Confidentiality Issues in Large, Multicenter Research Programs." *American Journal of Epidemiology* 152(4):371–78.

Curtis, Peter, Pamela Frasier, Adam O. Goldstein, Nancy E. Kreher, and Alfred Reid. 1996. "Consent Form Readability in University-Sponsored Research." *Journal of Family Practice* 42(6):606–11.

Doerr, Adam. 2010. "Newborn Blood Spot Litigation: 70 Days to Destroy 5+ Million Samples." February 2. http://www.genomicslawreport.com/index.php/2010/02/02/newborn-blood -spot-litigation-70-days-to-destroy-5-million-samples/.

Dresden, Graham M., and M. Andrew Levitt. 2001. "Modifying a Standard Industry Clinical Trial Consent Form Improves Patient Information Retention as Part of the Informed Consent Process." *Academic Emergency Medicine* 8(3):246–52.

Durant, Lauren E., Michael P. Carey, and Kerstin E. E. Schroder. 2002. "Effects of Anonymity, Gender, and Erotophilia on the Quality of Data Obtained from Self-Reports of Socially Sensitive Behaviors." *Journal of Behavioral Medicine* 25(5):439–67.

El Emam, Khaled, C. Ouellet, Luk Arbuckle, S. Samet, Ben Eze, Grant Middleton, L. Gaugette, et al. 2014. "Secure Surveillance of Antimicrobial Resistant Organism Colonization in Ontario Long Term Care Homes." *PLoS One* 9(4):e93285.

Esposito, James L., Edith Agard, and Ralph L. Rosnow. 1984. "Can Confidentiality of Data Pay Off?" *Personality and Individual Differences* 5(4):477–80.

Fidler, Dorothy S., and Richard E. Kleinknecht. 1977. "Randomized Response versus Direct Questioning: Two Data-Collection Methods for Sensitive Information." *Psychological Bulletin* 84(5):1045–49.

Ford, Carol A., Susan G. Millstein, Bonnie L. Halpern-Felsher, and Charles E. Irwin Jr. 1997. "Influence of Physician Confidentiality Assurances on Adolescents' Willingness to Disclose Information and Seek Future Health Care: A Randomized Controlled Trial." *Journal of the American Medical Association* 278(12):1029–34.

Frey, James H. 1986. "An Experiment with a Confidentiality Reminder in a Telephone Survey." *The Public Opinion Quarterly* 50(2):267–69.

Goodstadt, Michael S., and Valerie Gruson. 1975. "The Randomized Response Technique: A Test on Drug Use." *Journal of the American Statistical Association* 70(352):814–18.

Government of Ontario. 2004. *Personal Health Information Protection Act.*

Haer, Roos, and Nadine Meidert. 2014. "Undisclosed Privacy: The Effect of Privacy Rights Design on Response Rates." *Survey Practice* 7(2):1–5.

Hopper, K. D., T. R. TenHave, and J. Hartzel. 1995. "Informed Consent Forms for Clinical and Research Imaging Procedures: How Much Do Patients Understand?" *American Journal of Roentgenology* 164(2):493–96.

John, Leslie K., Alessandro Acquisti, and George Loewenstein. 2011. "Strangers on a Plane: Context-Dependent Willingness to Divulge Sensitive Information." *The Journal of Consumer Research* 37(5):858–73.

Joinson, Adam N., and Carina B. Paine. 2007. "Self-Disclosure, Privacy and the Internet." In *The Oxford Handbook of Internet Psychology*, edited by A. Joinson, K. McKenna, U. Reips, and T. Postmes. Oxford University Press. Oxford. 237–52.

Kosseim, Patricia, and Dara Jospe. 2011. "ARCHIVED—Speech: Banking for the Future: Informing Consent in the Context of Biobanks—January 21, 2011." January 21. https://www.priv.gc.ca/media/sp-d/2011/sp-d_20110121_pk_e.asp.

Laberge, Claude, Linda Kharaboyan, and Denise Avard. 2004. "Newborn Screening, Banking and Consent." *GenEdit* 2(3).

Lelkes, Yphtach, Jon A. Krosnick, David M. Marx, Charles M. Judd, and Bernadette Park. 2012. "Complete Anonymity Compromises the Accuracy of Self-Reports." *Journal of Experimental Social Psychology* 48(6):1291–99.

Lewandowsky, Stephan, Ulrich K. H. Ecker, Colleen M. Seifert, Norbert Schwarz, and John Cook. 2012. "Misinformation and Its Correction: Continued Influence and Successful Debiasing." *Psychological Science in the Public Interest* 13(3):106–31.

Mazar, Nina, On Amir, and Dan Ariely. 2008. "The Dishonesty of Honest People: A Theory of Self-Concept Maintenance." *Journal of Marketing Research* 45(6):633–44.

McDonald, Aleecia M., Robert W. Reeder, Patrick Gage Kelley, and Lorrie Faith Cranor. 2009. "A Comparative Study of Online Privacy Policies and Formats." *Lecture Notes in Computer Science* 5672/2009:37–55.

Minnesota Department of Health. 2012. "News Release: Minnesota Department of Health to Begin Destroying Newborn Blood Spots in Order to Comply with Recent Minnesota Supreme Court Ruling." January 31. http://www.health.state.mn.us/news/pressrel/2012/newborn013112.html.

Moher, Ester. 2013. "Perception of Risk of Disclosure of Health Information." Presentation presented at the Workshop on Risk Perception in IT Security and Privacy, Symposium on Usable Privacy and Security, Newcastle, UK, July 24.

Moher, Ester, and Khaled El Emam. In prep. "Readability and Privacy: How Improving Readability Attenuates Ironic Disclosure Problems." Manuscript.

Muhlenfeld, Hans-Ullrich. 2005. "Differences between 'Talking About' and 'Admitting' Sensitive Behaviour in Anonymous and Non-Anonymous Web-Based Interviews." *Computers in Human Behavior* 21:993–1003.

Nair, Kalpana, Donald Willison, Anne Holbrook, and Karim Keshavjee. 2004. "Patients' Consent Preferences Regarding the Use of Their Health Information for Research Purposes: A Qualitative Study." *Journal of Health Services Research & Policy* 9(1):22–27.

Peer, Eyal, Alessandro Acquisti, and Shaul Shalvi. Forthcoming. "'I Cheated, but Only a Little'—Partial Confessions to Unethical Behavior." *Journal of Personality and Social Psychology.* http://ssrn.com/abstract=2268571.

Public Works and Government Services Canada. 2005. *CIHR Best Practices for Protecting Privacy in Health Research.* Canadian Institutes of Health Research. Ottawa.

Reamer, Fredric G. 1979. "Protecting Research Subjects and Unintended Consequences: The Effect of Guarantees of Confidentiality." *Public Opinion Quarterly* 43(4):497–506.

Singer, Eleanor. 1978. "The Effect of Informed Consent Procedures on Respondents' Reactions to Surveys." *Journal of Consumer Research* 5(1):49–57.

———. 1993. "Informed Consent and Survey Response: A Summary of the Empirical Literature." *Journal of Official Statistics* 9(2):361–75.

Singer, Eleanor, Hans-Jurgen Hippler, and Norbert Schwarz. 1992. "Confidentiality Assurances in Surveys: Reassurance or Threat?" *International Journal of Public Opinion Research* 4(3):256–68.

Singer, Eleanor, Dawn R. Von Thurn, and Esther R. Miller. 1995. "Confidentiality Assurances and Response: A Quantitative Review of the Experimental Literature." *The Public Opinion Quarterly* 59(1):66–77.

Tracy, Paul E., and James Alan Fox. 1981. "The Validity of Randomized Response for Sensitive Measurements." *American Sociological Review* 46(2):187–200.

U.S. Department of Health and Human Services. 2006. *HIPAA Administrative Simplification.* 45 CFR Parts 160, 162, and 164. Washington, DC. http://www.hhs.gov/ocr/privacy/hipaa /administrative/privacyrule/adminsimpregtext.pdf

Warner, Stanley L. 1965. "Randomized Response: A Survey Technique for Eliminating Evasive Answer Bias." *Journal of the American Statistical Association* 60(309):63–69.

Wildeman, Sheila, and Jocelyn Downie. 2001. "Genetic and Metabolic Screening of Newborns: Must Health Care Providers Seek Explicit Parental Consent?" *Health Law Journal* 9:61.

Willison, Donald J., Karim Keshavjee, Kalpana Nair, Charlie Goldsmith, and Anne M. Holbrook. 2003. "Patients' Consent Preferences for Research Uses of Information in Electronic Medical Records: Interview and Survey Data." *British Medical Journal* 326:1–5.

Willison, Donald J., Lisa Schwartz, Julia Abelson, Cathy Charles, Marilyn Swinton, David Northrup, and Lehana Thabane. 2007. "Alternatives to Project-Specific Consent for Access to Personal Information for Health Research: What Is the Opinion of the Canadian Public?" *Journal of the American Medical Informatics Association* 14(6):706–12.

Willison, Donald J., Valerie Steeves, Cathy Charles, Lisa Schwartz, Jennifer Ranford, Gina Agarwal, Ji Cheng, and Lehana Thabane. 2009. "Consent for Use of Personal Information for Health Research: Do People with Potentially Stigmatizing Health Conditions and the General Public Differ in Their Opinions?" *BMC Medical Ethics* 10(10).

Woods, Kathryn M., and Regis J. McNamara. 1980. "Confidentiality: Its Effect on Interviewee Behavior." *Professional Psychology* 11(5):714–21.

Zhong, Chen-Bo, Vanessa K. Bohns, and Francesca Gino. 2010. "Good Lamps Are the Best Police: Darkness Increases Dishonesty and Self-Interested Behavior." *Psychological Science* 21(3):311–14.

PART VI **DECIDING FOR PATIENTS AND LETTING PATIENTS DECIDE FOR THEMSELVES**

Introduction

Christopher T. Robertson

Justice Cardozo famously wrote that "[e]very human being of adult years and sound mind has a right to determine what shall be done with his own body" (*Schloendorff v. Society of N.Y. Hosp.* 1914, 92). The chapters in this part return to this eternal theme, asking how behavioral economics can shape, or even supplant, those decisions.

In his chapter, Matthew J. B. Lawrence looks not at the patient's healthcare decisions, but rather her decisions about how insurance coverage disputes should be resolved. He suggests that a more dynamic process could help resolve the Medicare dispute backlog, by sorting out those (like some individual patients) who value robust dispute resolution procedures, including oral hearings, in contrast to others (like companies with thousands of claims) who are really just interested in recovering the aggregate value across all their claims, with a modicum of accuracy. For these latter claimants, efficient resolution can be achieved by sampling a few claims and then extrapolating to the remainder, just as social scientists routinely do, and as Medicare is now trying in a pilot program. What is true for Medicare is likely true for many other contexts of dispute resolution (see, for example, Jackson and Rosenberg 2007; Cheng 2012). I predict that we will see great experimentation around these sorts of sampling methodologies in the future, bringing the fundamental scientific method to the law.

Lawrence largely seems to assume that robust procedures are in the interests of individual claimants, but one attractive feature of his proposal is that they can simply vote with their feet. It may turn out that the preference for procedure is itself based on a false hope that the robust procedures will yield greater chances of winning.

Although Lawrence focuses mostly on the idea of using a particular default rule to achieve the self-sorting, it may be appropriate to use more aggressive mechanisms. Rather than requiring people to opt out of the slow and expensive hearings, if it turns out that most well-informed individuals choose the contrary, then it may be sensible to flip the default rule. Even more, it may be efficient to create a dynamic default rule, for example, assuming that those with multiple Medicare disputes are likely corporations with an overriding interest in efficiency, while those with only one Medicare dispute are likely individuals interested in robust oral procedures. More elaborate mathematical prediction models could be useful as well.

In the chapter that follows, Manisha Padi and Abigail R. Moncrieff ask about a policy intervention that overrides patient choice: a mandate. Here, it is not a mandate for any particular treatment, but rather just for insurance coverage. The standard story of why a mandate is necessary begins with a governmental commitment to getting everyone covered. As the Supreme Court explained, when the government chooses market-based regulations (guaranteed issue and community rating) as its mechanism to get everyone covered, these "reforms provide an incentive for individuals to delay purchasing health insurance until they become sick, relying on the promise of guaranteed and affordable coverage" (*National Federation of Independent Business v. Sebelius* 2012, 2585). The very idea of insurance as a way to manage risk is undermined if people can instead buy it only after the risk has materialized, and the mandate thus solves a collective action problem. As Justice Ginsburg explained, "[i]n the 1990's, several States—including New York, New Jersey, Washington, Kentucky, Maine, New Hampshire, and Vermont—enacted guaranteed-issue and community-rating laws without requiring universal acquisition of insurance coverage. The results were disastrous. All seven states suffered from skyrocketing insurance premium costs, reductions in individuals with coverage, and reductions in insurance products and providers. Several states that have attempted such market-based reforms without an individual mandate have experienced precisely the market failures that neoclassical economics would predict" (*National Federation of Independent Business v. Sebelius* 2012, 2614). Here then, the decision to decline health insurance can be overridden both for paternalistic reasons and to solve a collective action problem—causing those who will predictably benefit from insurance to pay for it.

A fundamental challenge for any choice architect is to determine which choices, or which policy mandates in lieu of choices, will be welfare enhancing. Padi and Moncrieff suggest that any evaluation of the insurance mandate should consider not just the benefits of solving a collective action problem to get people covered, but also must weigh the "experienced utility" of those who are subject to the mandate. And in a refreshingly simple approach they suggest doing so "simply by making the policy change and then asking individuals whether they are happier."

Going forward, much more work needs to be done to operationalize how exactly these survey questions would be posed and analyzed. One way to do such a study would be in blinded fashion, simply measuring happiness at one timepoint (say 2009, before the mandate) and measuring it again at another timepoint (say 2019, after the mandate comes into effect and its costs and benefits have materialized), and comparing the results to see if there has been a positive or negative change. One difficulty of this approach is that much else has changed during this time, including, for example, the fact that the unemployment rate has fallen by nearly half between 2010 and 2015 (a

problem of "confounding"). Moreover, ObamaCare is itself complex, making it difficult to extract the impact of the mandate in isolation. Padi and Moncrieff suggest
alternatively asking people more directly, "[a]re you better off than you were before
ObamaCare?" This approach is also confounded in the same ways, but even worse,
will be strongly affected by motivated reasoning. Individuals who favored Obama-
Care as policy will be hard pressed to admit that it made their lives worse, and vice
versa. So this method may collapse into being little more than an opinion poll about
whether people favored ObamaCare or not; it does not tell us whether they should
favor it because it is a welfare-enhancing policy. In this sense, social science degrades
into politics.

In her chapter, Sarah Conly focuses on the decision (or lack thereof) about whether
those living in permanent states of unconsciousness (persistent vegetative states or
states of coma) should receive ongoing care and sustenance to extend their lives, or
whether they should instead be caused to die, by removing such care and sustenance. Provocatively, Conly argues for the latter. She cogently maintains that much
of our current practice is based on a default rule favoring life-sustaining treatment,
one perhaps not justified by welfarist or autonomy-based considerations, or by distributive justice. Research by Scott Halpern, George Loewenstein, Kevin Volpp, et al.
has shown that "patients may not hold deep seated preferences regarding end-of-life
care" (Halpern, Loewenstein, Volpp, et al. 2013, 408). Indeed, in an experimental
setting in which seriously ill patients completed real advanced directives, the authors
found that changing the default option from life-extending care to comfort care
shifted the choices of about one-third of the patients toward comfort care (Halpern,
Loewenstein, Volpp, et al. 2013). Even without the nudge, 61% of respondents favored
comfort care. Although not focused on those in persistent states of unconsciousness,
this research supports Conly's insight that it may be worthwhile to shift toward a
default rule that such care will be withdrawn, for those that fail to state a contrary
preference in advance.

Nina A. Kohn's chapter takes a novel approach to the question of surrogate decision-
making. Her work is informed by an impressive body of social science research showing that surrogates often decide in ways that are contrary to the preferences of the
patients themselves, and instead project their own values and preferences onto the
patients for whom they are deciding. This is a breakdown in the principal-agent relationship, one that has been resistant to various interventions already tried. Kohn
ingeniously suggests that the better solution is to improve the matching between
principals and agents, so that they have aligned values.

As Kohn acknowledges, for this approach to work, we will need some mechanism
for identifying which values are important, and then measuring the held values for
both the principal and the agent. Future work will need to develop, and validate, this
methodology of eliciting the right values (predictive of healthcare decisions) and
matching principals to agents. I am imagining something like a dating website. The
suggestion is deeply subversive—is it possible that some stranger might actually be a

better surrogate for me than my own spouse, or my own child? The implication seems to be required by Kohn's analysis.

There are also practical questions. This elicitation mechanism will be more feasible for surrogates being chosen ex ante—each could fill out a survey instrument properly validated to elucidate the relevant values. But ex post, when a court is trying to appoint a surrogate for a patient who has failed to choose one herself, it is not clear how the patients' values can be observed by the court reliably. In practice then, we may instead have to resort to traditional lists of ranked surrogates, perhaps with a side constraint that some will be skipped over if they have known conflicts in the relevant domains (for example a spouse who is a member of one of the rare religious groups that opposes organ transplantation, for someone who is herself deeply committed to donation).

In the final chapter, Barbara J. Evans asks about whether the U.S. Food and Drug Administration (FDA) should override patients' decisions to access their own genetic information—both the raw data as well as interpretations as to the clinical significance of any observed variations. To be sure, the FDA has the authority to regulate medical devices, including those used to perform genetic sequencing, and has warned purveyors of direct-to-consumer genetics services that they may violate federal law if they make unapproved health claims about the significance of observed genetic variations, effectively shutting them down until they are able to substantiate their claims to the FDA. Recently, the FDA has shown that the premarket approval regime is minimally workable: it approved one company to sell a genetic test for a particular condition, Bloom Syndrome, which is quite rare (U.S. Food and Drug Administration 2015).

As Evans acknowledges, the FDA has a bona fide interest here since some such advice can be quite dangerous. An example may be helpful: prior to the FDA shutting them down, 23andMe provided consumers with information about whether they have a genetic variation associated with sensitivity to a commonly used blood thinning drug, warfarin (23andMe 2012). If that information is unreliable, it could cause patients to change their own dosage to their detriment, causing either blood clotting or excessive bleeding.

In a classic pattern of a regulatory dialectic, the FDA's pressure on companies like 23andMe may simply cause the market to disaggregate, so that the regulated companies that use medical devices are distinct from the unregulated companies that merely provide health information. Aside from statutory arguments that the latter group is untouched by the authority of the FDA, information providers also enjoy First Amendment protection, as Evans argues. Future work should explore alternative regulatory mechanisms, including the Federal Trade Commission's enforcement over "unfair competition" as well as tort law remedies for misrepresentation or breaches of implied warranties. The challenge for these regulatory mechanisms is, however, that they may put the burden on regulators to demonstrate that unsubstantiated health claims are actually false (Robertson 2014). Thus, ultimately, this market may rely on the capacity of patients to make wise decisions for themselves.

These chapters are linked only thinly by a focus on patient decision-making, and instances in which law may shape or altogether override those decisions. Together, however, they suggest a range of approaches available to policymakers to help ensure that decisions better serve the patient's own goals as well as the goals of social policy.

References

23andMeBlog. 2012. "Blood Thinners and the Genetics behind Drug Response." October 2. http://blog.23andme.com/health-traits/blood-thinners-and-the-genetics-behind-drug -response/.

Cheng, Edward K. 2012. "When 10 Trials Are Better Than 1000: An Evidentiary Perspective on Trial Sampling." *University of Pennsylvania Law Review* 160(4):955–65.

Halpern, Scott D., George Loewenstein, Kevin Volpp, et al. 2013. "Default Options in Advance Directives Influence How Patients Set Goals for End-of-Life Care." *Health Affairs (Millwood)* 32(2):408–17.

Jackson, Robert J., Jr., and David Rosenberg. 2007. "A New Model of Administrative Enforcement." *Virginia Law Review* 93:1983.

National Federation of Independent Business v. Sebelius, 132 S.Ct. 2566 (2012).

Robertson, Christopher T. 2014. "When Truth Cannot Be Presumed: The Regulation of Drug Promotion under an Expanding First Amendment." *Boston University Law Review* 94:545.

Schloendorff v. Society of N.Y. Hosp., 105 N.E. 92, 93 (N.Y. 1914).

U.S. Food and Drug Administration. 2015. "FDA Permits Marketing of First Direct-to-Consumer Genetic Carrier Test for Bloom Syndrome." February 19. http://www.fda.gov /NewsEvents/Newsroom/PressAnnouncements/UCM435003.

CHAPTER 18

Procedural Justice by Default
Addressing Medicare's Backlog Crisis

Matthew J. B. Lawrence

Medicare has a backlog crisis. When Medicare refuses to cover doctor-recommended healthcare, the claimant may seek de novo review before an administrative law judge (ALJ). But since Medicare started scrutinizing claims more closely in 2008, appeals are being filed four times faster than the ALJs can hear them. The queue today stands at three years, but the Medicare statute requires a decision in ninety days. Something must be done.

This chapter reframes Medicare's backlog crisis as a symptom of an underlying problem in the design of the coverage appeal process, to wit, the law provides the same costly and inefficient procedural protections to all claimants, even though most do not benefit from them. We offer many procedural protections (like an individualized hearing) even when they are not cost-effective because of the inherent, outcome-independent value of participation—the "day in court" ideal—but such protections are wasted when conferred on a claimant for whom process has no inherent value qua process. And that is the case for most Medicare appeals, 89% of which are brought by power wheelchair manufacturers, nursing homes, hospitals, state Medicaid agencies, and other providers, suppliers, or payers who usually benefit from the appeals process only when they win.

The challenge, then, becomes sorting the claimants for whom a hearing has inherent value from the claimants who would be no worse off having their claims resolved through a more streamlined, cost-effective process. Behavioral economics offers a way. Appeals should be given the full measure of procedural justice by default, but monetarily focused claimants should be incentivized with the promise of a cheaper, faster resolution and aggregation options to opt in to a fast-track actuarial appeals process that offers zero procedural protection and no hearing. This libertarian paternalistic approach would leverage differences between claimants who tend to be motivated by principle and those who tend to be motivated by money (such as susceptibility to status quo bias and ability to make use of economies of scale) to sift claimants for whom process has inherent value from those for which it does not.

Background

Like any entitlement program, Medicare's administrative task is ultimately to determine eligibility for and distribute taxpayer dollars. The administrative task for Medicare is complicated, however, by the fact that each recipient's entitlement is tied not to a precise statutory formula but instead to a standard that implicates professional judgment. Beneficiaries are entitled to coverage for all medical care they receive that is medically "reasonable and necessary" (42 U.S.C. §1395y(a)(1)(A)). That decision is initially made by doctors, not bureaucrats, which creates an administrative challenge for the Medicare program (Bagley 2013).

Medicare attempts in various ways to control the decisions of these "bedside bureaucrats" (Bagley 2013). A primary such means is to second-guess doctors' decisions about medical necessity, especially as to nonemergency big-ticket items like hospital admissions, long-term care, and motorized wheelchairs (77 Fed. Reg. 46,439 (Aug. 3, 2012)). The process by which Medicare does so is known as "utilization review."

Medicare hires private contractors to perform utilization review on the more than 1 billion claims for coverage that it receives each year (42 U.S.C. §1395ff(a)(2)(A)). These contractors are empowered to deny payment for treatments and services that are excluded by Medicare payment rules or that they themselves deem not to be medically "reasonable and necessary" (42 U.S.C. §1395y(1)(A)(1); 42 U.S.C. §1395kk-1(a)(3)).

In some cases, utilization review in Medicare is prospective, that is, it happens before care is delivered (Neumann, Rosen, and Weinstein 2005). Usually, though, Medicare utilization review is retrospective, happening after delivery. Either the beneficiary submits a claim for reimbursement or the provider (or supplier) does so, having taken "assignment" of the claim as a condition of service (a provider that takes assignment of a claim cannot charge the beneficiary if the claim is denied). In practice, the vast majority of claims are submitted by providers or suppliers.

Whether performed prospectively or retrospectively, utilization review affects Medicare claimants profoundly. Its direct effect is usually to make a claimant pay for healthcare herself (or itself). Its indirect effect is to influence (for better or worse) the ex ante healthcare choices of beneficiaries and especially providers who make treatment decisions in the shadow of utilization review (Naylor et al. 2012).

By statute (42 U.S.C. §1395y(a)(1)(A)), and constitutional mandate (*Schweiker v. McClure* 1982, 188), Medicare offers an adjudicatory process everywhere that it subjects doctors' treatment recommendations to utilization review, a way to appeal decisions denying coverage to a de novo hearing before an independent ALJ. The composition of Medicare's appeal workload, like that of its claimants, is dominated by provider-filed appeals. As shown in figure 18.1, at the time of the Office of Inspector

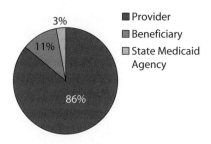

FIGURE 18.1 Percentage of appeals filed by type of appellant

General's 2012 Report, 11% of appeals were filed directly by beneficiaries challenging an adverse coverage determination, with the remaining 89% filed by either providers/ suppliers (86%) or state Medicaid organizations (3%). The provider/supplier category includes hospitals, nursing homes, durable medical equipment manufacturers (such as the now-defunct "Scooter Store" famous for its ubiquitous mid-day television commercials), and practitioners (U.S. Department of Health and Human Services Office of Inspector General 2012). The subject matter of appeals varies widely; disputes reflect disagreements about a patient's need for a motorized wheelchair, inpatient hospital admission, off-formulary drug, home health or rehabilitation services, particular treatment (such as bariatric surgery or sex change surgery), and so on.

As a check on utilization review, itself a primary means by which Medicare ultimately makes decisions about what to cover, Medicare's coverage appeals process plays a major role in the formation of Medicare policy through the piecemeal adjudication of claims. "Medicare coverage decision-making and appeals processes are the venues in which the battle over program costs, and ultimately the future design and content of the Medicare program, will play out" (Kinney 2003, 1511).

Unfortunately, Medicare's coverage appeal process is broken. As mentioned above, in the Affordable Care Act (ACA) and other enactments, Congress instructed the Centers for Medicare and Medicaid Services to step up its scrutiny of wasteful Medicare claims. It has done so, saving the taxpayers billions in the process (U.S. Department of Health and Human Services Office of Inspector General 2013). But that savings comes out of the pockets of providers and patients, who are having their claims denied increasingly often (again, for better or worse). At the same time, more beneficiaries are entering the Medicare program as the baby boom generation enters retirement (House Committee on Oversight & Government Reform 2014). Combined, these factors have led to a dramatic and steady uptick of appeals, totaling 545% from FY 2011 to FY 2013.

Under this new state of affairs, Medicare's Office of Hearings and Appeals is not capable of providing a hearing to every claimant who wants one. In 2013, for example, Medicare claimants filed appeals of decisions denying coverage four times faster than Medicare's ALJs could hear them, as shown in figure 18.2.

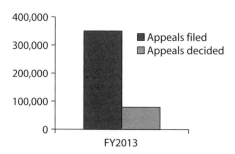

FIGURE 18.2 Medicare appeals filed and appeals decided

As a result, almost a million appeals and counting are waiting for a hearing (the federal courts process fewer civil cases in a year), and that number grows day by day (House Committee on Oversight & Government Reform 2014). As of July 2014, the Office of Medicare Hearings and Appeals was beginning to implement measures that it hoped would alleviate some of the backlog, such as a pilot project to try statistical sampling in limited cases. Such efforts, though, "are insufficient to close the gap between workload and resources" in the hearing process (House Committee on Oversight & Government Reform 2014). Related efforts by the Centers for Medicare and Medicaid Services to settle a significant block of cases in the backlog that resulted from a particular change in hospital billing rules (Abelson 2014), also will be insufficient either to bring capacity in line with demand or to clear the backlog. Meanwhile, claimants have filed suit seeking to compel swifter resolution of claims (*American Hospital Association v. Sebelius* 2014), pointing to the statutory mandate of a decision in ninety days (42 U.S.C. §1395ff; 42 C.F.R. 405.1016).

Problem: Wasted Procedural Justice

ALJ hearings are not the most cost-effective way to promote accurate coverage decision-making in the Medicare program. A number of reforms could produce greater error-correction bang for the administrative buck, from statistical sampling to paper hearings.

Our reason for offering claimants access to an individualized hearing before an ALJ is not efficiency. We do so because we believe these procedural protections are valuable for their own sake.

That there is a tension between efficiency and participation—in Medicare or anywhere—is hardly a novel insight about procedural design. But this is: in many Medicare coverage appeals, there is no such tension because access has no inherent value (or reduced value). So the procedural protections expended in many Medicare coverage appeals simply go to waste. If we can find a workable way to sort appeals in which procedural protections have inherent value from those in which they do not—the next part proposes a libertarian paternalistic way to do so—we can reduce the cost of processing coverage appeals and partially address Medicare's backlog.

ALJ Hearings Are Not the Most Cost-Effective Way to Resolve Claims Accurately

Participatory hearings are not the most cost-effective way to ensure accuracy in Medicare's administrative process. More streamlined administrative technologies could resolve claims as accurately, or nearly as accurately, as live hearings and would come at a fraction of the cost. For one, statistical sampling techniques (what Robert Bone calls "actuarial litigation" [Bone 1993]) could be used in order to determine the error rate for groups of appealed claims—say, knee brace claims in a given region—with reimbursement in the run of claims based on the rate of success for analogous claims in the sample.

Even for those cases not amenable to "actuarial litigation," individual adjudication could be streamlined significantly. In lieu of live hearings the efficiency track could employ the paper hearing process that the ACA sets up to resolve analogous healthcare coverage disputes in the private sector (Vukadin 2012). In this process, claimants would have their appeals decided solely on the basis of written filings by board-certified clinicians (Vukadin 2012). This process costs the private insurance companies required to use it about half as much as the live hearings currently used in Medicare, but does not appreciably diminish accuracy.

ALJ Hearings Are Justified by the Inherent Value of Participation

Our commitment to procedural justice, not feasibility, stands in the way of more efficient identification and correction of utilization review errors in Medicare. The inherent, outcome-independent value of process—the value of the "day in court"—can be understood in several ways, including its capacity to reaffirm the dignity of the aggrieved, as Mashaw understands it (Mashaw 1985), as a condition of the normative legitimacy of an adjudicatory body, as Solum does (Solum 2004), as satisfying a "preference for fairness," as Kaplow and Shavell understand it (Kaplow and Shavell 2002), or as the capacity of process to generate acceptance, as I argue elsewhere (Lawrence 2015). But however it is understood, the idea that process is inherently valuable counsels against reforms that trade access for efficiency (Bone 2011b).

The fact that Medicare coverage disputes implicate beneficiaries' deservedness for healthcare coverage makes the inherent value of participation especially pronounced. Beneficiaries' willingness to make use of a public entitlement program like Medicare may depend in part on the trust that they put in the operation of the program (Bertrand, Mullainathan, and Shafir 2004). Furthermore, managed care failed in part because its efforts to cut back on healthcare expenses, which sounded promising in theory, were subject to public outcries by disappointed claimants. If we hope not only to get coverage decisions right but also get them accepted by the people who matter—disappointed claimants—we must use every tool at our disposal.

The Inherent Value of Hearings Varies among Medicare Claimants

While some Medicare hearings may be justified by their inherent value, many Medicare claimants—in particular, large providers and suppliers—derive little or no such value from a hearing. As to such claimants, hearings can be a waste of time and money.

The inherent value of participation can be thought of in consequentialist terms, as the cathartic, soothing effect of being heard on a claimant who is bitterly disappointed by an outcome. It can also be thought of in deontological terms, as a condition of the dignity of the claimant required in order to make a decision about her life. On either view, participation has little or no value for many Medicare claimants.

At least three claimant traits tend, on either the consequentialist or the deontological view, to indicate that a Medicare claimant has lesser or greater capacity to derive inherent value from participating in a hearing. These are: (1) whether the claimant is a provider or a beneficiary; (2) whether the claimant is a corporate entity or an individual; and (3) whether the claimant is a repeat filer or a first-time filer. Providers tend to have a diminished capacity to benefit from participation as compared to beneficiaries because it is less likely a provider appeal is emotionally charged; providers are more likely to file appeals in the ordinary course of business and provider appeals tend to be pursued not by the doctor whose recommendation is in question but by a case manager in his office. Furthermore, from the dignitary perspective, the fact of assignment means that the issue at stake in a provider appeal is not whether the beneficiary is entitled to healthcare, but rather who should pay for healthcare that the provider already determined the beneficiary to be entitled to. As for corporate entities, they tend to benefit less from a hearing than individual claimants because in such an appeal the claimant itself—the corporate entity—has neither psychology nor human dignity, which diminishes the inherent value generated by providing a hearing to a corporate claimant by virtue of the claimant.

However it is understood, the inherent good that comes from giving an appellant her desired "day in court" does not obtain when a major device manufacturer or hospital group pursues a financially motivated appeal. A person or entity motivated to appeal in part by fairness may benefit from having her "day in court," whatever the outcome, but a sophisticated corporate entity that appeals only for money benefits only when it wins.

Solution: Procedural Justice by Default

At a minimum a substantial proportion of the hearings held in the Medicare appeals system are a waste of time and money. The way to address the backlog is to find a way to provide costly due process rights only for the small fraction of appeals where an individualized hearing has inherent value. If demand for justice is heterogeneous, then the supply of justice should be too.

The most apparent answer is to "sort" appeals, picking and choosing which ones Medicare should offer procedural protections and which ones can be handled in a more streamlined process designed to maximize efficiency. ALJs or some other entity could apply a standard to sort those appeals that get a hearing from those that do not. Or a blanket rule could be used to sort appeals without the need for individualized determinations, for example, providers might be forced to bring their appeals through a fast-track process, leaving individualized hearings for the appeals brought by beneficiaries.

Sorting poses challenges, however, which make it an unattractive fix. First and foremost, sorting would run counter to constitutional due process requirements, depending on the protections offered in the efficiency track (*Schweiker v. McClure* 1982, 188). Furthermore, individualized sorting would be intolerably costly and difficult; it is hard to tell whether a suit is motivated only by money or also by a grievance. And a blanket rule that forces provider-driven appeals into a process that providers deem less attractive might incentivize providers to stop taking assignment at all, closing off a practice that arguably benefits Medicare beneficiaries. Furthermore, some providers no doubt appeal for principled or emotional reasons (and some beneficiaries only for money), so a sorting rule would be both over- and under-inclusive.

Rather than actively sort claims, we can design the rules to "sift" passively among claims by inducing appellants to sort themselves. The theoretical literature on adjudicatory design discusses ways that rules can be designed to incentivize appellants to sift themselves for quality, that is, incentivize those with winning claims to sue (or appeal) and those with losing claims to decline to do so (Kaplow 2012; Hay 1996; Cameron and Kornhauser 2006). The same principle can be used to sift appeals in which procedural protections have the most value from appeals where such protections are not inherently valuable.

Mechanics of "Justice by Default"

Medicare should reform its appeals process to offer justice only by default. That is, all appeals should be defaulted into a procedural route that offers the full panoply of due process protections. But, the rules should offer an opt-in, "efficiency" track process that guarantees no procedural rights—not even the right to an individualized determination—but promises an overall likelihood of success equal to that of the "participation" track.

This approach would leverage status quo bias to sort claimants to ensure that only those claimants for whom a hearing is wasted would pursue the "efficiency" track, and therefore avoid the objection that such a system would come at the cost of claimants' participation interests. For those subject to status quo bias, default rules act functionally as mandates (Bubb and Pildes 2014). But for some actors the default is just that—a default—and for these actors the default is not paternalistic at all (Camerer et al. 2003). Because a default rule functions as a mandate only for those who are subject to status quo bias, it is "asymmetrically paternalistic" (Camerer et al. 2003).

Status quo bias actually reflects several phenomena that tend to cause people to follow the default—in behavioral parlance, to make the default "stick": (1) the endowment effect, which causes a person to value what she possesses more than what she does not possess, all else being equal (Korobkin 1998); (2) a signaling effect, because those with limited information take the default to reflect the policymaker's (or public's) opinion about the best option (Beshears et al. 2009); (3) a reputational effect, where a person worries about how others will perceive her if she opts out; and (4) inertia resulting from bounded rationality, where a person with finite attention chooses not to waste mental resources considering a departure from a status quo that she perceives to be adequate (Beshears et al. 2009).

The status quo will be least sticky for those Medicare claimants who stand to benefit least from procedural protections, for two reasons. First, other market failures that would tend to distort the demand for process downward—limited information and projection bias (Lawrence 2015)—are likely to be most present for those claimants who are also afflicted by status quo bias.

Second, several of the factors that make a default stick overlap with the factors that indicate enhanced inherent process value among Medicare claimants noted above. A corporate entity is both less likely to be susceptible to status quo bias (because it is less susceptible to the endowment effect) and less likely to derive inherent benefit from participation. Similarly, a repeat player is both less likely to be susceptible to status quo bias (because it has heightened incentive to become and remain informed, counteracting the default's signaling and inertia effects) and less likely to derive inherent benefit from participation. So, too, providers are both less likely to be susceptible to status quo bias (because they are in a better position to be informed about the process) and less likely to derive inherent benefit from participation.

Furthermore, to minimize the risk that claimants who would benefit from procedural protections opt out, the choice could be presented in a way designed to enhance its stickiness, that is, its tendency to be followed. This could be done both by making opt-out difficult (we could require a separate letter, rather than a check box [Ayres 2012]) and by framing the choice to discourage opt-out.

While status quo bias could be leveraged as a primary means of sorting claimants, additional means could be employed as well. A second sorting mechanism could be the use of incentives designed disproportionately to encourage repeat players, or those appealing multiple claims, to opt in to the efficiency track. Such entities are capable of benefiting from economies of scale in a way that one-off claimants are not. So the efficiency route should offer enhanced opportunities to take advantage of these, like exclusive aggregation mechanisms for consolidation and class treatment. This would give many financially motivated entities a targeted reason to opt for the efficiency route.

Costs and Benefits

Here are what I see as the benefits of the "justice by default" proposal:

Flexibility. Unlike ALJs, private contractors could quickly ramp up supply in response to increased demand. ALJs are hired for life and overseen by the Office of Personnel Management, making it difficult to increase hearing capacity in response either to unexpected jumps in demand or to temporary spikes (like the recent one in inpatient hospital claims). Private contractors would not be subject to this limitation.

Cost. Private contractors would review claims at a fraction of the cost of an ALJ hearing, and so would free up funds to allow Medicare to offer prompter hearings to the claimants who really benefit from them.

Expertise. Private contractors use reviewers with professional expertise in the medical specialty at issue, so the resulting decisions may be more accurate, not less.

Here are what I see as the downsides of this proposal, and why they are not prohibitive:

Variation. The private contractors might tend to grant appeals more often than ALJs, or vice versa, so claimants would pursue whichever route gave them the greatest anticipated likelihood of success. We could avoid this problem by randomly having some ALJ hearing decisions evaluated (purely for diagnostic purposes) by the private contractors, then tying contractor compensation to the similarity between their grant rates and the ALJs. The randomized study would also allow us to assure Medicare claimants that going without an ALJ hearing would not mean a diminished likelihood of success.

Claim selection. Claimants might try to pick-and-choose appeals, pursuing only the most sympathetic claims through an ALJ hearing. We could avoid this problem by requiring claimants to choose to opt in either for all of their claims in a given fiscal year or for none at all.

Private control of payment policy. Private contractors might make systematic errors in resolving Medicare claims, thereby distorting Medicare payment policy. We could avoid this problem by leaving in place the right to appeal a decision to the Departmental Appeals Board. We might even penalize contractors (perhaps significantly) for each reversal by the Departmental Appeals Board, thereby incentivizing them to align their decisions to its anticipated rulings.

Conclusion

In sum, Medicare should respond to the ongoing backlog by implementing a "default" approach to deciding which claimants to provide hearings for as described above. This would allow the claimants who really need it to receive something closer to an uncompromised hearing, without adversely affecting the overall accuracy of the administrative process or seriously threatening to deny hearings erroneously. It would thereby allow us to quickly ramp up our capacity to resolve Medicare claims while lowering the cost of deciding each claim, all without sacrificing procedural justice for the claimants for whom that most matters. The result would be a more just—or more modestly, a less unjust—administrative process.

References

Abelson, Reed. 2014. "Medicare Will Settle Short-Term Care Bills." *The New York Times*, August 29, B1. http://www.nytimes.com/2014/08/30/business/medicare-will-settle-appeals -of-short-term-care-bills.html.

American Hospital Association v. Sebelius, No. 14-cv-00851, ECF No. 1 (D.D.C. 2014).

Ayres, Ian. 2012. "Regulating Opt Out: An Economic Theory of Altering Rules." *Yale Law Journal* 121(8):2032–2116.

Bagley, Nicholas. 2013. "Bedside Bureaucrats: Why Medicare Reform Hasn't Worked." *Georgetown Law Journal* 101(3):519–80.

Bertrand, Marianne, Sendhil Mullainathan, and Eldar Shafir. 2004. "A Behavioral-Economics View of Poverty." *The American Economic Review* 94(1):419–23.

Beshears, John, James J. Choi, David Laibson, and Brigitte C. Madrian. 2009. "The Importance of Default Options for Retirement Saving Outcomes: Evidence from the United States." In *Social Security Policy in a Changing Environment*, edited by Jeffrey R. Brown, Jeffrey Liebman, and David A. Wise. University of Chicago Press. Chicago. 167–95.

Bone, Robert G. 1993. "Statistical Adjudication: Rights, Justice, and Utility in a World of Process Scarcity." *Vanderbilt Law Review* 46:561–97.

———. 2011a. "Normative Evaluation of Actuarial Litigation" *Connecticut Insurance Law Journal* 18(1):227.

———. 2011b. "The Puzzling Idea of Adjudicative Representation: Lessons for Aggregate Litigation and Class Actions." *The George Washington Law Review* 79:577–627.

Bubb, Ryan, and Richard H. Pildes. "How Behavioral Economics Trims Its Sails and Why." *Harvard Law Review* 127:1595–1678.

Camerer, Colin, Samuel Issacharoff, George Loewenstein, Ted O'Donoghue, and Matthew Rabin. 2003. "Regulation for Conservatives: Behavioral Economics and the Case for Asymmetric Paternalism." *University of Pennsylvania Law Review* 151:1211.

Cameron, Charles M., and Lewis A. Kornhauser. 2006. "Appeals Mechanisms, Litigant Selection, and the Structure of Judicial Hierarchies." In *Institutional Games and the US Supreme Court*, edited by James R. Rogers, Roy B. Fleming, and Jon R. Bond. University of Virginia Press. Charlottesville. 173–204.

Hay, Bruce L. 1996. "Contingent Fees and Agency Costs." *Journal of Legal Studies* 25(2):503–33.

House Committee on Oversight & Government Reform, Subcommittee on Energy Policy, Health Care & Entitlements. 2014. *Office of Medicare Hearings and Appeals Workloads: Hearing before the Subcommittee on Energy Policy, Health Care & Entitlements, 113th Congress*.

Kaplow, Louis. 2012. "Burden of Proof." *Yale Law Journal* 121:738–859.

Kaplow, Louis, and Steven Shavell. 2002. *Fairness versus Welfare*. Harvard University Press. Cambridge, MA.

Kass, Julie E., and John S. Linehan. 2012. "Fostering Healthcare Reform through a Bifurcated Model of Fraud and Abuse Regulation." *Journal of Health & Life Sciences Law* 5(2):75–129.

Kinney, Eleanor D. 2003. "Medicare Coverage Decision-Making and Appeal Procedures: Can Process Meet the Challenge of New Medical Technology?" *Washington and Lee Law Review* 60(4):1461–1512.

Korobkin, Russell. 1998. "Status Quo Bias and Contract Default Rules." *Cornell Law Review* 83:608–87.

Lahav, Alexandra D. 2008. "Bellwether Trials." *George Washington Law Review* 76:576–638.

Lawrence, Matthew. 2015. "Mandatory Process." *Indiana Law Journal* 90(1).

Mashaw, Jerry L. 1985. *Due Process in the Administrative State*. Yale University Press. New Haven, CT.

Naylor, Mary D., Ellen T. Kurtzman, David C. Grabowski, Charlene Harrington, Mark McClellan, and Susan C. Reinhard. 2012. "Unintended Consequences of Steps to Cut Readmissions and Reform Payment May Threaten Care of Vulnerable Older Adults." *Health Affairs* 31(7):1623–32.

Neumann, Peter J., Allison B. Rosen, and Milton C. Weinstein. 2005. "Medicare and Cost-Effectiveness Analysis." *New England Journal of Medicine* 353(14):1516–22.

Schweiker v. McClure, 456 U.S. 188 (1982).

Solum, Lawrence B. 2004. "Procedural Justice." *Southern California Law Review* 78:181–321, 181.

U.S. Department of Health and Human Services Office of Inspector General. 2012. "Improvements Are Needed at the Administrative Law Judge Level of Medicare Appeals." http://oig .hhs.gov/oei/reports/oei-02-10-00340.pdf.

———. 2013. "Medicare Recovery Audit Contractors and CMS's Actions to Address Improper Payments, Referrals of Potential Fraud, and Performance." http://oig.hhs.gov/oei/reports /oei-04-11-00680.pdf.

Vukadin, Katherine T. 2012. "Hope or Hype: Why the Affordable Care Act's New External Review Rules for Denied ERISA Healthcare Claims Need More Reform." *Buffalo Law Review* 60(5):1201.

CHAPTER 19

Measuring the Welfare Effects of a Nudge
A Different Approach to Evaluating the Individual Mandate

Manisha Padi and Abigail R. Moncrieff

Americans have a hard time evaluating the costs and benefits of ObamaCare's individual mandate—a law that requires everyone to carry health insurance or pay a tax. Indeed, debates over the mandate's worthiness present so many visions of its purposes that scholars have a hard time deciding what they should even measure to evaluate its success. Proponents have argued that the mandate is necessary to prevent adverse selection, a neoclassical economic justification. But a dearth of consistent empirical support for the neoclassical story and the technical nature of that story make it a hard sell for the courts, Congress, and citizens alike. Given the neoclassical story's shortcomings, some scholars (Moncrieff 2013) have turned to a behavioral account, arguing that the mandate is useful to correct mistakes in healthcare consumption choices. But this story may be impossible to prove empirically given the difficulty in distinguishing mistakes from preferences. Indeed, scholars are more generally embroiled in methodological and ideological debates that have ensnared nearly all behaviorally motivated policies. Given those difficulties, some scholars, including Cass Sunstein in the foreword to this volume, have proposed that nudges are means of decreasing decision costs, whether or not cognitive failures would have caused mistaken choices. But that story does not avoid the empirical difficulty of the pure behavioral account; it may be impossible for analysts to distinguish decision costs from preferences. Furthermore, all of these accounts fail to capture one important, overarching cost of the mandate: the subjective welfare loss that many Americans experience from the mandate's coerciveness.

Given the mandate's multifarious costs and benefits, traditional analytic models have a hard time determining whether the law produces a net welfare gain or loss. In this chapter, we argue that shifting from the standard "decision utility" approach to the newer "experienced utility" approach (Kahneman, Wakker, and Sarin 1997; Kahneman 2000; Kahneman and Thaler 2006; Kahneman and Sugden 2005; Kahneman and Krueger 2006) is the best means of capturing empirically all the effects of this highly contentious intervention. The experienced utility approach asks a much simpler question than the ones analysts have been tackling. The simple question, to paraphrase Ronald Reagan, is: "Are you better off now than you were before the mandate?" As we show here, this criterion can provide a common language between, on the one hand, those who stress the costs to liberty of paternalistic intervention and, on the other, those who feel that nudges can be justified. Although libertarians might disfavor coercive interventions despite net welfare gains and thus be unconvinced by evidence of improved experienced utility, the experienced utility criterion at least incorporates welfare losses from coercion. In addition, an experienced utility approach, although not a perfect methodology, can overcome the main empirical issues facing behavioral economics (Loewenstein and Ubel 2008). Finally, the experienced utility framework encompasses the traditional economic story of the mandate, providing the most general method for assessing its success.

The Mandate's Empirical Struggles

There are three prevalent narratives attempting to justify the individual mandate, but all suffer from empirical limitations. Here, we highlight those limitations to reveal the gaps in our understanding of the statute's merits. We consider, first, the neoclassical story that the mandate corrects adverse selection; second, the standard behavioral story that it corrects mistakes in healthcare consumption; and, third, the altered behavioral story that it decreases decision costs for insurance purchases.

Adverse Selection

The traditional economic justification for the mandate—on which the Obama administration relied in litigation (*Nat'l Fed'n of Indep. Bus. v. Sebelius* 2012, 2566)—is that, without it, adverse selection causes inefficiencies. The story is as follows: because high-risk individuals are more likely than low-risk individuals to benefit from insurance, policy writers assume that anyone buying on the individual market is going to be costlier than average to cover. Insurers thus charge more for individual policies, making their product even more unattractive to the healthy and driving healthy people out of risk pools. This problem is self-perpetuating. At best, adverse selection causes inefficiently high prices and smaller markets, and at worst, it causes insurance's risk-pooling mechanism to collapse (Cutler and Reber 1998). If insurance companies could be confident that healthy people participated, the price could decrease to a point that more low-risk individuals would gain value from coverage. Under a pure rational actor model, then, more people would purchase insurance if the market could overcome the collective action problem of adverse selection.

On this account, the mandate performs the standard governmental function of solving a collective action problem. It is similar to requiring all Americans to pay for national defense. Like mandatory contribution to national defense, the mandate relieves beneficiaries of universal participation from the responsibility of monitoring and punishing free riders.

Although this vision of insurance has gained wide consensus among economic scholars, its empirical foundations are not rock-solid. Indeed, this narrative rests on several unproven assumptions. First, it assumes that insuring every individual is socially optimal. That is, the story assumes that the cost of insuring each person, if the insurance company had perfect information such that policies could be priced perfectly, is less than the benefit of coverage to that person. But some people might not be worth insuring (Hendren 2013), and some might suffer subjective losses from insurance that outweigh its economic benefits. Second, the adverse selection story assumes that individuals have more information than insurance companies about their risks, making it hard for firms to protect themselves against high-risk patients through accurate pricing. But that assumption might not hold; insurers might know more than customers if actuarial studies do better than consumers at predicting risks.

Finally and most importantly, the traditional story assumes that people who buy insurance are sicker than people who do not. The theory of adverse selection rests on the assumption that sick people are more likely to benefit from insurance and are therefore more likely to buy it (Siegelman 2004). But that assumption might be false— or at least less problematic than it seems—if health insurance markets are also or instead subject to advantageous selection, which occurs if people who buy insurance are more risk-averse than those who do not (de Meza and Webb 2001; Finkelstein and McGarry 2006; Cutler, Finkelstein, and McGarry 2008; Huang, Liu, and Tzeng 2010). In that case, the insured might have a lower chance of getting sick than the uninsured because the same risk aversion that drove them to insure makes them less likely to engage in unhealthy behavior. That is, risk aversion might predict both insurance purchases and healthy behavior. If the true story of health insurance is one of advantageous rather than adverse selection, then the uninsured are sicker than the insured, and the mandate will result in increased prices. If the true story is one of mixed adverse and advantageous selection, then the uninsured are a mix of bad and good risks, and forcing them into pools will have unpredictable price effects.

In this framework, the standard economic model of gathering data on individual choices leaves significant gaps. A policymaker might look at claims data, for example, to try to detect information asymmetry between insurer and insured (Chiappori and Salanie 2000; Finkelstein and Poterba 2014). The literature assumes that the insured have better information, causing adverse selection, if the data show that individuals with generous plans submit more claims or more-expensive claims than those with less-generous plans. But that conclusion rests on an assumption that people with high health costs are naturally riskier or sicker. That might not be true. High health costs could instead indicate a moral hazard problem—that those with insurance are likely to be less careful with their health. Or health costs could arise from excessive doctor visits, which would be consistent with advantageous selection arising from high risk aversion; risk aversion could explain both a generous purchase and high healthcare costs. Standard analytical tools cannot distinguish between these accounts.

Standard Behavioral Story

The behavioral justification for the individual mandate focuses on its ability to correct three biases that might plague individuals' healthcare savings and consumption decisions: myopia, optimism, and inertia. Myopia describes the phenomenon of people valuing the close future significantly more than the far future, which might cause individuals to underinvest in their long-term health. Optimism bias describes systematic underestimation of risks, which might cause individuals to spend too little on risk mitigation such as preventive care or health insurance. Inertia describes individuals' difficulty in changing long-held habits, which might make it harder for those who have been uninsured to become insured or for those who lack exercise habits to develop them. These biases, among others, might cause individuals to make mistakes in healthcare savings and consumption choices, to their own long-run detriment.

The standard behavioral justification for the mandate rests on its mitigation of these biases' effects. The story goes like this: insurance forces young, healthy people to contribute to a stable insurance system, paying more than the actuarial value of their insurance today so that they can pay less when they are older and higher-risk.[1] The mandate thus redistributes from young to old within an individual life. Compulsory insurance over time acts like a savings mechanism, forcing individuals to overcome any myopia or optimism that otherwise leads them to under-save. Additionally, health insurance decreases the perceived cost of consuming preventive care. Because Obama-Care prohibits cost sharing for preventive care, the mandate requires all Americans to pay for such care through their premiums, increasing the odds that they will consume routine physicals despite myopic or optimistic undervaluation of risk.[2] Finally, the mandate helps overcome inertia by making it more valuable to change the habit of relying on emergency room care rather than insurance. The benefit of becoming insured now includes avoidance of a substantial fine, which could be enough to overcome inertia.

Unfortunately, standard empirical methods cannot demonstrate whether these biases affect choices in the absence of regulation, much less whether regulation works to correct them. Suppose a policymaker wants to estimate the effect of optimism on insurance purchases. Optimism, in this setting, would mean that individuals underestimated the ex ante probability of sickness and therefore bought too little insurance. An economist might try to measure this effect by observing the number of people who buy too little coverage relative to their realization of negative health events. But another plausible theory explains such observations: that people correctly estimate the ex ante probability but get an improbably high ex post realization of costs. The decision to buy less insurance coverage in that case is not due to bias but to a rational decision that nevertheless caused a loss. These two explanations are difficult, if not impossible, to separate using nonexperimental data since data can include, at most, the ex ante purchase and the ex post cost.

Moreover, even if survey data demonstrated that the individual's ex ante belief of his own chance of, say, a heart attack was lower than the "true" actuarial probability, there still would be no proof of irrationality. He might have recently heard from his doctor that his heart appeared exceptionally healthy on a stress test. That information could not be incorporated into actuarial tables or other observable indicators of statistical risk. Therefore, when the policymaker sees an individual who bought low insurance coverage and then had a heart attack, she cannot draw any firm conclusions about the existence or costs of optimism.

The behavioral literature reflects these shortcomings. A long line of research in economics, neuroscience, and psychology has observed optimism bias (Sharot 2011; Puri and Robinson 2007; Hamermesh 1985; Hurd and McGarry 2002; Manski 2004). These studies use survey data and biological techniques to elicit an individual's stated beliefs and those beliefs' evolution after changes in her risk profile. People often underestimate risks of bad shocks (Sharot 2011). In addition, many people interpret news about health and mortality optimistically, under-adjusting their beliefs about themselves (Hamermesh 1985; Hurd and McGarry 2002; Manski 2004). Even with this evidence, however, it is hard to establish a link between mistaken beliefs and mistaken choices (Besharov 2004).

Similarly, studies have found evidence of short-sighted, or myopic, behavior (Frederick, Loewenstein, and O'donoghue 2002; Kirby and Maraković 1995). Calibrations of nonexperimental data also provide some evidence that myopic models fit datasets better than classical models (Laibson, Repetto, and Tobacman 2001). A myopic decision-maker values tomorrow much less than today, but she values 100 and 101 days from now more similarly. This short-sighted behavior can cause regret; individuals make decisions for the future that seem rational today but that their future selves regret (Rasmusen 2012). This phenomenon suggests that governments can intervene beneficially by providing individuals with commitment devices. The literature has established the benefits of commitment devices in areas as diverse as smoking, exercising, and saving (Gruber and Kőszegi 2001; DellaVigna and Malmendier 2006; Ashraf, Karlan, and Yin 2006). However, even in such a well-developed literature, it is difficult to connect empirically the demand for commitment devices with cognitive failure. Behaviors that appear myopic might instead result from changes in individuals' beliefs or preferences. That is, someone who seems to make short-sighted decisions like overeating might have a rational belief that food or money could be scarce in future periods. Actions that appear myopic cannot definitively be linked to myopic utility.

Finally, inertia has been documented in the health insurance context in several cutting-edge papers. Abaluck and Gruber, in an influential paper, provided evidence that individuals do not optimize their choice of insurance coverage (Abaluck and Gruber 2011). But their conclusions were limited because, in their setting, it was difficult to disentangle behavioral bias from rational explanations. A later paper by Handel was able to isolate "mistakes" in health insurance choices, but he shows only that a cost exists when switching from the status quo (Handel 2013). The paper cannot establish whether choices result from rational recognition of switching costs or from psychological inertia. Although this research has proved fruitful in providing evidence of regret-worthy choices, it cannot demonstrate that psychological biases are to blame or that government intervention is beneficial.

In short, the behavioral literature has not been able to establish that de-biasing interventions make people better off.

Decision Costs

In an attempt to overcome these measurement problems, some scholars, including Cass Sunstein, have shifted their narrative, treating biases as decision costs rather than mistakes. The central problem with behavioral accounts is the difficulty proving that people make real-world choices based on mistaken beliefs rather than spending resources to overcome mistakes. Even if biases did not affect outcomes, however, they would affect costs. An optimistic person who wants to buy optimal insurance would need to discover and confront her true risks. Similarly, a person with myopia or inertia would need to figure out the true future value of insurance and preventive care. On this account, the individual mandate might improve welfare by decreasing decision costs, shifting the default from "no insurance" to "yes insurance."

This account of the mandate's function, however, is not free of empirical difficulties. Although this justification does not require demonstration that individuals make mistaken choices absent regulation, it does pose the difficult question of whether governmental choices are cheaper—in terms of both decision and error costs—than private choices. The validity of the central assumption that governmental decisions are cheaper depends on the preference heterogeneity among the population. If a single choice is right for everyone, then government benefits from economies of scale in making that choice for everyone. Coordinated decision-making is cost reducing and welfare enhancing when a uniform policy represents the best choice for everyone, particularly when the choice is complicated. If, however, choices are perfectly heterogeneous, then government needs to expend a lot of resources optimizing individual choices. Government might still be better at making choices for individuals if agents can obtain information or expertise at lower cost, but the introduction of agency costs is likely to make governmental decision-making costlier than individual decision-making when preferences are heterogeneous, even if individual decisions are prone to high error costs.

In order to assess this justification for the mandate, therefore, we would need to know how heterogeneous the needs and preferences of Americans are and how good government bureaucrats are at assessing individuals' needs and preferences. Those questions are difficult.

Applying Experienced Utility

One of the central dualities confronting policymakers who apply behavioral economics is the divergence between "experienced utility" and "decision utility" (Vitarelli 2010; Adler 2012–13). Neoclassical economics relies on the assumption that individuals maximize their "true" utility function, meaning that their choices reveal their preferences. This is the "decision utility" framework. Behavioral economics undermines this assumption by introducing the possibility that individuals' decisions reflect warped versions of their preferences, distorted by behavioral biases and cognitive limitations. If this is true, analysts can no longer use decisions to measure utility.

To address this problem, Daniel Kahneman and his coauthors coined the term "experienced utility" as an alternative for measuring welfare. Experienced utility is the subjective well-being that individuals obtain from a particular situation. The obvious issue, which has challenged economists for years, is that well-being is hard to measure. The preferred method is simply to ask people how happy they are, using various techniques. In the simplest framework, an individual's welfare maps exactly to his self-reported subjective well-being.[3]

Two literatures have developed in behavioral economics, one that attempts to remain in the traditional decision utility framework and another that embraces the experienced utility framework. No consensus has emerged as to which is more useful in analyzing policies like the mandate. Loewenstein and Ubel provide a middle ground, proposing a complex, blended criterion (Loewenstein and Ubel 2008). We posit, in contrast, that a straightforward adoption of experienced utility has a variety of key benefits, particularly when applied to nudges.

What role can the government play in de-biasing decisions? Many scholars have rallied behind the concept of "nudges"—minimal interventions that steer individuals toward rationality while preserving choice. A standard example is a default rule, which assigns the healthy "broccoli" choice as the default and puts the burden on the individual to change to an unhealthy "donut" choice. Another example is a sin tax, which increases the price of donuts relative to broccoli.

Proponents of nudges argue that individuals can still choose a donut or broccoli, but the intervention fights mistakes by making it easier to choose broccoli. Critics, however, argue that these interventions are based on the dangerous assumption that government knows people better than they know themselves. That assumption, the critics argue, renders nudges coercive and paternalistic—no better than any regulation that attempts to micromanage behavior. To resolve this debate, we must evaluate welfare effects. If a nudge's benefits are high enough, they could justify costs to autonomy.

But, as noted, empirical cost-benefit analysis has serious difficulties accounting for behavioral bias. The standard decision utility approach relies on the assumption that individuals maximize self-interest. That assumption, called "revealed preference," is used to translate observed choices into welfare. The idea is that actual decisions, such as how many donuts or how much broccoli individuals buy, give an accurate impression of how much individuals like broccoli and donuts. But if those actual choices are not perfectly utility maximizing, then the data are less useful in measuring welfare. When the revealed-preference assumption does not hold, it is nearly impossible to distinguish biased individuals from individuals who love donuts so much that they would rather be obese than give them up. In short, knowledge that biased people feel urges to eat unhealthy foods does not prove the converse: that individuals eating unhealthy foods are doing so because of biases.

Suppose that we do not want to take a stand on whether choices emerge from mistakes or preferences. Can the decision utility framework tell us whether a nudge is net beneficial? Decision utility shows only the amount of donuts and broccoli that people buy before and after a nudge. It does not allow us to disentangle the driver behind individuals' choices, whether biases, preferences, or real economic costs (such as greater travel distance to a greengrocer than a bakery). An intervention targeted to increase broccoli consumption might combat biases, but it might also hurt individuals who are happy with their current consumption—whose donut consumption is based on rational factors such as strong preferences or costs of acquiring broccoli. In short, to use decision utility here, the analyst has to decide ahead of time which biases individuals were facing; decisions themselves do not reveal biases. Complications such as multiple biases or heterogeneity across individuals could make her analysis computationally infeasible.

Under the experienced utility framework, the analyst has a much easier task. She can test the intervention's effects simply by making the policy change and then asking individuals whether they are happier. The following equation elucidates.

$$U_i(intervention) = U_i(no\ bias) - \Delta U_i(bias) + B_i(intervention) - C_i(intervention)$$

Here, U_i is the individual's utility, B the intervention's benefit, and C the cost. The decision utility approach tries to identify $U_i(no\ bias)$, individuals' utility level absent any bias, and $\Delta U_i(bias)$, the utility lost due to bias. It has proven difficult to demonstrate that $\Delta U_i(bias)$ is nonzero, let alone to calculate either number precisely. Even if analysts could resolve that issue, however, and if $B_i(intervention)$ could be established, legal scholars would hotly debate the intervention's costs, $C_i(intervention)$. Critics of nudges argue that one cost of intervention is the unquantifiable loss of freedom, which does not appear from choices.

The experienced utility approach does not attempt to identify each term of the equation separately. Instead, we take advantage of the fact that $U_i(no\ intervention) = U_i(no\ bias) - \Delta U_i(bias)$. Under standard cost-benefit analysis, an intervention is justified only if $B_i(intervention) > C_i(intervention)$. Therefore, government should enact a policy if

$$U_i(intervention) > U_i(no\ intervention)$$

In the case of paternalistic intervention, we can simply ask whether individuals are better off after the intervention.[4]

This approach is not without imperfections, as Loewenstein and Ubel have pointed out. One major issue is "habituation": the tendency of individuals to adjust happiness to accommodate changes (Loewenstein and Ubel 2008). Habituation is a concern in the long run; people can adjust to disability and extreme poverty, for instance, so it is likely that any utility change from a health insurance change will soon be absorbed into baseline utility. It might suffice to measure utility immediately before and after the change, depending on whether long-run benefits are expected. Another issue is that policies that take decisions away from individuals might improve welfare but enhance ignorance. Perceived utility is unlikely to account for knowledge gains from the process of decision-making, and when government makes decisions for individuals, it eliminates those learning benefits. This concern seems minor, however, related to the benefits of incorporating behavioral bias into a welfare criterion.

The experienced utility approach has several important advantages. It incorporates lost utility from lost autonomy. Therefore, scholars with different ideologies can use survey data to test how much individuals truly suffer from coercive governmental action. The approach also captures purely economic considerations such as high transportation costs, switching costs, or insurance costs, which can cause heterogeneous effects for different kinds of people. Finally, it captures behavioral bias only insofar as the intervention is successful in de-biasing. This approach thus identifies as such any severe bias that the intervention fails to correct. Some important economics papers have moved toward using the experienced utility approach in estimating the equilibrium effects of health policies (Gruber and Mullainathan 2005; Baicker et al. 2013). This approach should be broadly applied in analyzing any behavioral law.

Conclusion

Few policy innovations have proved as contentious as ObamaCare's individual mandate. Even among proponents, competing justifications make it difficult to demonstrate that it is improving social welfare. The easiest way to bridge these ideological divides and to assess the policy's results might just be to ask the people affected by the policy: "Are you better off than you were before ObamaCare?"

Notes

1. This story assumes that government does not change the rules before today's young people become old enough to benefit. That risk attaches to any public program, including Medicare and Social Security. But entitlement programs are generally sticky.
2. Because health insurance (unlike most kinds of indemnity insurance) covers routine maintenance and wear-and-tear and because ObamaCare forbids cost sharing for preventive services, insurance now reduces the point-of-consumption cost of preventive care to its time cost.

3. In economics overall, surveys are viewed as unreliable data sources. The concern is that surveys' writing and distribution methods can significantly impact responses. Moreover, individuals are often unaware of or deeply mistaken about basic facts, making it difficult to trust responses to subjective questions. In the experienced utility framework, however, these issues become a benefit. Individuals are experts on their own thoughts, so if there truly was a negative bias that a policy intervention successfully fought, survey responses would most accurately report it. A long line of literature has developed techniques for eliciting experienced utility.

4. Note that we consider this analysis at the individual level to accommodate any social welfare criterion that the policymaker prefers. Experienced utility frameworks are equally useful to a Rawlsian policymaker, who measures only the utility of the worst-off individual, as to a utilitarian policymaker, who weighs each utility equally. We do not mean to imply that government should intervene against an individual only if it would make that particular individual better off.

References

Abaluck, Jason, and Jonathan Gruber. 2011. "Heterogeneity in Choice Inconsistencies among the Elderly: Evidence from Prescription Drug Plan Choice." *The American Economic Review* 101(3):377–81.

Adler, Matthew D. 2012–13. "Happiness Surveys and Public Policy: What's the Use." *Duke Law Journal* 62:1509.

Angeletos, George-Marios, David Laibson, Andrea Repetto, Jeremy Tobacman, and Stephen Weinberg. 2001. "The Hyperbolic Consumption Model: Calibration, Simulation, and Empirical Evaluation." *Journal of Economic Perspectives* 15(3):47–68.

Ashraf, Nava, Dean Karlan, and Wesley Yin. 2006. "Tying Odysseus to the Mast: Evidence from a Commitment Savings Product in the Philippines." *The Quarterly Journal of Economics* 121(2):635–72.

Baicker, Katherine, Sarah L. Taubman, Heidi L. Allen, Mira Bernstein, Jonathan H. Gruber, Joseph P. Newhouse, Eric C. Schneider, Bill J. Wright, Alan M. Zaslavsky, and Amy N. Finkelstein. 2013. "The Oregon Experiment—Effects of Medicaid on Clinical Outcomes." *New England Journal of Medicine* 368(18):1713–22.

Besharov, Gregory. 2004. "Second-Best Considerations in Correcting Cognitive Biases." *Southern Economic Journal* 71(1):12–20.

Chiappori, Pierre-André, and Bernard Salanie. 2000. "Testing for Asymmetric Information in Insurance Markets." *Journal of Political Economy* 108(1):56–78.

Cutler, David M., Amy Finkelstein, and Kathleen McGarry. 2008. "Preference Heterogeneity and Insurance Markets: Explaining a Puzzle of Insurance." *The American Economic Review* 98(2):157–62.

Cutler, David M., and Sarah J. Reber. 1998. "Paying for Health Insurance: The Trade-Off between Competition and Adverse Selection." *The Quarterly Journal of Economics* 113(2):433–66.

De Meza, David, and David C. Webb. 2001. "Advantageous Selection in Insurance Markets." *RAND Journal of Economics* 32(2):249–62.

DellaVigna, Stefano, and Ulrike Malmendier. 2006. "Paying Not to Go to the Gym." *The American Economic Review* 96(3):694–719.

Finkelstein, Amy, and Kathleen McGarry. 2006. "Multiple Dimensions of Private Information: Evidence from the Long-Term Care Insurance Market." *The American Economic Review* 96(4):938–58.

Finkelstein, Amy, and James Poterba. 2014. "Testing for Asymmetric Information Using 'Unused Observables' in Insurance Markets: Evidence from the UK Annuity Market." *Journal of Risk and Insurance* 81(4):709–34.

Frederick, Shane, George Loewenstein, and Ted O'Donoghue. 2002. "Time Discounting and Time Preference: A Critical Review." *Journal of Economic Literature* 40(2):351–401.

Gruber, Jonathan, and Botond Köszegi. 2001. "Is Addiction 'Rational'? Theory and Evidence." *The Quarterly Journal of Economics* 116(4):1261–1303.

Gruber Jonathan, and Mullainathan Sendhil. 2005. "Do Cigarette Taxes Make Smokers Happier?" *The BE Journal of Economic Analysis & Policy* 5(1):1–45.

Hamermesh, Daniel S. 1985. "Expectations, Life Expectancy, and Economic Behavior." *The Quarterly Journal of Economics* 100(2):389–408.

Handel, Benjamin R. 2013. "Adverse Selection and Inertia in Health Insurance Markets: When Nudging Hurts." *The American Economic Review* 103(7):2643–82.

Hendren, Nathaniel. 2013. "Private Information and Insurance Rejections." *Econometrica* 81(5):1713–62.

Huang, Rachel J., Yu-Jane Liu, and Larry Y. Tzeng. 2010. "Hidden Overconfidence and Advantageous Selection." *The Geneva Risk and Insurance Review* 35(2):93–107.

Hurd, Michael D., and Kathleen McGarry. 2002. "The Predictive Validity of Subjective Probabilities of Survival*." *The Economic Journal* 112(482):966–85.

Kahneman, Daniel. 2000. "Experienced Utility and Objective Happiness: A Moment-Based Approach." In *Choices, Values, and Frames*, edited by Daniel Kahneman and Amos Tversky. Cambridge University Press. New York. 673–92.

Kahneman, Daniel, and Alan B. Krueger. 2006. "Developments in the Measurement of Subjective Well-Being." *The Journal of Economic Perspectives* 20(1):3–24.

Kahneman, Daniel, and Robert Sugden. 2005. "Experienced Utility as a Standard of Policy Evaluation." *Environmental and Resource Economics* 32(1):161–81.

Kahneman, Daniel, and Richard H. Thaler. 2006. "Anomalies: Utility Maximization and Experienced Utility." *The Journal of Economic Perspectives* 20(1):221–34.

Kahneman, Daniel, Peter P. Wakker, and Rakesh Sarin. 1997. "Back to Bentham? Explorations of Experienced Utility." *The Quarterly Journal of Economics* 112(2):375–405.

Kirby, Kris N., and Nino N. Maraković. 1995. "Modeling Myopic Decisions: Evidence for Hyperbolic Delay-Discounting within Subjects and Amounts." *Organizational Behavior and Human Decision Processes* 64(1):22–30.

Laibson, David, Andrea Repetto, and Jeremy Tobacman. 2000. "A Debt Puzzle." *NBER Working Paper* No. 7879.

Loewenstein, George, and Peter A. Ubel. 2008. "Hedonic Adaptation and the Role of Decision and Experience Utility in Public Policy." *Journal of Public Economics* 92(8): 1795–1810.

Manski, Charles F. 2004. "Measuring Expectations." *Econometrica* 72(5):1329–76.

Moncrieff, Abigail R. 2013. "The Individual Mandate as Healthcare Regulation: What the Obama Administration Should Have Said in NFIB v. Sebelius." *American Journal of Law and Medicine* 39:539–696.

Nat'l Fed'n of Indep. Bus. v. Sebelius, 132 S. Ct. 2566 (2012).

Puri, Manju, and David T. Robinson. 2007. "Optimism and Economic Choice." *Journal of Financial Economics* 86(1):71–99.

Rasmusen, Eric. 2012. "Internalities and Paternalism: Applying the Compensation Criterion to Multiple Selves across Time." *Social Choice and Welfare* 38(4):601–15.

Sharot, Tali. 2011. "The Optimism Bias." *Current Biology* 21(23):R941–R945.

Siegelman, Peter. 2004. "Adverse Selection in Insurance Markets: An Exaggerated Threat." *Yale Law Journal* 113:1223–81.

Vitarelli, Anthony. 2010. "Happiness Metrics in Federal Rulemaking." *Yale Journal on Regulation* 27:115.

CHAPTER 20

Better Off Dead
Paternalism and Persistent Unconsciousness

Sarah Conly

In this chapter, I argue that it is better for both the person and for society generally that those who are in permanent states of unconsciousness—persistent vegetative states (PVSs) or states of coma—should be dead rather than maintained on life support systems. To the extent that such people can remain alive without ventilators—as happened, say, to Karen Quinlan, who remained alive in a persistent vegetative state for almost ten years after the famous court decision allowed her parents to take her off a mechanical ventilator (*In Re Quinlan* 1976, 10)—it would be better if they were not: it would be better if they were denied other sorts of treatment that keep them alive, like nutrition and hydration, and in the end, better that they receive an injection that would cause a speedy death. At present, we encourage continuing care by making it the default option—in order to be removed from care a person needs an advance directive requesting that, or at least testimony to the effect that he did not want continued care, or a family that declines care on behalf of the patient. I argue that insofar as people (whether patients or family members) opt to have care continued in such conditions it is on the basis of bias and other irrationalities, and we should make the rational decision more attractive, whether through nudges or more stringent forms of interference.

Why?

Why do I favor killing off helpless people who mean to do no harm? There are three reasons: (1) there is no benefit to them in remaining alive in such a state; (2) while there are competent people who do request such treatment for their later, unconscious

I would like to thank Luke Cummiskey and participants in discussions at the University of Chicago, Princeton University, and Harvard University for their comments.

selves, they do this as a result of poor reasoning, which undercuts our prima facie obligation to respect their wishes; and (3) the costs to society of maintaining such people in a living state is not only very great, but a very great waste.

First, as to the value of life: there are any number of things that make human life valuable, and perhaps we each have our favorites. For some, life's value lies in its subjective quality: the experience of pleasure, or love, or aesthetic appreciation. For others, it is the capacity for choice, and in particular moral choice: that we can evaluate and choose according to that evaluation makes our lives uniquely worthwhile. For yet others, life is valuable because it allows the accomplishment of our goals, whether to climb Everest or to complete a novel. Whatever quality makes life valuable, though, that element is not present when we are in a state of permanent and deep unconsciousness. We have no experiences. We do not reflect and evaluate. We engage in no endeavors. We merely continue physically, and that not robustly. We cannot participate in any characteristically human activities.

And when we consider the reasons why we think of death as bad—that it eliminates agency, that it frustrates our ongoing projects, or that it simply deprives us of the possibility of worthwhile experiences, we see that existence in an unconscious state has the same effects. We cannot engage in mental operations, cannot bring about the things we intended to bring about, and cannot have experiences, and this is in a sense (although obviously not in the biological sense) the functional equivalence of death.

Yet, many people do not make advanced directives declining care if they should end up in a coma or persistent vegetative state. Some people, of course, do not make advance directives at all, and of those who do, some do not indicate that they would want care withheld under these circumstances. Why not, and what should we do about this?

This brings us to the second point: opting for long-term care in such cases is likely not to be a rational choice. In some cases this is because no reasoning is actually involved—the patient does not make an advance directive, or does so without really considering the options, or considers the options but reasons poorly in doing so. Irrational choices do not deserve the respect that rational choices do because they may not reflect the person's values or goals.

This is necessarily speculative. I do not know of any studies that have tried to discover what the thought processes are of those who choose not to decline care. Considerably more concern has been shown for the quality of reasoning, avowed or observed, of people who have declined care. There, attention has been paid—at least in some contexts—to whether the patient is depressed, whether the patient is under undue pressure from relatives to decline treatment, whether the patient actually understands the consequences of declining care, and so forth. This is especially true in cases where patients request physician-assisted suicide, but also happens in some cases where patients simply decline care that could keep them alive. The idea seems to be that while declining care suggests a frame of mind that is somehow suspect, requesting care is always reasonable.

However, there is no reason to assume that requests for care are somehow better based than requests that no care be received. As I have argued, existence in an unconscious state has none of the properties that make us value life, so when this is the future that life offers, there is no reason that self-interest should come down on the side of life; at best, the choice between continued existence in an unconscious state and death should be a toss-up, unless bias has entered in and corrupted reasoning. (We will see below that there are other reasons, though, to prefer death.) Thus it seems likely that those who request such care are either mistaken as to the facts or, even if possessed of the facts in some sense, are failing to grasp them in the way that allows them to have their proper weight in reasoning.

Patients may be particularly resistant to the truth of the matter—that in any qualitative sense their life is just as much over when they are alive but in a coma or a persistent vegetative state as when they are dead. Many of us may simply find it hard to imagine a world in which we are alive but unconscious for good. We have not, after all, ever experienced such a thing, and this makes it hard to imagine it in a vivid way. Patients and families alike sometimes cling to the belief that as long as the patient is alive, cure is possible. Perhaps science is just on the brink of regenerating brain tissue! Others, fueled by popular stories of reemergence, may think that living a normal life even after a prolonged state of unconsciousness is a realistic possibility (Swinburn et al. 1994). More people have probably seen Steven Seagal's *Hard to Kill* than have read about the actual medical prognoses of those in a coma or PVS. (Seagal's character suddenly awakens after being in a coma for seven years and immediately fights off would-be assassins using his IV pole as an aikido jo.)

However, this is all extremely improbable. Science is not on the brink of such a discovery. And even on the rare occasions when people regain some aspects of consciousness after prolonged unconsciousness, they do not typically regain a normal life, and often fade back into unconsciousness again. Chances of regaining consciousness are much less for those whose who are old, whose state is a result of illness (for example, a stroke) rather than traumatic injury, and who have been unconscious more than a year. Spontaneous recovery is just not something it makes sense to plan for. Naturally, we would want to consider the chances of recovery before withdrawing support from an unconscious person, but typically those who hope for recovery are relying on a false hope, driven by fear of death rather than medical prognosis.

It may seem hard to believe that people are making dispositions for the future in ignorance of what treatment will in fact bring. And since we all know we are going to die, it may seem unlikely that we are really engaged in irrational resistance to that fact. This, though, ignores our general ability to make irrational decisions in the face of our own intelligence and knowledge. Psychologists and behavioral economists have demonstrated that we often choose poorly when it comes to choosing means to our ends. We have a natural bent to poor reasoning in certain situations. My research has not uncovered studies on the role of cognitive bias in making decisions about care in terminal cases. We know a great deal about these biases in other decisions, though, and there is certainly no reason to think they would not play a role here.

The optimism bias makes us believe that we are less likely than others to undergo an unfortunate outcome. Wishful thinking makes us think that things will turn out the way we want them to. We suffer from "neglect of probability," whereby we ignore relevant information. We have a confirmation bias, wherein we tend to accept information as it supports our view, and discredit it when it does not. The availability bias makes us overestimate the likelihood of something happening when we have a stronger memory of its happening in the past—like exaggerating the chances of our recovering from a long-term coma because we have heard of one famous case. We suffer from focusing effect, in which we pay too much attention to one aspect of a situation (perhaps "I will not be dead!") at the expense of others ("I will not be conscious!"). And so forth. As I say, these biases do not appear to have been studied specifically in the choices of those who are making advance directives, but it seems easy to see how, especially in a situation clouded by dread and ignorance, they are likely to affect our choices and bring us to choose a situation that is not beneficial and has more costs than the alternatives

We know, after all, that we are good at believing two opposing things at once when we have a motivation to do so. Sometimes this is harmless: for example, we all believe that our children are especially talented and good, even as we believe that parental preferences for offspring are clearly a function of evolution. Too often, though, we may do this when it comes to death, believing we will die, but maintaining the belief that we can avoid death. Consider George Eliot's moving description of Mr. Casaubon's passing, as she says, through "one of those rare moments of experience when we feel the truth of a commonplace, which is different from what we call knowing it . . . When the commonplace 'We must all die' transforms itself suddenly into the acute consciousness 'I must die—and soon,' then death grapples us, and his fingers are cruel" (Eliot 1898, 442).

That we should try to avoid this consciousness of death is not surprising, and it is not always bad. Just as it is in our interests, in many contexts, to believe that our children are unusually wonderful, it may also behoove us for much of life to believe, in some sense, that we are not actually going to die. It may keep us from drowning our fears in alcohol, for example. But just as we need occasionally to grasp reality when it comes to our children, for their sakes, for our own sakes, and sometimes for the sake of others, we need also to acknowledge at a certain point that the kind of thinking that seeks to deny death is mistaken.

So, our decision to seek care in unconscious states may be based on irrational beliefs. It is likely to be irrational in another way as well. We know that in many cases continuing care is inconsistent with values that patients have seemed to hold deeply for many years. Patients in these states often have families for whom they have long felt responsible. The welfare of our children in particular matters a great deal to us. It seems likely that continued care for a parent (or partner or sibling or child) in an unconscious state will become extremely burdensome to the family whose happiness we have previously done so much to promote, while yielding nothing tangible to ourselves.

For one thing, such care is expensive. Even where we have insurance, institutional and medical costs may well exceed what insurance will pay (depending on how long the state of unconsciousness lasts before death is finally unavoidable). Of course, family members are certainly not legally bound to pay out of pocket for the continued care for a relative on life support. However, if that is what the relative has asked for in her advance directive, families may feel a moral burden to do so. This has either of two results: they pay the expenses, which will be extremely burdensome on all but the super-rich, or, they do not pay. If they do not, either because they are literally unable to, or because they decide that the benefit is not worth the cost, they are likely to feel guilty for discontinuing a treatment whose cessation means that their relative dies. They will feel they have been ungrateful because gratitude dictates "doing everything possible" for their relative, even when nothing useful actually is possible.

Second, even if medical finances are not a problem, there is a psychic cost to having a relative who is an unconscious state for a continued period of time. If you continue to visit, that is painful: for one thing, of course, it may be expensive and time-consuming. Beyond that, though, visiting patients who are unconscious has its own difficulties. They are not like themselves—they are not like the persons everyone knew. They do not look the same, and, obviously, they are not responsive. You are encouraged (in my experience, at any rate) to talk to them as if they were conscious, but the thought that they might actually be conscious—and confined, without the ability to move, to a bed in a facility for perhaps years, alone for most of the day without any stimulation— is at the same time devastating. If, on the other hand, they are not conscious, then what is the point of visiting? So, of course, you may choose to stop visiting—but this in turn can induce tremendous guilt. There is just no easy way. Who of us wants to put our child, our partner, our sibling, or our parent in this painful situation for an extended period of time, for no good to ourselves? Who wants to make their relationship with us a source of ongoing pain instead of pleasure? While we are conscious we benefit from others' care for us, even if we are disabled and cannot live as we once did—we know that we are cared for, and that we can give back the same kind of loving attention. Once consciousness is gone it is harder to maintain any belief in mutual benefit. There is a great deal said about death with dignity. Many would argue that it is less dignified to die a death that is inconsistent with the values of one's life.

Lastly, such care is a burden on society more generally. We are all aware of the rising costs of healthcare, and we know that insurance, which prevents individuals from having to pay out-of-pocket costs, is correspondingly becoming more and more expensive. Ending care for the permanently unconscious will certainly not solve the problem of healthcare expense, but it is certainly a very expensive species of care, with no benefits. The release of such money and such medical resources into the healthcare system could allow for cheaper, more effective treatments for others—others who would truly benefit. This is not a guarantee—we do not know where such funds will go. But if the costs are without benefit at present, it certainly seems likely that they would end up spent better.

It might be that no one of these considerations alone—that the treatment brings no benefit, that the choice to undergo it is irrational, and the fact that the treatment is so costly—would be sufficient to show that such treatment is wrong. Taken in combination, though, I believe they do.

Why Is This Not the Normal Policy in Healthcare?

The reasons for respecting wishes for prolonged care even in unconscious states are various, resting on both tradition and innovation in medical ethics.

The medical establishment is said to consider three things when formulating medical policy: (1) patient well-being; (2) patient autonomy; and (3) distributive justice (Buchanan and Brock 1990). While the parameters for medical decision-making these establish are generally good, they have so far not worked well in consideration of care of unconscious patients.

Patient Well-Being

The traditional dictum, "first do no harm," is still considered of prime importance. Doctors do not undertake treatments they believe to be more harmful than beneficial. Historically, since we did not have the means to keep patients alive in permanently unconscious states, life was considered generally beneficial, and death was considered generally a loss, so naturally physicians tried to avoid patient deaths. Now, though, the options have changed. We need to change our historical tendency to favor life in every condition, and to see that death in these cases is not a harm since it is no worse than a state of permanent unconsciousness.

Patient Autonomy

However, there are other issues that affect physicians' position on patient treatment. In the past few decades, physicians have embraced the idea of patient autonomy: that (within certain limits) the patient has the right to choose treatments according to her own judgment, and even when the physician thinks the patient's judgment is mistaken, that judgment has to be respected. No degree of benevolence is sufficient to justify treating the (competent) patient as less than a full agent. While doctors are free to try to persuade the patient to pursue another course, "even the irrational choices of a competent patient must be respected if the patient cannot be persuaded to change them" (Brock and Wartman 1990, 1595). The accepted ethical principle is that people "are entitled to autonomous determination without limitation on their liberty being imposed by others" (Beauchamp and Childress 1980, 59).

This stress on patient autonomy has many laudable aspects. However, as has been discussed above, we know more now about the actual process of decision-making than when this new movement of patient autonomy was growing. Cognitive deficits common to all of us may lead to even informed patients choosing very poorly in certain cases, even very important ones. While this is not true in every situation, it is true sufficiently often that we need to consider whether the whole "patient autonomy" movement was, in some sense, misguided. It depends. The patient autonomy movement did two things: it suggested that outcomes should be evaluated in terms of the patient's goals, rather than anyone else's goals, and it mandated that patient decisions should determine which course of treatment was preferable. I would argue that the first of these is indeed an improvement: what counts as a success must be a function of what the patient actually wanted since the life that is lived will be the patient's.

Respecting patient wishes when it comes to choosing means is quite different, however. The mistake of the patient autonomy movement was in thinking that the first principle—respect for patient decisions about outcomes—implied the second—respect for patient decisions about means. In fact, since actual decisions may not advance patient goals, respect for the achievement of goals does not entail respect for instrumental decisions (Conly 2013). Instead, in some situations, respect for the patient's goals may require disregarding the patient's choices as to means when that choice is incompatible with reaching the desired end.

Given this, the idea that we must respect the decision of the patient when that is ill-informed or irrational makes little sense. Of course, it would be wrong to override every irrational decision people make. It would drive us crazy, for one thing. We value our liberty to choose, as well as valuing our actual attainment of desired outcomes, and that is something to be considered very carefully. But we also know that in some cases we do not think that the value of liberty is enough to be worth the costs that allowing it will entail. We allow the refusal of futile treatments, even if the patient wants them—physicians have no obligation to provide medical treatment that is of no demonstrable benefit, and patients and families have no right to demand it (Miles 1992; Tomlinson and Brady 1990). If there is no medical benefit, the patient's values do not have to be considered. Of course, maintenance in unconscious states may appear not to be futile—it provides life, after all, rather than death. In effect it is futile, though, since a life of unconsciousness is qualitatively the same as death. We refuse futile treatments because they bring costs without benefits, so maintenance in permanently unconscious states should have the same status.

We may wonder as well about the nature of the advance directive. Does it respect autonomy to allow patients to enter into an expensive, life-long agreement that they will have no power to revoke? While we are reconciled to the fact that we cannot change certain things after our deaths, it seems a bit more peculiar that we may set up an arrangement that will last all of our lives, cost a huge amount, and yet be impossible to amend—especially, as in this case, when there are no benefits. We do not allow voluntary slavery contracts for a number of reasons, but one is that irrevocable contracts that determine your fate until death seem like a bad idea. Once we have signed an advance directive we are locked in to this for life, rendering it worse than any shifty life-long time-share we may be inveigled into by a nefarious salesman. Physicians are not nefarious salesmen, of course, and they do not encourage the pursuit of long-term care in an unconscious state. Still, such patients are locked in, as a result of a decision made without counseling, often as an addendum to a will concerning allocation of property, often without anyone present with relevant knowledge or skill, and there is no way they can get back to us and say, "This isn't what I was expecting, and I'd like to change my mind." (For a related discussion, see Ackerman 1981.)

Distributive Justice

This final consideration is in some ways the most delicate. Is it legitimate, in treating a patient, to consider how this treatment affects others—in particular, how much it costs others? This is delicate because, of course, when it comes to our relationship with our own physician we like to operate under the understanding that all he is considering is our own personal welfare. It is hard to trust a doctor with your health, much less your life, if you think he is balancing that against someone else's bottom line.

At the same time, at least in the United States, we all know that the cost of healthcare has become a great concern. There is a danger that healthcare costs may in some sense bust the bank, if not on a national scale, then at least on a local one. School systems, for example, have found the rise in healthcare costs for employees to be one of the biggest expenses they grapple with, and the fact that it rises sometimes by such huge percentages per year makes it all the harder to plan school budgets and to get the votes the budgets require. Businesses naturally grapple with the same difficulties as municipalities. Most people agree that it is a disproportionate amount of the American gross domestic product (GDP), and it is certainly one of the highest percentages of GDP spent by any country (World Bank 2014). Everyone seems to agree that we need to lower healthcare costs, and for many, the prospect of some sort of healthcare rationing seems inevitable. If rationing occurs, the idea would be to reduce or remove altogether treatments that are both very expensive and of little benefit.

Nonetheless, we have shown reluctance to institute any rationing, and in particular have shown reluctance to ration the care that goes to those in permanent unconscious states. For one, there is the appeal to our sensibilities of the helpless. When people are entirely dependent on us we feel especially responsible, and experience the "praiseworthy recognition of the extreme vulnerability of the incompetent individual" (Buchanan and Brock 1990 190). To cut costs here in particular may seem to strike at the defenseless. And we do not like the idea that doctors in particular might turn against the weak, and just for the sake of saving money.

This is fair. We do want to look out for the vulnerable, and we do want to recognize that there is always a temptation to take advantage of the vulnerable just because we can. It is a fair concern, but it is not a definitive concern. In a world of limited resources, we also need to consider social costs. Can we put a dollar amount on a human life? Yes and no. No, we cannot calculate precisely what a life is worth, whether it is a conscious life or an unconscious life. It does not really make sense, in a metaphysical sense, to speak of a life as being worth X number of dollars—the two cannot be compared. As to policy, though, when we are deciding how much to spend, we do such calculations every day. We do it when we determine how much to spend on road safety, for example. More money spent on construction—proper banking, lights, safety rails, road surfaces, and so on—means more lives saved, but we do not make the safest possible roads. We are willing to lose lives for relatively minor gains—for example, a higher speed limit that is more dangerous but allows most of us to arrive more quickly—and we are certainly willing to lose them when that saves large amounts of money. So, it is reasonable and familiar to consider when we want to save lives and how much we want to spend to save them: to consider the benefits and the costs. Costs are not merely to be considered in terms of dollars; after all, dollars spent on one thing means fewer to spend on other things, and so we lose services. If we eliminate a useless treatment that is also very expensive, and heath care costs go down, more people can afford better treatment, and can live longer and better lives.

It is also true that we do not want to lose our relationship of trust with our doctor. What this means, I think, is that individual doctors should not take it upon themselves to compare the costs of care to their patients to the benefits that might be brought if the same money were spent elsewhere. Such policies should be decided institutionally, whether that institution is the government or the American Medical Association. And such policies should be transparent—we are filled with distrust when it turns out we are not getting into what we thought we were getting into because someone has deceived us. But such policies can be transparent, so that our doctor has not stepped outside what is required by her general professional ethic. This in itself should not diminish our trust, insofar as we have such trust. After all, we already know our doctor will not do everything she can for us. She will not bump off the other doctor's patient to make his organs available when we need a transplant. She will not steal drugs, as easy as that might be, in order to reduce our personal healthcare costs. And so on; our care is always decided within a particular moral context, and no one considers that a disappointing failure of care.

Given the principles of medical ethics, then, it seems to me the consistent and workable practice society should adopt is to discourage the care of the permanently unconscious. We could simply make withdrawal of care at a certain point the default option. Or, we could make it more difficult to receive care, by requiring that those who want it show an overriding need—for example, membership in a religion or culture that forbids withdrawing care. Or, we could perhaps refuse insurance payments for continued care. We may have to learn what the most effective, least painful alternative is, but surely what we should not do is continue our present practice.

References

Ackerman, Terence. 1981. "Why Doctors Should Intervene." *Hastings Center Report* 12:14–17.

Beauchamp, Tom, and James Childress. 1980. *Principles of Biomedical Ethics.* Oxford University Press. New York.

Brock, Dan, and Steven A. Wartman. 1990. "When Competent Patients Make Irrational Choices." *New England Journal of Medicine* 322:1595–99.

Buchanan, Allen E., and Dan W. Brock. 1990. *Deciding for Others: The Ethics of Surrogate Decision Making.* Cambridge University Press. Cambridge.

Conly, Sarah. 2013. *Against Autonomy: Justifying Coercive Paternalism.* Cambridge University Press. Cambridge.

Eliot, George. 1898. *Middlemarch.* Dirigo Publishing Company. Boston.

In Re Quinlan, 70 N.J. 10 (NJ 1976).

Miles, Steven H. 1992. "Medical Futility." *Journal of Law, Medicine, & Ethics* 20:310–15.

Swinburn, J. M. A., S. M. Ali, and D .J. Banerjee. 1994. "To Whom Is Our Duty of Care?" *British Medical Journal* 318:1753–55.

Thaler, Richard, and Cass Sunstein. 2008. *Nudge: Improving Decisions about Health, Wealth, and Happiness.* Yale University Press. New Haven, CT.

Tomlinson, Tom, and Howard Brody. 1990. "Futility and the Ethics of Resuscitation." *Journal of the American Medical Association* 264:1276–80.

World Bank. 2014. "Health Expenditures, Total (% of GDP)." http://data.worldbank.dorg /indicator/SH.XPD.TOTL.ZS.

CHAPTER 21

Improving Healthcare Decisions through a Shared Preferences and Values Approach to Surrogate Selection

Nina A. Kohn

When patients lack capacity to make their own healthcare decisions, surrogate decision-makers must step in to do so. Whether the surrogate is an agent appointed by the patient, a guardian appointed by a court, or a default surrogate decision-maker selected according to state statutory law, it is generally agreed that the surrogate's primary goal should be to reach the decision the patient would have made if capable. Therefore, the conventional wisdom is that surrogate decision-makers should be selected based on their relationship to the patient, trustworthiness, and willingness to follow the patient's directions.

Unfortunately, the extensive social psychology literature on healthcare decision-making clearly shows that selecting surrogates based on such traits is insufficient to protect patients' wishes. Surrogates frequently make treatment decisions for patients that are inconsistent with patients' preferences even when explicitly instructed otherwise, and commonly recommended strategies for ameliorating this problem appear to have only limited effect.

This chapter shows that the likelihood that surrogate decisions will be consistent with patient preferences could be increased by selecting surrogates based, at least in part, on shared preferences and values. It therefore proposes an alternative model for surrogate selection that can guide individuals and courts in appointing surrogates, as well as policymakers seeking to improve healthcare decision-making. It then discusses

This chapter is based on an article in the *San Diego Law Review* entitled "Using Matched Values and Preferences to Select Legal Surrogates." It is dedicated to the memory of the late Professor Jeremy Blumenthal, a friend and esteemed colleague, who was the chapter's intended coauthor. Professor Blumenthal passed away before having the opportunity to contribute to the chapter directly, but it represents the evolution of ideas we arrived at jointly while coauthoring earlier work. All credit for it should thus be shared, although all errors are my own.

how individuals and judges could be encouraged to use this alternative model by introducing them to simple information that challenges their assumptions about surrogate decision-making.

The Current State of Surrogate Decision-Making

When individuals lack capacity to make healthcare decisions for themselves, the law enables third parties to gain authorization to make those decisions. Legally recognized surrogates for healthcare decision-making fall into three broad categories: (1) healthcare agents appointed by patients prior to the onset of cognitive incapacity through the use of a type of advance directive[1] known alternatively as a "healthcare proxy" or a "power of attorney for healthcare"; (2) court-appointed surrogates known as "guardians" who are empowered to act pursuant to a court determination that an individual is "incapacitated" and in need of a guardian; and (3) "default surrogate decision-makers" selected in accordance with state statutory law who are given the authority to act on the basis that an individual needs a surrogate but has neither an appointed agent nor a guardian. Close relatives—especially spouses and adult children—are the most commonly selected surrogates in all the situations.

The law governing surrogacy is shaped by an understanding that a primary goal of appointing a surrogate decision-maker is to ensure that treatment decisions made for a patient are those the patient would have made if able. Thus, state statutes that articulate decision-making standards for surrogate decision-makers typically require surrogates to use substituted judgment (that is, to make the decision they believe the patient would have made) where the patient's wishes are actually known and often where they are reasonably ascertainable. Consistent with this common approach, the Uniform Health Care Decisions Act instructs surrogates to make healthcare decisions "in accordance with the patient's individual instructions, if any, and other wishes to the extent known to the surrogate. Otherwise, the surrogate shall make the decision in accordance with the surrogate's determination of the patient's best interest" (National Conference of Commissioners on Uniform State Laws 1994).

Unfortunately, the extensive social science literature on surrogate decision-making in the healthcare context[2] strongly indicates that surrogates frequently fail to make "congruent" decisions, that is, decisions that are consistent with those patients would want made for themselves. A systematic review by Shalowitz et al. surveyed forty years of research on surrogate decision-making and found that surrogates predicted patients' treatment preferences with only, on average, 68% accuracy regardless of whether the surrogate was selected by the patient or according to a statutory hierarchy (Shalowitz et al. 2006). Notably, this rate of agreement is most likely significantly higher than the rate of actual, conscious agreement, as it fails to account for chance agreement.

Subsequent studies have further documented the failure of surrogates to accurately predict patient treatment preferences (for example, Bryant et al. 2013; Newman et al. 2012; Marks and Arkes 2008; Mantravadi et al. 2007; Ciroldi et al. 2007).

Multiple factors may explain the lack of congruence between decisions made directly by patients and those made by surrogates. A common explanation for incongruence is that the surrogate may simply be unaware of the patient's preferences due to a lack of prior discussion or the surrogate forgetting or misconstruing the content of conversations that did occur. Research suggests such unawareness may contribute to the problem, as numerous studies have shown that surrogates are often unaware of patients' treatment preferences or values even when they believe otherwise (for example, Reamy et al. 2011). Indeed, surrogates often have a false sense of confidence in the ability to predict patient preferences (Cicirelli 1992; Suhl et. al 1994; Uhlmann et. al. 1988).

Less benign factors, however, also appear to contribute to incongruence. Most notably, surrogates who disagree with patients' wishes or values may deliberately deviate from known patient preferences. Numerous studies have found that surrogates sometimes choose to ignore or override known patient preferences (for example, Vig et al. 2006), and such deviations can occur even in situations in which the deviation would not directly benefit the patient (Warren et al. 1986). At times, the surrogate may see such deviations as consistent with the patient's preferences because the surrogate believes the patient's preference would change if the patient better understood the situation at hand. Yet surrogates often plan to base their decisions about treatment at least partly on their own values (Vig et al. 2006).

However, perhaps the most important and consequential factor contributing to incongruence is that surrogates tend to project their own preferences onto patients. In a study of patients and individuals likely to be chosen as their surrogates, Zweibel and Cassel found that the likely surrogates predicted patient treatment preferences with only 63% accuracy (Zweibel and Cassel 1989). By contrast, there was a strong correlation between what surrogates said they would want for themselves and what they predicted the patients would want. Surrogates overwhelmingly (ranging from 93% to 95% of the time, depending on the scenario) selected the treatment for the patient that they indicated they would want for themselves in the same situation (Zweibel and Cassel 1989).

A similar pattern of projection was found in a 2001 study in which Fagerlin et al. paired undergraduate students with the students' parents and had the two discuss end-of-life issues together. Both were then surveyed as to the parents' preferences in a variety of serious healthcare situations. The study found that the best predictor of what the students thought their parents would want is what the students wanted for themselves. Indeed, although there was only a 64% rate of agreement between parents' preferences and students' predictions of parent preferences, there was a 78% rate of agreement between what students predicted parents would want and what students wanted for themselves (Fagerlin et al. 2001). The pattern was then repeated in a parallel study of older adults and their self-selected surrogates. While there was a markedly higher rate of congruence in this study (surrogates accurately predicted principals' preferences 72% of the time), the surrogates' preferences for their own care were still the best predictor of what the surrogate thought the principal would choose: 80% of the time, surrogates thought principals would choose what the surrogates wanted for themselves (Fagerlin et al. 2001).

Likewise, Moorman, Hauser, and Carr's analysis of data from 2,750 married couples in their mid-sixties found that spouses reported one another's preferences for life-sustaining care at a rate only slightly better than chance, and that the patterns of incongruence witnessed were consistent with spouses' projecting their own care preferences onto one another (Moorman, Hauser, and Carr 2009). Similarly, when McDade-Montez et al. asked newly married couples to predict one another's end-of-life preferences, they found that predictions of spouses' end-of-life treatment preferences were more closely related to individuals' own treatment preferences than to their spouses' treatment preferences (McDade-Montez et al. 2013). The researchers attributed these findings to individuals assuming that their spouses shared their beliefs.

Previous Strategies for Increasing Congruence

A common recommendation for increasing congruence in treatment decisions is to select surrogates based on their relationship with the patient. Thus, professionals advising those executing advance directives frequently advise selection of a trustworthy individual who knows the patient well and is familiar with the patient's wishes. This approach is also consistent with the statutory hierarchies for selecting surrogate decision-making statutes, and with current practices for appointing guardians for incapacitated persons. Unfortunately, although family members are more likely to predict patient treatment preferences than are physicians (Shalowitz et al. 2006; Coppola et al. 2001; Ouslander et al. 1989; Bedell and Delbanco 1984; Principe-Rodriguez et al. 1999; Seckler et al. 1991; Uhlmann et al. 1988), degree of relatedness does not appear to predict accuracy (Shalowitz et al. 2006). Thus, choosing family members as surrogates may be advisable, but degree of relatedness may not be a fruitful basis for choosing between relatives.

Another frequently recommended strategy for increasing congruence is for patients to discuss their wishes with their surrogates. Despite the proliferation of campaigns by nonprofit organizations to encourage such conversations, the evidence as to the efficacy of such discussion (for example, Suhl et al. 1994) is limited. Taken as a whole, the empirical literature on surrogate decision-making research strongly suggests that such discussions do little to increase the likelihood that the surrogate will make the decision that patient would have made (Moorman, Hauser, and Carr 2009; Ditto et al. 2001; Smucker et al. 2000; Fagerlin et al. 2002). This appears to be the case both where the patient and surrogate discuss the patient's specific treatment preferences (Ditto et al. 2001; Moorman, Hauser, and Carr 2009) and where they discuss the patient's values related to treatment (for example, Matheis-Kraft and Roberto 1997). There is some limited evidence that such discussion may improve surrogates' understanding of patients' personal beliefs about the process by which decisions should be made (Pearlman et al. 2005), but that this does not lead to improved congruency with regard to specific treatment decisions (Pearlman et al. 2005).

A third type of intervention designed to improve surrogates' substantive accuracy is to specifically instruct surrogates to use substituted judgment. There is evidence as to the effectiveness of this intervention (for example, Tomlinson et al. 1990; Whitton and Frolik 2012), but the size of the effect appears to be limited and the evidence itself is mixed, as some studies have failed to find it improves congruency (Hare et al. 1992).

Finally, some scholars have proposed replacing or supplementing surrogate decision-makers with alternative decision-making paradigms. For example, Houts et al., have suggested that higher rates of congruency could be achieved by basing treatment decisions on an actuarial model in which decisions are made by looking to what others are known to have chosen in like circumstances (Houts et al. 2002). However, this approach is unlikely to lead to a decision-making process that is more consistent with patient wishes even if it improves congruency as to treatment decisions. This is because an important goal—and in many cases the primary goal—for many patients is that their family, or certain family members, be involved in the decision-making process (Kelly et al. 2012; Fagerlin et al. 2002).

Thus, existing proposals to increase congruence may have some value, but do not do enough to lower the rate of incongruency. The following section therefore proposes a new approach to surrogate selection to supplement, if not replace, existing strategies for improving congruence.

A New Approach to Increasing Congruency
Capitalizing on Projection by Matching Values and Preferences

The repeated finding that surrogate decision-makers project their own preferences and values when making healthcare decisions for others suggests that surrogates chosen based on the extent to which they share the patient's preferences and values may be able to achieve the goal of congruent healthcare decisions at a far higher rate than surrogates selected based on conventional factors. Accordingly, surrogates should be selected based, at least in part, the extent to which they share treatment preferences. Where it is not possible to compare treatment preferences, or where an individual cares less about individual treatment decisions than about consistency with a set of values, then surrogates should be selected based on shared values.

Scholars frequently argue that surrogate decision-makers should consider patients' values when making decisions for patients, and some have explicitly suggested that a discussion of values should be part of the conversation that patients have with their surrogates. What this chapter proposes differs significantly in that it brings the role of values into the surrogate decision-making process at an earlier stage: to consider values not only when determining *how* the surrogate should act, but also to consider values when determining *who* should act as surrogate.

When matching surrogates and patients based on values, a perfect match is highly unlikely. Therefore, it will be important to identify the values that are most important for the patient and the surrogate to share. As a general matter, the greatest weight should be placed on values that have the greatest impact on the most important and fundamental treatment choices. Three types of values should thus be given special consideration: (1) values that are most predictive of treatment choices; (2) values that remain stable over time; and (3) foundational values that individuals employ to prioritize among other values. Values related to prioritizing among goals are important because many of the most difficult and fundamental treatment decisions involve making tradeoffs between desired outcomes—for example, between prolonging life and minimizing pain (Karel et. al. 2007).

Further research would be helpful to better understand which values are most important to treatment decisions, in part because current research on the impact of values on treatment decisions tends to examine the impact of patients' values and not the impact of surrogates' values. Nevertheless, existing research provides some insight into which types of values are likely to meet the criteria. McDade-Montez et al. found that differences in spirituality, moral strictness, and conservativeness between newlywed husbands and wives were correlated with wives making less accurate predictions of husbands' preferences (McDade-Montez et al. 2013). Thus, surrogates who are similar in terms of these three characteristics may be preferable to those who are not. Research indicating which values affect patients' own treatment choices (for example, Scheunemann et al. 2012) may also help identify values that are particularly important to share since surrogates project their own values.

Operationalizing Shared Preferences and Values Surrogate Selection

Methods for operationalizing a shared preferences and values approach to surrogate selection vary based on the type of surrogate in question. Individuals executing advance directives should favor surrogates with similar values and preferences. Thus, when deciding whom to appoint, individuals should discuss not only their own preferences but also the potential surrogate's preferences for her own care. Such discussions may be particularly valuable when young persons are being considered as surrogates, as some evidence suggests that younger surrogates may be more likely to project their values onto patients (Fagerlin et al. 2001). Similarly, courts should consider potential guardians' healthcare-related preferences and values; courts should favor appointment of individuals whose preferences for their own care mirror, or at least are closely aligned with, what the person subject to guardianship is known (or, if actual knowledge is not possible, reasonably believed) to have wanted. If the relevant preferences cannot be ascertained, courts should favor appointing individuals whose healthcare-related values appear consistent with those of the person subject to guardianship.

Finally, states should allow default surrogate decision-makers to be selected based in part on their personal beliefs, not merely their familial status.[3] Familial status is certainly relevant, in part because of human tendency to choose spouses and mates who share important values (McDade-Montez 2013). However, instead of prioritizing potential surrogates based solely on their relationship to the patients, states should consider authorizing a group of "interested persons" to, based on a facilitated discussion, select a surrogate for the patient whose relevant preferences and values most closely match those of the patient. A less radical alternative would be for states to continue to adhere to priority lists based on relationship but nevertheless allow the extent to which potential surrogates' preferences and values match those of the incapacitated patient to determine whom is selected as a surrogate within a common class (for example, which adult child or which sibling is selected).

Fully implementing a shared preferences and values approach to surrogate selection will require law reform. Changes to state statutes authorizing default surrogate decision-makers will be necessary in most jurisdictions. However, a shared preferences and values approach could be largely implemented without legal reform.

Most surrogate decision-makers are selected by patients themselves; thus, attorneys and others counseling individuals about advance planning can have a significant impact on surrogate selection by recommending that individuals consider potential surrogates' values when deciding whom to appoint. Specifically, those executing advance directives should be counseled to interview potential surrogates about what they would want done for themselves in situations of importance to the principal, and choose surrogates whose answers closely mirror theirs.

One way for attorneys and other counselors to encourage this approach to surrogate selection would be with a remarkably simple behavioral nudge: challenging individuals' assumptions about surrogates' behavior by introducing them to new information. Specifically, counselors should inform those selecting surrogates that relating treatment preferences to even well-meaning surrogates has little effect on increasing the likelihood that they will act accordingly, and that the best predictor of what surrogates choose for others is what they would choose for themselves.

While currently individuals select surrogates based primarily on familial relationship, this pattern of preference might well change if individuals had a more accurate understanding of how surrogates make decisions. Specifically, they might select different surrogates if they understood that even "trustworthy" and well-meaning family members frequently fail to act according to patient wishes, and that the best predictor of what surrogates choose for others is what they would choose for themselves. Especially given such information, prioritizing surrogates based on matched values and preferences might be very attractive to those executing advance directives. When surrogate selection is said to be based on "trust" or "loyalty," principals may send (or may fear sending) the message that family members not selected are somehow disloyal or untrustworthy. The ability to offer those rejected as surrogates an alternative explanation—one not based on such moral criticism—could hold significant appeal. By explicitly mentioning this emotional and relationship-protecting benefit, attorneys and other counselors could further encourage the use of a matched preferences and values approach.

Just as individuals could choose to use a shared preferences and values approach when selecting their own surrogates, judges could consider such factors when appointing surrogates. State guardianship statutes would need to be amended before judges could be required to consider shared values and preferences; however, judges could consider such factors even without legal reform because judges have significant discretion when choosing among potential guardians. If judges are to use their discretion in this matter, however, they need to be educated about the limitations of existing methods for selecting surrogates and about the phenomenon of projection. This education should be robust and evidence-based so that judges feel comfortable querying would-be guardians about personal beliefs; otherwise, such inquiries might well be considered inappropriate, irrelevant, or even prejudicial.

Of course, it will not be possible in any of the three systems to operationalize a shared preferences and values approach to surrogate selection with perfect accuracy. Even aside from the problem that no two people are exactly alike, assessing the degree to which preferences are shared is complicated by the fact that we can never truly know the preferences of incapacitated persons. Moreover, although values related to healthcare treatment tend to be relatively stable (Karel et al. 2007), health status interacts with people's healthcare preferences such that the value they place on their own life—and thus on potentially life-sustaining treatment—has a tendency to increase as health status worsens (Winter and Parks 2012).

Advantages of a Shared Preferences and Values Approach

In addition to increasing the likelihood that surrogates will make treatment choices that a patient would have made if capable, a shared preferences and values approach has the advantage of drawing attention to the value-laden nature of treatment decisions. This, in turn, may help surrogates recognize that they should consider patients' values, not simply medical information, when making treatment decisions.

Another advantage of a shared values and preference approach is that it may allow for more flexible decision-making. To protect their wishes, individuals are often urged to provide surrogates with explicit instructions as to the care that they do and do not wish to receive. Detailed instructions, however, may not result in treatment decisions that are consistent with patients' specific treatment preferences because such preferences often evolve over time.[4] In addition, many patients want surrogates to have the leeway to make context-specific decisions (Sehgal et al. 1992). Choosing a surrogate based on shared values may reduce the extent to which patients need, or feel they need, to reify treatment preferences in their advance directives, and thus may allow for the type of context-specific decision-making that patients often favor.

Conclusion

Surrogate decision-makers frequently fail to predict patients' treatment preferences, in part because they tend to project their own preferences onto patients. Healthcare decision-making for incapacitated persons can be improved by capitalizing on this tendency. Specifically, the likelihood that surrogates will make the decisions patients would make for themselves can be increased by selecting surrogates based, at least in part, on the extent to which they share the patient's treatment preferences. Where patients' specific preferences are not known, or where patients care less about specific treatment decisions than about making decisions consistent with their underlying values, surrogates should be selected based at least in part on the extent to which they share the patient's relevant values. Incorporating a shared preferences and values approach into the practice and law of surrogate selection could thus both increase the frequency with which surrogates make the decisions patients want made and facilitate more context-appropriate treatment decisions.

Fully incorporating a shared values and preferences approach into the law of surrogate decision-making would require legal reform, but the approach could be adopted in most instances with far less formality. Specifically, individuals and judges selecting among surrogates could be encouraged to use this alternative model by introducing them to simple information that challenges their assumptions about how surrogates make decisions. Thus, as with many other areas of healthcare-related behavior, decisions with regard to surrogate selection could be improved with a small nudge.

Notes

1. The term "advance directive" is a broad one that encompasses documents that appoint a surrogate healthcare decision-maker, documents that state future healthcare preferences (for example, living wills), and documents that do both (as is the case with most healthcare proxies).
2. The literature, of course, has significant limitations. It is impossible to conclusively determine whether or not a surrogate decision-maker has made the decision an incapacitated patient would have made for herself and thus the literature is, ultimately, speculative in nature. The literature is based largely on studies in which individuals with capacity predict their future treatment choices, and those choices are compared to those their surrogates report they would make under the same conditions. Such studies are premised on two potentially problematic assumptions: (1) that surrogates and patients have similar decision-making patterns in hypothetical situations and in actual treatment situations; and (2) that an individual's current, pre-incapacity wishes are strongly indicative of her subsequent, post-incapacity wishes.

3. Professor Blumenthal and I suggested this idea in an earlier article, including it as one of several ways default surrogate decision-making processes might be improved on (Kohn and Blumenthal 2008).
4. Especially in jurisdictions that require clear and convincing evidence of patient wishes to terminate life-sustaining treatment, including detailed instructions is nevertheless critical for patients who want to ensure that the surrogate will be permitted to terminate such treatment.

References

Bedell, Susanna E., and Thomas L. Delbanco. 1984. "Choices about Cardiopulmonary Resuscitation in the Hospital: When Do Physicians Talk with Patients?" *New England Journal of Medicine* 310(17):1089–93.

Bryant, Jessica, et al. 2013. "The Accuracy of Surrogate Decision Makers: Informed Consent in Hypothetical Acute Stroke Scenarios." *BioMed Emergency Medicine* 13:18.

Cicirelli, Victor G. 1992. *Family Caregiving: Autonomous and Paternalistic Decision Making.* Sage Publications, Inc. Newbury Park, CA. 104.

Ciroldi, Magali, et al. 2007. "Ability of Family Members to Predict Patient's Consent to Critical Care Research." *Intensive Care Medicine* 33(5):807–13.

Coppola, Kristen M., et al. 2001. "Accuracy of Primary Care and Hospital-Based Physicians' Predictions of Elderly Outpatients' Treatment Preferences with and without Advance Directives." *Archives of Internal Medicine* 161(3):431–40.

Ditto, Peter H., et al. 2001. "Advance Directives as Acts of Communication: A Randomized Controlled Trial." *Archives of Internal Medicine* 161(3):421–30.

Fagerlin, Angela, et al. 2001. "Projection in Surrogate Decisions about Life-Sustaining Medical Treatments." *Health Psychology* 20(3):166–75, 171.

———. 2002. "The Use of Advance Directives in End-of-Life Decision Making: Problems and Possibilities." *American Behavioral Scientist* 46(2):268–83, 275–76.

Hare, J., et al. 1992. "Agreement between Patients and Their Self-Selected Surrogates on Difficult Medical Decisions." *Archives of Internal Medicine* 152(5):1049–54, 1050.

Houts, Renate M., et al. 2002. "Predicting Elderly Outpatients' Life-Sustaining Treatment Preferences over Time: The Majority Rules." *Medical Decision Making* 22(1):39–52, 46.

Karel, Michele J., et al. 2007. "Three Methods of Assessing Values for Advance Care Planning: Comparing Persons with and without Dementia." *Journal of Aging & Health* 19(1):123–51, 145.

Kelly, Brenna, et al. 2012. "Systematic Review: Individuals' Goals for Surrogate Decision-Making." *Journal of the American Geriatrics Society* 60(5):884–95.

Kohn, Nina A., and Jeremy A. Blumenthal. 2008. "Designating Health Care Decision-Makers for Patients without Advance Directives: A Psychological Critique." *Georgia Law Review* 42:979–1018.

Mantravadi, Anand V., et al. 2007. "Accuracy of Surrogate Decision Making in Elective Surgery." *Journal of Cataract & Refractive Surgery* 33(12):2091–97.

Marks, Melissa A. Z., and Hal R. Arkes. 2008. "Patient and Surrogate Disagreement in End-of-Life Decisions: Can Surrogates Accurately Predict Patients' Preferences?" *Medical Decision Making* 28(4):524–31, 529.

Matheis-Kraft, Carol, and Karen A. Roberto. 1997. "Influences of a Values Discussion on Congruence between Elderly Women and Their Families on Critical Health Care Decisions." *Journal of Women & Aging* 9(4):5–22.

McDade-Montez, Elizabeth, et al. 2013. "Similarity, Agreement, and Assumed Similarity in Proxy End-of-Life Decision Making." *Family Systems & Health* 31(4):366–81, 377.

Moorman, Sara M., Robert M. Hauser, and Deborah Carr. 2009. "Do Older Adults Know Their Spouses End-of-Life Treatment Preferences?" *Journal of Aging Research* 31(4):463–91.

National Conference of Commissioners on Uniform State Laws. 1994. *Uniform Health-Care Decisions Act.*

Newman, Julia T., et al. 2012. "Surrogate and Patient Discrepancy Regarding Consent for Critical Care Research." *Critical Care Medicine* 40(9):2590–94.

Ouslander, Joseph G., et al. 1989. "Health Care Decisions among Elderly Long-Term Care Residents and Their Potential Proxies." *Archives of Internal Medicine* 149(6):1367–72.

Pearlman, Robert A., et al. 2005. "Improvements in Advance Care Planning in the Veterans Affairs System." *Archives of Internal Medicine* 165(6):667–74, 671.

Reamy, Allison M., et al. 2011. "Understanding Discrepancy in Perceptions of Values: Individuals with Mild to Moderate Dementia and Their Family Caregivers." *The Gerontologist* 51(4):473–483.

Principe-Rodriguez, Karen, et al. 1999. "Substituted Judgment: Should Life-Support Decisions Be Made by a Surrogate?" *Puerto Rico Health Sciences Journal* 18(4):405–9.

Scheunemann, Leslie P., et al. 2012. "The Facilitated Values History: Helping Surrogates Make Authentic Decisions for Incapacitated Patients with Advanced Illness." *American Journal of Respiratory and Critical Care Medicine* 186(6):480–86, 481.

Seckler, Allison B., et al. 1991. "Substituted Judgment: How Accurate Are Proxy Predictions?" *Annals of Internal Medicine* 115(2):92–98.

Sehgal, Ashwini, et al. 1992. "How Strictly Do Dialysis Patients Want Their Advance Directives Followed?" *Journal of the American Medical Association* 267(1):59–63.

Shalowitz, David I., et al. 2006. "The Accuracy of Surrogate Decision Makers: A Systematic Review." *Archives of Internal Medicine* 166(5):493–97, 494.

Smucker, William D., et al. 2000. "Modal Preferences Predict Elderly Patients' Life-Sustaining Treatment Choices as Well as Patients' Chosen Surrogates Do." *Medical Decision Making* 20(3):271–80, 273.

Suhl, Jeremiah, et al. 1994. "Myth of Substituted Judgment: Surrogate Decision Making Regarding Life Support Is Unreliable." *Archives of Internal Medicine* 154(1):90–96, 93, table 4.

Tomlinson, Tom, et al. 1990. "An Empirical Study of Proxy Consent for Elderly Persons." *The Gerontologist* 30(1):54–64, 59.

Uhlmann, R. F., et al. 1988. "Physicians' and Spouses' Predictions of Elderly Patients' Resuscitation Preferences." *Journal of Gerontology* 43(5):M115–M121, M117.

Vig, Elizabeth K., et al. 2006. "Beyond Substituted Judgment: How Surrogates Navigate End-of-Life Decision-Making." *Journal of the American Geriatrics Society* 54(11):1688–93.

Warren, John W., et al. 1986. "Informed Consent by Proxy: An Issue in Research with Elderly Patients." *New England Journal of Medicine* 315(18):1124–28, 1127.

Whitton, Linda S., and Lawrence A. Frolik. 2012. "Surrogate Decision-Making Standards for Guardians: Theory and Reality." *Utah Law Review* 2012:1491–1538.

Winter, Laraine, and Susan M. Parks. 2012. "Elders' Preferences for Life-Prolonging Treatment and Their Proxies' Substituted Judgment: Influence of the Elders' Current Health." *Journal of Aging & Health* 24(7):1157–78.

Zweibel, Nancy R., and Christine K. Cassel. 1989. "Treatment Choices at the End of Life: A Comparison of Decisions by Older Patients and Their Physician-Selected Proxies." *The Gerontologist* 29(5):615–21.

CHAPTER 22

Consumer Protection in Genome Sequencing

Barbara J. Evans

High-throughput DNA sequencing—also called next-generation sequencing, or NGS—rapidly tests all or part of a person's genomic DNA. A typical person displays on the order of 3 million genetic variants if the whole genome is sequenced, and an exome (the 1.5% of the genome that holds the roughly 20,000 human genes) typically contains around 10,000 variants (U.S. Food and Drug Administration 2014; Evans et al. 2014). There is wide debate about how to keep patients and research participants (together, "consumers") safe as this tsunami of genomic information rolls over them.

Genomic testing itself carries virtually no risk because it only requires a blood draw or other low-risk tissue sampling. The perceived consumer safety risks are in the nature of consequential harms that may occur if people react badly to information the tests reveal. Two major categories of risk are: (1) psychosocial harm if, for example, genomic information makes consumers anxious; and (2) harmful follow-up behaviors, such as pursuing unnecessary or injurious medical treatments to mitigate erroneously perceived health risks (see literature review in Evans 2014a). In 1999, the National Bioethics Advisory Commission noted that many experts "prefer to avoid such harms by controlling the flow of information to subjects and by limiting communications to those that constitute reliable information" (National Bioethics Advisory Commission 1999, 71).

From a First Amendment standpoint, the fact that information may cause psychosocial harm is a dubious basis for consumer safety regulations. The government does not have a substantial interest in keeping people from experiencing anxiety in response to factual information. "Speech remains protected even when it may . . . 'inflict great pain'" (*Sorrell v. IMS Health, Inc.* 2011, 2653). Claims about the clinical meaning of gene

This research was supported by the Greenwall Foundation and the University of Houston Law Foundation.

variants are subject to scientific uncertainty, but this fact alone does not make them inherently misleading in a way that avoids the First Amendment problem (see Evans 2014a for a review of cases). Moreover, the available evidence does not bear out that consumers actually experience the alleged psychosocial harms (Vayena and Prainsack 2013).

This leaves another possible rationale for consumer safety regulation: that it is necessary to prevent harmful follow-up behaviors in response to test results. The U.S. Food and Drug Administration (FDA) embraced this rationale, citing concern that consumers might seek inappropriate follow-up medical procedures in its 2013 warning letter to direct-to-consumer genetic testing service 23andMe (Gutierrez 2013) and in its 2014 discussion paper on NGS (U.S. Food and Drug Administration 2014). If the major goal in regulating NGS is to manage harmful post-testing behaviors, then behavioral economics offers a natural lens for focusing the ongoing debate about how NGS should be regulated.

This chapter explores current policies that aim to protect people from making bad medical decisions in response to uncertain genomic information. It specifically questions the choice architecture these approaches create and identifies several conceptual problems when applying these approaches to NGS. The chapter reframes the problem of making genomic testing safe for consumers and concludes that mere nudges may not suffice, if the goal is to transform the genomic testing industry in ways that can optimize consumer safety.

Protecting Consumers from Genetic Uncertainty

Many bioethicists, physicians, and scientists counsel against letting individuals receive genetic findings if the clinical significance is not well understood (see, for example, National Bioethics Advisory Commission 1999; Bookman et al. 2006; Fabsitz et al. 2010; Knoppers et al. 2006; Wolf et al. 2008). This approach seeks to protect people by controlling what they can be told or by channeling information through learned intermediaries whose involvement, it is hoped, may prevent bad medical decisions. The aim is to prevent people from using poorly validated, uncertain genetic information in self-destructive ways.

When a consumer undergoes NGS, the final laboratory report typically interprets the clinical significance of only a handful of the variants detected. At present, the vast majority of findings are variants of uncertain significance (VUS) and are not reported to the patient and doctor but may remain stored at the laboratory. These variants have unknown clinical validity and clinical utility/actionability. Clinical validity refers to the presence of a strong, well-validated association between a gene variant and a specific health condition or predisposition (Secretary's Advisory Committee on Genetic Testing 2000). It bears on whether a genetic finding has an "established" clinical meaning (Fabsitz et al. 2010, 575). Clinical utility or actionability, on the other hand, depends on whether medical science, at its current stage of development, offers options to mitigate the disease risks associated with a particular gene variant (Secretary's Advisory Committee on Genetic Testing 2000, 15). Fabsitz et al. defined "actionable" as meaning that "disclosure has the potential to lead to an improved health outcome; there must be established therapeutic or preventive interventions available or other available actions that may change the course of the disease," although some members of their working group dissented on the basis that personal meaning, such as usefulness in life planning, should also justify sharing information with individuals (Fabsitz et al. 2010, 575, 578).

Genomic science is in the earliest stages of its development. This was seen in guidelines the American College of Medical Genetics (ACMG) published in 2013 (Green et al. 2013) concerning the return of incidental findings in clinical genome sequencing. They concluded that 57 specific gene variants (involving 56 different genes) have a clear enough clinical validity and actionability to warrant a deliberate search whenever gene sequencing is performed. Another study identified 90 to 125 variants that merit evaluation for clinical significance during gene sequencing (Dewey et al. 2014). These figures are a mere sliver of the millions of possible variants.

The regulatory challenge is to protect individuals in the face of this systemic ignorance. Over the past twenty years there have been many calls for the FDA to regulate genetic tests as medical devices and conduct premarket review to ensure that tests have clinical validity before they can be marketed to consumers (see, for example, NIH-DOE Task Force 1997; Secretary's Advisory Committee on Genetic Testing 2000, 10–11). The FDA's 2014 framework for regulating laboratory-developed tests proposed to require proof of clinical validity before tests can be cleared or approved for clinical use (79 Fed. Reg. 59,776 (Oct. 3, 2014)). As applied to genomic testing, requiring premarket review of clinical validity has several conceptual problems—a point that even the FDA acknowledged in its later discussion paper on NGS (U.S. Food and Drug Administration 2014).

Dubious Consumer Protection

If the FDA required premarket review of claims that gene variants have clinical validity, laboratories would be unable to give consumers any information about the potential health impact of variants whose significance is uncertain or not yet well established. This would create a choice architecture in which individuals would be allowed to make medical decisions based on their genetic information only when the available data are capable of supporting a wise decision. Giving people clinically valid information does not, of course, guarantee that they will make good choices based on it, but it does tend to prevent bad choices, albeit through the brute force tactic of suppressing individual choice altogether. The problem is that this approach eliminates the possibility that people might make good decisions—either directly, based on the available if fuzzy data, or indirectly because they feel empowered and interested in their health.

There is growing awareness that paternalistic understandings of patient well-being may be counterproductive in the face of behavior-dependent chronic diseases, against which physicians may have little to offer beyond general "do's" and "don'ts" that patients themselves are expected to monitor and enforce (Christenson, Grossman, and Hwang 2009). Restricting patients' access to information casts them as inept and dependent and works against the sense of self-mastery patients need in order to manage their ongoing wellness. More broadly, shifting from a disease-oriented model of medicine to a more prospective, wellness-oriented approach requires active patient involvement (Snyderman and Yoediono 2008) that requires patient data access. Embracing these concepts, the U.S. Department of Health and Human Services (HHS) issued a final rule (79 Fed. Reg. 7290–7316 (Feb. 6, 2014)) amending two of its regulations: the Health Insurance Portability and Accountability Act (HIPAA) Privacy Rule (45 C.F.R. Parts 160, 164) and the Clinical Laboratory Improvement Amendments (CLIA) of 1988 regulations (42 C.F.R. Parts 493). The changes expand consumers' direct access to their own genetic and other diagnostic information held by HIPAA-covered laboratories. HHS acted out of concern that barriers to laboratory data access were "preventing patients from having a more active role in their personal healthcare decisions" (79 Fed. Reg. 7,290 (Feb. 6, 2014)).

Laboratory-held data, as noted earlier, may include uninterpreted variant data that were stored at the lab but not included in the final test report. Thus, consumers now may be able to discover gene variants they possess, yet the FDA's proposed policies apparently would limit what they can be told about the potential clinical significance of those variants. Premarket review may frustrate consumers without necessarily protecting them: variant files are typically stored in electronic form, and consumers who want to explore the meaning of their variants seemingly could avail themselves of unregulated on-line genetic interpretation services or transmit their files offshore for interpretation if the FDA's premarket review process prevents domestic laboratories from making clinical claims.

Lack of Scalability

The bioethical debate about return of incidental findings in genomic research (Wolf 2008; Wolf et al. 2008) has helped shape the debate about regulation of genomic testing more generally, including in the clinical setting. This is not necessarily desirable because the two contexts differ in important ways. Deciding whether to return an incidental genetic finding to a particular patient or human research subject is a small-scale problem. The genetic test already has been performed, and the question is whether a specific finding should be shared with the tested individual. An ethical review body, when making this decision, possesses perfect information about which gene variant the individual actually possesses. Clinical validity and actionability only need to be assessed for that specific gene variant. It is known that research subject A carries genetic variant X, and the question is whether variant X is well enough understood to warrant returning this information to subject A. That is a narrowly bounded inquiry.

This same basic approach—requiring prior proof of clinical validity—is not scalable to the far larger problem of deciding whether a new genetic test can safely be sold to consumers. A new genetic test—even if it is a test for a single gene—may detect hundreds of variants of that gene, all having different levels of clinical validity and utility/actionability. The concepts of clinical validity and utility have meaning only at the level of specific gene variants. These concepts are indeterminate for the gene itself, with all its conceivable variants, and for a genetic test, which may detect a whole array of variants of each gene that it examines. Health characteristics do not actually depend on genes because we all have the same genes; our health instead depends on which variants we have, and even when a variant is known, its clinical impact may depend on its interactions with other genes and environmental exposures as well as on the consumer's clinical history (U.S. Food and Drug Administration 2014). The concept of clinical validity becomes murky when applied to genomic testing.

The FDA's premarket review process has merit as applied to single-analyte in vitro diagnostic test, such as a strep test or a test to detect the presence or absence of a particular gene variant. But there are over 20,000 human genes, and each of them can be defective in a multitude of ways. Each gene, in effect, comprises an entire fleet of variants; individual patients are like passengers who ride on different variants in that fleet. Under its premarket review process, the FDA can clear or approve a new genetic test based on evidence that *one* of the gene's variants has clinical validity. Premarket review does not, however, ensure safety and effectiveness of the entire fleet. The agency does not—and indeed cannot—require evidence establishing the clinical validity of every variant genomic testing may detect because the full range of variations in a particular gene can only be discovered after the test is in wide commercial use.

As applied to genetic tests, the FDA's premarket review process is analogous to a hypothetical airline safety regulation that requires each airline to prove that *one* of its planes is airworthy. Passengers who end up on that plane will be safe, but what about the others? An FDA-cleared or approved genetic test only returns well-validated results for patients who, after testing, turn out to have the discrete gene variant(s) for which the FDA reviewed evidence of clinical validity and utility. The fact that the test is safe and effective for those patients does not imply that it is safe and effective for all. Patients carrying the gene's other possible variants will receive clinically nonvalidated results, even though the test is FDA-cleared or approved. They may gain a false sense of security upon learning that they do not have the specific deleterious mutation(s) for which the FDA reviewed evidence, even if they have an even worse mutation whose clinical significance is not yet known. Premarket review is simply not the right tool for assessing clinical validity of genomic testing; the problem demands an ongoing process of evidence generation throughout the postmarketing period after tests are cleared or approved (Evans, Burke, and Jarvik 2015).

Unlearned Intermediaries

The scalability problem suggests a useful role for learned intermediaries to help guide patients' decisions in response to genomic test results. Consumers initially seemed comfortable with this approach. A 1998 survey of patient attitudes found that 70% viewed their primary care doctor as their first choice for information about genetic issues, and 80% had confidence that their primary care provider could advise them on these matters (Secretary's Advisory Committee on Genetic Testing 2008). Unfortunately, a 1999 National Cancer Institute study of 1,251 randomly selected physicians found that only 40% of primary care doctors and 57% of tertiary care doctors felt qualified to recommend genetic tests for cancer susceptibility, and 75% of the surveyed physicians bemoaned the lack of clear management guidelines for patients with positive test results (Secretary's Advisory Committee on Genetic Testing 2008).

Ten years after those surveys, patients and patient advocates commenting in the recent CLIA-HIPAA rulemaking uniformly supported direct patient access to laboratory data (Individual Comments 2011). Some claimed strong dignitary, liberty, and even property interests in access to their own test results. Others—and this was particularly true of self-identified chronic-disease patients—doubted whether physicians reliably interpret and convey information that patients need to know and argued that, to be safe, patients must monitor decision-making by harried, overworked medical professionals (Individual Comments 2011). In the preamble to the CLIA-HIPAA final rule, HHS cited empirical evidence that physicians fail to inform patients of abnormal test results about 7% of the time (79 Fed. Reg. 7293 (Feb. 6, 2014)). Patients worry that physicians' paternalistic aspirations outstrip physicians' actual competence to protect them. All the patients who commented in the proceeding wanted direct, disintermediated access to their own test information.

The central safety problem—now and for many decades into the future—is that there are so many conceivable variants of the roughly 20,000 human genes, yet so little understanding of what most of them mean in terms of their impact on human health. At this primitive stage of the genomic era, learned intermediaries are little wiser than the rest of us. To borrow words from Nietzsche, the godlike learned intermediary of twentieth-century medicine is dead.

Evolving Industry Structure

The CLIA-HIPAA amendments enhance individual access to uninterpreted genomic data and may stimulate demand for stand-alone genomic interpretation services to help clarify the meaning of the data people receive. The unbundling of genomic testing and interpretation already was under way before these changes went into effect. It may render traditional health and safety regulatory strategies obsolete.

A recent landscape analysis examined sixty-eight companies that are active in one or more of the vertically related segments of the genome sequencing industry (Curnutte et al. 2014). An upstream supply segment sells equipment and consumables (such as sequencing instruments, software, and reagents) for use in genome sequencing. A pre-analytic phase involves collecting, shipping, and processing patients' biospecimens prior to sequencing at a laboratory. The analytic or test administration phase performs sequencing, alignment, and base calling. Post-analytic segments identify the patient's variants, interpret their significance, prepare reports, and store data (Curnutte et al. 2014, 981).

Of the sixty-eight companies examined, only a handful display vertical integration into most or all segments of the business (Curnutte et al. 2014). Forty-one of the companies conduct sequencing—that is, they operate laboratories engaged in test administration. These forty-one companies differ in the degree to which they are integrated downstream into genomic interpretation and data storage. Ten of the forty-one laboratories offer unbundled sequencing—in other words, they provide "data-only" services that produce sequencing data without interpreting the clinical significance of variants detected. Conversely, the landscape analysis found twenty-one companies that provide unbundled interpretation services without administering tests (Curnutte 2014).

Several factors are driving this unbundling of test administration and genomic interpretation (Evans 2014b). Court decisions in *Association for Molecular Pathology (AMP) v. Myriad Genetics* (2013, 2107) and *Mayo Collaborative Services v. Prometheus Laboratories* (2012, 1289) weakened patent protections and fostered competitive entry into some industry segments. Another crucial factor is that sequencing data, if consistently formatted, have the potential to be interoperable across companies. Results of traditional (nongenetic) laboratory tests tended not to be interoperable because laboratories used different reagents and testing processes with different reference ranges for a positive test result. Labs could not necessarily interpret the clinical significance of each other's uninterpreted test results. In contrast, the line-up of a patient's genomic nucleotides is a fact of nature. Assuming a laboratory used analytically valid methods that correctly identified the patient's variants, any number of service providers may be able to interpret the clinical significance of those variants. As HHS noted in the CLIA-HIPAA preamble, "[p]atients today are much better informed and have access to interpretive information on laboratory results from many sources, including the internet" (79 Fed. Reg. 7295 (Feb. 6, 2014)). Patients no longer must rely on the lab that performed a test to interpret its meaning for them.

The major patient safety challenge in sequencing does not relate to detecting variants. The FDA notes that there are some unresolved challenges in assessing the analytical validity of genomic tests (U.S. Food and Drug Administration 2014), but sequencing technology is capable of detecting which variants a person has with a fair degree of accuracy; if in doubt, the variants can be confirmed using other accepted technologies like Sanger sequencing or an alternative FDA-cleared sequencing analyzer. The real safety challenge lies in genomic interpretation: will consumers receive accurate advice about what their gene variants mean?

Stand-alone interpretation services threaten to slip through the sieve of existing health and safety regulatory frameworks. If interpretation is not tied to a testing device or laboratory testing process, it seemingly eludes the jurisdiction of the CLIA and FDA regulations (Javitt and Corner 2014). Attempts to regulate it also raise subtle First Amendment concerns. Genomic interpretation is in the nature of speech (Evans 2014a). If courts view it as the practice of medicine, genomic interpretation is potentially regulable as professional speech; however, the right regulators seemingly would be the state medical practice boards, and intrusive CLIA or FDA regulation arouses federalism concerns (Evans 2014a). If interpretation is treated as commercial speech, it can be federally regulated, but only within constitutional constraints. Blocking all discussion of variants that lack well-established clinical validity appears to violate these constraints, although regulators may be able to impose less-extensive restrictions, such as requiring frank disclosure of the uncertainties inherent in genomic interpretation (Evans 2014a). If courts venture farther and conclude that compiling and distributing current scientific hypotheses and conclusions about the meaning of specific gene variants is pure speech, this could virtually foreclose the regulation of stand-alone genomic interpretation services, to the extent their activities fit that description (Evans 2014a).

The safety-critical segment of gene sequencing (genomic interpretation) is separable from the business activities that current regulations were designed to regulate (supply of devices and consumables in the case of the FDA's regulations, and test administration in the case of CLIA). In this respect, the current regulatory frameworks are obsolete.

Reframing the Consumer Safety Challenge

Ensuring the best attainable protection for persons who undergo genomic testing requires regulators to engage with a neglected policy challenge. That challenge is to craft policies that will, as quickly as possible, reduce the high level of uncertainty that presently surrounds the clinical significance of genomic findings. Current policies focus on optimizing the choices patients and research subjects make in the face of this uncertainty, taking a static view of the uncertainty itself and treating it as a parameter over which policymakers have no control (Evans, Burke, and Jarvik 2015). Policymakers' only role is to manipulate consumers' choices by blocking their access to information that regulators deem too uncertain or by inserting intermediaries who may help consumers respond to uncertainty in a rational way (Evans, Burke, and Jarvik 2015).

The flaw of these approaches was captured by the geneticist Greg Lennon: "It's not reasonable to think there's some specific date—May 18, 2035—that the genome will all make sense, and that's the day you are allowed to see it" (Regalado 2014b). Current policies leave regulators passively waiting for a hypothetical future date when genomic uncertainty will be resolved. Then, the FDA can clear all genetic tests before they go on the market, consumers can hear their results, and the world once again will be safe for the First Amendment.

Policymakers obviously cannot, by stroke of a regulatory wand, banish the uncertainty of genomic interpretation, but there is a way that they could hasten its resolution. That way lies in implementing appropriate data access policies. Genomic uncertainty is dynamic. It grows smaller whenever a laboratory or an informaticist notices a new, statistically significant association between a gene variant and a health impact (Evans, Burke, and Jarvik 2015). Industry participants that have integrated downstream into data storage control crucial data resources. These resources make it possible to infer the clinical significance of novel gene variants, so that variants of uncertain significance are gradually transformed into variants of known significance. That knowledge, in turn, is the crucial input to make genomic interpretation as safe and effective as it can be at any given point in time. Genomic uncertainty can be conquered, but only by sharing information, including findings about the clinical significance of novel gene variants and the underlying data needed to reproduce and validate those findings (Evans 2014c).

Patient safety is optimized when all providers of genomic interpretation services render state-of-the-art services informed by the best available data about the clinical significance of all gene variants that any laboratory has previously detected (Evans 2014c). Regulatory policies that limit flows of information to consumers do nothing whatsoever to achieve this optimum. The right policy focus, instead, is to facilitate flows of information among suppliers of genomic testing services. The relevant choice architecture to manipulate is not the choices patients face as they respond to genomic uncertainty. The real challenge is to create choice architectures that encourage parties who know the clinical significance of specific gene variants to share their knowledge to facilitate high-quality, state-of-the-art genomic interpretation for all. Solving the data-sharing problem is the key to solving the health-and-safety problem.

Entities such as the National Institutes of Health (NIH) have promoted policies requiring data to be deposited into publicly accessible genomic data commons (Contreras 2014). These policies apply, however, only to data generated with public research funds—which accounts for a large share of genomic data generated in the past. That is starting to change, however, as gene sequencing moves into wider clinical use. As it does so, an ever-greater share of the available sequencing data will be generated at commercial clinical laboratories that are not bound by NIH data-sharing policies (Evans, Burke, and Jarvik 2015).

According to a recent estimate, 228,000 human genomes were sequenced by researchers around the globe by 2014 (Regalado 2014a). Inferring the clinical significance of gene variants requires extremely large-scale data resources, including data for hundreds of thousands to millions of people (Shirts et al. 2014). Research funding agencies like the NIH ultimately cannot pay to sequence the vast number of genomes that need to be studied in order to clarify the clinical significance of people's gene variants. Present uncertainties can only be reduced by harnessing data generated in clinical as well as research settings—that is, by harnessing proprietary data as well as data generated with public research funds (Evans, Burke, and Jarvik 2015).

The barriers to data access can be summarized as follows. Obviously, there are privacy concerns about sharing people's genomic and clinical data. Well-designed distributed data network infrastructures can mitigate these concerns, as was done in the FDA's large-scale Sentinel System drug safety surveillance system (McGraw, Rosati, and Evans 2012), but the infrastructure creation requires large investments of capital and cooperative effort (Evans 2014c). None of the sector-specific regulatory agencies that oversees genetic testing has authority to marshal the needed cooperation, investments, and data sharing (Evans 2014c). Commercial laboratories have no legal obligation to share what they know, and they face strong commercial incentives not to do so (Kularni and Ma 2013). Privacy laws further impede data sharing among HIPAA-covered clinical laboratories, and Omnibus revisions to the HIPAA Privacy Rule fell far short of creating a data-pricing structure that can incentivize the needed data sharing and provide sustainable financing for ongoing data infrastructure operations (Evans 2014c).

To make genomic interpretation safe for consumers, it is essential to address the industry's data access and infrastructure issues. After *Verizon Communications v. Law Offices of Curtis V. Trinko*, courts in the United States may be reluctant to intervene if laboratories that control crucial genomic data resources refuse to deal with competitors that need access. Making genomic interpretation safe for consumers ultimately may require regulatory solutions resembling nondiscriminatory access requirements imposed in other major infrastructure industries such as electric power transmission, natural gas pipelines, and telecommunications (Evans 2014c). Such solutions are not mere nudges; they apply legal coercion to ensure nondiscriminatory access to resources necessary to the public's convenience, safety, and health.

Conclusion

The goal of consumer safety regulation for genomic testing should be to ensure high-quality, state-of-the-art genomic interpretation services for all who undergo gene sequencing. This requires policies to ensure that all suppliers of genomic interpretation services have access to critical data resources—including proprietary data held by commercial clinical laboratories—on reasonable, nondiscriminatory terms. To achieve this, Congress may need to implement an economic regulatory scheme, as it has done in other critical infrastructure industries (Evans 2014c). Policymakers should not rule out noncoercive, market-oriented solutions, such as appropriate data-pricing schemes to incentivize voluntary data sharing. They should be aware, however, that the genomic testing industry differs from some other infrastructure industries in which coercive access solutions worked effectively because genomic data infrastructures are still in their early stages of development, with large future investments required. Dynamic efficiency is thus a concern, and forced data sharing could backfire if it deters investment in developing needed data resources and data infrastructures. Policymakers should nudge data holders to share data but understand that if nudges fail, consumer safety may ultimately require more forceful regulatory solutions. Consumers are not made safe by suppressing what they can be told. Rather, they are made safe by ensuring that what they are told is informed by the best available evidence.

References

Association for Molecular Pathology v. Myriad Genetics, Inc., 133 S.Ct. 2107 (2013).

Bookman, Ebony B., et al. 2006. "Reporting Genetic Results in Research Studies: Summary and Recommendations of an NHLBI Working Group." *American Journal of Medical Genetics Part A* 140(10):1033–40.

Christenson, Clayton M., Jerome H. Grossman, and Jason Hwang. 2009. *The Innovator's Prescription: A Disruptive Solution for Healthcare.* McGraw-Hill. New York. 160.

Contreras, Jorge L. 2014. "Constructing the Genome Commons." In *Governing Knowledge Commons*, edited by Brett M. Frischmann, Michael J. Madison, and Katherine J. Strandberg. Oxford University Press. New York. 99–135.

Curnutte, Margaret A., et al. 2014. "Development of the Clinical Next-Generation Sequencing Industry in a Shifting Policy Climate." *Nature Biotechnology* 32(10):980–82.

Dewey F. E., et al. 2014. "Clinical Interpretation and Implications of Whole-Genome Sequencing." *Journal of the American Medical Association* 311:1035–45.

Evans, Barbara J., 2014a. "The First Amendment Right to Speak about the Human Genome." *University of Pennsylvania Journal of Constitutional Law* 16(3):549–636, 568–83.

———. 2014b. "Mining the Human Genome after Association for Molecular Pathology v. Myriad Genetics." *Genetics in Medicine* 16(7):504–9.

———. 2014c. "Economic Regulation of Next-Generation Sequencing." *Journal of Law, Medicine, and Ethics* 42(Suppl.):51–66.

Evans, Barbara J., Wylie Burke, and Gail P. Jarvik, 2015. "The FDA and Genomic Tests—Getting Regulation Right." *New England Journal of Medicine* 372:2258–64.

Evans, Barbara J., Michael O. Dorschner, Wylie Burke, and Gail P. Jarvik. 2014. "Regulatory Changes Raise Troubling Questions for Genomic Testing." *Genetics in Medicine* 16(11):799–803.

Fabsitz, Richard R., et al. 2010. "Ethical and Practical Guidelines for Reporting Genetic Research Results to Study Participants: Updated Guidelines from a National Heart, Lung, and Blood Institute Working Group." *Circulation: Cardiovascular Genetics* 3(6):574–80.

Green, Robert C., et al. 2013. "ACMG Recommendations for Reporting of Incidental Findings in Clinical Exome and Genome Sequencing." *Genetics in Medicine* 15(7):565–74.

Gutierrez, Alberto. 2013. FDA Warning Letter to Ann Wojcicki, CEO, 23andMe, Inc. November 22. http://www.fda.gov/iceci/enforcementactions/warningletters/2013/ucm376296.htm.

Individual Comments. 2011. http://www.regulations.gov (referencing rulemaking file CMS-2011-0145), at document references CMS-2011-0145-0022, CMS-2011-0145-0035, CMS-2001-0145-0039, CMS-2011-0145-0063, CMS-2011-0145-0073, CMS-2011-0045-0079, CMS-2011-0145-0090, CMS-2011-0145-0104, CMS-2011-0145-0105, CMS-2011-0145-0120, CMS-2011-0145-0166.

Javitt, Gail H., and Katherine Strong Carner. 2014. "Regulation of Next Generation Sequencing." *Journal of Law, Medicine, and Ethics* 42(Suppl.):9–21, 17.

Knoppers, B. M., et al. 2006. "The Emergence of an Ethical Duty to Disclose Genetic Research Results: International Perspectives." *European Journal of Human Genetics* 14(11):1170–78.

Kularni, Samarth, and Philip Ma, eds. 2013. *Personalized Medicine: The Path Forward.* McKinsey & Company. New York. 34.

Mayo Collaborative Services v. Prometheus Laboratories, Inc., 132 S.Ct. 1289 (2012).

McGraw, Deven, Kristen Rosati, and Barbara Evans. 2012. "A Policy Framework for Public Health Uses of Electronic Health Data." *Pharmacoepidemiology & Drug Safety* 21(Suppl.):18–22.

National Bioethics Advisory Commission. 1999. *Research Involving Human Biological Materials: Ethical Issues and Policy Guidance, Vol. 1.* 71–72.

NIH-DOE Task Force (Joint National Institutes of Health–Department of Energy Working Group on Ethical, Legal, & Social Implications of Human Genome Research). 1997. Chapter 2 of *Promoting Safe and Effective Genetic Testing in the United States*, edited by Neil A. Holtzman and Michael S. Watson. http://www.genome.gov/10002404.

Regalado, Antonio. 2014a. "EmTech: Illumina Says 228,000 Human Genomes Will Be Sequenced This Year." *MIT Technology Review.* September 24. http://www.technologyreview.com/news/531091/emtech-illumina-says-228000-human-genomes-will-be-sequenced-this-year/.

———. 2014b. "How a Wiki Is Keeping Direct-to-Consumer Genetics Alive." *MIT Technology Review.* October. http://www.technologyreview.com/featuredstory/531461/how-a-wiki-is-keeping-direct-to-consumer-genetics-alive/.

Secretary's Advisory Committee on Genetics, Health, and Society (SACGHS). 2008. *U.S. System of Oversight of Genetic Testing: A Response to the Charge of the Secretary of Health and Human Services.* Pp. 151–52. http://osp.od.nih.gov/sites/default/files/SACGHS_oversight_report.pdf.

Secretary's Advisory Committee on Genetic Testing (SACGT). 2000. *Enhancing the Oversight of Genetic Tests.* P. 15. http://oba.od.nih.gov/oba/sacgt/reports/oversight_report.pdf.

Shirts, B. A., et al. 2014. "Large Numbers of Individuals Are Required to Classify and Define Risk for Rare Variants in Known Cancer Risk Genes." *Genetics in Medicine* 16(7):529–34.

Snyderman, Ralph, and Ziggy Yoediono. 2008. "Perspective: Prospective Health Care and the Role of Academic Medicine: Lead, Follow, or Get Out of the Way." *Academic Medicine* 83(8):707–14.

Sorrell v. IMS Health, Inc., 131 S. Ct. 2653, 2670 (2011) (quoting *Snyder v. Phelps*, 131 S. Ct. 1207, 1220 (2011)).

U.S. Food and Drug Administration. 2014. "Optimizing FDA's Regulatory Oversight of Next Generation Sequencing Diagnostic Tests—Preliminary Discussion Paper." December 29. http://www.fda.gov/downloads/medicaldevices/newsevents/workshopsconferences/ucm427869.pdf.

Vayena, Effy, and Barbara Prainsack. 2013. "Regulating Genomics: Time for a Broader Vision." *Science Translational Medicine* 5(198):198ed12.

Verizon Communications Inc. v. Law Offices of Curtis V. Trinko LLP, 540 U.S. 398 (2004).

Wolf, Susan M. 2008. "The Challenge of Incidental Findings." *Journal of Law, Medicine, and Ethics* 36(2):216–18.

Wolf, Susan M., et al. 2008. "Managing Incidental Findings in Human Subjects Research: Analysis and Recommendations." *Journal of Law, Medicine, and Ethics* 36(2):219–48, 235.

PART VII **DEFAULTS IN HEALTHCARE**

Introduction

Gregory Curfman

In making choices about healthcare, framing a decision as an opt-in or an opt-out may have important consequences for patients, providers, and the healthcare system as a whole. The opt-in approach has the advantage that it preserves active choice and avoids the criticism of paternalism. If, however, the choice is complex or difficult, the opt-in approach runs the risk of a wrong decision that may cause harm. In contrast, the opt-out approach may help to prevent a potentially harmful decision, while still preserving the option to overrule the default and make a different choice. This is why an opt-out default rule is sometimes, but not always, an attractive option in the healthcare setting.

Default rules have been used to accomplish various healthcare goals. For example, they have been applied to encourage the use of interventions that improve healthcare, to reduce the use of interventions that may be hazardous, and as a way to control healthcare spending and potentially benefit society as a whole. An example of the first application is a default rule that patients will receive pneumococcal vaccination unless they opt out, which may protect patients from acquiring this potentially serious bacterial infection. A default rule that intravenous catheters in hospitalized patients must be replaced on a fixed schedule may help to reduce catheter-associated infections. And a default to fill prescriptions with generics unless the provider overrides the default rule would help to reduce spending on prescription drugs. In each of these cases, defaults are used as nudges, but choice is preserved.

Even though default rules preserve choice, they have proved to be effective in influencing decision-making because of people's biases when faced with a making a choice. One such bias, called status quo bias, reflects the tendency for people to leave things as they are (inertia). Another type of bias, called omission bias, reflects an underlying fear of making an error of commission, and making things worse. Thus, even though default strategies preserve choice, people may be inclined to stay with the default.

The following two chapters provide further insights into the use of defaults in the healthcare setting. In "Forced to Choose, Again: The Effects of Defaults on Individuals in Terminated Health Plans," Anna D. Sinaiko and Richard J. Zeckhauser discuss the implications of a default to traditional Medicare when a person terminates from a Medicare Advantage plan; and in "Presumed Consent to Organ Donation," David Orentlicher provides an interesting examination of the controversial issue of a default policy regarding organ donation.

Although presumed consent for organ donation (an opt-out policy) is practiced in many European countries, law in the United States assumes that people do not want their organs to be removed after death unless they have given specific permission (an opt-in policy). While an opt-out policy would theoretically increase the supply of organs for transplantation and may save lives, it has been controversial in the United States and has never been implemented. Orentlicher points out that people may be more supportive of opt-out default policies if they are aimed to improve outcomes for the individual. In the case of organ donation, however, an opt-out default is solely altruistic and has no direct benefit to the potential donor. Some also worry about the definition of death ("brain death" versus "cardiac death") that might be applied for the trigger to harvest organs.

In a similar vein, Sinaiko and Zeckhauser examine default rules in health insurance. Medicare Advantage plans, which are administered by private insurers and typically offer more benefits than traditional Medicare, are often preferable to a substantial number of elderly people. The default to traditional Medicare may not fit the healthcare preferences of a person who has terminated a Medicare Advantage plan, which changes the network of available physicians. Instead, Sinaiko and Zeckhauser suggest the possibility of a "smart default," in which a system could analyze the degree of overlap in physician networks across Medicare Advantage plans in an area. They posit that an even more sophisticated algorithm could consider the person's previous physicians. A smart-default system could place a person into the plan most similar to the terminated plan, or into the plan where the physician network had the greatest degree of overlap with the previous plan. Traditional Medicare would be employed only as a backup to the selection by the smart default. The authors suggest that smart defaults would add nuance to default systems and may better meet the needs of consumers of healthcare.

Defaults as applied to healthcare decisions may serve a valuable purpose by "nudging" people toward decisions beneficial to their overall health, avoiding choices that may be adverse to their health, and benefiting society by controlling healthcare costs. The interesting chapters by Sinaiko and Zeckhauser, and by Orentlicher, remind us, however, that defaults may also have unintended consequences that need to be carefully considered before a default policy is put in place. In some circumstances, especially when the default option does not benefit the individual, an opt-out approach may not be widely acceptable. In other cases, smart defaults, which may refine the default process and sharpen the default decision, may be a preferable alternative. Given their potential benefits, we may fully anticipate that default options will continue to be part of the landscape in healthcare decisions.

CHAPTER 23

Forced to Choose, Again
The Effects of Defaults on Individuals in Terminated Health Plans

Anna D. Sinaiko and Richard J. Zeckhauser

The Affordable Care Act (ACA), the most significant U.S. health policy measure since Medicare was enacted in 1965, aims to improve outcomes in the market for health insurance and to reduce dramatically the percentage of uninsured people in the United States. At its center is the extension of private health insurance through new health insurance marketplaces, where regulated health plans are sold through a web-based portal and are subsidized based on enrollee income. Plans offered in the non-group market (both within and outside the marketplaces) must cover a defined essential benefit package and must be classified into one of four cost-sharing tiers (platinum, gold, silver, or bronze) that are defined by actuarial value, where the least generous plans (those offered in the bronze tier) are required to provide coverage for, on average, 60% of an individual's health costs.

In 2014, 3.8 million more Americans had health insurance than in the previous year, and more than 7 million individuals enrolled in health insurance plans through ACA marketplaces. However, 2.6 million people—18.6% of all individuals enrolled in a non-group health plan in 2013—received a notice canceling their plan for 2014 because it failed to meet the coverage requirements of the ACA (Clemans-Cope and Anderson 2014). Insurance coverage in the non-group market has always encountered frequent disruptions (Sommers 2014). However, the driver behind these cancellations is new: the requirements of federal legislation, specifically the ACA. Moreover, this tally does not count another group facing plan terminations driven in part by the ACA: individuals whose employers stopped offering coverage. Their numbers are not known.

Research for this essay was supported by the National Institute of Aging (P01 AG032952). We are grateful to Richard Frank for comments and helpful conversations on early versions of this work. Jeff Souza provided excellent research assistance. All errors are our own.

Media attention pushed these cancellations to the forefront of the policy debate, raising the possibility that the ACA hurt large numbers of individuals. Stories of terminated individuals were prominent in the news in the fall of 2013. The story that profiled Jeff Learned of California was typical. On bemoaning his need to find a new plan for his teenage daughter, who has a health condition that has required multiple surgeries, he complained: "I don't feel like I need to change, but I have to" (Appleby and Gorman 2013). Another representative news piece involved Valentina Holroyd, a 58-year-old from San Ramon, California, who, following the termination of her plan from Kaiser Permanente, faced either a 29% premium increase plus additional costs to enroll in a plan offering equivalent coverage, or an increase in deductible from $1,000 to $5,000 for a plan offering an equivalent monthly rate to her terminated plan (Luhby 2013). Such media coverage implied that taking people out of a health plan that they had selected for themselves and forcing them to choose a different one was inherently a bad thing. But was it?

Whether or not plan terminations are, in economic terms, welfare reducing is an empirical question that depends on individual outcomes following the terminations. To examine this, we label as "terminated choosers" the individuals who selected a health plan in a prior period that is no longer offered. Hence, they are forced to choose again. Whether terminated choosers are worse off following a termination depends first on whether they stay insured or become uninsured, and second, if they stay insured, whether they end up in a plan that is inferior to their previous plan. Although the answers to these questions are important, no literature currently exists on the impact of the choice environment and defaults on terminated choosers.

Health insurance in the United States is increasingly offered in exchange settings, where plans will regularly enter and exit the market—whether for economic reasons or because of regulatory impositions—and where the number of clients in terminated health plans is likely to continue to grow. Private insurance exchanges, where employers can give their employees vouchers and let them shop among exchange plans for health and/or dental benefits, are gaining popularity among firms as a way to increase choice while controlling employer costs. The Medicare program includes two exchange settings, one for private health plans (Medicare Advantage) and one for prescription drug plans (called Part D). Finally, several states are introducing exchanges into their Medicaid programs, whether by offering choices of Medicaid-managed care plans (Florida) or by enrolling newly eligible Medicaid individuals into plans offered in the ACA marketplace (Arkansas). In any exchange setting, some plans will be terminated, forcing significant numbers of individuals to select new health plans.

In this chapter, we argue that whether a plan's cancellation harms terminated choosers depends not only on the remaining alternatives in their choice sets, but also on the choice architecture and on whether the terminated choosers make active or passive decisions. More specifically, terminated choosers who fail to make an active choice may be subject to defaults, which have been shown to powerfully influence choices. If the default is contrary to an individual's original preferences, the nudge it represents may diminish the terminated chooser's welfare.

We first discuss how terminated choosers differ from other consumers in health insurance markets, and then analyze how default options affect consumers generally and terminated choosers specifically, for whom the interplay among preferences, search frictions, and defaults is unique. The experience of terminated choosers in the Medicare Advantage program serves as our case study. We conclude with a discussion of policy alternatives for choice architecture and defaults that could be implemented in health insurance markets to improve outcomes for future terminated choosers.

What Is Different about Terminated Choosers?

Terminated choosers differ in a few important ways from those who are selecting a plan from a set of options for the first time, individuals we label "original choosers." First, other factors being equal, having one's plan terminated is experienced as much worse than having chosen originally from a set of alternatives that did not include that plan. The principle describing this phenomenon is loss aversion: a preference for avoiding losses because the disutility associated with surrendering an object is greater than the utility associated with acquiring it (Tversky and Kahneman 1991). The disparity between losses and gains can be demonstrated by a thought experiment: imagine a college student who had narrowly decided to take course "L." Course "L" was then withdrawn, but courses "M," "N," and "O" were offered. For the student conjecturing about the benefits of the withdrawn course, none of the new offerings is viewed as an equal replacement; in part, the gap is due to loss aversion. Likewise, in a health insurance market, the loss of a chosen plan is likely to outweigh the benefits of a few added plans.

Terminated choosers also differ from original choosers because they had the opportunity to make an active choice among alternatives in a prior period, which provides information about their preferences. In a health insurance market, individuals who select a plan reveal their preferences regarding the management of their care, their access to physicians, and their tolerance for risk, all of which are relevant to the preferred new plan for a future period.

Preferences for health insurance are known to be "sticky," which has implications for terminated choosers. Status quo bias describes the disproportionate adherence of earlier entrants to their previous choices, in contrast to the distribution of selections made by new entrants in a market (Samuelson and Zeckhauser 1988). Such persistence may reflect a rational reliance on an informal assessment of search and transition costs combined with uncertainty about alternative options, or it may reflect a sensible conclusion that options change slowly and that people's preferences remain fairly consistent. However, status quo bias may also be driven by loss aversion, by the tendency of individuals to avoid the regret occasioned by learning that their initial choices were poor, or because individuals weight errors of commission (switching plans when they should not) far more than errors of omission (failing to switch when they should).

For terminated choosers, status quo bias reinforces the preference to remain in their terminated plans. Thus far, in the health insurance literature, status quo bias has been studied as a force for inertia, where the choices of individuals already engaged in a market are compared to those of new entrants. We have no evidence of how status quo bias affects terminated choosers—individuals who are forced to make choices because their current selections are no longer available. In these situations, individuals cannot resurrect the status quo; they cannot reproduce their original health plan choices. Not only will elements of the new choices be different (locations, physicians, etc.), but there is an additional psychological effect as terminated choosers move away from a prior reference point. When a terminated chooser faces a range of new plan choices, some similar to the original choice, some not, it is likely that the forces of status quo bias will push in the direction of choosing similar substitutes.

The Power of Defaults and Terminated Choosers

In decision-making, the default option is the selection individuals will be assigned if they fail to choose an option on their own. Defaults have been found to influence outcomes in a range of consequential decisions, including retirement savings and organ donations. Madrian and Shea's (2001) study of participation in an employer's 401(k) program found that participation increased by 50% when the default was changed so that new employees were enrolled unless they elected to opt out. Johnson and Goldstein (2003) found that rates of organ donation are significantly higher in countries where the default is a consent to donate organs, rather than the opposite.

If rational prescriptions were followed, positioning an alternative as a default would not affect its likelihood of being chosen.[1] Thus, evidence that defaults are powerful adds to the growing evidence that consumers often depart from rational prescriptions when making decisions. Defaults influence decisions, in part, because they are perceived as being endorsed by authorities (such as financial planners, personnel officers, and policymakers) who "know what is best for us" (Frank 2007; Goldstein et al. 2008). Defaults also get status quo recognition; an alternative choice risks a significant and regrettable error of commission (Samuelson and Zeckhauser 1988).

The "nudge" concept was developed to counter decision-making errors. It guides policymakers on ways to structure choice architecture and, in particular, on setting defaults to lead to the most effective choices by consumers (Thaler and Sunstein 2008). A default policy may be chosen to maximize individual welfare, or to take a broader societal view and consider as well benefits and costs to external parties, including government. A default may assure that some option is chosen, or the default outcome may be no involvement, as with many employer-based insurance programs, such as those for long-term care.

Goldstein et al. (2008) present a taxonomy of default options including mass defaults, which are the same for all consumers of a product, and personalized defaults, which are tailored to individuals. Smart defaults attempt to optimize for the community on average (if a mass default) or for the individual (if personalized).

Mass defaults are used most prominently for individuals making first-time choices. Thereafter, persistent personalized defaults are common: individuals not choosing are assigned the same choice they made in the prior period, on the theory that what they wanted previously is what they would want now. Employee benefits, often involving multiple products, represent a situation where persistent defaults are widespread.

In considering the right default for terminated choosers, a persistent default is not possible. However, the appropriate default for a terminated chooser may differ from the optimal default for original choosers. Unless the terminated chooser is being terminated from a prior default plan, the terminated chooser has shown a preference among the choices available, and this active choice provides prima facie evidence that the prior default was not her preferred choice. Moreover, that choice provides information that could help determine a personalized default.

The percentage of a population that elected a choice other than the default is also relevant. If 95% of people had accepted the prior default, this would suggest that the default choice served the population well since some who would have chosen actively obviously preferred it. It would also indicate that a particular terminated chooser who was part of the 5% who opted out of the default was an outlier. In these cases, using the same highly popular default as a mass default for terminated choosers might be reasonable. The small percentage of contrary outliers could still actively choose an alternative other than the default, as they had done previously.

However, when a sizable percentage of clients previously opted away from the initial default, utilizing information from prior choices might be worth the effort. The Medicare and Medicare Advantage market illustrates a situation where a large and growing portion of consumers opt away from the original default. From 2003 to 2008, the number of first-time Medicare enrollees who chose a Medicare Advantage plan grew from 11% to 21%.

This pattern indicates that traditional Medicare, the default for first-time choosers, was increasingly selected against, to the point where one in five beneficiaries selected an alternative. As a result, making the additional effort to personalize defaults for terminated choosers within this population might be desirable; that is, the terminated choosers would be better off in expectation if they were assigned a default option determined by considering their past choices rather than an undifferentiated mass default to traditional Medicare. There is a potential welfare loss when traditional Medicare is made the default because some terminated choosers are likely to end up in the default option either because they responded to the "authoritative" pressure of the nudge, or because they failed to make an active choice, perhaps because they were not paying attention or perhaps because of cognitive decline associated with aging. The default to traditional Medicare does avoid the danger of individuals' mistakenly being left without health insurance, a danger that arises in other health insurance markets, but so too would a more personalized default. We now analyze the Medicare Advantage case study in greater detail.

Case Study: A Mass Default Gone Wrong—Terminated Choosers in Medicare Advantage

The Medicare Advantage program gives Medicare beneficiaries the option to choose a private health plan instead of fee-for-service traditional Medicare. Medicare Advantage plans must provide benefits that are at least actuarially equivalent to traditional Medicare. The vast majority of Medicare Advantage plans have been managed-care plans, primarily HMOs (health maintenance organizations), which use primary-care gatekeeping, utilization management, and selective provider networks to reduce healthcare spending. In exchange for these restrictions, Medicare Advantage beneficiaries typically avoid either traditional Medicare's substantial cost sharing or its premiums for supplementary coverage. Medicare Advantage plans fully cover their enrollees' medical care. Medicare Advantage beneficiaries also usually enjoy coverage for some additional services, such as vision and hearing. Medicare Advantage plans receive in return a risk-adjusted, monthly, per-enrollee payment from the Medicare program.

Since 2003, increasing numbers of Medicare beneficiaries have found the Medicare Advantage program to be preferable to traditional Medicare. From 2003 to 2008, Medicare Advantage program enrollment more than doubled, increasing from approximately 4.5 million beneficiaries in 2003 to 9.9 million in 2008. This growth is a result of three forces: large numbers of new Medicare beneficiaries, an increasing preference for Medicare Advantage among new beneficiaries, and more switchers from traditional Medicare to Medicare Advantage relative to individuals making the opposite switch (table 23.1). The increasing popularity of Medicare Advantage was likely due to two factors. First, in 2003, Congress passed the Medicare Modernization and Improvement Act, which increased payment rates paid to Medicare Advantage plans. That, coupled with regulatory provisions, led to plans being established with richer benefit packages than traditional Medicare, in the form of reduced out-of-pocket costs and extra benefits (Medicare Payment Advisory Committee 2007, 2009). Second, the variety of Medicare Advantage plan options expanded substantially. Medicare Advantage began to include preferred provider organization (PPO) plans, managed-care plans with less restricted physician networks, and private fee-for-service (PFFS) plans that, from 2003 to 2008, were similar to traditional Medicare. They offered fee-for-service coverage, but without any provider restrictions. Apart from their specific reasons for selecting Medicare Advantage plans, all of these plans' beneficiaries revealed that they preferred an Medicare Advantage plan to traditional Medicare.

Generally, insurers contract with Medicare to offer a specific type of plan (HMO, PPO, or PFFS) in a county, but they frequently offer multiple plans with different names

Table 23.1. *Medicare Beneficiary Transitions in and out of Medicare Advantage, 2003–8*

	2003	2004	2005	2006	2007	2008
Age 65	1,630,443	1,695,993	1,683,276	1,735,996	1,830,302	2,041,461
Percent into MA	11.0%	11.2%	12.9%	16.0%	19.0%	21.1%
Percent into TM	89.0%	88.9%	87.2%	84.0%	81.0%	78.9%
In MA in prior year and age 66+	4,330,876	4,211,538	4,330,177	4,772,588	5,575,978	6,402,756
Percent transition from MA to TM	10.6%	7.7%	6.7%	7.8%	7.2%	7.2%
N transitioning from MA to TM	459,073	325,552	288,390	371,785	403,701	463,560
In TM in prior year and age 66+	22,875,785	23,365,548	23,681,460	23,610,252	23,241,231	22,931,475
Percent transition from TM to MA	0.8%	1.2%	2.3%	3.9%	3.9%	4.0%
N transitioning from TM to MA	178,431	271,040	532,833	918,439	906,408	908,086

Source: Author's calculations from Medicare enrollment files (100% sample).

Notes: MA, Medicare Advantage; TM, traditional Medicare. Sample includes those whose original reason for entitlement was reaching age 65. Beneficiaries eligible for Medicaid (dual-eligibles) were excluded.

and variable benefits under each contract. As with any marketplace for health insurance, each year some insurers choose not to renew their contract. From 2008 forward, exits from the Medicare Advantage program became more common, primarily because of legislation that changed the amounts that plans were paid and the ways plans were regulated.[2] Some counties experienced more exits than others, though beneficiaries in all counties continued to have access to at least one Medicare Advantage plan of each plan type from 2007 to 2010 (Medicare Payment Advisory Committee 2011).

An insurer must notify beneficiaries when a plan terminates and must explain that they can change to traditional Medicare or choose another Medicare Advantage plan from a provided list of plans available in the service area. Beneficiaries have approximately four months to choose a new plan. In all cases the beneficiaries remain insured by Medicare, as those who do not actively choose for themselves are automatically enrolled in traditional Medicare. This is an example of a mass default.

Medicare's current policy to massively default to its own program is in many ways a conservative choice. Having terminated choosers default into traditional Medicare mimics the default facing original choosers. Traditional Medicare offers the widest physician network, and is thus the most liberal in terms of physician access. In addition, unlike an implicit default, under which terminated choosers who failed to select a new option for coverage would lose their health insurance coverage, this default seeks to avoid harm by keeping beneficiaries enrolled in health insurance.

However, having traditional Medicare as the default option for terminated choosers fails to consider that the terminated choosers originally chose to enroll in Medicare Advantage rather than in traditional Medicare. Valuable information is thus ignored. In addition, a higher proportion of Medicare Advantage as opposed to traditional Medicare clients enroll in Medicare Part D; Part D offers prescription drug coverage at heavily subsidized rates, and thus reflects an appropriate choice for most individuals. However, following an Medicare Advantage plan termination, the current default into traditional Medicare does not include prescription drug coverage. Neither does it cover several additional benefits that are included in the majority of Medicare Advantage plans. Thus, the mass default plan is both actuarially less favorable and less generous than the plan terminated choosers chose previously. Terminated choosers who enter traditional Medicare can elect to enroll in a prescription drug plan, but this requires active choice on their part and does not occur should the terminated chooser passively accept the default.

What is the impact of having traditional Medicare as the default for terminated choosers of Medicare Advantage? We find a moderate impact on the transitions of beneficiaries from terminated plans in Medicare Advantage to traditional Medicare. An analysis of the choices made by nearly 233,000 terminated choosers who were enrolled in an Medicare Advantage plan that included Part D prescription drug coverage from 2006 to 2010 finds that large percentages of terminated choosers, including 95% of beneficiaries terminated from an HMO in 2006 and 83% of beneficiaries terminated from an HMO or PFFS plan in 2009, actively chose to select a new Medicare Advantage plan (Sinaiko and Zeckhauser 2014). These active choices by terminated choosers likely stemmed from the same preferences that had led to their choices to enroll in Medicare Advantage during earlier periods. The persistent preferences of these individuals were perhaps magnified by status quo bias, the proclivity of individuals to stick to their original plan or a close substitute. This bias has been shown to exist, for some combination of rational and irrational reasons, among Medicare beneficiaries (Sinaiko, Afendulis, and Frank 2013; Afendulis, Sinaiko, and Frank 2014).

However, we also observe that some beneficiaries were likely affected by the nudge, which is exercised through the default policy. Even with such high rates of terminated choosers returning to Medicare Advantage, terminated choosers were more likely to be enrolled in traditional Medicare in the year following their plan terminations than were non-terminated choosers. Moreover, 21% of terminated choosers who enrolled in traditional Medicare dropped Part D coverage, whereas only 2% of those actively choosing to stay in Medicare Advantage dropped it. This is likely due to passive acceptance of the default (and some general susceptibility to nudges) because enrollment in Part D requires active selection of a Part D plan within a finite period of time, whereas terminated choosers who passively accepted the default and were assigned to traditional Medicare would end up without Part D coverage.

As we mentioned briefly above, all of the beneficiaries in this study were terminated from a plan that included prescription drug coverage. If judged from the standpoint of the individual beneficiaries, the current nudge into traditional Medicare without actuarially favorable Part D prescription drug coverage almost certainly represents a welfare loss from their prior position of being enrolled in an Medicare Advantage plan with drug coverage. Improving the default provisions for terminated choosers in the Medicare Advantage program would, therefore, have the potential to improve significantly the welfare of the affected individuals.

Can We Design a Better Nudge for the Medicare Program?

The current mass default of terminated choosers into traditional Medicare mimics the default option for original choosers and is thus administratively simple. It also preserves beneficiary access to familiar physicians because, while traditional Medicare covers services provided by any physician who accepts Medicare, Medicare Advantage plans use networks that exclude some physicians. Finally, by allowing beneficiaries a period of time in which they can choose a new plan for themselves (an opt out), the current policy avoids the significant error of putting beneficiaries into traditional Medicare when they strongly prefer an alternative and are sufficiently alert to make an alternative choice.

A default away from a terminated chooser's original choice could serve as a beneficial wakeup call if the persistent enrollment of Medicare beneficiaries in the same health plans over time was overwhelmingly due to status quo bias (and not their preferences). Given that health insurance plans and individuals' conditions change regularly, the terminated chooser's original plan might no longer be optimal. If so, a default away from his original plan could force a reevaluation of his enrollment decision. However, our work elsewhere (see Sinaiko and Zeckhauser 2014) finds that rates of reenrollment in Medicare Advantage plans by terminated choosers are high (as described above). Moreover, they are greater than rates of reenrollment into Medicare Advantage by beneficiaries who voluntarily switch out of their Medicare Advantage plans (that is, voluntary switchers are more likely to transition to traditional Medicare) and greater than rates of take-up of Medicare Advantage by newly eligible Medicare beneficiaries. This evidence suggests that when forced to reevaluate, terminated choosers still choose an Medicare Advantage plan. Status quo bias, even if it is powerful, is at worst minimally harmful.

Using traditional Medicare as a mass default also minimizes government financial outlays; insuring a beneficiary in traditional Medicare costs the government less than in an Medicare Advantage plan. However, this disparity has been shrinking from 2008 to 2014, and further narrowing is expected (Henry J. Kaiser Family Foundation 2014). Nonetheless, Medicare Advantage is unpopular in some political circles, and policymakers who prefer Medicare to be an overwhelmingly public program would find the default into traditional Medicare politically favorable.

Despite these policy and political advantages, the current policy of default into traditional Medicare is far from optimal. It ignores available information about beneficiaries' preferences among plans. More specifically, a second Medicare Advantage plan is likely to be more similar to a terminated chooser's original choice than is traditional Medicare in several consequential ways (for example, covered benefits and cost-sharing requirements) and, therefore, better suited to the beneficiary. The failure of the current default to include or even attend to the highly subsidized Part D pharmaceutical coverage, whether due to a desire to mimic the original default (which also excludes Part D coverage), to respond to some political interests, or to hold down government expenditures, has a strong negative consequence. That policy fails to best serve the well-being of individual Medicare recipients. Moreover, given that consumers have been found to be susceptible to nudges, particularly in arenas, such as health insurance, that are characterized by complex information, the welfare-attending need for an alternative default is clear.

What would the optimal policy for terminated choosers in Medicare Advantage look like? It would include an explicit default into some form of insurance that would yield maximum expected benefits for the inevitable individuals who will fail to choose a new plan for themselves. A choice architecture that employs a personalized smart default that takes account of individual starting positions, preferences, and expected needs (Smith, Goldstein, and Johnson 2009) can be used to allow terminated choosers the opportunity to select a new Medicare Advantage plan or enroll in traditional Medicare. The nudge for beneficiaries who fail to make an active choice for themselves should be back to Medicare Advantage with a plan that includes Part D prescription drug coverage.

As insurers end plans that they find unfavorable to them and as regulations force plans out of existence, terminated choosers will represent a significant component in other government-sponsored health insurance markets, as well as in their purely private counterparts. The experiences and outcomes for terminated choosers in these other markets should be analyzed to inform the design of optimal choice architecture for Medicare. Indeed, smart defaults are already being used in some public health insurance programs, such as the California Demonstration Project to Integrate Care for Dual Eligible Beneficiaries (the Cal MediConnect program). There, eligible individuals are being passively enrolled in health plans using an "intelligent assignment" process that analyzes the individuals' recently used providers and matches those providers to the physician networks of participating plans (California Department of Health Care Services 2014). This smart default includes the opportunity for individuals to opt out and actively select their own plans. In cases where they fail to do so, the default places them in plans that prioritize continuity of care. Research should examine outcomes for consumers in these programs.

Implementing a smart default in Medicare would take some work. It would be a complicated system to organize, and careful attention would need to be paid to educating beneficiaries on the process and on their options so as to maximize their well-being. Administrative complications would arise because physician networks differ across Medicare Advantage plans, and because different individuals would be defaulted into different plans. However, smart defaults are feasible and, in this case, would be preferable to the current system. A smart default system could analyze the degree of overlap in physician networks across Medicare Advantage plans in an area. An even more sophisticated algorithm could consider the physicians the individual has previously used. Possible policy alternatives could default a terminated chooser into the plan most similar to the just-terminated plan, or into the plan where the physician network had the greatest degree of overlap with the prior plan. Traditional Medicare would be employed as a backup only if there were no reasonable fit.

Upgrading the default provisions for terminated choosers in the Medicare Advantage program has the potential to improve significantly the welfare of the affected individuals. The addition of a smart default modification to Medicare's architecture for terminated choosers would be an effective step toward the expressed goal of beneficial healthcare for all Americans. As such, it would also serve as a template for defaults in other insurance programs.

Notes

1. This assumes no (or minimal) search and transaction costs associated with learning about and selecting alternatives.
2. The Patient Protection and Affordable Care Act (ACA) of 2010 reduced payments to Medicare Advantage plans relative to traditional Medicare. This legislative measure led to

less availability of HMO and PPO plans (Afendulis, Landrum, and Chernew 2012). The payment reductions, along with provisions in the Medicare Improvements for Patients and Providers Act (MIPPA) of 2008 that imposed a network requirement on PFFS plans, likely resulted in fewer PFFS plans being offered.

References

Afendulis, Christopher C., Mary Beth Landrum, and Michael E. Chernew 2012. "The Impact of the Affordable Care Act on Medicare Advantage Plan Availability and Enrollment." *Health Services Research* 47(6): 2339–52.

Afendulis, Christopher, Anna Sinaiko, and Richard Frank. 2014. "Dominated Choices and Medicare Advantage Enrollment." National Bureau of Economic Research Working Paper No. 20181.

Appleby, Julie, and Anna Gorman. 2013. "Thousands of Consumers Get Insurance Cancellation Notices Due to Health Law Changes." *Kaiser Health News.* October 21. http://www.kaiserhealthnews.org/stories/2013/october/21/cancellation-notices-health-insurance.aspx.

California Department of Health Care Services. 2014. Duals Demonstration Memorandum of Understanding (MOU). www.dhcs.ca.gov/Pages/demoMOU.aspx.

Clemans-Cope, Lisa, and Nathaniel Anderson. 2014. "How Many Nongroup Plans Were Canceled? Estimates from December 2013." Health Affairs Blog. http://healthaffairs.org/blog/2014/03/03/how-many-nongroup-policies-were-canceled-estimates-from-december-2013.

Frank, Richard G. 2007. "Behavioral Economics and Health Economics." In *Behavioral Economics and Its Applications*, edited by Peter Diamond and Hannu Vartiainen. Princeton University Press. Princeton, NJ.

Goldstein, Daniel G., Eric J. Johnson, Andreas Herrmann, and Mark Heitmann. 2008. "Nudge Your Customers toward Better Choices." *Harvard Business Review*:99–105.

Henry J. Kaiser Family Foundation. 2014. "The Role of Medicare Advantage." *Journal of the American Medical Association* 312(10):990.

Johnson, Eric J., and Daniel Goldstein. 2003. "Do Defaults Save Lives?" *Science* 302:1338–39.

Luhby, Tami. "Obamacare Pricier for Some Individual Buyers." 2013. *CNN Money.* October 29. http://money.cnn.com/2013/10/29/news/economy/obamacare-insurance/.

Madrian, Brigitte C., and Dennis F. Shea. 2001. "The Power of Suggestion: Inertia in 401(k) Participation and Savings Behavior." *Quarterly Journal of Economics* 116(4):1149–87.

Medicare Payment Advisory Commission. 2009. *Report to the Congress: Improving Incentives in the Medicare Program.* Medicare Payment Advisory Commission. Washington, DC.

———. 2007. *Report to Congress: Medicare Payment Policy.* Medicare Payment Advisory Commission. Washington, DC.

———. 2011. *Report to Congress: Medicare Payment Policy.* Medicare Payment Advisory Commission. Washington, DC.

Samuelson, William, and Richard Zeckhauser. 1988. "Status Quo Bias in Decision Making." *Journal of Risk and Uncertainty* 1:7–59.

Sinaiko, Anna D., Christopher C. Afendulis, and Richard G. Frank. 2013. "Enrollment in Medicare Advantage Plans in Miami-Dade County: Evidence of Status Quo Bias?" *Inquiry* 50(3):202–15.

Sinaiko, Anna D., and Richard Zeckhauser. 2014. "Selection Effects versus Default Power: The Choices of Terminated Medicare Advantage Clients." Unpublished Working Paper, Harvard University.

Smith, N. Craig, Daniel G. Goldstein, and Eric J. Johnson. 2009. "Smart Defaults: From Hidden Persuaders to Adaptive Helpers." INSEAD *Business School Research Paper No. 2009/03/ISIC.* http://papers.ssrn.com.ezp-prod1.hul.harvard.edu/sol3/papers.cfm?abstract_id=1116650.

Sommers, Benjamin D. 2014. "Insurance Cancellations in Context: Stability of Coverage in the Nongroup Market Prior to Health Reform." *Health Affairs* 33(5):887–94.

Thaler, Richard H., and Cass R. Sunstein. 2008. *Nudge: Improving Decisions about Health, Wealth, and Happiness.* Yale University Press. New Haven, CT.

Tversky, Amos, and Daniel Kahneman. 1991. "Loss Aversion in Riskless Choice: A Reference-Dependent Model." *Quarterly Journal of Economics* 106(4):1039–61.

CHAPTER 24

Presumed Consent to Organ Donation

David Orentlicher

In the search for reforms that will increase the supply of organs for transplantation in the United States, observers often endorse "presumed consent" policies that reverse the usual presumption for organ retrieval (Dukeminier and Sanders 1968; Gill 2004; Muyskens 1978). Currently, U.S. law assumes that people do not want to donate at death unless they have expressed a desire to donate.[1] Under a presumed consent system, which many European countries employ, the law assumes that people want to donate at death unless they have expressed their objection to donation. Presumed consent replaces an "opt-in" regime with an "opt-out" nudge. While presumed consent seems promising both in theory and in practice, careful consideration suggests that it can raise serious concerns for many people, making its adoption politically difficult. And these concerns reflect the fact that presumed consent is a poor fit with prominent versions of nudge theory.

Arguments Favoring Presumed Consent

There is much to commend presumed consent. As its proponents point out, presumed consent has a number of apparent virtues. Most importantly, presumed consent might save many lives, by ensuring that more organs are transplanted from deceased individuals. Thousands of organs go unused every year because people do not authorize organ retrieval before they die and either their families are not asked to provide authorization or family members do not agree to donation when asked.[2] Under presumed consent, the failure to obtain explicit consent would not prevent

I am grateful for comments and assistance from Kent Holloway, Steve Johnson, Mark Paster, and Christopher Robertson.

organ retrieval. As long as the deceased person had not objected to organ donation while alive, the person's organs could be taken for transplantation.

Moreover, presumed consent would increase the organ supply while still preserving personal autonomy. People who do not want their organs taken could opt out of donation. Presumed consent allows people to determine their destiny by doing nothing, by affirmatively choosing donation, or by registering their objections to transplantation.

And presumed consent appears to reflect public sentiment. Survey data suggest that presumed consent is more consistent than an opt-in system with individual preferences about organ donation. Indeed, more than 62% of adult Americans report that they have granted permission for donation on their driver's license or through other means, and nearly 60% of those who have not granted permission state that they definitely or probably would want their organs retrieved after their deaths for transplantation (U.S. Department. of Health and Human Services 2013, 18, 24–25).[3] Thus, nearly 85% of adult Americans indicate a willingness to donate their organs after death.[4] And, in fact, in recent years, there has been a sharp increase in the number of organs that come from "designated donors," people who gave actual consent before their deaths. From 2007 to 2013, the percentage of organs from designated donors more than doubled, from 19% to 43% (Donate Life America 2014, 1). Survey data from Europe also indicate that presumed consent is more consistent than actual consent with public preferences. The data there suggest that countries with presumed consent do a better job than those with opt-in systems at maximizing the percentage of people whose wishes about organ donation are respected (Ugur 2014, 11). Switching to an opt-out nudge in the United States might ensure that more organ retrieval decisions vindicate individual self-determination.[5]

Presumed Consent and Behavioral Economics

Presumed consent appears to receive support not only from empirical data but also from principles of behavioral economics. As Richard Thaler and Cass Sunstein observe, presumed consent seems to be a useful public policy "nudge" (Thaler and Sunstein 2008, 173–82).

Like other scholars, Thaler and Sunstein worry about distortions in individual decision-making. While traditional economic thinking supposes that people act rationally in the pursuit of self-interest, human frailties impose impediments to decision-making that can cause people to make choices that do not actually reflect their true interests (Thaler and Sunstein 2008, 6–8). Nudges can help overcome these impediments to autonomous decision-making. Ultimately, a key goal of nudging is to help individuals make better choices "as judged by people themselves" (Sunstein 2014, 17)— not according to the judgment of others, such as the government (Thaler and Sunstein 2008, 5; Loewenstein et al. 2012, 2).[6] And nudges are especially useful when they also can yield substantial benefits for social welfare, as when more organs are available for transplantation.

In the case of organ donation, at least three of the common impediments to authentic decision-making are important. First, people are prone to "status quo bias"—people tend to stick with their current situation even if they would choose an alternative option were they required to choose between the two possibilities (Thaler and Sunstein 2008, 34; Camerer et al. 2003, 1224–26). Hence, "default" positions are powerful nudges. Many people will stay with an option simply because that is where they started (Thaler and Sunstein 2008, 35). In the case of organ donation in the United States, where the default position is not to donate, many people may not express their true preference to be an organ donor and transplantable organs may be wasted. The survey data previously discussed provide empirical support for this possibility, and experimental study data also suggest that default positions play a very important role in organ donation decisions (Johnson and Goldstein 2003). The importance of default options is amplified by the fact that people often assume that default positions are chosen for good reasons and therefore see the defaults as reflecting recommended action (Johnson and Goldstein 2003, 1338; Thaler and Sunstein 2008, 35).

Authentic decision-making also can be compromised by the difficulty people experience when weighing present costs and benefits with future costs and benefits. On one hand, people may have trouble delaying gratification; on the other hand, they may be quick to postpone pain. As a result, people tend to "over-indulge" in activities that have immediate benefits and delayed costs and "under-indulge" in activities that have immediate costs and delayed benefits. Decisions about organ donation can fall into the "under-indulge" category. Many people are reluctant to confront their mortality (Cohen 1989, 10–11)—hence, organ donation decisions can be distorted by the immediate discomfort that people face when contemplating death.

A third impediment to authentic decision-making is the fact that a decision about organ donation after death is implemented only once. With other kinds of decisions, people receive feedback about their choices and can make adjustments for future decisions (Thaler and Sunstein 2008, 74–75). If a menu selection does not taste good, people can make another selection the next time they dine at the restaurant. But once a person dies and the decision is made whether to retrieve the person's organs, there never is another chance to reconsider the matter. Mistakes cannot be corrected with one-shot decisions such as organ donation. Hence, it is especially important that people make their truly preferred choice when they decide about organ donation, and nudges may be useful in promoting authentic decision-making.[7]

Concerns about Presumed Consent

While presumed consent seems to hold considerable promise, there are important responses to the arguments for its adoption. For example, opt-out policies may disfavor minorities and the indigent, who are less likely to donate and may not realize that they need to express their objections to donation (Siminoff and Mercer 2001, 382). In addition, while opt-out policies appear to better reflect public preferences overall, that may not actually be the case. People often respond to surveys with what they perceive as the socially favored answer, leaving a false impression of their actual views and behavior (Fisher 1993). While 62% of adult Americans report that they have consented to posthumous organ donation, only 48% of Americans age 18 years or older are included in state organ donor registries (Donate Life America 2014, 5).[8] If actual consent to donation is an accurate measure of public preferences, then there is not a majority of the public willing to donate organs after death. And even if a majority of the public prefers donation, more mistakes might result from opt-out policies. Using survey data on presumed consent in Europe, researchers compared the likelihood that objectors would fail to register their opposition in presumed consent countries with the likelihood that willing donors would fail to register their agreement in actual consent countries. The estimated risk of error was higher for presumed consent (Ugur 2014, 11).

In any event, it is not clear that presumed consent actually would result in more organ transplants. While it is true that organ retrieval rates are higher in countries with presumed consent laws, the reasons for the higher retrieval rates may lie elsewhere than in the presumption of consent. Some studies find a meaningful effect from presumed consent legislation—organ donation rates may increase by one-quarter to one-third from presumed consent (Abadie and Gay 2006, 610; Ugur 2014). Other studies, however, do not find that presumed consent legislation increases donation rates (Coppen et al. 2005). Other factors, such as the infrastructure for organ transplantation or the likelihood that a person's organs will be suitable for transplantation, may explain the differences in retrieval rates between presumed consent and actual consent countries (Coppen et al. 2005, 1277–78; Rithalia et al. 2009). Indeed, it is clear that countries can achieve high retrieval rates without presuming consent (Rudge and Buggins 2012, 144).

The Spanish experience is illustrative. Spain has had the highest rates for organ retrieval (Abadie and Gay 2006, 606), and its high rates often are attributed to presumed consent legislation that was enacted in 1979. However, the country does not operate an opt-out registry, nor does the government employ public awareness campaigns to advise citizens about the law. In practice, families always are asked for consent, and the family's wishes prevail (Fabre, Murphy, and Matesanz 2010, 922). Spain's retrieval rate did not actually rise until 1989—ten years after adoption of presumed consent—when other changes were implemented. In particular, Spain has a highly organized national transplant system, with active and well-trained transplant coordinators at every hospital where organs are retrieved (Fabre, Murphy, and Matesanz 2010, 923). It may be that these other policy changes rather than presumed consent are responsible for Spain's high retrieval rates (Boyarsky et al. 2012).

The U.S. experience is consistent with this view. Organ procurement rates vary from state to state and can be increased by greater efforts to ensure that organ procurement organizations are aware of potential donors and that healthcare providers involve organ procurement professionals in discussions with family members. In Massachusetts, an intensive effort to increase organ donation rates resulted in an increase in the donation rate from 44% to 60% (Koh et al. 2007, 33).[9] Broader implementation of successful approaches to discussions with families is an important way to increase organ retrieval rates. For example, researchers have found that families are more likely to consent when the discussion about the person's death is separated from discussions about organ donation, when organ procurement professionals participate with hospital staff in the donation discussion, and when the request for donation takes place in a quiet, private setting (Gortmaker et al. 1998, 214).

Even with all of the responses to the arguments for presumed consent, there is an additional important reason to think that there may be some value to presumed consent legislation. Its very existence sends a message to family members deciding about organ donation that donation is the socially preferred choice. Family members may be more likely to agree to organ donation in presumed consent countries simply because of the "signaling" effect of the law. Hence, even though physicians typically ask for family consent in presumed consent countries when the deceased person did not register an objection to donation, despite the fact that consent is supposed to be presumed in such situations, the presumed consent legislation may increase the likelihood that actual consent is obtained. There is empirical evidence in support of this possibility, as long as the decision maker is aware of the presumed consent rule (Shepherd and O'Carroll 2013).

Poor Fit with Nudge Theory

While there are good reasons to think that the system of organ donation would benefit from presumed consent nudging, organ donation appears to be a poor fit for nudge theory (Korobkin 2009, 1678–79). As discussed, a key goal of nudging is to help people overcome common distortions in decision-making and realize their true preferences. That is much easier to accomplish when we are dealing with decisions about people's self-interest. We can be much more confident that we are helping people make choices according to their own judgment when we are helping them pursue their own interests. On the other hand, when we are helping people be more altruistic, as with organ donation, we have to worry whether we are helping them act against their own interests. People do many altruistic things, such as making charitable donations, and they often feel better for having done so, but they forgo even more opportunities for altruistic behavior because their self-interest trumps their inclination to serve the interests of others. While fostering altruistic behavior may in fact help promote the true preferences of many people, we should be less confident about that than about the possibility of promoting people's true preferences by fostering self-interested behavior.

In fact, the most persuasive examples that Thaler and Sunstein offer for public policy nudges are examples that involve nudges to help people promote their own interests. Thaler and Sunstein discuss employers who sign new workers up for the company's pension plan unless the workers opt out of the plan (Thaler and Sunstein 2008, 108–9), health insurers who summarize the terms of their policies in simplified and standardized ways so that prospective purchasers can easily compare the benefits and costs of different policies (Thaler and Sunstein 2008, 173–74), and school cafeterias arranging their food displays to make it more likely that students will choose fruits and vegetables (Thaler and Sunstein 2008, 1).

But imagine how people would react to similar policies that pushed people to be altruistic and promote the interests of others. For example, consider the following variation on the retirement plan contribution nudge. Instead of payroll deductions funding the employees' retirement plan, there would be payroll deductions for a food pantry established by the employer for needy families in the community. From every worker's paycheck, a small percentage of the employee's salary would be withheld and donated to the pantry, with the employer matching the donation, unless the employee expressly opted out of the food pantry nudge. Such a policy would be much more controversial than a retirement plan nudge, as are other actual or proposed policies to take people's dollars to meet the needs of other persons (Robertson 2009, 18). Public attitudes toward presumed consent have become more favorable in recent years, but nearly half of U.S. adults oppose adoption of presumed consent (U.S. Department of Health and Human Services 2013, 47–51).

To be sure, presumed consent does not require people to become organ donors after death. It may encourage organ donation, but individuals remain free to opt out of donation. Moreover, there is an important role for government policies that encourage people to act altruistically and make sacrifices for the benefit of others. Thus, for example, people receive tax deductions for their charitable contributions. We should not limit public policies only to those that facilitate self-interested decision-making (Loewenstein et al. 2012). As Russell Korobkin has observed, there is room for policies of "libertarian welfarism," according to which government uses nudges when they will promote social welfare at a small cost to individual welfare (Korobkin 2009, 1680).[10] One also can argue that presumed consent does not really entail any tradeoffs among individuals. A person may be worse off for having to be an organ donor after death, but that diminution in interest may be more than compensated for by the adoption of presumed consent. Having an opt-out rule may make it more likely that an organ will be available for transplantation if the person needs a new organ while still alive. In other words, a presumed consent policy may represent a desirable form of insurance for protecting people in the event of organ failure.

Nevertheless, there are important reasons to be concerned about presumed consent even if we recognize a role for government policies that promote altruistic behavior or even if we take a broader view of self-interest. First, people often have strong feelings about their bodily integrity after death, an individual interest that is given great weight in American ethics and law.[11] In addition, while there are risks of error with any policy, the risks of error may be more serious in a system of presumed consent than in a system of actual consent. Under the current system, potential organ donors know that their desire to be an organ donor after death may be unfulfilled even when they have agreed to be an organ donor (failed efforts to opt in). In a presumed consent system, potential non-donors would know that their rejection of organ donation might not be respected even when they have registered their objections (failed efforts to opt out). The anxiety from the possibility of unwanted organ retrieval could easily be greater than the anxiety from losing the chance to be an organ donor. Indeed, many people worry that if they are perceived as potential organ donors, physicians may be less aggressive with efforts to prolong their lives once their prognoses become grim (Scandroglio et al. 2011, 160; Korobkin 2009, 1679). Consciously or subconsciously, their doctors may be more interested in seeing them become organ donors than in keeping them alive. Of course, a similar risk exists under a system of actual consent, but one would expect the risk to be heightened under a system of presumed consent. If it is true that presumed consent results in more organs being retrieved, then physicians would assume that the odds of donation are greater under presumed consent when a patient dies. Presumed consent policies address concerns about suboptimal care by allowing people to register their objections to donation, but physicians may not realize that the objections were lodged.

There are some data consistent with the sense that the distress to donation objectors under presumed consent is more substantial than the distress to donation consenters under actual consent. While there have been a number of lawsuits brought by family members when a dead person's organs or tissues were removed without consent (Orentlicher, Bobinski, and Hall., 2013, 414–24)—and the lawsuits persisted even when unsuccessful for many years[12]—there are not comparable lawsuits brought by family members when organs have not been removed despite the decedent's or family's wishes for donation.[13] And in a study of public attitudes toward presumed consent, study participants viewed such a system as likely to produce more organs for transplantation than a system of actual consent, but concerns about the morality of presumed consent diminished the participants' enthusiasm for the policy (Robertson, Yokum, and Wright 2014, 102). For many study participants, the possibility that organs would be taken over a decedent's objections provoked feelings of outrage (Robertson, Yokum, and Wright 2014, 121).

We already have experience with harms to people from policies of presumed consent. At one time, presumed consent laws were common in the United States for deceased persons who were undergoing autopsies by coroners or medical examiners. But there were some notorious cases of trafficking in cadaveric corneas by coroners who took steps to ensure that they would remain unaware of objections to donation by decedents or families. As a result, drafters of the Revised Uniform Anatomical Gift Act eliminated the presumed consent provisions for medical examiners and coroners. Most states have followed the Gift Act's lead and repealed their presumed consent provisions (Orentlicher, Bobinski, and Hall 2013, 423–24).

The experience with organ retrieval after "cardiac death" also provides a note of caution about physicians and organ retrieval boundaries. While organ donation after death usually occurs after the donor is declared dead because of the total loss of brain function ("brain death"), it is becoming more common to retrieve organs from patients within a few minutes after their hearts beat for the last time ("cardiac death") (Dominguez-Gil et al., 2011). Ordinarily, the loss of cardiac function results in the deterioration of organs, but if the patient loses cardiac function while in an operating room, the organs can be removed before they deteriorate. Hence, when end-of-life care is discontinued, and patients are taken off a ventilator, if the patient or family has agreed to organ donation, the ventilator withdrawal can be performed in an operating room, and the organs retrieved for transplantation.

Here is the problem. Surgeons usually wait for five minutes after the heart stops beating before removing the person's organs. But as Jerry Menikoff has observed, the cessation of brain function often takes longer than five minutes after the heart stops beating (Menikoff 2002, 14–17). And under the prevailing rationale for defining death, patients are not dead until their brains have stopped functioning. In this view, we are alive not simply because some of our cells are functioning, but because our brains organize the cellular and organ activities of our bodies in a way that allows us to function as an integrated whole. Cessation of cardiac activity, then, represents death only insofar as it is an indirect reflection of the cessation of brain activity (Orentlicher, Bobinski, and Hall 2013, 390–91). Accordingly, if organs are taken before brain function completely subsides, the patient is alive in an important sense even if the patient satisfies the cardiac definition of death. In other words, the declaration of death after five minutes is consistent with the letter of the law but not its spirit. Of course, this pushing of boundaries has occurred in both actual consent and presumed consent countries, and so cannot be attributed to the adoption of presumed consent. Nevertheless, the fact that physicians are inclined to push some boundaries with respect to organ retrieval suggests that it may not be prudent to make it easier for physicians to push or even cross other organ donation boundaries.

There is an additional concern about presumed consent policies for organ donation. As discussed above, presumed consent policies may encourage donation by signaling donation as the socially preferred choice. On the other hand, the signaling effect may be diluted—or even overwhelmed—by an undesirable "crowding-out" effect. That is, efforts to push people in a socially desired direction may diminish a person's willingness to make the desired decision—nudges may crowd out altruistic inclinations. For example, people may be more likely to reject donation when they feel they are being pressured to donate rather than being free to choose donation fully voluntarily (Underhill, this volume). Indeed, when Brazil tried to implement a presumed consent regime in which objections could be lodged only by individuals for themselves, it provoked a backlash among the public, leading many people to register as non-donors. The public reaction led to the repeal of the presumed consent law (Csillag 1998).

Conclusion

For many reasons, presumed consent has been controversial as a reform for increasing the supply of transplantable organs. Viewing the issue through the lens of behavioral economics helps explain why presumed consent is problematic for many people. If our goal in changing default rules is to compensate for defects in human decision-making, we can be much more confident about default rules that help individuals pursue their self-interest than about default rules that might entail a sacrifice of self-interest in favor of the interests of others. And this is especially the case when people worry that the sacrifice could entail harms to personal health.

That said, maintaining the status quo of actual consent also entails harms to personal health, with many lives lost because usable organs are not donated for transplantation. The important questions for policymakers are the extent to which alternative policies can yield the same increase as presumed consent in organ donation rates and how the disadvantages of the alternative policies compare with the disadvantages of presumed consent.

Notes

1. Family members can give consent to donation after the person's death for people who did not express their preferences while alive.
2. Failure to obtain consent from the family is the leading reason why organs are not retrieved after death (Kemp 2008, 1578).
3. With more and more people registering their consent to organ donation, one might wonder whether we even need presumed consent. Switching to presumed consent still could be valuable. Surveys may overestimate the number of people who have consented to organ donation. Moreover, a substantial number of Americans have not agreed to be organ donors.
4. If 62.3% of Americans have granted permission and 59.2% of the other 38% would definitely or probably want to have their organs donated (U.S. Department of Health and Human Services 2013, 18, 24–25), that yields a level of support of 84.8%.
5. To judge the appropriateness of a presumed consent policy, one might also ask not whether people want to be organ donors after death but whether they support the adoption of presumed consent. On the latter question, there still is majority support, but barely, with about 51% of the U.S. public supporting presumed consent (U.S. Department of Health and Human Services 2013, 48).
6. To be sure, it is controversial whether it is possible or appropriate to reserve nudges for situations in which they promote individual self-interest. Nudge theory may at once promise too much and seek too little. As Mark White has observed, proponents of nudges overestimate their ability to identify policies that promote individual self-interest (White, this volume). On the other hand, why limit nudging to the promotion of self-interested behavior?

Nudges also can promote conduct that benefits society as a whole, even if doing so contravenes the interests of some people. If the status quo privileges some at the expense of the majority, and a simple nudge can privilege the majority at the expense of some, then there is much to be said for employing the nudge. But for purposes of this chapter, I aim to take Thaler and Sunstein and like-minded scholars on their own terms and show how presumed consent does not fit well with nudge theory.

7. In fact, there is some room for correction. After a person dies, family members can consent to organ donation. Even if the deceased individual did not "opt in" to organ donation, family members can choose donation on the decedent's behalf. Nevertheless, just as people are influenced by default rules for themselves, they are influenced by default rules for others (Thaler and Sunstein 2008, 179–80).

8. The 48% may represent an underestimate since it includes people who have signed up for organ donation when obtaining a driver's license or enrolled in a state organ donor registry online but not people who have expressed their willingness to donate only through their living wills.

9. However, the donation rate declined when the intervention was discontinued (Koh et al. 2007, 33).

10. Public policies that *require* people to make sacrifices for the benefit of other persons also are important. Taxes must be collected to fund programs that provide food, shelter, and healthcare for the poor.

11. Thus, we let people or their families decide whether their organs can be taken after death even though there is no harm to a dead body from having its organs taken and even though the lives of other people could be saved by transplanting the organs.

12. State supreme courts in Florida, Georgia, and Michigan rejected causes of action for families after the unauthorized taking of corneas from decedents several years before the U.S. Court of Appeals for the Sixth Circuit recognized procedural due process protections for family members (*State v. Powell* 1986; *Georgia Lions Eye Bank, Inc. v. Lavant* 1985; *Tillman v. Detroit Receiving Hospital* 1984; *Brotherton v. Cleveland* 1991).

13. Family members did sue when an organ was transplanted in a stranger instead of a designated recipient (*Colavito v. New York Organ Donor Network, Inc.* 2006, 713). In addition, an organ procurement organization might sue to ensure that a person's consent to donate is not overridden by family members after the person's death (Manning 2013).

References

Abadie, Alberto, and Sebastien Gay. 2006. "The Impact of Presumed Consent Legislation on Cadaveric Organ Donation: A Cross-Country Study." *Journal of Health Economics* 25:599–620.

Boyarsky, Brian J., Erin C. Hall, Neha A. Deshpande, R. Lorie Ros, Robert A. Montgomery, Donald M. Steinwachs, and Dorry L. Segev. 2012. "Potential Limitations of Presumed Consent Legislation." *Transplantation* 93:136–40.

Brotherton v. Cleveland, 923 F.2d 477 (6th Cir. 1991).

Camerer, Colin, Samuel Issacharoff, George Loewenstein, Ted O'Donoghue, and Matthew Rabin. 2003. "Regulation for Conservatives: Behavioral Economics and the Case for 'Asymmetric Paternalism.'" *University of Pennsylvania Law Review* 151:1211–54.

Cohen, Lloyd R. 1989. "Increasing the Supply of Transplant Organs: The Virtues of a Futures Market." *George Washington Law Review* 58:1–51.

Colavito v. New York Organ Donor Network, Inc., 860 N.E.2d 713 (N.Y. 2006).

Coppen, Remco, Roland D. Friele, Richard L. Marquet, and Sjef K. M. Gevers. 2005. "Opting Out Systems: No Guarantee for Higher Donation Rates." *Transplant International* 18:1275–79.

Cruzan v. Director, Missouri Dept. of Health, 497 U.S. 261 (1990).

Csillag, Claudio. 1998. "Brazil Abolishes 'Presumed Consent' in Organ Donation." *The Lancet* 352:1367.

Dominguez-Gil, Beatriz, Bernadette Haase-Kromwijk, Hendrik Van Leiden, James Neuberger, Leen Coene, Philippe Morel, Antoine Corinne, Ferdinand Muehlbacher, Pavel Brezovsky, Alessandro Nanni Costa, Rafail Rozental, and Rafael Matesanz on behalf of the European Committee (Partial Agreement) on Organ Transplantation. Council of Europe (CD-P-TO). 2011. "Current Situation of Donation after Circulatory Death in European Countries." *Transplant International* 24:676–86.

Donate Life America. 2014. "2014 National Donor Designation Report Card." Accessed January 20, 2015. http://donatelife.net/wp-content/uploads/2014/06/Report-Card-2014 -44222-Final.pdf.

Dukeminier, Jesse, Jr., and David Sanders. 1968. "Organ Transplantation: A Proposal for Routine Salvaging of Cadaver Organs." *New England Journal of Medicine* 279:413–19.

Fabre, John, Paul Murphy, and Rafael Matesanz. 2010. "Presumed Consent: A Distraction in the Quest for Increasing Rates of Organ Donation." *British Medical Journal* 341: 922–24.

Fisher, Robert J. 1993. "Social Desirability Bias and the Validity of Indirect Questioning." *Journal of Consumer Research* 20:303–15.

Georgia Lions Eye Bank, Inc. v. Lavant, 335 S.E.2d 127 (Ga. 1985).

Gill, Michael B. 2004. "Presumed Consent, Autonomy, and Organ Donation." *Journal of Medicine & Philosophy* 29:37–59.

Gortmaker, Steven L., Clare L. Beasley, Emile Sheehy, Barbara A. Lucas, Lynette E. Brigham, Ake Grenvik, Russel H. Patterson, Norman Garrison, Peter McNamara, and Michael J. Evanisko. 1998. "Improving the Request Process to Increase Family Consent for Organ Donation." *Journal of Transplant Coordination* 8:210–17.

Johnson, Eric J., and Daniel Goldstein. 2003. "Do Defaults Save Lives?" *Science* 302:1338–39.

Kemp, Clinton D., Bryan A. Cotton, J. Chad Johnson, Michelle Ellzey, and C. Wright Pinson. 2008. "Donor Conversion and Organ Yield in Traumatic Brain Injury Patients: Missed Opportunities and Missed Organs." *Journal of Trauma-Injury Infection & Critical Care* 64:1573–80.

Koh, Howard K., Marsha D. Jacobson, Anne Marie Lyddy, Kevin J. O'Connor, Sean M. Fitzpatrick, Milly Krakow, Christine M. Judge, Hillel R. Alpert, and Richard S. Luskinet. 2007. "A Statewide Public Health Approach to Improving Organ Donation: The Massachusetts Organ Donation Initiative." *American Journal of Public Health* 97:30–36.

Korobkin, Russell. 2009. "Libertarian Welfarism." *California Law Review* 97:1651–85.

Loewenstein, George, David A. Asch, Joelle Y. Friedman, Lori A. Melichar, and Kevin G. Volpp. 2012. "Can Behavioural Economics Make Us Healthier?" *British Medical Journal* 344:e3482.

Manning, Allison. 2013. "Family Loses Fight to Keep Son's Organs from Donation." *Columbus Dispatch*, July 12. Accessed March 15, 2015. http://www.dispatch.com/content/stories/local/2013/07/11/Judge-ordered-family-to-let-brain-dead-son-donate-organs.html.

Menikoff, Jerry. 2002. "The Importance of Being Dead." *Issues in Law & Medicine* 18:3–20.

Muyskens, James L. 1978. "An Alternative Policy for Obtaining Cadaver Organs for Transplantation." *Philosophy & Public Affairs* 8:88–99.

OPTN DSA Dashboard Report. http://www.aopo.org/related-links-data-organ-donation-transplantation-a40.

Orentlicher, David. 2009. "Presumed Consent to Organ Donation: Its Rise and Fall in the United States." *Rutgers Law Review* 61:295–331.

Orentlicher, David, Mary Anne Bobinski, and Mark A. Hall. 2013. *Bioethics and Public Health Law.* 3rd ed. Aspen. New York.

Rithalia, Amber, Catriona McDaid, Sara Suekarran, Lindsey Myers, and Amanda Sowden. 2009. "Impact of Presumed Consent for Organ Donation on Donation Rates: A Systematic Review." *British Medical Journal* 338:a3162.

Robertson, Christopher T. 2009. "Why Intuitions and Metaphysics Are the Wrong Approach for Health Law: A Commentary on Delaney and Hershenov." *The American Journal of Bioethics* 9(8):18–19.

Robertson, Christopher T., David V. Yokum, and Megan S. Wright. 2014. "Perceptions of Efficacy, Morality, and Politics of Potential Cadaveric Organ-Transplantation Reforms." *Law and Contemporary Problems* 77:101–29.

Rudge, Chris J., and Elisabeth Buggins. 2012. "How to Increase Organ Donation: Does Opting Out Have a Role?" *Transplantation* 93:141–44.

Scandroglio, Barbara, Beatriz Domínguez-Gil, Jorge S. López, María O. Valentín, María J. Martín, Elisabeth Coll, José M. Martínez, Blanca Miranda, María C. San José, and Rafael Matesanz. 2011. "Analysis of the Attitudes and Motivations of the Spanish Population towards Organ Donation after Death." *Transplant International* 24:158–66.

Shepherd, Lee, and Ronan E. O'Carroll. 2013. "Awareness of Legislation Moderates the Effect of Opt-Out Consent on Organ Donation Intentions." *Transplantation* 95:1058–63.

Siminoff, Laura A., and Mary Beth Mercer. 2001. "Public Policy, Public Opinion, and Consent for Organ Donation." *Cambridge Quarterly of Healthcare Ethics* 10:377–86.

State v. Powell, 497 So. 2d 1188 (Fla. 1986).

Sunstein, Cass R. 2014. *Why Nudge?: The Politics of Libertarian Paternalism.* Yale University Press. New Haven, CT.

Thaler, Richard H., and Cass R. Sunstein. 2008. *Nudge: Improving Decisions about Health, Wealth, and Happiness.* Yale University Press. New Haven, CT.

Tillman v. Detroit Receiving Hospital, 360 N.W.2d 275 (Mich. 1984).

Ugur, Zeynep B. 2014. "Does Presumed Consent Save Lives? Evidence from Europe." *Health Economics.* October 2.

U.S. Department of Health and Human Services: Health Resources and Services Administration, Healthcare Systems Bureau. 2013. "2012 National Survey of Organ Donation Attitudes and Behaviors." http://organdonor.gov/dtcp/nationalsurveyorgandonation.pdf.

CONTRIBUTORS

DAVID A. ASCH, University of Pennsylvania; Philadelphia Veterans Affairs Medical Center

JERRY AVORN, Program On Regulation, Therapeutics, And Law (PORTAL), Division of Pharmacoepidemiology and Pharmacoeconomics, Department of Medicine, Brigham and Women's Hospital and Harvard Medical School

JENNIFER BLUMENTHAL-BARBY, Baylor College of Medicine

ALEXANDER M. CAPRON, Gould School of Law and Keck School of Medicine, University of Southern California

NITEESH K. CHOUDHRY, Program On Regulation, Therapeutics, And Law (PORTAL), Division of Pharmacoepidemiology and Pharmacoeconomics, Department of Medicine, Brigham and Women's Hospital and Harvard Medical School

I. GLENN COHEN, Petrie-Flom Center, Harvard Law School

SARAH CONLY, Bowdoin College

GREGORY CURFMAN, Harvard Medical School

KHALED EL EMAM, Children's Hospital of Eastern Ontario; Privacy Analytics, Inc.

BARBARA J. EVANS, University of Houston Law Center

NIR EYAL, Harvard T. H. Chan School of Public Health

ANDREA FREEMAN, University of Hawai'i at Mānoa William S. Richardson School of Law

ALAN M. GARBER, Harvard University

JONATHAN GINGERICH, University of California, Los Angeles

MICHAEL HALLSWORTH, The Behavioural Insights Team; Imperial College London

JIM HAWKINS, University of Houston Law Center

DAVID HUFFMAN, University of Oxford

DAVID A. HYMAN, University of Illinois

JULIKA KAPLAN, Baylor College of Medicine

AARON S. KESSELHEIM, Program On Regulation, Therapeutics, And Law (PORTAL), Division of Pharmacoepidemiology and Pharmacoeconomics, Department of Medicine, Brigham and Women's Hospital and Harvard Medical School

NINA A. KOHN, Syracuse University College of Law

RUSSELL KOROBKIN, University of California, Los Angeles, School of Law

JEFFREY T. KULLGREN, VA Center for Clinical Management Research; University of Michigan Medical School; Institute for Healthcare Policy and Innovation, University of Michigan

MATTHEW J. B. LAWRENCE, Petrie-Flom Center, Harvard Law School

GEORGE LOEWENSTEIN, University of Pennsylvania; Carnegie Mellon University

HOLLY FERNANDEZ LYNCH, Petrie-Flom Center, Harvard Law School

ESTER MOHER, Children's Hospital of Eastern Ontario; Privacy Analytics, Inc.

ABIGAIL R. MONCRIEFF, Boston University School of Law

DAVID ORENTLICHER, Indiana University Robert H. McKinney School of Law and Indiana University School of Medicine

MANISHA PADI, MIT Department of Economics; Yale Law School

CHRISTOPHER T. ROBERTSON, University of Arizona, James E. Rogers College of Law

AMEET SARPATWARI, Program On Regulation, Therapeutics, And Law (PORTAL), Division of Pharmacoepidemiology and Pharmacoeconomics, Department of Medicine, Brigham and Women's Hospital and Harvard Medical School

ADITI P. SEN, University of Pennsylvania

NEEL SHAH, Harvard Medical School; Ariadne Labs for Health Systems Innovation

ZAINAB SHIPCHANDLER, Rice University

ANNA D. SINAIKO, Harvard T. H. Chan School of Public Health

DONNA SPRUIJT-METZ, Center for Economic and Social Research and Keck School of Medicine, University of Southern California

CASS R. SUNSTEIN, Harvard University

THOMAS S. ULEN, University of Illinois at Urbana-Champaign and University of Illinois

KRISTEN UNDERHILL, Yale Law School

KEVIN G. VOLPP, University of Pennsylvania; Philadelphia Veterans Affairs Medical Center

MARK D. WHITE, College of Staten Island/City University of New York

DAVID V. YOKUM, U.S. Social and Behavioral Sciences Team

JENNIFER L. ZAMZOW, Carnegie Mellon University

RICHARD J. ZECKHAUSER, Harvard Kennedy School, Harvard University

INDEX

The letter *t* following a page number denotes a table; the letter *f* denotes a figure.

biases (cont.)

and persistent unconsciousness, 12, 289–90; in policymaking processes, 45; pro-consumption, 147; in relative value health insurance, 24; status quo bias, 270–72, 323–24, 328–29, 334, 341, 347–48n6; systematic, 151; in utility, 67–68. *See also* cognitive bias

bioequivalent drugs, 159–61, 167

bioethics, 233–34, 312

Biologics Price Competition and Innovations Act (BPCIA), 162

biosimilar drugs, 159

blood and bone marrow donation, 195–96

bodily integrity, 89, 345

bonus incentives, 198

bounded rationality: in choice architecture, 15–16; and cognitive scarcity, 152; in decision simplification, 21, 22; in food policy, 126; in food selection, 131; in procedural justice, 271

brand name drugs, 163, 165–66, 167

burdens: of care for unconscious patients, 291–92; cognitive, 9–10, 33, 35, 145, 146–47, 148–54, 176–77; of intervention, 117; in motivational crowding out, 192–93, 196

campaign contributions in food policy, 133, 134

CareCredit, LLC, 172, 174–75, 176, 179–80

carrot-and-stick model, 3–6, 7, 32, 62, 190

Cassel, Christine K., 299

Charness, Gary, 203

Childress, James F., 113

choice: paradox of, 150–51; in rationality theory, 4–5

choice not to choose: as active choice, xii–xiii; defined, xxiv–xxvnn1–2; freedom in, xx, xxiii; in paternalism, xvii–xix, xxi–xxiv; regret in, 153; sanctions for, xiv–xv, xxii

choice overload, 146, 148–49, 150–52

chronic disease, 312, 314

Clinical Laboratory Improvement Amendments (CLIA), 312, 314, 316

coercion: of choice, xi, xiii, xv–xvi; in ethical frameworks, 114; in experienced utility, 276, 283; in government regulation, 16; individual mandate as, 12, 18; manipulation as, 85; nudges as, 72; political morality of, 97

cognitive bias: in care of unconscious patients, 289–90; in drug prescription, 163, 168; in food selection, 126; in healthcare financing, 10; in nudging, 72, 73–74; and personal interests, 56; and scarcity, 152–53; in utility, 67–68

cognitive dysfunction, 72, 73–74, 234, 235, 293

coma patients. *See* unconsciousness, persistent

commercial manipulation, 86, 92–93

commodification of human organs, 196

commodities, subsidized, 124–25, 128, 133

Community Living Assistance Services and Supports Act (CLASS), 62–63

complexity: of healthcare decisions, 75, 152; of incentives and motivation, 191

confidentiality, 11, 244–53, 249f

confirmation bias, 45, 49n6, 175, 235, 290

Connolly, Terry, 154

consent: explicit, 339–40; informed, 219, 239–40, 252–53; presumed, 19–20, 21, 244, 324, 339–47, 347n3; in procedural justice, 117

consent forms, 11, 246, 249–53, 251f

consumer-directed healthcare (CDHC), 22

Consumer Financial Protection Bureau (CFPB), 172, 177, 179–80

consumers: and the ACA, 65–66; and coerced choosing, xv; in DNA sequencing, 309–19; and medical credit, 172–81; and nutrition labeling, 132; overconsumption by, 33; protection of, 179–80

context: in credit decisions, 177–78; cultural, 120, 121; in decision-making, 105, 106; in information disclosure, 246, 249; of manipulation, 89–90; medical, 144; of public health, 111; socioeconomic, in food policy, 109, 132, 133–34; surrogates' decisions, 304–5

cost-benefit analysis: of the ACA individual mandate, 275–83; of caring for unconscious patients, 291–92, 293, 294–95; in cost sharing, 147, 149; of drug selection, 168; in ethical analysis, 116, 118; in human choice, 4–5; by patients, 9–10; in policy paradigms, 21–23, 29, 30; in presumed consent, 341, 344; of procedural justice by default, 272

cost-effectiveness, 22–23, 162, 267–68

costs: and the ACA individual mandate, 278–80, 282; ACA reducing, 283n2; and behavior change, 143–44; of care for unconscious patients, 12, 288, 291, 294–95; in choice architecture, 146–55; of choosing, xxi; and consumer credit, 172–81; of cost sharing, 154; default rules in, 323; in food selection, 126; generic drugs in, 158–68; of healthcare reform, 27–28, 34; of Medicare Advantage plans, 335; of presumed consent, 21; in procedural justice, 272

cost sharing: alternatives to, 148–49; as choice architecture, 145, 146–55; in consumption, 34, 148; in healthcare reform, 28; in patient choices, 10

counterfactual thinking, 149, 151, 154

counterproductive policies, 43–44, 45

credit, consumer, 10, 144–45, 172–81

Credit Service Organizations, 180

critiques, 8–9, 42, 56, 57, 83–93

crowding in, 203, 211–12

crowding out, 6, 10–11, 187–88, 190–99, 202–12, 212–13n1, 346

Daniels, Norman, 117

data: in affective forecasting, 228–29; collection of, 66–67, 209–10, 213n4; from DNA sequencing, 317–18; in doctor-patient relationships, 233–42; and the individual mandate, 277–80; secondary uses of, 244–45; small, 11, 236–38, 240–41; from surveys, 284n3

death: in organ donation, 324, 346; or persistent unconsciousness, 287–96

deceitful manipulation, 89–90

deception, benevolent, 120

decision aids in affective forecasting, 226, 228–29

decision simplification, 7, 21–24

decision utility model, 281–83

deductibles, 22, 28, 33, 146

default choices/rules: in the ACA, 56, 62–64, 69; and active choosing, xi–xiii, 323–24, 330; authoritative, 105; behavioral economics of, 60–61, 64–65; choice architects in, xvi–xvii; in choice-requiring paternalism, xix; in debiasing decisions, 281; democratic control of, 57, 98, 100–101; in drug prescription, 168; dynamic, 259–60; in end-of-life care, xix–xx, 287; in food selection, 126–27; in healthcare reform, 35; in libertarian welfarism, 18–19; in manipulation of patients, 13–14; in market failure, 32; as nudges, 324–25; in organ donation, 13–14, 19–20, 99, 106n2, 324, 329, 339–47; in personalized paternalism, 240; political morality of, 103–4; in procedural justice, 269–72; as simplified active choosing, xvii; smart, 324–25, 330; sticky, 60, 61, 65; in surrogacy, 298, 303; and terminated insurance plans, 326–36; and unconscious patients, 261, 295

deferred-financing plans, 174–75, 178, 179–80

democratic control, 57, 97–103, 106

dependent insurance coverage, 62–63, 66

dignity, 268–69, 291, 314

direct engagement in decision-making, 104–5

disabilities, 222

disclosure: in consumer credit, 174, 179–80; of health information, 11, 244–53, 249f; of nudges and responsibility, 103; risk of, in consent forms, 252; rules of, in costs, 143

disease prevention, 28–29, 109, 110–11, 112–21

disempowerment critique, 42

disincentives, 121n3, 146, 239

disrespect, 90–91, 100–101, 103

distributional function, 147

distributive justice, 116–17, 292, 294–96

disutility, 146, 148–49, 151–52, 153, 154, 328

DNA sequencing, 13, 309–19

doctor-patient relationships: affective forecasting in, 11, 222–30, 230–31n4, 230n2, 231n5; benign manipulation in, 93; collaboration in, 219–21; credit in, 172–73; goal setting in, 220–21, 235; mobile devices and small data in, 233–42; and permanent unconsciousness, 294–96; privacy in, 244–53

drugs, prescription, 10, 158–68, 333–34

Duflo, Esther, 112–13, 117

economic incentives, 28, 42, 128, 190

economic models, 4–6

effectiveness: of the ACA, 61–67; of electronic data, 237; in ethical frameworks, 113; evidence in maximizing, 43; of generic drugs, 158; of incentives, 187, 205–12; measuring, 65–67; of paternalism, 128, 129, 131–33, 241–42; of treatments in affective forecasting, 231n5

efficiency, 4, 28, 259–60, 267–68, 270–72, 318

ego-protection, 248

electronic devices, 236–38

electronic health records (EHRs), 167–68, 236–37

emotions: as cognitive burden, 35; in decision-making, xviii, 72–73, 75, 77, 78, 105, 225; in ethics, 56, 58; in food selection, 126–27, 131; manipulation of, 92–93; in Medicare appeals, 269, 270; in personalized paternalism, 238; predicting, 220–21, 223–24, 229; in surrogate selection, 304

empiricism: on the ACA, 65–67; in behavioral economics, 4, 41–43, 65; on choice overload, 150; on cognitive scarcity, 152–53; on consumer credit, 177–78; in measuring effectiveness of nudging, 61–64; on motivational crowding out, 191; in rationality theory, 5; into utility of the individual mandate, 275–80; in weight loss motivation, 202–12

employer mandates, 32, 62–63, 104

end-of-life care, xix–xx, 299–300, 346

endogenous preference formation, 194, 198

endowment effect, 271

environmental factors: as data, 233, 237, 238; in food selection, 124–25, 126–27, 131–32; and personal responsibility, 46–47

epistemology: in behavioral policy, 5, 6–7; in cost sharing, 147, 148, 154–55; in normative critiques, 8; of nudging, 73–74

e-prescribing systems, 162–63, 167–68

Epstein, Richard, 59

errors: in active choosing, 328–29; in affective forecasts, 30, 223–24, 226, 227–28; biases in, 275, 278–80; cost of, 280; in Medicare claims,

errors (cont.)
268, 272; or preferences, 280–82; preventing, 45–46, 60, 323; risk of in organ donation, 341–42, 345

Estrin, Deborah, 237–38

ethics: in affective forecasting, 223; of behavioral economics, 8–9; of benign manipulation, 83–93; in cases of permanent unconsciousness, 295–96; in DNA sequencing, 312; in doctor-patient relationships, 233–34; in drug prescription, 165–68; emotions in, 56, 58; in food policy, 110, 124–34; of incentives, 112–21, 165–67; of informed consent, 252–53; of nudging, 73–74; of paternalism, 241–42; of policy mandates, 110–11; in vaccination policy, 9, 112–21

exchanges, health insurance, 62–64, 65–66, 327

expansion of health insurance, 27–28, 31, 61–62

experienced utility, 275–76, 281–83, 284nn3–4

externalities in choice architecture, 18, 20–21, 24, 25

extrinsic motivation, 187–88, 191–92, 194, 205–7, 206t

Fagerlin, Angela, 299–300

False Claims Act, 164

family: in organ donation, 343, 347nn1–2, 358n7, 358n11; as surrogates, 298, 300, 303–4; and unconscious patients, 289, 290–91, 293

fast food, 124–25, 128, 129, 132–33

Fershtman, Chaim, 198

fertility clinics, 172, 173, 178

finances, 9, 10, 152–53

financial incentives: in consumer credit, 180; in drug prescription, 159, 163–68; in healthcare reform, 27–28, 33–34, 36; in high-value care, 196; in motivational crowding out, 187, 188; in weight loss, 202–12

financing. See credit, consumer

First Amendment and DNA sequencing, 309–10, 316

Fischer, Michael A., 162–63

Flynn v. Holder, 195

follow-on biologic drugs, 158–59, 162, 166–67

follow-up behaviors and genome sequencing, 309–10

food: assistance programs, 124–25, 132–34; industry, 9, 131–33; in oppression, 133–34; policy on, 9, 109, 110, 124–34; selection of, 125–27, 131–33

Food and Drug Administration (FDA), 129–30, 262, 312–13, 316

Food Stamp Program, 124, 126–27

formulary support in drug substitution, 162–63, 167–68

freedom, 91–92, 110, 293, 314

freedom of choice, xi–xii, xiii, xx, xxii, 73–74, 239

generic drugs, 10, 101–2, 158–68

genome sequencing/information, 13, 262, 309–19

genuine nudges, 83–93

Gneezy, Uri, 203

Goldstein, Daniel, 19, 329–30

Gorin, Moti, 85

government: in choice architecture, 15–16; in de-biasing decisions, 281; libertarian paternalism by, 16–18; in nudging, 98; role of, 6–7; using behavioral economics, 40–48. See also regulation, government

Gruber, Jonathan, 279–80

guardians. See surrogacy/surrogates

habit formation, 203, 211–12

habituation in experienced utility, 283

halo effect, 10, 175, 180

Handel, Benjamin R., 280

Hanlester Network v. Shalala, 164–65

harm prevention, 47–48

Hatch-Waxman Act of 1984, 158

Hausman, Dan, 87, 89, 97

Health and Human Services, Department of, 195, 312, 314

healthcare agents. See surrogacy/surrogates

healthcare reform, 27–36. See also Affordable Care Act (ACA)

health disparities and race, 134

Health Insurance Portability and Accountability Act (HIPAA), 237, 245, 312, 314, 318

health maintenance organizations (HMOs), 331, 336–37n2

health outcomes: in affective forecasting, 228–29, 231n5; big data in, 236; and credit, 178; doctor-patient relationships in, 221; financial incentives in, 212; and food policy, 125, 131; generic drugs in, 164, 166; and goals, 125, 293

Healthy Behavior Incentive Protocol, 197

helplessness, learned, 194–95

heterogeneity: of biases, 68; of cognitive processes, 187; in cost sharing, 154; in crowding out, 209; in decision simplification, 21, 24; in healthcare exchanges, 66; in motivation, 213n5; of preferences, 280

heuristics, 5, 6, 15, 21, 151, 152, 235

high-value healthcare, 148, 196

Hill, Thomas, 85

Houts, Renate, 301

image-spoiling, 193, 196, 198

immunization policy, 9, 112–21. See also vaccination

incentives: in aggressive soft paternalism, 128; in consumer credit, 180; in cost sharing, 147; in crowding out, 10–11, 187, 190–99; economic, 28, 42, 128, 190; effectiveness of, 187, 202–12; endogenous preference formation in, 194; ethics of in vaccination, 112–21; for genomic data sharing, 318; impact of, 204; in manipulation, 3; in Medicare appeals processes, 271–72; nonfinancial, 28, 32–33, 35; for prescribing drugs, 159, 163–67, 168; and vulnerability, 113, 121. *See also* financial incentives

income level, 23, 131, 132, 133

India, vaccination study in, 9, 112–21

individual choice: democratic control of, 97–98, 100–103; and genetic information, 262; in insurance plans, 326–36; and mandates, 260; in Medicare disputes, 259–60; in persistent unconsciousness, 287–96. *See also* autonomy

individual mandate: and adverse selection, 32, 275, 276–79; as coercion, 12, 18; justification of, 278, 285; measuring success of, 143–44, 275–83; utility of, 260–61, 275–83

individuals: interests of and nudging, 72–79; in paternalism, 17, xviii; welfare of, 329, 335, 336

industry, 9, 131–33, 314–18

inertia, 271, 278, 279–80, 329

information: access to and use of, 11, 309–19; in affective forecasting, 228–29, 230; asymmetry in, 31, 277; in autonomy, 120; in bounded rationality, 15; in choosing surrogates, 303; disclosure of, 85–86, 120, 244–53, 249f; electronic, 237; and food, 125–26, 127, 131–32; in generic drug prescription, 162–63, 168; genetic, 309–19; in incentives, 116; in manipulation, 13; in market failure, 33–34; and rational selection, 99; in smart defaults, 335

informed consent, 219, 239–40, 252–53

infrastructure, 318–19, 342

in-kind rewards, 198

Institute of Medicine, 45–46

institutional review boards, 245

insurance: cost sharing in, 146–55; decision simplification in, 7, 22; default rules in, 13, 324, 326–36; design of, 148; disputes over coverage in, 259–60; exchanges, 62–64, 65–66, 327; expansion of, 27–28, 31, 61–62; in healthcare reform, 30, 31–36; markets for, 30, 336; morality of nudges in, 103–4; risk managed by, 260; terminated, 326–36, 336–37n2; wellness programs in, 196–97

interoperability of genetic test results, 315

intervention ladder (Nuffield Council), 113, 119–20

interventions: in affective forecasting, 227–29, 230–31n4; behavioral, 29–30; in credit markets,

178; in the decision utility model, 282; in the doctor-patient relationship, 236–37, 238, 241, 323; ethics of, 117–18, 121; in irrational behavior, 30; as manipulation, 94n1; salience of, 102; sustainability of, 203

intrinsic motivation, 187–88, 192

irrationality, 30, 178, 288–92, 340–41

Iyengar, Sheena, 150

Johnson, Eric, 19, 329

judgment: of Medicare eligibility, 265–67; and nudges, 86–87, 99; substituted, 298, 301

justice: in ethical frameworks, 110, 113, 115t; procedural, 117, 264–73; in vaccination, 111, 116–17

justifications: behavioral, 278–80; of benign manipulation, 93; of the individual mandate, 278, 285; normative, 20; of nudges, 72–79; overjustification, 193–94

Kahneman, Daniel, 281

Kass, Nancy E., 113

Katz, Jay, 238–39, 240

Kessler, David, 131–32

knowledge base, 65–67, 224–25, 230

knowledge problem, xii, 144–45

Ledgerwood, David M., 204

legitimacy, 110, 111, 113, 115t, 119–20, 268

Lennon, Greg, 316

Lepper, Mark R., 150

liability in prescribing generics, 164–65

liberal neutrality, 56, 73

libertarian critiques of nudging, 98–99

libertarian paternalism: best interests in, 17–18, 24; in choice architecture, 16–18, 55; defined, 7; in freedom of choice, xi; as manipulation, 87; in Medicare appeals, 265; and no-donation default, 20; nudges as, 68, 72; in nutrition labeling, 131

libertarian welfarism, 7, 18–21, 344

life-satisfaction scores, 222

life-sustaining treatments, 222

Litvak, Kate, 67

Loewenstein, George, 4, 261, 281, 283

long-term care, declining of, 288–92

loss aversion, 328–29

low-value healthcare and cost sharing, 148

Madrian, Brigitte C., 329

majoritarian defaults, 100–101

managed-care plans in Medicare Advantage, 331

mandates, 32, 62–63, 84, 104, 110, 198. *See also* individual mandate

Mani, Anandi, 152

manipulation: in advertising, 88, 93, 94n3; affective forecasting in, 230n2; agendas in, 92, 94n11; benign, 57, 83–93; context of, 177–78; defined, 85, 86; in doctor-patient relationships, 235; of extrinsic motivation, 194; framing as, 94n2; in healthcare policy, 8–9; incentives in, 3; interventions as, 94n1; nudges as, 57, 72, 74, 84–87; of patients, 12–14; of personal health decisions, 77; position against, 87–90; in vaccination policy, 109–10

manipulation critique, 42

Mann, Ronald, 178

marketing strategies, 124–26, 158, 173

markets: efficiency in, 4; in food policy failures, 109, 132–33; in healthcare reform, 30–34; for health insurance, 30, 336; in regulations, 260; self-pay, 172–81

Mayo Collaborative Services v. Prometheus Laboratories, 315

Mazar, Nina, 246

mechanisms: in affective forecasting, 223–24; of crowding out, 195–97, 212; of disutility, 154; for surrogacy, 261–62

Medicaid, 62–64, 66, 165, 197, 327

medical necessity, 22–23

medical science, 75, 129

Medicare: Accountable Care Organizations, 33; appeals in, 12, 264–73, 266f; competition in, 31; defaults in, 330–31, 334–36; disputes about, 259–60; exchanges in, 327; Office of Hearings and Appeals, 266–67; Part D, 161, 165, 333–34, 335

Medicare Advantage: ACA in termination of, 336–37n2; beneficiaries' transitions in, 332t; choice overload in, 150; default rules in, 324; exchanges in, 327; market, 13, 31; mass default in, 331–34; opting into, 330

Medicare and Medicaid Services, Centers for, 266–67

Medicare Modernization and Improvement Act, 331

mental accounting, 126, 127

mHealth, 11, 221, 236–37

Mill, John Stuart, xviii

misreporting of information, 246

mistakes. *See* errors

mobile devices, 11, 236–38, 240–41

moral hazard, 33–34, 177, 178, 277

morality: incentives in, 190; of manipulation, 85–86; nudges in, 86–87, 91, 103–4; political, 97–106; of presumed consent, 345; in quality of life, 288; and signaling effects, 192–93

motivated reasoning. *See* rationalizations

motivation: changes in over time, 206–9, 208f, 213n4; in ethical analysis of vaccination,

115–16; extrinsic, 187–88, 191–92, 194, 205–7, 206t; financial, 269; in generic drug promotion, 166; heterogeneity in, 213n5; intrinsic, 187–88, 190–99, 202–12, 206t, 213n4

motivational crowding out. *See* crowding out

myopia, 174–75, 278

Myriad Genetics, Association for Molecular Pathology v., 315

narrow therapeutic index (NTI) drugs, 159–60, 167

National Bioethics Advisory Commission, 309

National Cancer Institute, 314

National Center for Behavioral Economics, 221

National Institutes of Health, 221, 317

National Organ Transplant Act, 195

negative externalities, 18, 20, 49n8

neoclassical law and economics, 10–11, 15, 30, 67–68, 275, 281

neutrality in choice architecture, 21

next-generation sequencing (NGS), 13, 309–19

non-educative nudges, 85–86

non-rational processes, 99

normative critiques of behavioral economics, 8–9

Nudge: Improving Decisions about Health, Wealth, and Happiness (Sunstein & Thalor), 17, 35–36, 42, 72, 340, 344

nudges, definitions of, 84, 121n1, 147

nutrition: in illness and death, 134; labeling, 9, 125–26, 129, 131–32; policy on, 109, 110, 125; report cards in, 127

Nutrition Labeling and Education Act (NLEA), 126

ObamaCare. *See* Affordable Care Act (ACA)

obesity, 29, 46–47, 124–25

objections to cost sharing, 147–48

obligations: in DNA sequencing, 318; and legitimacy, 115t, 119; to permanently unconscious patients, 287–88, 293; of physicians in affective forecasting, 220, 222–24, 226–27, 230; social, 33; to vulnerable populations, 116–17

optimism, 174–75, 177–78, 179–80, 278–79, 290

opting in, 62–63, 69, 270–71, 323

opting out: as adverse selection, 32; behavioral economics of, 60–61; as choice, xiii; in choice architecture, 68–69; errors prevented by, 323; of insurance, 260; in Medicare appeals process reform, 271; of organ donation, 324, 341–42, 344

organ donation: altruism in, 6, 198, 343–44, 346–47; and crowding out, 193, 194; defaults in, 13–14, 19–20, 99, 106n2, 324, 329, 339–47; family in, 2, 343, 347n1, 358n7, 358n11; harms resulting from, 345–46; incentives for, 190, 195–96; presumed consent rule in, 339–47

Orszag, Peter, 28
out-of-pocket costs, 9–10, 22, 28, 163–64, 166
outsourcing of decision-making, 149, 151, 153
overconsumption, 33
overprescribing, 166

paradigms of choice architecture, 15–25, 29f, 301
passive decisions, 327–28
Patel, Miteesh S., 163
paternalism: and active choosing, xi–xiii;
    aggressive soft, 125–26, 128–29; asymmetrical,
    271; beneficent, 234–35; and choice, xvii–xix,
    xxi–xxiv; in choice architecture, 68; coercive, 7,
    18; defined, xvii–xviii; in doctor-patient
    relationships, 219–20; in food policy, 9, 125–30;
    gentle soft, 125–28, 131–33; hard, 125, 129–30;
    in healthcare reform, 36; personalized, 238–42;
    in setting defaults, 61
Patient Protection and Affordable Care Act
    (PPACA). See Affordable Care Act (ACA)
patients: affective forecasts by, 11, 224–25; best
    interests of, 78, 230, 234; and credit, 174;
    decisional burdens of, 9–10; empowerment of,
    220; in healthcare reform, 36; manipulation of,
    12–14; monitoring of, 241; nudging of, 239–41;
    physicians' obligations toward, 220, 222–24,
    226–27, 230; preferences of, 235–36, 297–301.
    See also doctor-patient relationships
pay-for-performance programs, 165, 196, 197
payment method innovations, 125–26
penalties, xiv–xv, 3, 32, 104, 110
personal beliefs, 109–10, 114, 117–18
personal choice, 125, 128, 130, 133–34, 280
personal interests, 56, 75–76
personalized defaults, 330–31, 335–36
persuasion, rational, 102
Petry, Nancy M., 204
Pettit, Philip, 91
pharmaceutical marketplace, 160–61
physician networks, 324, 334, 336
physicians: in affective forecasting, 11, 222–30;
    and behavioral economics, 234–36; and choice
    overload, 151–52; as conduits to services, 219; in
    healthcare reform, 36; as intermediaries in
    DNA sequencing, 314; in Medicare claims, 265;
    in organ donation, 345, 346; in personalized
    paternalism, 240; prescribing practices of, 10,
    158–68, 167t; and third-party credit, 172–74,
    175–76. See also doctor-patient relationships
policymakers, 4, 67–68, 74, 76, 87
political economy perspective, 58
positive externalities, 18–19, 20–21, 24
poverty, 116–17, 118, 121, 132
precommitment devices, 29
predictions. See affective forecasts

preferences: adaptation of, 196; aggregation of,
    101; applicability of data on, 220; in decision
    utility, 281; in doctor-patient relationships,
    235–36; endogenous, 194; in food selection, 131;
    idiosyncratic, 23; revealed, 281–82; shared, in
    surrogacy, 297–305; social, 194, 343, 346; in
    status quo bias, 334; sticky, 131, 328–29
preferred provider organizations (PPOs), 331,
    336–37n2
prescription drugs, 10, 158–68, 333–34
presumed consent rule, 19–20, 244, 324, 339–47,
    347n3
preventive care, 28–29, 143, 278, 280
price: in food selection, 131, 132; of insurance
    premiums, 149; of prescription drugs, 158, 160;
    transparency in, 147
primary care physicians, 219, 314
privacy, 120, 237, 244–53, 318
private fee-for-service (PFFS) plans, 331
private insurance, 22–23, 326–28
procedural justice, 117, 264–73
projection in surrogacy, 304–5
proportionality, 91
providers of healthcare, 266, 269, 270, 271
psychology, 34–35, 190–92, 203, 329
psychosocial harm from DNA sequencing, 309–10
public health, 93, 109–11, 112–21

quality-adjusted life years (QALYs), 22–23
quality of life, 11, 225, 227–30, 230–31n4, 288

Randomized Control Trials, 41, 44
rational actor model, 276
rational choice: in declining care, 288–92;
    defaults in, 329; in food selection, 131; and
    manipulative nudges, 87; in medical credit,
    174–77, 178; nudges in, 97–98; outsourcing of,
    149; overload in, 150, 151; respect for, 98–103;
    in status quo bias, 328
rational choosers, 84, 85
rational economic model, 4–5
rationalizations, 5, 261
rationing, distributed, 147, 149, 294–95
Reb, Jochen, 154
Redelmeier, Donald A., 151–52
regret, 151, 153–54, 279
regulation, government: ACA as, 59; biases in, 68;
    in choice architecture, 16; of commercial firms
    in food policy, 110; of consumer credit, 172,
    179–80; cost savings in, 280; evidence in,
    41–43; of generic drugs, 159–60; of genetics
    services, 262, 310, 312, 316–17, 318; in hard
    paternalism, 129–30; libertarian paternalism as,
    16–18, 55; mandatory, 60–61; market based,
    260; nudges as, 57–58

relationships: consumer credit in, 172–73, 175–76, 178; and data, 238–42; in ethical frameworks, 113–14; in legitimacy, 119–20; in surrogacy, 261, 297, 303; in trust and transparency, 120

relative value health insurance (RVHI), 22–24

reputational effects of incentives, 193, 198, 271

research ethics boards, 245

resources, cognitive, 153, 176–77

respect, 87, 98–103, 293

responsibility: in active choosing, xviii–xix; in consumer credit, 173; and disclosure of nudges, 103; in government policy, 46–47; in narratives of food oppression, 133–34; shared, in healthcare reform, 33

right to choose, 68–69

risk aversion, 23, 118, 277

risks: and benevolent deception, 120; of disclosure, in consent forms, 252; in DNA sequencing, 309–10; of errors in organ donation, 345; in ethical frameworks, 114; financial, 148; of generic drugs and biologics, 166–67; insurance managing, 260; pooling of, 31, 32; underestimation of, 278–79

role-modeling as benign manipulation, 93

Rothschild-Stiglitz equilibrium, 31

safety: in anonymity and confidentiality, 245, 246, 252; of consumer access to genetic testing, 309–19; of follow-on biologics, 162, 167; of generic drugs, 158, 159–60, 161, 166; in healthcare decisions, 23

salience: in affective forecasting, 229; choice architecture, 6; of credit, 176; of decision-making, 58; of incentives, 212; in rationality theory, 5

self-control, 126, 131, 197–98

self-determination, 188, 193–94, 196, 197, 198

self-image, 193, 197, 198, 248

self-interest, 281–82, 289, 343–45, 347, 347–48n6

self-pay markets, 172–81

self-surveillance, 236, 237

Seva Mandir, 112–13, 114–16, 119–20

Shafir, Eldar, 151–52

Shalowitz, David I., 298

Shea, Dennis F., 329

Shiffrin, Seana, 104

signaling effects, 188, 192–93, 196–97, 271, 343, 346

The Silent World of Doctor and Patient (Katz), 238–39, 240

simplified active choosing, xiii, xvii

Skinner, Quentin, 91

small data, 11, 236–38, 240–41

Social and Behavioral Sciences Team, 41

social norms, 33, 35, 192–93, 196

social psychology in public policy, 40–41

soda tax (Berkeley, CA), 128

soft paternalism, 61, 111, 125–26, 129, 131–33

Special Nutritional Assistance for Women and Children, 132

speech, freedom of, 128, 316

state law in surrogacy, 297, 298, 300, 303–4

statistical tests in weight loss study, 206

Stenner, Shane P., 163

stereotyping in food oppression, 133, 134

stewardship model of ethics, 113

structural constraints/factors in food selection, 132–33

subjective expected utility, 15, 21, 24

subsidies: in food policy, 124–25, 128, 130, 133; in healthcare reform, 27, 29–30, 31, 33

substituted judgment, 298, 301

Sunstein, Cass R.: on disrespect of autonomy, 91; on manipulation, 85–86; on modeling and predicting behavior, 4; *Nudge*, 17, 35–36, 42, 72, 340, 344

Supplemental Nutrition Assistance Program (SNAP), 124

surrogacy/surrogates, 12–13, 261–62, 297–305

surveys, 203–6, 284n3, 340, 341–42

symmetric information and monitoring, 33–34

task danger, 196

taxation, 128, 198

technocratic defense of behavioral science, 42–43

terminated choosers, 326–34

terminated health plans, 326–36

testing: of behavioral economic theory, 144; of generic drugs, 159–60; presumed consent in, 244

Thaler, Richard: on choosing not to choose, 153; on modeling and predicting behavior, 4; *Nudge*, 17, 35–36, 42, 72, 340, 344

third-party financing, 172–81

threats, 114, 118. *See also* coercion

time: and choice overload, 151; in food policy, 132; inconsistency, 118–19

transparency: in cases of permanent unconsciousness, 294; in ethical frameworks, 110, 113, 115t, 120; and information disclosure, 244–46; of pricing in cost sharing, 147; in procedural justice, 117; in responsibility, 102–3; in self-pay markets, 178

treatments: and affective forecasting, 231n5; in decision simplification, 22–23; denial of, 287; life sustaining, forcing of, 222; medical credit in, 175; in Medicare claims, 265–66; in relative value health insurance, 23–24; surrogates in deciding, 297–305; values in, 304–5